THE PAROUSIA IN THE NEW TESTAMENT

SUPPLEMENTS

TO

NOVUM TESTAMENTUM

VOLUME XIII

LEIDEN
E. J. BRILL
1966

THE PAROUSIA
IN
THE NEW TESTAMENT

BY

A. L. MOORE

LEIDEN
E. J. BRILL
1966

CONTENTS

ACKNOWLEDGEMENTS

The author readily acknowledges that he alone is responsible for blemishes in this book. But his interest in the subject of N.T. eschatology he owes to his esteemed teacher, Revd. C. E. B. Cranfield, M.A., Senior Lecturer in Theology in the University of Durham, for whose constant advice and friendship he is ever grateful. He wishes to thank his wife for her patient encouragement and help throughout; and his brother, Revd. C. G. Moore, M.A., Rector of Stone, for his forbearance in allowing his Curate time to complete this study. He regrets that the important work by Prof. G. E. Ladd, *Jesus and the Kingdom. The Eschatology of Realism*, S.P.C.K., 1966, came to his notice too late for reference to be made to it in this book.

CHAPTER ONE

INTRODUCTION

The present interest in eschatology [1] owes much to J. Weiss and A. Schweitzer.[2] The question they raised was that of the overall structure and significance of New Testament eschatology, but this was bound to involve considerable examination of the idea of the Parousia in particular.

Surprisingly this renewal of interest has not fostered in the church a firmer conviction regarding the Parousia expectation. In fact the idea of the Parousia, at least in the form in which traditionally it has been expressed, has had to face many criticisms from various quarters.

From within the realm of critical theological investigation the Parousia hope has encountered considerable opposition. Schweitzer maintained that Jesus held to a Parousia hope only because it formed part of the contemporary Jewish apocalyptic which he accepted, and that such first century apocalyptic has no place in Christian thought. This view, introduced into this country with varying sympathy by W. Sanday and F. C. Burkitt,[3] is expressed strongly to-day by M. Werner and others.[4] An apologetic elimination of the Parousia hope, or at least a radical re-interpretation of its traditional expression, has flourished particularly in the

---

[1] For recent reviews of the eschatological thought of the past 50-60 years cf. e.g., J. W. Bowman, 'From Schweitzer to Bultmann', in *T.T.* XI 1954 pp. 160ff. G. R. Beasley-Murray, 'A Century of Eschatological Discussion', in *E.T.* LXIV 1953, pp. 312ff. D. J. Selby, 'Changing Ideas in N.T. Eschatology', in *H.T.R.* L 1957 pp. 21ff. W. D. Niven, 'After 50 Years: VI Eschatology and the Primitive Church', in *E.T.* L 1938-9 pp. 325ff. F. F. Bruce, 'Eschatology', in *L.Q.H.R.* 1958 pp. 99 ff. Fison, *Hope*, pp. 51ff. Kümmel, *Promise*, pp. 15ff. Rich, *Die Bedeutung*, pp. 1-3. Wilder, *Eschatology*, pp. 60ff. W. Schweitzer, *Eschatology and Ethics*.

[2] Cf. esp. Weiss, *Predigt* and *Urchristentum*; Schweitzer, *Quest* and *Mystery*.

[3] Cf. Sanday, *Life*. Burkitt, *Beginnings*, and *Jesus Christ*. (Burkitt wrote the Preface to the English translation 'The Quest of the Historical Jesus').

[4] Cf. Werner, *Formation*, and *Der protestantische Weg des Glaubens*, I, also U. Neuenschwander, *Protestantische Dogmatik der Gegenwart und das Problem der biblische Mythologie*. Buri, *Die Bedeutung*.

Anglo-Saxon world through the work of C. H. Dodd, followed by
T. F. Glasson and J. A. T. Robinson.[1] A somewhat similar re-
interpretation has been expressed on the Continent by E. von
Dobschütz and R. Otto, and, most recently, by J. Jeremias.[2]
Behind these views one can discern the pressure of evolutionistic
materialism and of the whole secular climate of thought.[3] Even
more apparent is the pressure of a secular philosophy behind the re-
interpretation of eschatology in terms of existentialism. This, not
unheralded before 1939, has been expressed most radically and
consistently during and following the second world war by R. Bultmann [4] and has many adherents to-day.[5]

Other factors also have tended to weaken the church's Parousia
hope. The contemporary concentration of the church on its worship
directs attention away from a future end-expectation, and although
this concentration is especially marked in Roman catholic circles [6]
it is not by any means unknown in Anglicanism.[7]

The church seems to have slackened its grasp upon the Parousia
hope under pressure from materialistic thought;[8] and western

---

[1] Cf. Dodd, *Parables*; *Preaching*. Glasson, *Advent*. Robinson, *In the End*;
Coming. Also, Guy, *Last Things*. Duncan, *Jesus*. Sharman, *Son of Man*.
Cadoux, *Theology*. Hunter, *Parables*.

[2] Cf. von Dobschütz, *Eschatology*. Otto, *Kingdom of God*. Jeremias, *Jesus
als Weltvollender*; *Parables*.

[3] e.g. Glasson, *Advent*, pp. 232ff. Robinson, *In the End*, pp. 17-24.

[4] Cf. *Glauben und Verstehen*; *Offenbarung und Heilgeschehen*, — *Die Frage
der natürlichen Offenbarung*; *New Testament and Mythology* (in *Kerygma*, ed.
Bartsch); *Primitive Christianity*; 'History and Eschatology', in *N.T.S.* 1954,
pp. 5-16; *History and Eschatology*.

[5] Cf. esp. E. Fuchs, 'Die Frage'; 'Christus'. E. Lohse, 'Lukas als Theologe
der Heilsgeschichte', in *Ev. T.* XIV 1954 pp. 256ff.; 'Zur N.T.' lichen Eschatologie', in *V.F.* 1956 (Jahresbericht 1953-55) pp. 184ff. Conzelmann,
'Gegenwart'; *Luke*. Bornkamm, *Jesus*; 'Enderwartung'. Käsemann, 'Problem'. Macquarrie, *An Existentialist Theology*; *Demythologizing*. Robinson,
New Quest; *Mark*. *Kerygma*, ed. Bartsch I and II.

[6] Cf. e.g. E. Quinn, 'The Kingdom of God and the Church in the Synoptic
Gospels', in *Scripture* IV 1949-51, pp. 237ff.

[7] Cf. Robinson, *Coming*, p. 15. Fison, *Hope*, p. 65 and below, p. 64.

[8] Cf. Roberts, *Jesus*, pp. 115f. Cairns, *Image*, pp. 206ff. George, *Communion*,
p. 25. G. Rupp, 'The Doctrine of Man: the Christian and Secular Eschatologies', in *E.T.* LXI 1950 pp. 100f. Reinhold Niebuhr, 'The Christian Faith
and the Economic Life of Lberal Society', (in *Goals*, ed. A. Dudley Ward).
D. L. Munby, *Christianity and Economic Problems*, pp. 267ff., gives a brief
account of the relation of the christian parousia hope to economic and social
thought.

capitalism, naturally biased towards conservatism, has hardly encouraged the church to re-affirm its hope in the impending judgement and renewal of the present world order.[1] Some recent 'bomb
psychosis' has given rise to a form of secular apocalypticism to
which, usually, the churches have responded with nervous in-
decision.[2]

Some sects have consistently maintained a Parousia hope, but too
often their fanaticism (sometimes morbid, sometimes comic) and
their concentration upon dates, has meant that they have failed
to see or proclaim the implications of the impending end for present
life, thought and obedience.[3]

Existentialist and materialistic philosophies have, however,
succeeded in shaking the church's confidence in the Parousia hope
(at least in the form 'he shall come again to judge both the quick
and the dead') generally only at an intellectual level. Certainly
on the plane of general congregational life and thought there is a
tendency to ignore the Parousia expectation. Following the Evanston Conference in 1954 some widespread interest in this theme was
aroused,[4] but this was only temporary. Yet there seems to be no
parallel, on the congregational level, to the intellectual antagonism

---

[1] The idea of a future golden age is more readily acceptable on communist
soil with its concern for the community and its forward direction (cf. E.
Heimann, 'Comparative Economic Systems', in *Goals*, ed. A. Dudley Ward)
than on the soil of private enterprise and the fulfilment of personal ends.
The way in which Protestantism and capitalism readily co-exist (cf. Heimann's essay, above, and J. C. Bennett, 'A Theological Conception of Goals
for Economic Life', in *Goals*, ed. A. Dudley Ward) is relevant for the assessment of Bultmann's popularity to-day (with its expressly individualist
interest). Rich, *Die Bedeutung*, p. 21, rightly points out that there can be
no private Parousia hope.

[2] Cf. J. Foster, 'Eschatology and the Hope of the New World', in *E.T.*
LIV 1942-3, pp. 10 ff.

[3] Cf. Glasson, *His Appearing and His Kingdom*, pp. 43ff.

[4] The theme of the Conference was, 'Christ, the hope of the world'.
Preparatory to it appeared:—Minear, *Christ the Hope of the World* (Bibliography); *The Meaning of Hope in the Bible* (Ecumenical Studies Geneva,
1952), being the report of two preparatory meetings convened by the Study
department of the W.C.C., in Zetten (15-19 April, 1952) and in Drew
University, U.S.A., (5-6 June, 1952); W. Schweitzer, *Eschatology* (Ecumenical Studies, Geneva, 1951); 'The Nature of Christian Hope', in *Ecumenical Review* 3, 1952, pp. 282f (being preparatory suggestions from Lesslie Newbigin, Edmund Schlink, Roger Mehl and D. F. McKinnon); *T.T.*, Oct 1953,
was devoted to the Evanston theme. See also the report, *Evanston Speaks*.
Fison, *Hope*. Minear, *Christian Hope*. Brunner, *Eternal Hope*.

towards the traditional Parousia hope, and there is no general movement aimed at removing it from the creeds. Unfortunately there is little positive integration of the Parousia hope into the life, thought and work of the church.

This, surely, has resulted in a serious impoverishment of the church's witness. The conviction underlying this thesis is certainly that a real and extensive impoverishment *must* follow from a weak, indifferent or uninformed Parousia hope, or from the abandonment —for whatever reason—of the Parousia expectation altogether. The intense urgency with which the church should undertake its tasks of repentance and of missionary proclamation of the gospel, is weakened if not entirely lost. This thesis, therefore, seeks to pose and probe again the question as to the authenticity of the Parousia hope in the New Testament.

We begin (in chapter 2) with the background of the New Testament expectation, tracing the hopes expressed in the Old Testament and inter-testamental periods. Then we examine recent views which evacuate the Parousia hope of its traditional place and significance.

First (in chapter 3) we discuss the thesis maintained by Schweitzer and others that Jesus held to an expectation which, by subsequent events, was proved false; and that the church from the first has failed to appreciate the true significance of this (so-called) "life of misunderstanding". They assert that not the Parousia hope but the example of living with an unfulfilled vision, is the inspiration of Christ's life and death for to-day. But this assertion we find altogether inadequate.

Next (in chapter 4) we examine the thesis that the early church wholly misunderstood Jesus' hope, falsely attributing to him the idea of a physical return to earth for judgement and renewal. We suggest that 'Realised Eschatology', so ready to affirm the real inbreak of the divine into the world in the person and work of Jesus Christ, is strangely docetic with regard to the Parousia.

Thirdly (in chapter 5) we discuss Bultmann's demythologized eschatology. The questions, whether Jesus' entire concept of the future has always been wrongly evaluated, and whether it behoves us to re-interpret his expectation in the terms offered by Bultmann, are both answered in the negative.

At this point (chapter 6) we venture to suggest that the Parousia hope belongs to the very fabric and substance of the New Testament, in all its parts, and to the very fabric and substance of Jesus' own thought and teaching in so far as it is possible to reconstruct this.

One of the most outstanding difficulties concerned with the New Testament Parousia expectation is the apparent insistence upon the *nearness* of the end. This difficulty, long recognised,[1] has often played a decisive role in interpreting and evaluating the New Testament hope as a whole. Involved in the three interpretations of eschatology already mentioned above are real attempts at elucidating this imminence—resolving it variously as a mistaken, but essential ingredient in Jesus' thought; as the early church's error; or as the expression in temporal terms of a supra-temporal impingement of the eternal order on man. Besides these interpretations, a number of scholars are prepared to see the imminence simply as a peripheral mistake on Jesus' part. But our examination of this view (in chapter 7) seeks to show that problems and questions, more radical than is usually supposed, arise in this case. Some relate the imminence to events *other than* the Parousia—to the Resurrection, the fall of Jerusalem, Pentecost, or the church's mission; or to two or more of these events taken together. But these interpretations we find unconvincing.

In chapters 8 and 9 we re-examine this element of imminence, seeking to determine whether the early church (in the first instance) believed that the Parousia would definitely occur within a specified time, or whether its imminent expectation was *un*delimited and altogether differently orientated. Following this, in chapters 10 and 11 we press the same questions further, asking whether Jesus himself expected the Parousia to occur within a set period of time, or whether his hope was differently orientated.

In the light of this discussion we draw (in chapter 12) a number of conclusions having a bearing upon the life of the church in the present. It is thereby hoped to show how directly relevant the Parousia hope is for the life of the church. The Parousia hope was, we believe, one of the driving forces behind the early church's life and obedience and behind its missionary zeal.[2] Perhaps by probing these questions and problems again, some light may be shed

---

[1] J. Kiss, 'Zur eschatologischen Beurteilung der Theologie des Apostels Paulus', in *Z.s.T.* XIV 1938, pp. 379ff., emphasises this.

[2] Cf. Cullmann, 'Eschatologie und Mission im N.T.', in *Evang. Missionsmagazin*, 1941, pp. 98-108; and below, chapter 4, p. 60.

on the motive which should drive the church to the same primary
tasks [1] with urgency and responsibility, and yet with freedom and
confidence.

---

[1] The absolute centrality of mission in the church's life and work is often
acknowledged—cf. e.g. H. Kraemer, *The Christian Message in a non-Christian World*, pp. 24-30. M. Warren, *The Triumph of God*, pp. 103-4. *The
Lambeth Conference Report*, 1958, pp. 2, 75. *Evanston Speaks* pp. 32-33—but
usually, in practice, remains peripheral.

CHAPTER TWO

THE BACKGROUND OF THE NEW TESTAMENT EXPECTATION

As a preface to our examination of the New Testament expectation, a brief review is here undertaken of the expectation in the
Old Testament and in the inter-Testamental period (as it is found
in Apocalyptic in Wisdom literature, in Hellenistic Judaism, in
Rabbinic Judaism, and in particular group movements).

EXPECTATION IN THE OLD TESTAMENT

The central concern of the Old Testament is the sovereignty of
God.[1] The actual phrase 'the Kingdom of God' (מלכת יהוה) is
seldom used in a religious sense prior to Daniel,[2] but the *concept*
is certainly early and central.[3] General agreement exists to-day
that the phrase means primarily 'sovereignty' as a characteristic of
JHWH and only secondarily a territory and a people wherein this
sovereignty is displayed and acknowledged.[4] It is, therefore, better
to speak of 'the sovereignty' than of 'the kingdom' of God.

This concept of God's sovereignty is related in the Old Testament
to Israel's past, present and future.

The relation to the past

In the creation stories of Genesis, as also in such isolated references
as Ps. 104,5; 119,90; Is. 47,16; I Chr. 29,11, etc., we find Israel's
conviction that the act of creation attests God's sovereignty in
and over nature.[5] But it was in the Covenant in particular that
Israel saw the sovereignty of God displayed; in the establishment

---

[1] Cf. Jacob, *Theology*, p. 37; Davidson, *Theology*, pp. 1-4; Eichrodt,
Theology, pp. 512ff.; Anderson, 'Hebrew Religion', pp. 308f.; Hebert,
Authority, pp. 47ff; Köhler, *Theology*, pp. 30ff.

[2] Cf. von Rad, in *T.W.N.T.* I, p. 569.

[3] Cf. the use of מלך in the names of national gods among Israel's neighbours; cf. von Rad, in *T.W.N.T.* I, p. 567.

[4] Cf. Dalman, *Words*, p. 94; von Rad, in *T.W.N.T.* I, pp. 564ff; Flew,
Church, p. 28; Richardson, in *T.W.B.*, pp. 119ff.; etc.

[5] Cf. Orr, in *H.D.B.* II, pp. 844ff.

of Israel as His people God's Lordship was expressed and given form and location.[1] It is to this election of Israel in sovereign love that the prophets look back, seeing in it the basis of God's concern with Israel's history and of the obligations of service imposed on Israel.[2]

The relation to the present

The Old Testament recognises that in every present moment Israel exists under God's kingship.[3] This is declared both by prophet and priest.[4] The nature of this kingship and its moral and religious implications comprise the burden of the prophetic message; JHWH is *now* King over Israel, therefore Israel must obey his commands.[5]

Recently the role of the cultus in Israel's life and the development of its religious ideas has been increasingly recognised. It appears that some Psalms reflect a cultic pattern, the centre of which concerned the (?annual) enthronement of the king (? at the New Year Festival), through which ritual the present kingship of JHWH was both personified and assured.[6]

Since *malkuth*, as it is applied to God, means primarily 'sovereignty' as distinct from 'a kingdom', it follows that human disobedience cannot affect JHWH's kingship, either to annul it or to establish it.[7] At the same time, every movement in the history of Israel

---

[1] See e.g., Ex. 19, 5; Deut. 14, 2; 26, 18; Ps. 135, 4. cf. Köhler, *Theology*, pp. 60-74; Eichrodt, *Theology*, pp. 36 ff.; Jacob, *Theology*, pp. 209ff. It is significant that the Deuteronomist uses the phrase 'at that time' (בעת ההוא) 16 times, indicating that the establishment of the Covenant was 'the classic time' of God's activity (cf. Marsh, in *T.W.B.* pp. 258f.).

[2] Cf. e.g., Hos. 11, 1ff., Mal. 1, 2; Is. 51, 2; Amos 3, 2; Hebert, *Authority*, p. 55; Eichrodt, *Theology*, pp. 58f.

[3] Cf. Köhler, *Theology*, p. 66; Eichrodt, *Theology*, pp. 70ff., p. 92.

[4] Cf. e.g., Is. 6, 5; I Chr. 29, 11;

[5] Cf. Eichrodt, *Theology*, pp. 316ff; Snaith, *Ideas*, pp. 51ff.; Robinson, *Religious Ideas*, pp. 154f.

[6] Engnell, *Studies*, pp. 43ff., is prepared to speak of the king in this respect as the personal incarnation of God; cf. similarly Bentzen, *King*, p. 37; Mowinckel, *Psalmenstudien* II, passim; Pedersen, *Israel*, III-IV, passim; H. J. Kraus, *Die Königsherrschaft Gottes im A.T.* passim; Jacob, *Theology*, pp. 262-270. Criticism of this reconstruction is offered by e.g., Eissfeldt, 'Jahve als König', in *Z.A.W.* XLVI, 1928 pp. 81-105; Snaith, *Studies in the Psalter*, and *Jewish New Year Festival*; Anderson, 'Hebrew Religion', pp. 297ff.
A bibliography of selected works to 1955 is given in Jacob, *Theology*, p. 279.

[7] Cf. Flew, *Church*, p. 28; Eichrodt, *Theology*, pp. 457ff.; Jacob, *Theology*, p. 105; Snaith, *Ideas*, pp. 94ff.

was motivated by the need to make clear in the pattern of Israel's life, the truth that JHWH was the sovereign Lord.[1] The reciprocity of the Covenant relationship meant that JHWH was not simply king *per se*, but that this kingship should be manifestly acknowledged in Israel's history:[2] Israel's drastic failure in this respect was regarded as the cause of all national disasters. Such failure *concealed* JHWH's kingship and compromised his sovereignty and resulted in this sovereignty being displayed now primarily through judgement.[3] It also hid JHWH's sovereignty from the eyes of the surrounding nations and was regarded as a slight upon JHWH himself.[4]

This failure and subsequent ambiguity became particularly apparent at the time of the Babylonian captivity. During the exile and in the post-exilic period great emphasis was laid upon the need to acknowledge JHWH's kingship *in the present*.[5] Isaiah's concept of a 'remnant' was extended, and legalistic separatism and pietistic particularism received much emphasis, the intention being that, if not in all Israel, then at least in a group within Israel, JHWH's kingship might be openly acknowledged.[6]

The relation to the future

The growth in Israel's religious consciousness of an expectation of a future manifestation of the Kingdom of God has been ascribed variously to a number of factors. Some suggest the ethical fulfilment of the purpose of creation, coupled with the non-realisation of this fulfilment in Israel's empirical life.[7] Others suggest Israel's understanding of its Covenant relationship; i.e. 'because Israel belongs to JHWH and can depend on Him, it has a future'.[8] Israel's eventual understanding of JHWH's transcendence has also been suggested.[9] Another suggestion is Israel's human aspiration

---

[1] Cf. Eichrodt, *Theology*, pp. 45-69.

[2] Cf. Köhler, *Theology*, pp. 64ff.; Robinson, *Religious Ideas*, p. 41; Eichrodt, *Theology*, pp. 36ff.

[3] Cf. Eichrodt, *Theology*, pp. 462ff., *Interpretation*, pp. 66ff., Köhler, *Theology* ,pp. 209ff.

[4] Cf. esp. Is. 52, 5-6; Ezek. 36, 20; (cf. Rom. 2, 24!). cf. Vriezen, *Theology*, pp. 228ff., Rowley, *Israel's Mission*, passim.

[5] Cf. Cook, *Old Testament*, pp. 195ff., Eichrodt, *Theology*, pp. 467ff.

[6] Cf. Cook, *Old Testament*, p. 194; Snaith, *Cyrus*, pp. 71-87.

[7] Cf. Orr, in *H.D.B.* II, pp. 844ff.

[8] Robinson, *Religious Ideas*, p. 185.

[9] Cf. Otto, *Kingdom of God*, pp. 40f., similarly Heim, *Jesus the Lord*, p. 27.

after world renewal.[1] Popular hope in the overthrow of Israel's enemies in a world catastrophe has also been put forward as the cause.[2] Some argue that eschatology arose through the cult; it was a projection into the future of what had been dramatically represented in the cult.[3] Yet again, Israel's theocentric understanding of history has been suggested.[4] Others argue that eschatology arose through the recognition that God must meet Israel's failure to acknowledge his sovereignty by an unambiguous manifestation of it throughout the world.[5]

It is possible that many of these features played a part in the development of Israel's eschatology. But in view of the fact that eschatological expectation deepened and prospered during and following the exile,[6] it seems likely that the two last suggestions were most influential and themselves encouraged the particular reading of history embodied in the first two suggestions.

Although there is a growing admission that the roots of Israel's eschatological hope go back far in its history,[7] it remains a fact that the experience of the exile intensified the problems of evil and of human failure [8] and intensified this forward look towards a future goal of history.[9] There is an increasing longing for the time when God would make his Kingship unambiguously clear.[10]

---

[1] Cf. Althaus, *letzten Dinge*, p. 7; Althaus sees all eschatology as having this same origin, though he adds (p. 11) that in Israel, the Covenant relationship gave specific content to the O.T. hope.

[2] Cf. e.g., Gressmann, *Der Ursprung der israelitisch-jüdischen Eschatologie;* and concerning this, Anderson, 'Hebrew Religion', pp. 303f.

[3] Cf. Mowinckel, *Psalmenstudien* II. Mowinckel maintains that Israel's eschatology arose through the meeting of the Canaanite cyclic view of history with the historical view characteristic of Israel. Contrast Johnson, *Sacral Kingship*, passim; Anderson, 'Hebrew Religion', p. 304.

[4] Cf. Rowley, *Faith*, p. 177; North, *Interpretation*, pp. 126ff.

[5] Cf. Richardson, in *T.W.B.* pp. 119ff.; von Rad, in *T.W.N.T.* I, pp. 567ff., Vriezen, *Theology*, pp. 351f., Köhler, *Theology*, pp. 218f.

[6] Cf. Snaith, *Cyrus*, pp. 88-94; and see below pp. 18 ff., concerning the rise of apocalyptic.

[7] Cf. Rowley, *Faith*, p. 177; Eichrodt, *Theology*, pp. 385f., Anderson, 'Hebrew Religion', pp. 303ff. (Dr. Anderson has some qualifications to make concerning this contemporary tendency).

[8] Cf. Whitley, *Exilic Age*, p. 100; Rops, *Israel*, pp. 214f., Bright, *History*, p. 350f.

[9] This intensification is expressed to some extent in legalism (e.g. Ezra's promulgation in 444 BC), to some extent in mysticism or personal pietism (e.g. Job, Ps. 73); perhaps too, an element of stoic resignation entered in (cf. Ecclesiastes) (cf. Manson, *Teaching*, p. 151). But see further below, p. 19.

[10] Cf. Mic. 4, 2; Is. 2, 3; Jer. 3, 17; etc. von Rad, in *T.W.N.T.* I, p. 567; Rowley, *Faith*, pp. 181ff.

Three further matters concerning Israel's hope in the manifestation of God's kingship must be mentioned. They are 1) the central figure in the expected End-drama: 2) the content of Israel's expectation: 3) the scope of this future expectation.

1) *The central figure in the expected End-drama*:

One strand in the traditions looks for JHWH himself to visit his people.[1] It is possible that disillusionment with Israel's kings and the reinterpretation of the cultic Psalms encouraged this conception; from the proclamation 'JHWH has become king' comes the hope 'JHWH will become king'[2]. This expectation lays weight on the End as a time of the peculiar activity of *God*.[3]

There is also a 'messianic' expectation, and here the problem arises as to the significance of the king's role in the cult and its relation to 'messianic' expectation. It is beyond the scope of the present survey to dwell on this [4] and a few tentative remarks must suffice. On the one hand there appears to be a development through cultic practice, whereby the idea of the king as representative of JHWH's Lordship could come to be thought of as 'Messiah'.[5] As disillusionment grew through experience of the monarchy, and in

---

[1] Cf. Is. 44, 6-23; 46, 9-13; 52, 7-9; Zech. 1, 3; 1, 16-17; etc., and the expression 'the day of JHWH', Amos 5, 18; etc.

[2] Cf. Is. 24, 23; 33, 21-22, Zeph. 3, 15f., Zech. 14, 16; etc. cf. Otto, *Kingdom of God*, p. 35.

[3] Cf. Is. 18, 7; Jer. 3, 17, Joel 3, 15-17, etc., cf. Marsh, in *T.W.B.* pp. 258f.

[4] Detailed discussion may be found in Mowinckel, *Psalmenstudien* II, and *He that cometh*; Gressmann, *Der Messias*; Bentzen, *King*; Ringgren, 'König und Messias' in *Z.A.W.* 64, 1952, pp. 120-147; and *Messiah*; Johnson, *Sacral Kingship*; Jacob, *Theology*, pp. 327ff (plus bibliography pp. 342f.)

[5] Mowinckel (*He that cometh*, passim) argues that since the term 'Messiah' involves eschatology it cannot be used of the contemporary Israelite king. Bentzen (*King*, p. 37), however, commenting on the role of the king in the cult, maintains that 'the Psalms experience in living actuality what eschatology expects. Therefore the king of the Psalms is in the main the same . . .' (similarly Engnell, *Studies*, pp. 176f.). Ringgren rightly points out that the simple application of the term 'messianic' to the king's cultic role does not necessarily mean that the role is considered 'prophetical' or eschatological; he notes that Engnell states, 'By messianism I mean elaborate king ideology' (Ringgren, *Messiah*, p. 24, referring to Engnell, *Studies*, p. 43, n 3.). Anderson ('Hebrew Religion', p. 305) therefore contends that 'it can only make for confusion' if the words 'Messiah' and 'messianic' are used 'in any other than a future sense'. At the same time, as Rowley (*Faith*, p. 192) maintains, the royal Psalms may well be regarded as 'messianic' in setting before the king in the cult both a pattern for himself and an ideal hope for the future, the latter aspect predominating in post exilic times.

due course as the monarchy ceased, a 'messianic' future hope arose.[1]
On the other hand, there is the expectation of a future Davidic
king,[2] which suggests that the specific promises given to David[3]
have been applied to the general 'messianic' hope.[4] If the references
to a 'Messiah' are not abundant, this may be due to the complexity
of Israel's expectation.[5] Certainly the Old Testament expectation is
fuller than the usage and occurrence of the technical term 'Messiah'
might suggest.[6]

Then there is the concept of the 'Servant of JHWH' (עבד יהוה).
The major problem is to determine the subject of the Servant Songs
of Deutero-Isaiah.[7] Various former or contemporary historical
figures have been suggested; also, Israel itself, an ideal remnant, an
abstract ideal, or a hoped for group or individual.[8] Actually for our
purposes the problem is peripheral; for although the Christian
church has, from the beginning, 'seen an impressive foreshadowing
of Christ' in these songs,[9] there is in fact 'little to connect the
Servant superficially with the Davidic leader, and it is not surprising that there is no solid evidence that the two were identified
in pre-Christian times . . .'.[10]

The expression 'Son of Man' (בר־אנש בן־אנוש בן־אדם.) must concern
us rather more fully, and particularly three problems arising from
its occurrence in Daniel.[11] First, the problem whether the term in

---

[1] Cf. Ringgren, *Messiah*, pp. 23ff.

[2] Cf. Is. 9, 6ff.; Mic. 5, 1-5, etc. Whereas the king is termed JHWH's
anointed, the expected Davidic king is nowhere in the O.T. referred to
technically by this term; cf. Rowley, *Faith*, p. 188; Campbell, in *T.W.B.*,
pp. 44f.

[3] Cf. II Sam. 7, 12; Jer. 17, 25; 33, 17; Amos 9, 11; Hos. 3, 5; Ezek. 45, 8.

[4] Cf. Ringgren, *Messiah*, pp. 25-38; Robinson, *Religious Ideas*, pp. 199f.

[5] Cf. Campbell, in *T.W.B.*, p. 44.

[6] This is illustrated not only by other terms but also by all the material
collected in Klausner, *Messianic Idea*.

[7] i.e. Is. 42, 1-4; 49, 1-6; 50, 4-6; 52, 13-53, 12.

[8] For an exhaustive survey of interpretations cf. North, *The Suffering
Servant in Deutero-Isaiah*, pp. 6-116; see also Zimmerli and Jeremias, in
T.W.N.T., V, pp. 655ff., and *Servant*, pp. 23-24; Lundhagen, *The Servant
Motif in the Old Testament*, Campbell, in *T.W.B.* pp. 223f.

[9] Campbell, in *T.W.B.* p. 224.

[10] Rowley, *Faith*, p. 197. For a full discussion of the significance of the
'Servant of JHWH' in the O.T. cf. the works cited above n. 8, and
Snaith, 'The Servant of the Lord', pp. 187ff. Lindblom, *Servant Songs*;
Eichrodt, *Theology*, pp. 483ff. (Lindblom, *Servant Songs*, pp. 105f. and
Zimmerli and Jeremias, *Servant*, pp. 105f., include bibliographies.)

[11] Elsewhere in the O.T. the title is used infrequently (except in Ezekiel)
as a synonym for man (e.g. Ps. 8, 4). Bentzen (*King*, p. 43) maintains that

Daniel is corporate or individual. T. W. Manson's 'corporate' thesis [1] has received many advocates.[2] There is, however, evidence to suggest that the Son of Man in Daniel is an individual,[3] though a representative figure,[4] for the four beasts (7, 3-8) are described (in v 17) as 'four kings' (ארבעה מלכין) suggesting 'the possibility of interpreting "one like unto a Son of Man" in v. 13 as the ruler of the "Saints of the Most High", who appears as their representative, rather than as identical with them'.[5]

Secondly, there is the problem whether the Son of Man in Daniel is a Messianic figure, or not. Mowinckel sharply distinguishes between 'Messiah', a figure which he sees developing from sacral kingship themes adopted by Israel into its cultus, and 'Son of Man' which he regards as arising from the eastern 'primal man' concept. Riesenfeld and others take the opposite view.[6] Bentzen, on the other hand, cites Pss. 8, 4-5 and 80, 17-18 as occasions when the king is termed Son of Man, suggesting that the two concepts at least run parallel.[7] Some association between an idealised king expectation and this Son of Man in Daniel who enters upon a future 'kingship' seems likely [8] though there are obvious differences.[9] Of the two terms, Son of Man is the more inclusive and is capable of taking up into itself the older hope of a 'Messiah' in the narrower sense.

The final problem is whether or not the Son of Man and the idea

---

the term is used of the king (and thus with messianic overtones at least) in Pss. 8, 4-5, 80, 17-18. Cf. further Vriezen *Theology*, p. 367.

[1] *Teaching*; and 'The Son of Man in Daniel, Enoch and the Gospels', in *B.J.R.L.* XXXII, 1950, pp. 174ff.

[2] Cf. those cited by Higgins, 'Forschung', p. 126.

[3] Mowinckel, (*He that cometh*, p. 352) says the expression in Daniel is corporate but that this is a reinterpretation of an individual concept which existed c 200 B.C. cf. also Jacob, *Theology*, p. 341.

[4] Cf. e.g. Cullmann, *Early Church*, p. 130; Taylor, *Names*, p. 26 Cranfield, *Mark*, p.274; Barrett, 'Background', p. 17 n. 39.

[5] Cranfield, *Mark*, p. 274.

[6] Cf. Higgins 'Forschung', p. 122.

[7] For a survey of these views see Higgins, '*Forschung*' p. 122; cf. Emerton, 'The Origin of the Son of Man Imagery', in *J.T.S.* IX 1958. Bentzen, *King*, p. 75; *Commentary*, p. 63.

[8] Cf. Vriezen, *Theology*, p. 367; Jacob, *Theology*, pp. 341f.

[9] Jacob, *Theology*, p. 342 writes, 'The Son of Man is, then, a real king, his function overlaps the Messiah's, but by giving him the title of man the author of the book of Daniel seeks to disentangle Messianism from national ties and to link it with the universal outlook of Genesis.'

of suffering are brought together in Daniel. Rowley [1] denies any connection, because 'the saints suffered before the appearance of the Son of Man . . .' On the other hand, if the Son of Man is understood as the peoples' representative, then the connection is close, for he comes as representative of the *suffering* saints. [2]

One further title must be considered under this section; the term 'Son of God' (בֶּן אֱלֹהִים). [3] Its application to the king (Pss. 2 and 89) suggests a certain messianic overtone. [4] It is interesting that the idea of kingship runs through, and therefore to some extent unites, the terms Son of Man, Son of God and the future Davidic Messiah.

2) *The content of Old Testament expectation*:

Israel's hope in the final manifestation of God's sovereignty involved the expectation both of judgement and of vindication. To recognise God as righteous [5] meant drawing the conclusion that all iniquity must fall under his judgement. Amos (5, 18) fulminates against the failure to take this fact seriously. Social injustice (cf 5,11f. and Is. 3,15, 5,8 etc.) and idolatry (cf Amos 5,23, Is. 2, 17f. etc.) cannot be set aside by mere religious conformity (Amos 5,22) but must lead to the revelation of God's judgement upon them. [6] Therefore the expected intervention of God in Israel's history would not simply involve the exaltation of Israel and the destruction of her enemies, but would include judgement upon *Israel*. [7]

The threat of judgement, however, does not eclipse the hope of restoration and the fulfilment of JHWH's promise to bless and to

---

[1] *Servant*, p. 62.

[2] Cf. Dodd, *According to the Scriptures*, p. 117; Davies, *Rabbinic Judaism*, p. 280; Cranfield, *Mark*, p. 275; Barrett, 'Background' pp. 2f.

[3] For its various applications — to the true Israel, the remnant, Israel as a whole, angels, etc. — cf. Taylor, *Names*, p. 52.

[4] Manson, *Jesus*, p. 103, connects the title with the 'halo of religious significance surrounding the person of the Davidic prince in Israel', and thinks that it was therefore 'through Scripture a Messianic potential'.

[5] Cf. Snaith, *Ideas*, pp. 51ff.; Köhler, *Theology*, pp. 209f., etc.

[6] Cf. esp. Is. 2, 12 where the unambiguous reversal of human unrighteousness is promised.

[7] The same opening formula of judgement is applied by Amos to the nations (1, 3-2,3) as to Israel and Judah (2, 4-16). Cf. North, *Interpretation*, p. 64; Eichrodt, *Theology*, pp. 464-7.

establish his people.[1] Alongside the expectation of doom stands that
of glory.[2] This hope certainly intensified during and through the
experience of the Exile, but the distinction is only one of degree.
Behind the expectation of a final, unambiguous manifestation of
God's kingship in these two forms lies the perception that this
same kingship is *already* being displayed in judgement and mercy
though, in the present, only in a provisional and equivocal way.[3]

3) *The scope of Old Testament expectation*:

Israel's peculiar consciousness of God and of themselves as his
people, involved for them a sense of priority.[4] The priority in
judgement was not by any means regularly perceived,[5] and the
priority in blessing was not infrequently expressed negatively;[6] at
times, however, it was understood in a more positive manner.[7]

The awareness that JHWH is not solely concerned with Israel, or
at least does not concern himself with Israel in isolation from her
neighbours, goes back 'long before the time of the Deuteronomist'.[8]
The promise 'and in thee (thy seed) shall all the families of the
earth be blessed'[9] emphasises that the Covenant between JHWH
and Abraham had some significance for the whole of mankind.[10]
If this is only implicit universalism, the 8th century prophets are
explicit that the future holds in store JHWH's acknowledgement
by all men.[11] The scope of JHWH's kingship already embraced all

---

[1] Cf. Robinson, *Religious Ideas*, pp. 197f., Davidson, *Theology*, p. 377;
North, *Interpretation*, pp. 130f.

[2] Even in Amos this subsequent glory is not lacking if the last five verses
are authentic. (Edghill, *Commentary*, *ad loc*, thinks they were inserted by
a different writer who regarded punishment as 'a means of purification,
even preservation'. Similarly, Cripps, *Commentary*, *ad loc*; Harper, *Commentary*, p. cxxxiv; Smith, *Twelve Prophets* I, pp. 199-205; Vriezen,
however, thinks it more probably 'a message from the prophet which he
passed on in the circle of his disciples'; *Theology*, p. 359).

[3] Cf. Eichrodt, *Theology*, pp. 67, 461; Vriezen, *Theology*, p. 229.

[4] Cf. Köhler, *Theology*, pp. 79ff., Martin-Achard, *Israel*, pp. 32ff., Bosch,
Heidenmission, pp. 19ff.

[5] Cf. above, n. 1; Eichrodt, *Theology*, p. 471; North, *Interpretation*, p. 64.

[6] E.g. in the overthrow of Israel's enemies, Zech. 14, etc.

[7] E.g. in descriptions of universal peace and harmony centring on the
glorified city of Jerusalem, Is. 9, 6-7. 17, 25-26.

[8] Rowley, *Faith*, p. 183.

[9] Gen. 12. 3. 18, 18. 22, 18. 26, 4. 28, 14.

[10] Cf. Martin-Archard, *Israel*, p. 35.

[11] Cf. Jer. 16, 19; Ps. 22, 7; Zech. 8, 22; Zeph. 3, 10; North, *Interpretation*,
pp. 72-74; Robinson, 'The Modern World', pp. 346ff., Rowley, *Faith*, p. 180.

natural phenomena;[1] therefore the prophets could not stop short of speaking of the future manifestation of God's kingship as embracing all nations and the entire cosmic order.[2]

It was with a view to this ultimate end that Israel's role in the world was occasionally understood as one of mission.[3] This is especially the case with Deutero-Isaiah.[4] At the same time, whatever stress was laid upon Israel's mission and on acceptance by the Gentiles of JHWH's rule, the coming age of glory was never regarded in the Old Testament as anything but the sole gift of God; always the day of JHWH is a day of special *divine* activity.[5]

It remains now only to draw out of this survey three points which elucidate the significance of the Old Testament hope.

Firstly, the contrast between the kingship of JHWH acknowledged by Israel's 'prophets' in the present, and that to which they look forward in the future, is essentially a contrast between concealed and revealed kingship. Kingship as a characteristic or attribute of JHWH could not be thought of as at one time partial, and later complete;[6] the contrast could only be between present hiddenness and future manifestation.[7] Already through the Covenant relationship JHWH's sovereign rule was manifested; but the manifestation was clouded by the partiality of Israel's response, and the sphere of the relationship was in any case limited to Israel. The expected revelation would involve an open recognition by all.[8]

Old Testament eschatology is eschatology and not simply mysticism,[9] so that the tension arising from the contrast between hidden and revealed lordship is a tension between what *is now*, and what *will be then*. The unambiguous revelation and acknowledgement of JHWH's lordship was awaited *not* in mystical perception

---

[1] E.g. I Kings 17, 14. 16; II Kings 1, 10f; 2, 8; etc. Ezra 1, 1; Jer. 1, 15; Is. 44, 24f.

[2] Cf. Is. 11, 10; Dan. 7, 27, etc. Rowley, *Faith*, p. 180; Köhler, *Theology*, pp. 85-98; North, *Interpretation*, pp. 76-78.

[3] Cf. Bosch, *Heidenmission*, pp. 17ff., Cook, *Old Testament*, p. 156; Jeremias, *Promise*, pp. 58f., Vriezen, *Theology*, p. 230; Browne, *Early Judaism*, pp. 1ff.

[4] Cf. Is. 45, 22; 42, 6; 43, 10; 49, 6; and the Servant Songs in toto.

[5] Cf. Bosch, *Heidenmission*, p. 28; Davidson, *Theology*, pp. 374f.

[6] Cf. Köhler, *Theology*, p. 31.

[7] Cf. von Rad, in *T.W.N.T.* I p. 567.

[8] Cf. e.g. Jer. 31, 34; Is. 2, 2. Köhler, *Theology*, p. 230; Smith, *Commentary*, Isaiah 2, 2; ad loc.

[9] Cf. Eichrodt, *Theology*, p. 176.

of the truth by individuals but in the future inbreaking of God into history in an unmistakable manner.[1]

Finally, the contrast between concealed and revealed, and the tension between 'now' and 'then', arise from the fact of divine promise and the assurance of divine fulfilment. Israel's hope was never founded on human optimism, nor upon any reading off from nature of a certain evolutionary tendency, or the like; nor was the expected future conceived as a human goal nor even the reward of human obedience and activity. The hope persisted rather *in spite of* these factors, being based entirely on the promise of God through his covenant relationship with Israel. The conviction that God's past promises *will be* fulfilled gives to prophecies of coming judgement their sense of imminence.[2] This 'nearness' is made, to some

---

[1] The problem of the O.T.'s understanding of time obviously calls for consideration at this juncture, but it would be beyond the bounds of this survey to do more than draw attention to recent lines of enquiry. Cullmann (*Time*, pp. 51ff.) contrasts the Biblical time conception with that of Greek thought, maintaining that in the Bible 'because time is thought of as an upward sloping line, it is possible here for something to be "fulfilled"; a divine plan can move forward to complete execution . . .' Modifications, or criticisms, of this thesis are offered by Marsh (*Fulness*), Boman (*Hebrew Thought*), Ratschow ('Anmerkungen' in *Z.T.K.* LI, 1954, pp. 36ff.), Eichrodt ('Heilserfahrung' in *T.Z.* XII, 1956, pp. 104ff.), Minear ('The time of hope' in *S.J.T.* VI, 1953, pp. 337ff.), and most recently by Barr (*Biblical Words*). Barr is critical of the semantic methodology underlying Culmann's thesis (cf. Barr's *Semantics*). Marsh, arguing that the O.T. is dominated by the idea of 'real' time (paralleling the N.T. 'kairos' concept), holds that the O.T. is not concerned with chronological time (*Fulness*, p. 20). Similarly, Boman (*Hebrew Thought*) p. 137 elucidating O.T. time from the subjective side, argues that 'time is something qualitative' for the Israelites, 'because for them it is determined by its content'. Ratschow thinks in terms of 'time for' and 'time not for', though recognising that the O.T. knows of chronological time too, whereby 'time for' and 'time not for' is objectivised. Both Boman (*Hebrew Thought*, p. 141) and Eichrodt ('Heilserfahrung', pp. 118f.) are critical of Marsh's dismissal of chronological time in the O.T., and they are concerned with the relationship between the 'kairoi' and chronological time; with the relationship of a psychological time-view to the idea of an objective time-sequence. Eichrodt maintains that it is in the encounter of faith that man perceives that God's acts in history do not occur sporadically or disconnectedly, but that he has provided a framework in which these acts can connectedly proceed in the form of a salvation-history; that there is a real past and a real 'not yet' — although the O.T. recognises that men are able to participate in a 'supra-temporal' salvation ('Heilserfahrung', p. 125); cf. Boman, *Hebrew Thought*, p. 143 (It is surprising that Boman nowhere mentions P. S. Minear's article which has much in common with his own view.)

[2] Cf. Ezek. 30, 3; Is. 13, 6; Joel 1, 15; 2, 1; 3, 14; Obad. 15; Zeph. 1, 14; etc.

2

extent, to appear simply an astute reading of the political situation at particular moments. Actually, the situation itself was taken as a sign of God's readiness to fulfil his promises; the situation did not give rise to the imminent hope, but rather the imminent hope gave rise to the particular understanding of the situation as a 'sign'.[1]

Expectation in the Inter-Testamental period

1. *Expectation in Apocalyptic*

Apocalyptic[2] has three roots. There is, in the first place, Old Testament prophecy. In common with prophecy, apocalyptic sought to declare and relate God's word to the men of its generation.[3] To some extent there is a concern to re-interpret unfulfilled promises,[4] a process already begun by Ezekiel. The scope of prophecy embraced past, present and future, and this total sphere is also apocalyptic's concern. Thus the older tendency to eliminate any predictive element from prophecy[5] is as erroneous as the suggestion that apocalyptic is concerned only with the future.[6] There are, of course, differences, but these are mainly of emphasis: apocalyptic is *especially* concerned with the future and lays more stress on the expected age of bliss as a divine irruption into history than do the prophets.[7] But its basic presuppositions it shares with the prophets of the Old Testament.[8]

---

[1] Cf. Köhler, *Theology*, pp. 87f.; Davidson, *Theology*, pp. 379ff. 381; Bosch, *Heidenmission*, p. 18.

[2] Apocalyptic properly begins with Daniel. Most scholars regard the apocalyptic passages in Joel, Zech. 9-14 and Is. 24-27 as transition passages, for whilst these passages are certainly 'apolacyptic' in character, there is more to the apocalyptic of Daniel, etc., than these passages contain. cf. Rowley, *Relevance*, p. 23; Frost, *Apocalyptic*, pp. 45f., Welch, *Visions*, pp. 32ff., North, *Interpretation*, pp. 119f. Köhler, *Theology*, p. 225; Jacob, *Theology*, p. 319.

[3] Cf. Welch, *Visions*, pp. 32f.; Charles, *Development*, p. 14; Oesterley, *Apocrypha*, p. 96.

[4] E.g. Dan. 9, 2; which 'corrects' Jer. 29, 10. Cf. Charles, *Eschatology*, p. 185; Snaith, *Cyrus*, pp. 100ff.; (Lake, *Introduction*, p. 200 goes too far in saying, 'Apocalyptic . . . arose during the Greek period, chiefly in order to explain the non-fulfilment of prophecy . . .')

[5] Cf. Charles, *Commentary on Daniel*, p. xxvi; cited by Rowley, *Relevance*, p. 35, n. 1; Kent, *Growth*, p. 134.

[6] Cf. Kent, *Growth*, p. 134; Cook, *Old Testament*, p. 207.

[7] Cf. Charles, *Eschatology*, p. 193; *Development*, p. 22; Oesterley, *Apocrypha*, p. 97.

[8] Welch, *Visions*, pp. 32ff., draws the two very close. For a discussion of the relation of prophecy to apocalyptic cf. Charles, *Eschatology*, pp. 173ff.,

In the second place, some foreign influence is likely to have affected the rise of apocalyptic,[1] but it is difficult to determine to what exact extent.

In the third place, apocalyptic was motivated by circumstance. The problems of sin and of righteous suffering (and hence of the equivocation of God's kingship in Israel) increased to an unprecedented degree under the circumstances leading to the Maccabean revolt,[2] and to this root apocalyptic owes more than to prophecy or foreign influence. In the situation of near despair, apocalyptic brought a message of imminent hope, its purpose being to sustain fainting faith in the moment of doubt.[3] Concentration upon the future is basically due to the contemporary situation in which faith in the sovereign rule of God was radically being called in question. The portrayal of future events is given for this purpose and *not* for its own sake.[4] Whatever 'fantastic' details apocalyptic might contain, its expectation cannot be summarily dismissed, nor should it be scorned as a decline from the high spiritual insights of Old Testament prophecy.[5]

The chief themes of apocalyptic [6] which concern us here are, the Kingdom of God, the element of imminence, and the central figure in the End-drama.

The expression 'the Kingdom of God' 'hardly ever occurs in apocalyptic, though the thing itself is presupposed'.[7] The primary

---

Development, pp. 12ff. Oesterley, *Apocrypha*, pp. 96f., Rowley, *Relevance*, pp. 13ff., Frost, *Apocalyptic*, pp. 11f., 46ff.

[1] Cf. Rowley, *Relevance*, p. 40; Oesterley, *Apocrypha*, p. 91; Snaith, *Cyrus*, pp. 94ff., Frost, *Apocalyptic*, pp. 71ff.

[2] Cf. Brockington, *Apocrypha*, p. 6; Frost, *Apocalyptic*, pp. 8ff.

[3] Cf. Rowley, *Relevance*, p. 36; Oesterley, *Apocrypha*, p. 97; North, *Interpretation*, p. 136.

[4] H. T. Andrews, 'Apocalyptic Literature' in Peake's *Commentary* (unrevised ed.) p. 423 (quoted, North, *Interpretation*, p. 139) quite misunderstands the apocalyptist's intention. His motivation is *not* morbid resignation or boredom, *nor* incurable curiosity or speculation, but, in the difficulties of the contemporary situation, to re-affirm God's sovereignty.

[5] As, e.g., in Cook, *Old Testament*, pp. 207f., contrast Welch, *Visions*, pp. 34f. For details of the imagery one may cf. Oesterley, *Apocrypha*, p. 97; Otto, *Kingdom of God*, p. 37; etc.

[6] For full details cf. Oesterley, *Apocrypha*, 101-112; Frost, *Apocalyptic*, passim. but esp. pp. 242-258; North, *Interpretation*, pp. 132-140; Charles, *Development*, pp. 47-159; *Eschatology*, pp. 157ff., Lake, *Introduction*, pp. 203-208; Bouset, *Religion*, pp. 242-289.

[7] Charles, *Development*, p. 48.

meaning is still that of God's kingship[1] though the idea in its
eschatological aspect as much as in its present involves much more
explicitly than before a 'kingdom', a sphere and people in which this
rule is manifested.[2] A characteristic feature is its supernatural
quality;[3] the earth as the sphere of God's future rule seems to
become less and less suitable [4] and the scene of the future consummation is laid more often than before in a radically transformed
earth.[5] The coming of this Kingdom is conceived variously. Sometimes it is expected in a sudden catastrophic moment,[6] sometimes
it is preceded by the so-called Messianic kingdom, during which
it is often anticipated progressive work would take place.[7]

Characteristic of apocalyptic expectation is the sense of imminence.[8] To suppose that this intense hope was based simply on a
longing for better times would be to miss the point entirely.[9] The
hope was built upon the conviction that God is already God, and his

---

[1] Cf. Dalman, *Words*, pp. 91ff.; Edersheim, *Life*, p. 270.

[2] Cf. Dalman, *Words*, p. 137; Charles, *Development*, pp. 48ff. (the development is here perhaps over-emphasised); Otto, *Kingdom of God*, pp. 36f.

[3] Cf. Otto, *Kingdom of God*; p. 40; Oesterley, *Apocrypha*, p. 97; Bousset,
Religion, p. 242.

[4] Cf. Oesterley, *Apocrypha*, p. 97; North, *Interpretation*, p. 136. Yet God's
Lordship over the *present* is still recognised (the demand for repentance, for
instance, is in no way minimised; cf. Test. Dan. 6, 4, Jud. 23, 5; Ass. Moses
1, 18 etc.) cf. Charles, *Development*, p. 30; Stauffer 'Das theologische Weltbild
der Apokalyptik', in *Z.s.T*. VIII, 1931, pp. 201ff.

[5] Though Oesterley, *Apocrypha*, pp. 97f. overstresses this transcendent
note. Rowley, *Relevance*, p. 165, n. 1 refers to the argument put forward by
N. Messel, that 'the Kingdom is uniformly thought of as an earthly one'. The
idea of a transformed heaven and earth is quite distinct from the idea of an
abandonment of the universe, cf. further, Frost, *Apocalyptic*, pp. 21ff.

[6] E.g. I Enoch 83-90; cf. Frost, *Apocalyptic*, p. 21.

[7] E.g. II Bar. 40, 3; I Enoch 90, 33; 38; Jub. 23; 26-28. A similar pattern
is sometimes found although there is no actual Messiah, as e.g. in I Enoch 91,
12; Ass. Moses 10, 7-10, etc. cf. Frost, *Apocalyptic* p. 22; Walker, *Hebrew Religion*, pp. 47ff., Klausner, *Messianic Idea*, pp. 222ff., Charles, *Eschatology*,
pp. 208ff; Bousset, *Religion*, Anhang, pp. 286-289 and see further below,
p. 29.

[8] Cf. Rowley, *Relevance*, p. 25; Welch, *Visions*, p. 36; Frost, *Apocalyptic*,
pp. 20-33; Oesterley, *Apocrypha*, pp. 97, 99; Snaith, *Cyrus*, pp. 100ff;
Bousset, *Religion*, p. 249.

[9] Snaith, *Cyrus*, pp. 96ff., and Frost, *Apocalyptic*, pp. 356f., give the
impression that this expectation arises from the selfish desire for national
aggrandisement. Actually, it is based on the covenant promises and that
which they involve. cf. Charles, *Eschatology*, pp. 241ff., Oesterly, *Apocrypha*,
p. 97; and note the idea of a mission to the Gentiles, not wholly lacking—
cf. Frost, *Apocalyptic*, p. 41; Bosch *Heidenmission*, pp. 35-39.

control in history an established fact. This, in conflict with the
blatant denial of such rule and control by evil forces, was essentially the motive force behind apocalyptic.

The urgency sometimes takes the form of chronological calculations. This, in turn, leads to re-interpretations of 'faulty' predictions.[1] But this intense concentration was not allowed to diminish
present obedience,[2] nor were the chronological calculations the
primary matter.[3]

Concerning the central figure in the awaited End-drama there
is considerable variation. In some visions the figure of Messiah
is entirely absent.[4] In such cases 'the kingdom was always represented as under the immediate sovereignty of God'.[5] Where Messiah
is spoken of he is sometimes represented as a supernatural figure [6]
who 'arises'[7] and who perhaps had some form of pre-existence.[8]
Where he is pictured as a human figure [9] his lineage acquires some
significance: the old expectation of an ideal Davidic king appears,[10]

---

[1] Cf. Jer. 25, 11 and 29, 10 with Dan. 9, 24-27; II Bar. 36-40 and II Esdras
10, 60-12, 35. Cf. Box, *The Ezra Apocalypse*, pp. 35ff.

[2] Cf. Oesterley, *Apocrypha*, p. 99 cf. the stress upon the Law, I Enoch
5, 4; 99, 2; 99. 14; Sib. Or 3, 27f. II Esdras 9, 7-12, etc.; and the asceticism
advocated in, e.g., I Enoch 108, 7; Ass. Moses 9, 6; etc.

[3] Box, *The Ezra Apocalypse*, pp. 35ff., overemphasises such calculations.
Contrast Charles' virtual omission of this element. The ease with which
predictions could be re-calculated (cf. Snaith, *Cyrus*, pp. 100ff.) witnesses
to the fact that the Apocalyptic writers maintained a certain detachment
from the strict consequences of their chronological calculations.

[4] Cf. Daniel, Jubilees, Enoch 1-36, 91-108, Ass. Moses, Slav. Enoch,
Baruch (though here a Messianic Kingdom is mentioned; cf. 4, 25; 31ff.
4, 36-5, 4) Charles, *Eschatology*, pp. 235f. thinks that the hope of a Messiah is
not abandoned in Jubilees: contrast Pfeiffer, *History*, p. 50.

[5] Charles, *Development*, p. 76. cf. Vriezen, *Theology*, p. 369.

[6] Oesterley, *Apocrypha*, p. 107 says this is 'characteristic of the Apocalyptic literature taken as a whole'. But apart from the figure of the Son of
Man in I Enoch and the 'Blessed Man' of the Sibylline Oracles (5 : 414ff.),
the figure of the Messiah is more often regarded as human, though endowed
with outstanding characteristics (cf. Test. Levi 18, 10ff. etc.) cf. Frost,
Apocalyptic, p. 240; Walker, *Hebrew Religion*, p. 50.

[7] Cf. Test. Dan 5, 10. Ps. Sol. 17, 47, etc.

[8] II Bar. 29, 3 speaks of 'The Messiah (who) shall begin to be revealed'
at the appointed time, though this does not necessarily involve the idea of
pre-existence: cf. Oesterley, *Apocrypha*, p. 106; Walker, *Hebrew Religion*,
p. 48; Sjöberg, *verborgene Menschensohn*, pp. 42f. 56. Parallel to the hints
at pre-existence there are hints of a return to heaven—cf. II Bar. 30, 1.
contrast II Esdras 7, 29-30.

[9] Cf. II Bar. 29-30, the Salathiel Apoc., II Esdras 3-10, etc.

[10] Cf. I Enoch 90, Test. Jud. 24, Test. Simeon 7, 2, Test. Levi, 8, 14 etc.
(where Charles, *Development*, p. 80, suggests the references are due mainly

whilst sometimes the lineage is traced to Levi.[1] The Messiah's character is essentially two-fold. On the one hand he is to war against the enemies of the righteous saints [2] (the prophetic conjunction of political and religious aims is not altogether lost sight of [3]), and on the other hand he is to be endowed with the Spirit [4] so as to be able to obey God's will,[5] 'working righteousness and mercy',[6] being 'pure from sin so that he may rule a great people'.[7]

As for the term 'Son of Man', its use in Daniel has already been discussed,[8] and in apocalyptic it 'did not become a Messianic title'.[9] The term occurs in I Enoch and II Esdras, and a similar expression 'Blessed Man' is found in the Sibylline Oracles. In Enoch [10] the term takes up the attributes and functions of the

---

to literary reminiscence). This concept reappears in literature of the 1st Century A.D. (cf. additions to the Testament of the 12 Patriarchs—Test. Jud. 24, 5-6. etc.).

[1] Cf. Test. Reuben 6, 7ff. Test. Dan 5,10, etc. Many think that this is due to a 're-adaptation of the messianic idea, due to the occupation of the throne and high priesthood by the Hasmonaean house, giving rise to the substitution of a scion of the house of Levi for a scion of the house of David' (Rowley, *Relevance*, p. 27), (cf. similarly Charles, *Development*, pp. 80-90, esp. pp. 83-4). Following disillusionment in the Maccabean leaders, the Davidic descent was re-asserted, though a total abandonment of the Levitic lineage did not occur—hence sometimes the two are juxtaposed (cf. Test. Reuben 6, 10-11, Test. Simeon 7, 2). K. G. Kuhn, however, interprets this as a union of two ideas, of a priestly Messiah on the one hand and of a political Messiah on the other (cf. 'The Two Messiahs', in *N.T.S.* 1954-6, pp. 168ff., and see also below under 'Expectation in the Qumran Community').

[2] Cf. Jubilees 18, Test. Jos. 19, 8, I Enoch 90, 19, etc.—the purpose being ultimate peace, cf. I Enoch 94, 4. 1,8. Sib. Or. 3: 373-376. Ps. Sol. 17, 37f.

[3] Cf. Rowley, *Relevance*, pp. 15ff.

[4] Cf. Ps. Sol. 17, 42, 18.8.

[5] Cf. Sib. Or. 3 : 655f.

[6] Cf. Test. Naph. 4, 5.

[7] Ps. Sol. 17, 41. Cf. Test. Jud. 24, 1. Test. Levi 18, 7. Ps. Sol. 17, 31. Cf. Oesterley, *Apocrypha*, pp. 105f. Sometimes—generally in early apocalypses—the Messianic kingdom occurs where the Messiah is absent (cf. Charles, *Eschatology*, pp. 241ff.), and was generally temporally unlimited. In later apocalypses the duration is variously limited (cf. Snaith, *Cyrus to Herod*, pp. 104f. Lake, *Introduction*, p. 206, who suggest that this development was due to a coalescing of views). Later the idea even of a temporary Messianic kingdom is abandoned (cf. Charles, *Development*, p. 62).

[8] Cf. above pp. 12ff.

[9] Cf. Dalman, *Words*, p. 249.

[10] The term occurs in 46, 4. 48, 2. 62, 5; 9; 14. 63, 11. 69, 26-27. 70, 1 and 71, 1 (cf. also 62, 7 where the demonstrative is omitted). Cf. Charles, *Pseudepigrapha*, p. 214.

Messiah and brings other features besides,[1] thus at least giving
the term a 'Messianic significance'. It has been argued that the
Son of Man here should be identified with Enoch himself,[2] but this
is very unlikely.[3] He is a supernatural figure and pre-existence
in some form is attributed to him.[4] His work and character are
closely allied to God's own:[5] he is the Christ (48, 10), the Righteous
One (38, 2), the Elect One (40, 5). He is to judge the world and is
revealer of all things and champion of the righteous.[6] (It is disputed
whether or not the idea of suffering enters into the presentation of
the Son of Man in Enoch, but the question cannot be entered into
here).[7]

---

[1] Cf. Dalman, *Words*, p. 243, 'It is clear, at all events, that "son of man"
is not taken for granted by the author as an already established title for
the Messiah. But it is not to be denied that the author, though in this part
of the Similitudes he avoids every other Messianic title, really imputes to the
"son of man" a Messianic significance'. Cf. also Charles, *Pseudepigrapha*,
p. 214: Oesterley, *Apocrypha*, pp. 105f. *Judaism*, pp. 155-159. Cranfield,
Mark, p. 273. Sjöberg, *verborgene Menschensohn*, p. 44. *Menschensohn*,
pp. 169ff. Glasson, *Advent*, pp. 28ff. Frost, *Apocalyptic*, pp. 224, 228 (who
maintains that 'the Son of Man who was great enough to sit in JHWH's
seat, would have little difficulty in attaching the Davidic Messiah to his
person', p. 228).

[2] The identification is made by Charles, *Pseudepigrapha*, *ad. loc.* Otto,
Kingdom of God, pp. 201ff. Sjöberg, *Menschensohn*, pp. 186ff (and concerning
Sjöberg, cf Frost, *Apocalyptic*, pp. 220f). T. W. Manson, 'The Son of Man in
Daniel, Enoch and the Gospels', in *B.J.R.L.* XXXII, 1950, pp. 171ff. M.
Black, 'The son of Man in the Old Biblical Literature', in *E.T.* 1948, LX.

[3] The only basis is in 71, 14 where Charles emends to 'this is' instead of the
'thou art' of the text. Against Charles cf. Higgins, in *N.T. Essays*, p. 58
note 134-5; Manson, *Jesus*, p. 120; Dalman, *Words*, p. 244; Rowley, *Relevance*, p. 56.

[4] Cf. 48, 2; 3. 46, 1-2. 49, 2. 62, 7. 70, 1. Cf. Sjöberg, *verborgene Menschensohn*, p. 44, n. 5 and p. 45. Frost, *Apocalyptic*, pp. 218f. Otto, *Kingdom
of God*, p. 188 (who speaks of an 'ideal pre-existence which passes over into
a mysterious sort of present existence'). Preiss, *Life in Christ*, p. 50. Klausner,
Messianic Idea, pp. 290ff. Bousset, *Religion*, p. 263.

[5] He is to receive the homage of all men, will judge all men, condemning
and slaying the wicked and rewarding the just. cf. Frost. *Apocalyptic*,
pp. 218ff. Klausner, *Messianic Idea*, pp. 291f.

[6] Cf. Charles, *Pseudepigrapha*, p. 214 (note on 46, 2-3). For his judgement
cf. 38, 2. 39, 6. 53, 6. Wisdom, cf. 49, 1ff. 51, 3. Power, cf. 49, 3. 52, 6. For
his work as revealer cf. 64, 3. 49, 2. etc. and for his work as champion cf. 39,
7. 48, 4. 51, 5. 53, 6. etc.

[7] Bevan, *Jerusalem*, p. 162 says there is 'no hint of incarnation of abase-
ment . . . no shadow of death . . .' Jeremias and Zimmerli, *Servant*, pp. 59ff.
contend that numerous parallel expressions in the Servant Songs of Deutero-
Isaiah and I Enoch 'Son of Man' passages point to the conclusion that Son
of Man and Servant of God are here combined for the first time. But contrast

In the vision of II Esdras 13 the 'likeness of a man' (איז דמות דבר
נשא) [1] rises from the sea causing consternation (v. 4), anihilating
the wicked who dare to war against him (vv. 5-11) and gathers
together the 'multitude which was peaceable' (v. 12). In the interpretation which is given it is said that the Son of Man is the 'messianic' deliverer [2] 'Whom the Most High is keeping many ages' (v. 26)
and who is to come to judge and establish his Kingdom.[3]

There is mention of a 'Blessed Man' in the Sibylline Oracles
(5, 414), but in view of the fact that he is said already to 'have
come from the plains of heaven . . .' and also that the section is
to be dated about 125 A.D. (and possibly is of Christian origin),
the passage can help little in determining pre-Christian hopes.[4]

The term 'Son of God', although 'through Scripture (cf. Ps. 2,
89, 26-27) a Messianic potential',[5] seems to have been made little
use of in Apocalyptic expectation.[6]

Similarly the concept 'Servant' appears to have been another
Messianic potential which was not generally taken up by Apocalyp-

---

Sjöberg, *Menschensohn*, pp. 116ff. and *verborgene Menschensohn*, pp. 70f.
Otto, *Kingdom of God*, p. 255. Some think that suffering at least looms in
the background here—cf. Cranfield, *Mark*. p. 275; Davies, *Rabbinic Judaism*,
p. 279 and p. 280, n. 1.

[1] Dated by Charles in the 1st Century AD but before 70. Cf. *Eschatology*,
pp. 337f. Similarly Oesterley, *Apocrypha*, pp. 514f. who dates it just prior to
A.D. 70; contrast Brockington, *Apocrypha*, pp. 25f. who dates it about
100 A.D.

[2] Cf. Oesterley, *Apocrypha*, p. 516. Pfeiffer, *History*, p. 84.

[3] Charles, *Pseudepigrapha*, p. 616 suggests that in its earliest form this
material contained ideas of an 'Urmensch' which ultimately developed into
the heavenly Messiah figure. Cf. also *Development*, p. 242: Klausner, *Messianic
Idea*, p. 353 (who concludes that oriental influences of some kind lie behind
this passage). Jeremias, in Erlöser und Erlösung im Spätjudentum und
Urchristentum, *D.T.* II, 1929, pp. 106ff., wants to connect the Son of Man
here with suffering. Sjöberg, on the other hand, denies the connection—
'Der verborgene Messias wird nach ihm nicht im Hades, sondern im Himmel
von Gott aufbewahrt' (*verborgene Menschensohn*, p. 47, n. 4). But the argument that elsewhere in II Esdras the Son of Man is reserved in heaven
until his appearing amongst men does not exclude the possibility, surely, that
this appearing might occur through a process and in a context of suffering.

[4] Cf. Charles, *Development*, p. 226. Pfeiffer, *History*, pp. 226ff.

[5] Manson, *Jesus*, p. 103.

[6] Cf. Test. Jud. 24, 2. Ps. Sol. 17, 28f., 30. 18, 4. Test. Jud. 24, 3. Test. Levi
18, 8. Oesterley's translation of II Esdras 7, 28 (cf. *Apocrypha*, p. 517) is
rejected by Taylor, *Names*, p. 53, n. 2 and cf. further Sjöberg, *verborgene
Menschensohn*, p. 47, n. 1. Klausner, *Messianic Idea*, p. 358. Jeremias and
Zimmerli, *Servant*, pp. 49f.

tic.[1] II Bar. 70, 9 mentions 'My servant Messiah', but the authenticity of the verse is questionable.[2] II Esdras 7, 28f.[3] reads in the
Ethiopic 'My servant' and in 7, 30 this servant dies. But this is
hardly a description of Messiah in terms of the suffering servant of
Deutero-Isaiah even if a link is facilitated.[4]

We see, then, that the pattern of expectation and the pattern
of ideas concerning the Kingdom of God found in the O.T. re-
appear here. There is a concern with the past: older prophecy is
re-interpreted to be sure—but it *is* older prophecy. The Apocalyptists based their work on that which had gone before them.[5] Further,
they wrote from an historical standpoint. This was more than a
literary device for it betrays an awareness that in the past outstanding events in Israel's life could be found those acts of God
whereby he made known to the nation his Lordship over it: and
that those acts were the basis on which any confident expectation
that God would one day intervene to make clear his Lordship,
could be founded.

There is also concern for the present: the faithfulness to the
Covenant relationship of at least the remnant of Israel must be
upheld—there is not the least tendency to antinomianism in
the face of the expected catastrophic intervention—rather the
reverse, in as much as the coming climax was expected to reveal
the moral demands of God, already valid and binding.[6]

The future contains the key to the present and the past: all
the equivocation would one day be put to an end through the
divine intervention in history for the sake of manifesting the
Kingship of God. In judgement and blessing he would manifest his
Lordship, and this would involve a total transformation of the

---

[1] Cf. Jacob, *Theology*, p. 342.

[2] Charles, *Pseudepigrapha, ad loc*, counts the verse a later interpolation:
'verse 10 is the natural sequence to verse 8.'

[3] Cf. also 13, 32; 37; 52. 14, 9. Jeremias and Zimmerli, *Servant* p. 45,
n. 163, p. 49.

[4] I.e. there is no explicit redemptive suffering here. Cf. Klausner, *Messianic Idea*, p. 361. Sjöberg, *verborgene Menschensohn*, p. 257. Nevertheless the
title is perhaps helpful in facilitating a subsequent union of the two concepts
—cf. Jeremias and Zimmerli, *Servant*, pp. 59f. Cranfield, *Mark*, p. 277.

[5] Cf. the interest in the chronology of the past as well as of the future.
Cf. Frost, *Apocalyptic*, p. 20.

[6] Hence the dual themes of pessimism (perhaps better designated realism)
regarding this world and 'now': and optimism (perhaps better described as
faith) regarding the future—cf. North, *Interpretation*, p. 136.

present situation, hence the picture of world renewal enhanced sometimes by the idea of an entirely supernatural realm.[1]

Whether God would act directly or mediately through an appointed representative, it is essentially *divine* activity which is awaited. The expectation is held with particular intensity and the end is thought to be imminent. But the basis of this is not a desire for a time chart, but rather the conviction that it is unfitting and intolerble that God's Lordship should be made so ambiguous by the ascendency of the wicked and the suffering of the righteous and that therefore he must and will quickly intervene to change the situation and make himself manifest.[2]

2. *Expectation in Wisdom literature*

In the later wisdom writings particularly, although the Hebrew characteristics remain,[3] 'we certainly find . . . positions taken up which show to some extent a departure from traditional Judaism'.[4] There is still a concern with the past, for wisdom itself is culled from past experiences and traditions,[5] and there is also the idea of wisdom operative in creation.[6] There is a strong emphasis upon the present. Human conduct and right behaviour is its chief concern.[7] This is certainly practical [8] and has a universal appeal and relevance,[9] but it is not entirely correct to see this as thoroughly anthropological, for it is sufficiently Hebrew to retain God as its basis,[10] exalting law and obedience to law as the height of wisdom.[11] The future expectation is, however, slight.[12] The reason appears

---

[1] Cf. Frost, *Apocalyptic*, pp. 20ff.

[2] The contrast therefore, between now and then, which has been traced in the O.T. understanding of God's kingship is found here too.

[3] Cf. Snaith, *Cyrus to Herod*, p. 163: Oesterley, *Jews*, p. 234: Box, *Judaism*, p. 118.

[4] Cf. Oesterley, *Apocrypha*, p. 245. Cf. also Pfeiffer, *History*, pp. 64ff. Rankin, *Wisdom*, p. 5. Baumgartner in *The Old Testament and Modern Study*, pp. 210ff. Box, *Judaism*, p. 118.

[5] Cf. e.g. the title 'Pirqe Aboth'—sayings of the fathers.

[6] Cf. Snaith, *Cyrus to Herod*, p. 177. Oesterley, *Apocrypha*, p. 248.

[7] Cf. Snaith, *Cyrus to Herod* p. 166. Cook, *Old Testament*, p. 204. Oesterley, *Apocrypha*, p. 236. Box, *Judaism*, p. 119. Rankin, *Wisdom*, p. 3.

[8] Cf. Box, *Judaism*, p. 119.

[9] Cf. Baumgartner, in *The Old Testament and modern Study*, p. 211. Cook, *Old Testament*, p. 204. Box, *Judaism*, p. 119.

[10] Cf. Oesterley, *Apocrypha*, p. 214.

[11] Cf. Snaith, *Cyrus to Herod*, p. 166. Pfeiffer, *History*, p. 64.

[12] Cf. Rankin, *Wisdom*, p. 3. Klausner, *Messianic Idea*, p. 252.

to be the emphasis upon the present and present behaviour and, of course, apocalyptic writings could be said to balance the deficiency here.[1]

3. *Expectation in Hellenistic Judaism*

Already the influences at work during the Hellenistic period have been seen in apocalyptic and wisdom writings. It is only necessary to add a note concerning other minor or peripheral evidence.[2] First Philo [3] who, though to some extent a unique phenomenon,[4] must be accepted as the chief monument of Hellenistic Judaism.[5] In combining the religious understandings of Hebrew and Greek,[6] Philo retained a respect for the law and an obedience to it, and the fundamental conviction in a transcendent God.[7] He held, too, a national hope for the future[8]—but his chief element of hope was personal, involving ecstacy,[9] mysticism [10] and illumination [11]. Secondly, the mystery religions which held a fascination for the Graeco- Roman world.[12] Essentially, however, the mystery cults were individualistic and aimed at a mystic incorporation into the divine.[13] The Corpus Hermeticum [14] which reflects such 'syncretistic Mystery cult' views [15] has as its chief end and aim knowledge (γνῶσις) of God.[16] Then, the fourth Eclogue

---

[1] There is no reason to suppose that the wisdom writers of the hellenistic period were ignorant of or antagonistic to apocalyptic expectations.

[2] For a discussion of the expectation in Hellenistic Judaism in more detail, cf. Box, *Judaism*, pp. 72ff. Oesterley, *Jews*, pp. 19ff. Pfeiffer, *History*, pp. 181ff.

[3] Cf. Oesterley, *Apocrypha*, pp. 61ff. *Jews*, pp. 20ff. Snaith, *Cyrus to Herod*, p. 173. Bousset, *Religion*, pp. 438f., 452ff. Pfeiffer, *History*, pp. 197ff.

[4] So Oesterley, *Apocrypha*, pp. 61f. Bousset, *Religion*, p. 438; contrast, Kennedy, *Mystery Religions*, p. 64.

[5] So E. Bevan, *Later Greek Religions*, p. 98.

[6] Cf. Bousset, *Religion*, p. 440. Goodenough, *Philo*, pp. 97ff.

[7] Cf. Oesterley, *Apocrypha*, p. 64. Bousset, *Religion*, p. 439.

[8] Cf. Goodenough, *Philo*, pp. 113f.

[9] Cf. Bousset, *Religion*, p. 449. Bevan, *Religions*, p. 98.

[10] Cf. Kennedy, *Mystery-Religions*, pp. 65ff. Bousset, *Religion*, p. 452.

[11] Cf. Oesterley, *Apocrypha*, p. 65.

[12] Cf. Kennedy, *Mystery-Religions*, p. 20. Pfeiffer, *History*, p. 147.

[13] Cf. Bousset, *Religion*, p. 290. Pfeiffer, *History*, p. 148.

[14] Reitzenstein, *Die hellenistische Mysterienreligionen*, 1910, p. 33 dates the material as 1-3rd centuries A.D. Kennedy, *Mystery-Religions*, pp. 104ff. argues for about 300 B.C. — 300 A.D.

[15] Cf. Kennedy, *Mystery-Religions*, p. 104.

[16] Cf. Kennedy, *Mystery-Religions*, p. 109.

of Vergil presents the hope of a 'golden age' but in fundamental contrast to apocalyptic expectation; although it is on a cosmic scale it is the hope of revolution from within rather than of intervention from without.

Still, therefore, an interest is found in past, present and future. The past is the time of God's working in Israel (cf the 'historical' writings of Hellenistic Judaism).[1] The present is the occasion when men are required to live a virtuous life by practice of wisdom. The future is viewed primarily as the ultimate end of human aspiration (rather than as the movement of God towards the world). The contrast of hidden and revealed is not at all prominent, and the tension between a 'now' and a 'then' gives way to one between 'here' and 'there'.[2] Instead of confidence in God's fulfilment of given promises, we find rather striving after the attainment of human longings.[3]

4. *Expectation in Rabbinic Judaism*

A hard and fast division is not here intended between apocalyptic and Rabbinic expectations,[4] and only the main outlines of expectation will be noted[5] (the material does not offer us systematics but does allow us to distil certain ideas).[6]

The meaning of *Malkuth* is still 'rule', 'sovereignty'.[7] It is not

---

[1] Cf. Pfeiffer, *History*, p. 200.

[2] Boman, *Hebrew Thought*, pp. 161ff. accepts the Greek idea of a 'flight from this wretched world into the blessed timeless Beyond' (p. 163) as a parallel to the Hebrew 'now'—'then' contrast, both of which, he says, are subsumed under the Christian idea of Revelation in Christ, and he argues on these lines against Cullmann (*Christ and Time*). In fact he appears to be at cross-purposes, for Cullmann is not suggesting that the Hebrew 'now'—'then' contrast excludes a 'here'—'there' contrast, and his point is only that the Hebrew does not long for absorption into the divine nor for an abandonment by God of this world, but looks for a future inbreak into history in fulfilment of Covenant promises.

[3] The contrasts may be overdrawn, but the differences are none the less real; cf. Schmidt, in *T.W.N.T.* I, p. 574.

[4] Davies, *Rabbinic Judaism*, p. 9 writes, 'The Pharisees . . . would not only be cognisant of apocalyptic speculation but in varying degrees doubtless attracted by it.' Cf. also Lake, *Introduction* pp. 202f.

[5] Cf. S.-B. *Kommentar*: Bonsirven, *Judaïsme*: Davies, *Rabbinic Judaism*. The difficulty in using the Mishnah as evidence for 1st century Rabbinic views is noted. Cf. Danby, *Mishnah*, pp. xiii ff. Davies, *Rabbinic Judaism*, p. 3.

[6] Montefiore, *Judaism and Hellenism*, p. 139 calls the material 'as a whole, rambling, discursive, inartistic, amorphous!'

[7] Cf. Kuhn, in *T.W.N.T.* I, pp. 570f. Dalman, *Words*, pp. 96f.

so prominent in Rabbinic Judaism as in the N.T. proclamation.
It has past, present and future reference. As for the past, God
is regarded as Creator-King. On account of the fall of man he
limited his kingship, but a significant step forward came with
Abraham.[1] In its present application, the *Malkuth* JHWH takes on
two senses. First, it is now an eternal reality.[2] Secondly, it can
be accepted or rejected in the present by acknowledgement and
obedience or their opposites.[3] The characteristic feature of the
present Lordship is, however, its hiddenness,[4] and in this respect
the old problem of suffering was acutley felt.[5] With reference
to the future, there is an attempt to some extent to unite various
ideas.[6] The coming aeon is spoken of as the heavenly realm into
which the Righteous enter on dying:[7] it is also the final aeon which
lies beyond the days of the Messiah.[8] The scope of the future
expectation varies, but generally a certain prominence attaches
to Israel.[9] The hope does not mean that the present is a matter
for indifference.[10] The coming aeon could and should be prayed

---

[1] Cf. S.-B. *Kommentar*, I, p. 172.

[2] Cf. Targum Onkelos of Ex. 15, 18. Cf. Bousset, *Religion*, pp. 374f.

[3] Acceptance in point of fact comes to mean recognition of monotheism
and the Shema. Cf. Kuhn, in *T.W.N.T.* I, p. 572. S.-B. *Kommentar*, I, p. 177.
Bonsirven, *Judaïsme*, pp. 77ff.

[4] Cf. S.-B. *Kommentar*, I. p. 178.

[5] Cf. S.-B. *Kommentar*, I, p. 178.

[6] Cf. S.-B. *Kommentar*, IV, pp. 799ff.

[7] Cf. S.-B. *Kommentar*, IV, pp. 968ff.

[8] Sometimes this is thought of as *not* immediately following the advent
of the Messiah, though the usual view is that the coming age 'unmittelbar
an die Tage des Messias anschliessen werde und dass sein Beginn zugleich
die Erneurung der Welt bedeute' (S.-B. *Kommentar*, IV, pp. 969f.). There is
a splitting up of future expectation into the 'days of the Messiah' followed by
the 'final aeon'. Behind this lies the attempt to harmonise the expectation
of a direct intervention of JHWH himself, with that of his action through
a mediator (cf. Dalman, *Words*, pp. 269f. S.-B. *Kommentar*, IV, pp. 968ff.
Kuhn, in *T.W.N.T.* I, p. 573. Bousset, *Religion*, p. 238). It is perhaps strange
that 'nirgends erscheint etwa der Gedanke, dass das Königsreich des Messias
die מלכת שמים sei, oder dass der Messias durch sein Wirken die שמים
מלכת herbeiführe, o.ä.' (Kuhn, in *T.W.N.T.* I, p. 573).

[9] Cf. Sanh. 10, 1. 'All Israel has a share in the coming Aeon.'

[10] Some references suggest that it is only human sin which holds back the
coming aeon (cf. S.-B. *Kommentar*, IV, p. 30 and Excursus pp. 977ff.), whilst
others without going this far give human obedience a significant place. Yet
other references show that the divine initiative in the whole matter was not
lost sight of.

for.[1] The characteristic of its coming would be the manifestation of God's (already real) Kingship.[2]

The central figure of the end is variously portrayed. The 'Son of David' concept of the Messiah occurs (cf Ps. Sol. 17, 21) in pre-Christian times—more frequently in post Christian Jewish writings.[3] Not infrequently the figure of Messiah is clothed with the character of the old idealised King expectation.[4] His work includes political aspects, though this is only a part of his total concern.[5] His work in judgement varies according to the position given to the Messianic Kingdom in relation to the final aeon. Variation is found also concerning his pre-existence.[6] The term 'Son of Man' was not a regular Jewish designation, though for example in Rabbinic 'messianic' interpretation of Dan. 7, 13 the term seems 'certainly sometimes' to have been understood to 'denote the Messiah'.[7] The term 'Son of God' is used with reference to Israel as a whole, as the people of God,[8] but it is evident that 'Son of God was not a common Messianic title.[9] As for the 'Servant' concept, there is no general or frequent or obvious connection in Rabbinic literature of about the 1st century of the Messiah with the figure of the Servant of Deutero-Isaiah.[10]

---

[1] Cf. the 11th prayer of the Shemoneh Esre; cf. S.-B. *Kommentar*, I, p. 178. Kuhn, in *T.W.N.T.* I, p. 572.

[2] Cf. Dalman, *Words*, p. 100. Bonsirven, *Judaïsme*, p. 157. Kuhn, in *T.W.N.T.* I, p. 572. S.-B. *Kommentar*, I, p. 178.

[3] Cf. S.-B. *Kommentar*, I, p. 525 and IV, pp. 968f.

[4] Cf. S.-B. *Kommentar*, IV, pp. 872f.

[5] Cf. Dalman, *Words*, pp. 297f.

[6] Cf. Dalman, *Words*, pp. 300f. Sometimes the idea of pre-existence is lacking, cf. Dalman, *Words*, p. 302.

[7] So Dalman, *Words*, pp. 244ff. who sets out the evidence for Rabbinic interpretations of Dan. 7, 13. Cf. also Manson, *Jesus*, Appendix C, pp. 173ff. Davies, *Rabbinic Judaism*, pp. 279ff. Albright *From Stone Age to Christianity*, p. 292 (who think the terms 'Son of Man' and 'Messiah' merged in the pre-Christian era: contrast Rowley, *Relevance*, p. 29).

[8] Cf. S.-B. *Kommentar*, III, pp. 17ff. Dalman, *Words*, pp. 268ff.

[9] Manson, *Jesus*, pp. 105f. similarly Dalman, *Words*, p. 272; S.-B. *Kommentar*, III, p. 20.

[10] Manson, *Jesus*, pp. 168ff., sets out the evidence showing how in the Targum on Is. 52, 3-53, 12 all the elements of suffering are attributed to Israel or the heathen nations. He nevertheless asserts that 'in Biblical and Jewish belief the ideas Son of God, Servant of the Lord and Son of Man, however separate they may have been in origin, had come to signify only variant phases of the one Messianic idea . . .' (op. cit. p. 110). Certainly it is true that the figures of Messiah and Servant are at least brought into close contact in the Targum and therefore an identification of the two seems to be partially facilitated.

There is evidence that some circles engaged in speculations and reckoning the date of the end.[1] On the other hand there is also evidence that some rejected entirely such attempts.[2] This reckoning hints at an earnest desire for the coming of the End, similar to the urgency manifest in apocalyptic. Further evidence can be found in the frequent prayers where the longing for God quickly to bring in his kingdom finds voice.

5. Expectation amongst particular groups

a. The Qumran Community.[3]

Only the briefest sketch can here be given of the various elements in this community's expectation.[4] God's rule is again comprehended under a three-fold pattern. In the past God made known his Lord-

---

A fairly detailed discussion of attempts to find an actual identification in early Rabbinic literature is given by Davies, *Rabbinic Judaism*, pp. 275ff. He quotes Volz (*Jüdische Eschatologie*, p. 237) as giving an often drawn conclusion, 'Von einem Leiden des Messias ist in unserer Periode noch nicht die Rede. Is. 53 hat man erst später mit dem Messias in Verbindung gemacht'. He hesitatingly reject's King's argument (E. H. King, *Yalḳuṭ on Zechariah*, 1882, pp. 85ff.) that a 'Messiah ben Joseph' (usually given a 2nd century dating) can be found in our period: and he accepts Rowley's refutation of the thesis that Taxo in the Ass. Moses is to be seen as a suffering servant in 2nd Isaiah's sense. He concludes that 'the assumption is at least possible that the conception of a suffering Messiah was not unfamiliar to pre-Christian Judaism' (op. cit. p. 283). Cf. further, Jeremias in *Mélanges offerts à M. Goguel*, pp. 118f., for similar views. Contrast Sjöberg, *verborgene Menschensohn* pp. 256ff. 264ff.

[1] Cf. S.-B. *Kommentar*, IV, pp. 799ff. Bonsirven, *Judaïsme*, pp. 161ff.

[2] Cf. S.-B. *Kommentar*, IV, p. 1013.

[3] The question as to the identity of this community with the Essenes is here peripheral. A comparison of the sources of information on the Essenes (Josephus Ant. XII: v. 9. XV: x. 4f. XVIII: i. 5. Wars II: viii.2-13. Philo in Eusebius, Pliny, Natural History V : 17) with the scrolls is enough to show that 'the correspondence between the ideas of the Brotherhood and those that obtained generally in Palestine during the Graeco-Roman age and that survive sparodically among the more exotic sects is especially striking in the field of eschatology' (Gaster, *Scriptures*, p. 32). And this general correspondence includes the more particular similarity with the Essenes. Qumran expectation we shall take to be representative of all such communities.

[4] For fuller discussion cf. esp. Dupont-Sommer, *Dead Sea Scrolls*: Rowley *The Zadokite Fragment and the Dead Sea Scrolls*: Bruce, *Second Thoughts on the Dead Sea Scrolls*: Allegro, 'Further Messianic References in Qumran literature', in *J.B.L.* LXXV, 1956, pp. 182ff. References to the Scrolls will be made according to the system listed by R. de Vaux, 'Fouille au Khirbet Qumran', in *R.B.* 1953, p. 88.

ship especially to Israel's leaders, and in particular in the establishment of the Covenant by which Israel became a people 'unto God'
and received the expression of his will.[1] In the present we find a
double understanding: on the one hand God's sovereignty was
thought to be acknowledged in the community itself, in the faithful
remnant whose 'main purpose was to exemplify and promulgate
the true interpretation' of the Law,[2] and whose life reflected this
submission in obedience to God's rule. On the other hand, there is
a recognition that God's present Lordship is but an aspect of his
eternal sovereignty.[3] This Lordship is not generally recognised
because at present Belial holds sway in the world.[4] Therefore there
is also a future aspect to the Kingdom, the expectation that God
would one day put an end to the present ambiguous situation and
reveal himself as Lord in the punishment of the wicked and 'the
blessing of the faithful. The future age was expected to come into
being through the mediation of a Messiah, variously conceived. We
meet again the expectation of two Messiahs, one of Levi and one of
Judah,[5] the significance of which is not entirely clear. The relation

---

[1] Cf. the Oration of Moses, and see Gaster, *Scriptures*, pp. 225ff. cf. also
the fact that the Community was founded upon Scripture and its interpretation. Cf. Burrows, *Scrolls*, pp. 247ff.

[2] Cf. Gaster, *Scriptures*, p. 15.

[3] Cf. I. Q.S. iii.

[4] Cf. I. Q.S. xii, 2. C.D. iv, 12.

[5] The expectation is already found in the Testament of the 12 Patriarchs
of a Levitical Messiah alongside a Kingly descendant of Judah. In an older
recension of the Testaments (fragments found in Qumran) this Levitical
Messiah is himself both priest *and* king (cf. Test. Reub. 6, 7-12). Elsewhere
the priest Messiah of Levi is superior to the kingly (cf. Test. Jud. 21, 1-15.
Test. Naph. 5, 1-3). The Zadokite Document in its mentions of 'Messiah
from Aaron and Israel' 'might be thought to point more naturally to one
Messiah: but in the light of cognate references in other Qumran texts a
strong case can be made out for understanding them to point to two Messiahs—a Messiah of Aaron and a Messiah of Israel' (Bruce, *Biblical Exegesis*,
p. 44). This twofold expectation is linked in I.Q.S. with the hope of a prophet (cf. I.Q.S. ix, 11) and this threefold expectation is supported by I.Q.
Testimonia referring to the coming prophet (Dt. 5, 25-26, 18, 18f.) the
coming Messiah of Jacob (Num. 24, 15-17) and the coming priest of Levi
(Dt. 33, 8-11), the last having the preeminence.
   The teacher of Righteousness is connected with the coming Messiah in
some way. Dupont-Sommer 'believes that the writer of the Damascus Document expected the teacher of righteousness to return at the end of the world
as the Messiah. To support this view he quotes the expression "from the
gathering in of the unique teacher to the arising of the Messiah from Aaron
and from Israel", but this implies a distinction between the unique teacher
and the Messiah rather than their identification. Believing that the teacher

of the Messiah to a (? the) Teacher of Righteousness is also disputed.
No use of the term 'Son of Man' in a Messianic connection is made,
but it may be that it remained a potential. Some references seem
to regard the whole community as 'suffering servant',[1] and it is
possible that in I.Q.Sa. 53, 14 we have a reference to a priestly
Messiah identified with the suffering servant—which could be a
category for the community and for an expected individual.[2]

The intensity of the community's hope is reflected in the careful
and detailed preparations for the work of its members in the
messianic woes.[3] There is, in the community, a tension between the
present and future. And whilst there is no indication that the
present was regarded with indifference, there is certainly a straining
after that which is to come.

b. The Zealots.[4]

Here we can confidently trace a doctrine of the sovereignty of
God over the past life of Israel, and an awareness that this
sovereignty is inadequately acknowledged in the present. But
what the Zealot expectation for the future was, is a problem. It is
usually said that they sought to establish the Messianic Kingdom.[5]
Their first aim, however, seems to have been simply the recovery
of a theocratic government on the former pattern. If this was confused with the hope of the messianic kingdom,[6] there still seems
reason to distinguish the two ideas and to accept the theocratic
as the Zealot's primary aim.[7]

---

of righteousness was put to death in 65-63 B.C. Dupont-Sommer infers that
the end of the world was then expected very soon . . .' (Burrows, *Scrolls*,
pp. 265f. Dupont-Sommer's reconstruction of the community's hope has
received little support; cf. Burrows, *Scrolls*, p. 266).

[1] I.Q.S. 3, 6-12, 4, 20-21, 5, 6-7. 9, 3-5.

[2] Bruce, *Biblical Exegesis*, p. 62.

[3] Cf. I.Q.M. *passim*. Gaster, *Scriptures*, p. 258 writes, 'To men who believed
that the Final Age was indeed at hand, preparations for this war were a
matter of imminent and urgent concern.'

[4] I.e. ζηλωτής קנא. Josephus says the term was applied to the anti-Roman
party from the time of Judas' revolt.

[5] Cf. Angus, in *E.R.E.* XII, pp. 849f. Cullmann, *State*, pp. 8ff.

[6] Cf. Cullmann, *State*, p. 9.

[7] J. N. Schofield, *The Historical Background to the Bible*, p. 292 writes,
the Zealots were 'ready to support any self-styled Messiah or prophet who
proclaimed the imminent coming of God and the establishment of His
Kingdom.' But there is no evidence that they regarded any of their own

They reveal an intense religious zeal and maintain a definite conjunction of political and religious hopes. They also reveal deep dissatisfaction with their present situation, in as much as it departed from the theocratic situation of former times where God's Lordship over Israel was more faithfully set forth than it could be under Roman rule. But as an extreme nationalist wing of Pharisaism it seems unlikely that they would have entertained hopes of forcing in the messianic age, and therefore their significance for our survey here is slight.

---

leaders as Messiah, until the Bar Kochba rising in 132 A.D. (cf. Duncan, *Son of Man*, p. 67). There is, similarly, no evidence that Zealots immediately hailed John the Baptist as leader or Messiah.

CHAPTER THREE

CONSISTENT ESCHATOLOGY

In its historical context, Schweitzer's interpretation of New Testament eschatology can be seen as a reaction against 19th century immanentism and liberalism. His thesis is as follows.

John the Baptist thought of himself as a prophet. Jesus alone (because of his messianic consciousness) saw him as 'Eljah'.[1] Jesus believed himself to be the Messiah-designate [2] and had a lively awareness of the nearness of the Kingdom of God and of his own glorification. But first repentance must be proclaimed and effected,[3] Jesus leading the way. Thus he effected a synthesis of prophetic and apocalyptic eschatologies.[4] Through his mighty works he prepared for the Kingdom's dawning.[5] The mission of the twelve was 'the last effort for bringing about the Kingdom'.[6] Yet the expected advent delayed and Jesus came to realise that only through his own affliction would the kingdom dawn. The entry into Jerusalem was his 'funeral march to victory'[7] and he died confidently expecting as the immediate consequence the dawning of the Kingdom and his own 'coming' as Messiah. Jesus' expectation proved wrong.[8] It was his peculiar consciousness—a secret awareness progressively disclosed to Jesus at his baptism, to the three at the Transfiguration, to the Twelve shortly afterwards and through Judas to the authorities [9]—which gave rise to this false expectation.

Schweitzer extends his thesis to include a study of Paul in which he assumes 'the complete agreement of the teaching of Paul with that of Jesus' (meaning that Paul's thought was thoroughly Hebraic, and dominated by eschatology).[10] Paul (in Schweitzer's

---

[1] Cf. Mk. 9, 11-13. Mtt. 11, 7ff. 11, 14 Ἡλείας ὁ μέλλων ἔρχεσθαι.
[2] Cf. *Mystery*, pp. 185f., pp. 254ff.
[3] Cf. *Mystery*, pp. 94f.
[4] Cf. *Mystery*, p. 256.
[5] Cf. *Mystery*, pp. 256f.
[6] Cf. *Mystery*, p. 261.
[7] Cf. *Mystery*, p. 267.
[8] Cf. *Quest*, p. 369.
[9] Cf. *Mystery*, pp. 185ff., 214ff.
[10] Cf. *Mysticism*, p. vii.

view) regarded Jesus' death as the inauguration of the Messianic era [1] and believed that an 'overlap' of aeons had occurred whereby the present world order continues, but its relevance is lost to those who are 'in Christ'.[2] This 'overlap' must cease when Jesus enters fully into his Kingdom [3] and this event was regarded as imminent. The lingering power of the angels over the elect mattered little: [4] the sacraments are temporary *ad hoc* institutions; [5] ethics, now based on the past inauguration, are but interim ethics,[6] and the present allows mystical union with Christ whereby one is here in this world, but also transcendently with Christ.[7]

Following upon the loss, in the 2nd century, of 'the expectation of the immediate dawn of the Messianic Kingdom',[8] Paul's thought (according to Schweitzer) was misunderstood, was Hellenised and translated into non-eschatological terms. The process was begun before the hope in a speedy coming of the Kingdom died, so that when the continued Parousia delay led eventually to the abandonment of an eschatological hope, a Hellenistic dogmatic system replaced it without disturbance.[9] The process of change can be traced through Ignatius and Polycarp, Justin and John.[10]It was facilitated because Paul's mysticism made Hellenisation possible.[11] We must turn to Paul for the gospel of Jesus: but only to 'the authentic Primitive Christian Paulinism',[12] for Greek, Catholic and Protestant theologies 'all contain the gospel of Paul in a form which does not continue the gospel of Jesus but displaces it'.[13]

Recently F. Buri has supported Schweitzer's thesis. He upholds its recognition of the centrality of eschatology in the New Testament, of the centrality for Jesus' and for Paul's thought of a temporally delimited *Naherwartung* [14] and of the centrality for the life

---

[1] Cf. *Mysticism*, p. 64.
[2] Cf. *Mysticism*, p. 192.
[3] Cf. *Mysticism*, p. 63.
[4] Cf. *Mysticism*, p. 65.
[5] Cf. *Mysticism*, p. 22.
[6] Cf. *Mysticism*, pp. 297ff.
[7] Cf. *Mysticism*, pp. 3ff.
[8] Cf. *Mysticism*, p. 39.
[9] Cf. *Mysticism*, p. 336.
[10] Cf. *Mysticism*, pp. 341ff., 348ff.
[11] Cf. *Mysticism*, p. 372.
[12] Cf. *Mysticism*, p. 392.
[13] Cf. *Mysticism*, p. 391.
[14] Cf. *Die Bedeutung*, pp. 25ff.

and growth of the early church of the Parousia-delay crisis.[1] He realises that the weakest point in Schweitzer's thesis is its failure to offer any full and sustained interpretation of the Jesus of history for present faith. Schweitzer's reverence for life maxim is more practised than expounded.[2] Buri seeks to overcome this deficiency by introducing Bultmann's hermeneutic principle of existential interpretation. 'The New Testament', he argues, 'must be understood as referring to the individual and total human situation present and future, and not—directly—to world history'.[3] The basis of eschatology is anthropological: it is the 'will for life fulfilment' in the present, despite the discouragement of knowledge. The essence of New Testament eschatology (he maintains) is the overcoming of knowledge by will, and this is expressed in the form of Judaic apocalyptic. But we can substitute for this form the recognition of each present moment as a creation of God, and hence we can achieve a reverence for each moment as a creation divine. The achievement of all this is precisely what the New Testament means when it speaks of being 'in Christ'.[4]

Schweitzer concentrated upon the initial stage of the development of dogma through Jesus and Paul. Building on this, subsequent development has been reconstructed, notably, by M. Werner. In the 'elucidation of the inner causes of Hellenisation', Werner argues, we need some overall understanding of the ministry and message of Jesus and the thought of Paul which may serve as our point of departure.[5] Werner believes that Schweitzer's thesis provides this.[6] His own contribution may be summarised as follows: 'Jesus was wholly at one with late-Jewish apocalyptic in ... fundamental outlook'.[7] Because Jesus, the Apostles, Paul and the entire early church were all dominated by the conviction that the End and the Parousia of Jesus as Messiah were immediately to occur, the delay caused an enormous crisis for the church which led to:

---

[1] Cf. *Die Bedeutung*, p. 27. Buri rejects all attempts to remove this expectation from the centre of the N.T. as 'embarrassment solutions'.

[2] Cf. *My Life and Thought*, pp. 183ff.

[3] Cf. 'Das Problem', pp. 97ff.

[4] Cf. *Die Bedeutung*, pp. 127ff., 164ff.

[5] It is Werner's contention that Harnack, Loofs, and Seeberg fail at precisely this point: *Formation*, p. 6.

[6] Cf. *Formation*, p. 9.

[7] Cf. *Formation*, p. 14.

a. falling away of many and the rise of 'heretics' (properly, according to Werner, self-designated 'seekers').[1]

b. the abandonment of the old 'eschatological' understanding of the gospel.[2]

c. the reconstruction of belief primarily in terms of Jesus' person (originally conceived as a 'high angelic being') and of Jesus' work (originally conceived eschatologically) in noneschatological categories.[3]

Werner maintains that we must return 'to that situation in which the Primitive Christian faith, after the death of Jesus, found itself so involved with the problem of the continuing delay of the Parousia'[4] in an effort to perceive what the 'present significance of this Primitive Christianity' is, now that the content of 'the apocalyptic-eschatological ideas ... in their original form are no more, as such, to be reckoned as Christian truth'.[5] The task is simply sketched in three pages of postscript.[6]

Our criticism of Consistent Eschatology is most conveniently undertaken in two areas of concern, methodology and interpretation. First, we consider methodology. Werner recognises that since Schweitzer's day form criticism demands comment, but he concludes that where form criticism is used against Schweitzer it is, generally, wrongly turned into an historical criterion.[7] Schweitzer, to be sure, was a forerunner of the form critics in attacking all subjective criteria of literary judgement, but he failed in that he did not apply his searching criticism of others, to himself. His literary method led him, for instance, to accept the form of the Sermon on the Mount and of the charge to the Twelve (Mtt. 10) as authentic. In both cases, form criticism—without turning itself into an historical criterion—shows us the fragmentary nature of the material.[8]

---

[1] Cf. *Formation*, pp. 44ff.
[2] Cf. *Formation*, pp. 71ff.
[3] *Formation* pp. 72ff.
[4] Cf. *Formation*, p. 327.
[5] Cf. *Formation*, p. 327.
[6] Cf. *Formation,* pp. 328ff.
[7] Cf. *Formation*, p. 11.
[8] Cf. Glasson, *Advent*, p. 103. Kümmel, *Promise*, pp. 63ff. Grässer, *Problem*, pp. 18ff. Michaelis, *Matthäus*, II, p. 93. Flückiger, *Ursprung*, p. 26, who all maintain the composite character of Mtt. 10.

In two important instances Schweitzer suspended his literary criterion in favour of historical presuppositions. He combined Mtt. 10 with Mk. 6, though on literary grounds this is quite unjustified,[1] and he transferred the Transfiguration scene to a period preceding the conversation on the way to Caesarea Philippi, though there is no literary ground for doing so.[2]

The historical criterion which Schweitzer selected 'from within the tradition' [3] is the apocalyptic of contemporary Judaism. But the selection of this as the measure of the authenticity of New Testament material raises three important questions:

i. Is such a narrow and precise criterion necessary?

ii. Is its selection justified in view of the complexity of thought in contemporary Judaism? [4]

iii. Can such a criterion allow even the possibility of any *sui generis* element in Jesus' life and work?

In its application the criterion has radical effects which seem increasingly questionable. For example, Schweitzer rejects in the Synoptic material the birth narratives as unauthentic: yet there are commentators who find grounds for treating these narratives with much more respect.[5] The fourth Gospel, on Schweitzer's criterion, is entirely removed from material bearing on the actual life of Jesus: [6] yet the historical value of the Fourth Gospel is being increasingly recognised.[7] As a further example, Schweitzer's criterion rules the 2nd Epistle to the Thessalonians as non-Pauline because 'it explicitly opposes the idea that the return of Jesus is immediately at hand, and enumerates all that must happen before that Day can dawn (II Thess. 2, 1-12)'.[8] The Epistle, however, *can* be interpreted quite adequately as Pauline.[9]

On the basis of this historical criterion a picture of Jesus as an apocalyptic *Schwärmer* emerges with which certain elements of the New Testament do not accord: these elements are therefore

---

[1] Cf. e.g. Flückiger, *Ursprung*, p. 25. Kümmel, *Promise*, pp. 62f.

[2] *Mystery*, p. 180. Schweitzer admits as much.

[3] Cf. Werner, *Formation*, p. 15.

[4] Cf. above, chapter 2, pp. 18ff.

[5] Cf. e.g. Creed, *Luke, ad loc.* Manson, *Luke*, pp. xxf.

[6] Cf. *Mystery*, p. 9. Werner, *Formation*, p. 47.

[7] Cf. Barrett, *John*, pp. 116ff. Strachan, *Fourth Gospel*, pp. 27ff. Howard, *Fourth Gospel*, pp. 18f.

[8] Cf. *Mysticism*, p. 42.

[9] As e.g. by Lauk, *II Thessalonicher*, pp. 9ff. Oepke, *Thessalonicher*, pp. 128ff.

designated 'later interpretation'. A first century acpocalyptic *Schwärmer*, however, is no less an arbitrary creation than (for example) a nineteenth century Idealist, or a twentieth century Jesus of existentialism.[1] Schweitzer's antithesis between the (so-called) historical facts of the Synoptics and the (so-called) theological idealisation of the remainder of the New Testament is not a *necessary* antithesis.[2] Further, Werner's antithesis between Jesus and all subsequent dogma is not a *necessary* antithesis.[3] It is at least possible that cleavage, where it is definitely to be found, is due to alien influences rather than to any inner need for re-interpretation.[4]

We turn now to criticism of interpretation. In representing apocalyptic as the dominating feature of Jesus' thought, Schweitzer omits to notice the considerable variety of expectation contained within contemporary apocalyptic writings.[5] Most significantly, the work of the Messiah is never represented in apocalyptic as 'forcing in the kingdom', and the idea of a secret life of humiliation prior to exaltation is, generally, lacking.

In selecting apocalyptic as the dominating feature of Jesus' thought world, Schweitzer neglects other prominent aspects of first century Judaism: traditionalism, for instance, amongst the Sadducees, legalism amongst the Pharisees and syncretism where Hellenistic influence thrived. Schweitzer himself noted the inadequacy of apocalyptic in interpreting Jesus' thought, but only conceded that Jesus combined with it the older prophetic ethics.[6] The New Testament contains hints (at least) that apocalyptic was not the all dominating factor either in Jesus' thought or in the contemporary situation, which Schweitzer imagined it to be. The common people, for example, who both 'heard Jesus gladly' (Mk. 12, 37) and who 'went out unto' John the Baptist 'and were baptised of him, confessing their sins' (Mk. 1, 5) are never represented as acclaiming

---

[1] Cf. Cullmann, *Unzeitgemässe Bemerkungen*, pp. 266ff.

[2] Cf. Burkitt's preface to the English *Quest*, and G. Seaver's unsuccessful criticism of this (in *Schweitzer*, p. 201).

[3] One need only compare the entirely positive evaluation of the rise of christian dogma in terms of the elucidation of its inherent significance in Jesus' person and work, in accord with his own self-understanding, offered by Turner, *Pattern*, to see how arbitrary and self-imposed are these antitheses.

[4] Cf. Cullman, 'Das Wahre', pp. 171ff. who cites the lack of discernment of the continuing work of the Holy Spirit as one cause.

[5] Cf. above, chapter 2, pp. 18ff.

[6] Cf. *Mystery*, pp. 256ff. *Mysticism*, pp. 8off.

the Baptist as 'Messiah',[1] nor do they suggest that Jesus is more than a 'John the Baptist, or Eljah, or one of the prophets' (Mk. 8, 28). Had apocalyptic had such a general, dominating influence, it is difficult to understand why John was held only as a prophet, and neither he nor Jesus attracted messianic acclaim.[2] The disciples, too, do not appear to have been entirely bound by apocalyptic speculation. Matthew ὁ τελώνης (Mtt. 10, 3), for instance, would have had little in common with the Pharisees amongst whom apocalyptic most probably had some favour. Simon the Zealot (Lk. 6, 15, Acts 1, 13), or ὁ Κανανα̃ος (Mk. 3, 18. Mtt. 10, 4) was a member of the political zealot group, and others (Judas Iscariot, Simon Peter, the two sons of Zebedee) might perhaps have been:[3] according to our survey of this group, its aims were primarily political, its interest quite different from apocalyptic. Jesus himself, also, though most likely influenced by apocalyptic [4] would hardly have attended only to this pressure. It is clear that he would have been to synagogue services from childhood [5] and must have been thoroughly familiar with the Pentateuch and Prophets through the lessons, and with Rabbinic Targumim through the sermons.[6] Surely, these will have influenced him too.

It is specially questionable whether apocalyptic can prove an adequate key in probing Jesus' self-understanding. Difficulties clearly arise in interpreting the (so-called) messianic secret. In Schweitzer's view the secret consists in Jesus' belief that he was Messiah-designate.[7] This, he argues, is a secret 'of necessity' because it is inexpressible.[8] Yet Schweitzer's thesis of a double consciousness, which he propounds as a rationale of the secret,[9] might be expected to have served as a medium for its communication.[10]

---

[1] Neither in the N.T. nor in Josephus.

[2] Even if the Entry into Jerusalem is understood (with many commentators) as openly messianic, this is not necessarily contradicted: but it is possible that the event was *not* so understood by the bystanders: cf. Cranfield, *Mark*, pp. 352ff.

[3] Cf. Cullman, *State*, pp. 15ff.

[4] Cf. Cranfield, *Mark*, p. 275.

[5] Cf. Luke's explicit statement, 4, 16.

[6] Cf. W. Bacher, in *H.D.B.* IV, pp. 640ff.

[7] Cf. *Mystery*, p. 254.

[8] Cf. *Mystery*, p. 186.

[9] Cf. *Mystery*, p. 187.

[10] Schweitzer's argument runs:

a. The secret is inexpressible, hence it *is* a secret.

Further, it is this secret which, according to Schweitzer, Judas betrayed: apparently he *was able* to express it. In fact there is no justification in the Synoptics for holding that this *is* what Judas betrayed.[1] Moreover, the variety and character of terms used or accepted by Jesus regarding his person and work weigh against Schweitzer's analysis of Jesus' self-consciousness. Chief of these is his characteristic self-designation *Son of Man*. The present and future usages of this can be reconciled if we say, *not* 'Jesus expected to be revealed as the Son of Man when the Kingdom dawned', but rather, 'Jesus as Son of Man already (though now in humiliation) expected to be revealed as Son of Man in glory'.[2] Perhaps, too, Jesus saw his work in the light of the *Servant* of Deutero-Isaiah. In the Baptism narrative (Mk. 1, 11 par.) the baṯ-ḳôl contains an allusion to Is. 43, 1.[3] 'The voice from heaven . . . comes to Jesus as a summons to accept the task of the one who is addressed in the same way at the beginning of the ebed-Jahweh hymns in Is. 42, 1. Jesus was therefore conscious at the moment of his baptism that he had to take upon himself the ebed-Jahweh role'[4] Again, in the last supper (Mk. 14, 24, Mtt. 26, 28, Lk. 22, 20. cf I Cor. 11, 24) all four accounts agree [5] in mentioning both the covenant (διαθήκη) and vicariousness (ὑπὲρ ὑμῶν, ὑπὲρ πολλῶν, περὶ πολλῶν). Though several allusions are probably intended,[6] Otto [7] and Cullmann [8] find

---

b. This secret is difficult for us to understand, but everyone then held a 'double consciousness' theory which made the matter intelligible.

[1] Flückiger, *Ursprung*, p. 35 argues that Schweitzer has begun with the idea of 'betrayal' and so thinks in terms of a 'secret', whereas the idea of παραδίδωμι means 'jemanden ausliefern, übergeben, in die Hände spielen . . .' Such a claim to Messiahship could not, of course, have been condemned as blasphemy. It was surely the claim to Sonship which led to this charge. Cf. Flückiger, *Ursprung*, p. 36.

[2] Cf. Cullmann, *Christology*, p. 164. Cranfield, *Mark*, pp. 276ff. Preiss, *Life in Christ*, pp. 43ff.

[3] The apparent reference to Ps. 2, 7 may not be intended—cf. Cranfield, *Mark*, p. 55. Contrast Glasson, *Advent*, p. 119 who thinks 'the combination of these two passages is a stroke of genius'; similarly Schniewind, *Markus*, pp. 12ff.

[4] Cullmann, *Christology*, p. 67. Cf. *Baptism*, pp. 16f. Cranfield, *Mark*, pp. 54f.

[5] With the exception of the D text of Luke.

[6] To the Sinai Covenant (Ex. 24, 6-8) in τὸ αἷμα . . . . τῆς διαθήκης (Mk. 14, 24): to the Covenant foretold in Jer. 31, 31 in I Cor 11, 25, as well as to the Servant Songs, Is. 53, 12. 42, 6. 49, 8.

[7] *Kingdom of God*, pp. 289ff.

[8] *Christology*, p. 65.

certain reference to Is. 42, 6 and 49, 8 where it is actually the servant who is given 'for a covenant of the people'.[1] This vicarious element seems to be present similarly in the λύτρον ἀντὶ πολλῶν of Mk. 10, 45.[2] It is at least possible that some relationship existed in Jesus' mind between his understanding of himself and the person of the 'ebed JHWH'.[3] The term *Son of God* might also be mentioned here. Schweitzer maintained that Jesus became conscious at his baptism of his status as Messiah-designate: the baṭ-ḳôl,, however, 'confirms his already existing *filial* consciousness'.[4] The Transfiguration, similarly, is not a revelation of his status as Messiah-designate, but a confirmation of his Sonship. It is as Son that the demons recognise him (Mk. 5, 7. 3, 11, etc.). It is as 'Christ ὁ υἱὸς τοῦ Εὐλογητοῦ' that he is condemned (Mk. 14, 61 par.).[5] Other designations such as *Rabbi, Master, Prophet*, which other people used of Jesus and which were not altogether repudiated by him, suggest that Jesus was able to create impressions familiar to diverse traditions in Jewish life and thought, and was apparently not unwilling to do so. All these terms indicate that Jesus saw himself as more than Messiah-designate.[6] The terms of Apocalyptic

---

[1] This is contested by e.g. Flew, *Church*, pp. 103f. But a consciousness of vicarious suffering in the establishment of a new covenant seems most probably to be present in Jesus' words.

[2] Of which Cullmann, *Christology*, p. 65 writes, 'Here we have the central theme of the ebed Jahweh hymns, and this is a clear allusion to Is. 53, 5. It is as if Jesus said, "The Son of Man came to fulfil the task of the ebed Jahweh"'.

[3] Cf. further Zimmerli and Jeremias, in *T.W.N.T.* V, pp. 636ff. and *Servant*. Manson, *The Servant Messiah*. Cullmann, *Christology*, pp. 51ff. For the contrary view, cf. Hooker, *Jesus and the Servant*: Barrett, 'The Background of Mk. 10, 45', in *N.T. Essays*, pp. 1ff.

[4] Cranfield, *Mark*, p. 55.

[5] Some of these passages seem to draw the Servant and the Son together. At the baptism the baṭ-ḳôl might be said to confirm a filial consciousness in a context of dedication to the mission of the servant. In the case of the Transfiguration, the confirmation of Sonship is linked, at least in Luke, to the mission of suffering (cf. ἔλεγον τὴν ἔξοδον αὐτοῦ, ἣν ἤμελλεν πληροῦν): cf. also Mtt. 11, 25-30 where an expression of filial consciousness is followed by a passage (vv. 28-30) reminiscent of the mission of the Servant (cf. esp. 'for I am meek and lowly' Is. 50, 6. 53, 3f.).

[6] We may note also such references as Mtt. 12, 42 = Lk. 11, 31. Mtt. 13, 16. Lk. 10, 21ff. Mtt. 19, 16ff. = Lk. 18, 18f (where Jesus' answer couples, as on a par, obedience to the commandments and allegiance to himself). Mk. 2, 6ff., where, even if the term Son of Man is a gloss (cf. Rawlinson, *Mark, ad loc.* Taylor, *Mark, ad loc.* Cranfield, *Mark ad loc.*) the proclamation of forgiveness cannot be questioned; here—if not blasphemy (the answer of

are also seen to be insufficient, and the future tense not comprehensive enough, to express Jesus' consciousness of his own person and work.

When Jesus' self-consciousness is understood in wider terms then the secret of his person becomes intelligible, and is better formulated as the Son of God secret. It consists in the fact that 'God was in Christ' (II Cor. 5, 19): in him was the Eschaton—yet not in glorious majesty but in the form of a servant 'to save his people from their sins' (Mtt. 1, 21. Mk. 2, 6).[1] It arises from the fact that Jesus, Son of God assumes the role and mission of the Servant, and it is sustained in order that the divine mystery of election (of 'calling' and of 'faith') might be operative. Contrary to Schweitzer's thesis, Jesus did not seek to force in the Kingdom [2] but declared it to be present already in his own person and work (we shall have to expand on this later).

Jesus' death can hardly be interpreted (as Schweitzer wishes) as meaning for Jesus 'saving others from the Messianic woes'.[3] Apocalyptic expectation does not anticipate such a Messianic work. If λύτρον is to be identified as meaning אשם (in Mk. 10, 45) a sin-offering,[4] then the matter is even more definite, for nowhere in the gospels or in late Jewish apocalyptic is the bearing of Messianic woes referred to as a sin-offering;[5] and precisely in the context of Mk. 10, 45 the Messianic woes are *not* mentioned. It is, surely, because Schweitzer's interpretation underemphasises the grace-motif in Jesus' death that he resorts to his thesis of reverence for life, and Werner (following Buri) turns to Jasper's existentialism.[6]

Schweitzer maintains that Jesus expected one single event following his death (the End, involving the general resurrection and his own glorification). We shall argue that apparent references

---

the scribes)—is an indication of the presence of the final rule of God (cf. Schniewind, *Markus*, p. 23).

[1] Cf. further Schniewind, *Markus*, pp. 41ff. (on Mk. 4, 11f.) Torrance, in *S.J.T.* III, 1950, pp. 298ff. Cranfield in *S.J.T.* V, 1952, pp. 49ff. Preiss, *Life in Christ*, pp. 43ff. Cullmann, *Christology, passim*.

[2] Flückiger, *Ursprung*, p. 38 (and note 57) rightly argues that even in terms of apocalyptic such a mission is unthinkable.

[3] Cf. *Mystery*, pp. 266f.

[4] With Jeremias and Zimmerli, in *T.W.N.T.* V, pp. 709ff. and Cranfield, *Mark*, p. 342. contrast Büchsel, in *T.W.N.T.* IV, pp. 341ff.

[5] Cf. Flückiger, *Ursprung*, p. 33, pp. 8off.

[6] The evacuation of a gospel motif is found also in late Jewish apocalyptic (cf. Enoch 98, 10. 53, 2. 60, 6. 62, 9. II Esdras 5, 17f.).

to a speedy coming of the End do not necessitate this view [1] and that there is evidence that Jesus expected a *Zwischenzeit* and made provision for such.[2] Schweitzer appears to allow one group of references (which he interprets as forecasting a speedy End) to rule out another group (which might be taken as indicating an interval before the End) and this is an instance of quite unsatisfactory 'monist' thinking.[3] Taken in conjunction with the soteriological interpretation of Jesus' mission and death, the provision of an interim in which the call to repentance and faith is made possible, is entirely intelligible. The grace-motif of Jesus' life and work is seen to be continued and made effectual in the grace-character of the interim. Divorced, as in Schweitzer's thesis, from such a soteriology, the expectation of an interval must be quite incomprehensible.

The reconstruction of Paul's thought in terms of consistent eschatology is questionable at many points. Werner (less cautiously than Schweitzer) maintains that Paul held Jesus to be an angelic power. To be sure, a certain subordination of the Son to the Father is present (cf. e.g. I Cor. 15, 28). But an angel Christology, as such, seems to be excluded by, for example, Phil. 2, 6 ff. Rom. 8, 37-39, etc. The appellation κύριε could conceivably reflect the occasional apocalyptic usage with reference to angels, but is much more likely to follow the frequent usage [4] of the Old Testament in connection with God; ὁ κύριος, never used in the Old Testament or in apocalyptic literature of an angel, *is* on the other hand the well-used expression for God.[5] Other titles with a wealth of significance are applied to Jesus in the New Testament [6] and these must influence our understanding of any 'angel' category of interpretation.

Schweitzer [7] and Werner [8] claim that Paul understood Jesus' death and resurrection as the initiation of the End of the world, and that he saw Jesus' resurrection as the literal beginning of

---

[1] See below, pp. 177ff.
[2] See below, pp. 95ff.
[3] Cf. Schuster, in *Z.N.W.* XLVII, 1956, pp. 1ff.
[4] Even more frequent than in apocalyptic itself as Werner admits.
[5] Cf. Michaelis, *Zur Engelchristologie*, pp. 61ff.
[6] Cf. Taylor, *Names*: Cullmann, *Christology*.
[7] Cf. *Mysticism*, pp. 54f.
[8] Cf. *Formation*, p. 72.

the general resurrection. Werner [1] finds this especially in Gal. 6, 14.
But, as Flückiger [2] says, there is no mention here of a process nor
of an immediate continuation.[3] Contrary to Schweitzer Paul seems
to have expected not the completion of a process, although the
present involves a process of events—in individual believers (cf
Rom. 13, 11ff.), in the church (cf. II Cor. 10, 16. Rom. 9-11), and
in the world (cf. Rom. 8, 20. II Thess. 2). He rather contrasts past
hidden events [4] with their expected future *unveiling*: the undeniable
manifestation of the One in whom the End events have occurred—
hence he awaits Jesus himself, and 'in glory'.[5]

The contention that at certain points in the Epistles we find
Paul's confident belief that the End must come within a short and
limited period must be discussed later.[6] To anticipate our argument, we suggest that whilst Paul regarded the speedy return of
Christ as a real possibility, he nowhere maintained it as certain
or necessary, either in his early letters or in his late ones.

Consistent Eschatology concludes that the delay of the Parousia
created a total, crucial and indeed fatal crisis in the life of the
early church.[7] This, however, elevates one single area of thought into
the central problem of the church and ignores a welter of problems
concerning faith and life (much more deserving to be termed
'crises') which faced the church in its early years, and in the light
of which the development of dogma should also be viewed. Fore-

---

[1] *Formation*, p. 73.

[2] *Ursprung*, p. 49.

[3] Flückiger, *Ursprung*, p. 49 writes, 'Allerdings scheint Werner der Mei-
nung zu sein, dass Paulus diese Katastrophe für ein sehr langsam fortschrei-
tendes Geschehen angesehen habe, da der Galaterbrief immerhin zwei Jahr-
zehnte nach der Passion Jesu abgefasst worden ist, zu welcher Zeit eine
Verwandlung der Welt noch nicht erkennbar war. Vorsichtig redet er dann
auch nur von einem "Beginn" der kosmischen Endereignisse, obschon
Gal. 6, 14 mit keinem Wort auf eine bloss beginnende Handlung schliessen
lässt.'

[4] Cf. Col. 2, 3. 'Wisdom and knowledge hidden in Christ.' Col. 3, 4. 'the
life hidden in Christ'. Col. 4, 3-7 the gospel 'hidden in them that are
perishing', 'treasure in earthen vessels'. Phil. 2, 6ff. Rom. 3, 2f. II Cor. 8, 9.

[5] Cf. I Cor. 1, 8. 13, 10-12. Col. 3, 4. etc. Paul awaits an *open* judgement
which will one day be given, cf. Rom. 2, 16. I Cor. 1, 8. 3, 13. 4, 5. When also
the full blessing of redemption won through Christ's death and resurrection
would be experienced, cf. I Cor. 4, 5. 5, 6. II Cor. 1, 10. 1, 14. 4, 14.
Eph. 2, 7. 6, 8. When all things would be renewed, cf. Phil. 3, 20-21. I Cor.
15, 28. Col. 1, 17. 2, 15. 3, 1. Eph. 1, 20f. Phil. 2, 9f.

[6] Cf. below, pp. 108ff.

[7] Cf. Schweitzer, *Mysticism*, pp. 39ff. 336ff. Buri, *Die Bedeutung* pp. 27ff.
Werner, *Formation*, pp. 43ff.

most amongst these we mention Judaizing and the tendency towards legalism, giving rise to the problem of the relationship of Jew and Gentile Christians: Gnosticism, leading to the abandonment both of the reality of Christ's past (Docetism) and also of the future hope (pure mysticism), and giving rise to the problem of holding fast to the 'tradition' in the face both of Gnostic eclecticism and also of certain Christian attempts at apologetics: Antinomianism, leading to the abandonment of ethics and giving rise to the problem of maintaining a dialectic of the freedom of the gospel and the obligation of obedient faith: economic communism, leading to the abandonment of personal possessions (Acts 4, 32ff.) and producing 'busybodies' (II Thess. 3, 11) and giving rise to the problem of rightly dispensing charity.

These problems, arising from within and from without the Christian community must, surely, be considered as stimuli towards the formation of explicit statements of faith and order, before one supposed crisis (namely that of a Parousia delay) is set up as *the* central impulse. On the thesis of Consistent Eschatology it remains a problem why the Christian sect did not go the way of other disappointed apocalyptic groups whose chosen Messiah had failed them, and in part return to orthodox Judaism, in part linger on as a sect until finally dying out. Gamaliel's argument (Acts 5, 35ff.) is based on correct premises backed by precedents and is a valid one. The presence of confessional statements of an early date [1] indicates that it is at least possible and legitimate to understand the growth of Christian dogma as the explication of what was, from the first, true—though for a while only implicit.[2]

Werner himself cites examples [3] of what he calls the translation 'of the logic of the Parousia expectation into practice', creating groups fired with expectancy and manifesting either an ascetic world-abandonment or an antinomian world-affirmation, and he recognises that such movements 'produced great harm'. Surely, had the Christian community held a similar apocalyptic fervour it too would have expressed its logic in practice and stopped work to await its Lord! Yet from the first, it seems, the Christian

---

[1] Cf. e.g. Phil. 2, 6ff. Cullmann, *Confessions, passim.*

[2] Turner, *Pattern*, pp. 20 ff. cf. p. 22, 'There are more points of contact between the N.T. and the later church than he (Werner) seems to allow.'

[3] He cites Montanus: and two cases related by Hippolytus in his commentary on Daniel (under IV. 18, 1ff. 19, 1ff). Cf. *Formation*, p. 41.

community in its entirety attached firm importance to the present as having an especial place in the total salvation-history.

Consistent Eschatology must further reckon with the difficulty that in spite of being founded (apparently) upon disappointment, the church—to a greater or lesser extent, here and there, and from time to time—continued to live and suffer, to work and witness in a way hardly consistent with such an origin and foundation. Schweitzer and Werner think that disappointment led to Hellenisation. But it is at least possible that Hellenisation came about through 'human faithlessness', which is also an adequate explanation of the loss of expectancy in the church's faith and life.[1]

Few writers would deny the value of the impulse given to New Testament study by Schweitzer and other exponents of Consistent Eschatology. Nor would they deny the necessity of taking seriously the eschatology of the New Testament. But the narrowness and one-sidedness of the methodology involved and of the interpretation offered is very apparent.[2] The expectation of apocalyptic (certainly as Schweitzer understands it) cannot do justice to the soteriological understanding of Jesus' life and death which we find throughout the New Testament. Nor can it account for the fact that in spite of hope such as we find expressed in Acts 1, 6, the early church neither awaited whatever the future should hold with an abandonment of present responsibilities, nor did it die out its 'natural' way, as other disillusioned enthusiastic movements did.

---

[1] Cullmann, in *K.r.S.* XI, 1942.
[2] Cf. Niebuhr, *Christ and Culture*, pp. 34ff.

CHAPTER FOUR

REALISED ESCHATOLOGY

From the view that Jesus erred in expecting a Parousia, we turn to the view that the early church erred in its hope. Realised Eschatology has found considerable support, especially in the Anglo Saxon world.[1] Its foremost exponent, Professor C. H. Dodd [2] maintains that in Jesus' ministry 'the kingdom of God has finally come . . . In the ministry of Jesus Christ the divine power is released in effective conflict with evil.' This is the fixed point of his exegesis, provided, as he claims, by the 'clear and unambiguous' passages [3] and supported by a particular interpretation of the parables. Dodd holds that Jesus' expectation for the future was three-fold:

a. His own coming death.[4]
b. Impending disaster for the Jews.[5]
c. Survival of death, and the triumph of God's cause in his own person.[6]

The earliest Christian preaching, which Dodd reconstructs from Acts 1-11 [7] remained true (according to Dodd) to this teaching. However, within a few years—'once the tremendous crisis in which they felt themselves to be living'[8]—had passed, that which had originally been understood as one whole process was broken up into

---

[1] Cf. Bibliography in Kümmel, *Promise*, p. 2, n. 3, though this is not exhaustive: R. Otto and E. von Dobschütz are not included (cf. Barrett, in *S.J.T.* VI, 1953, p. 153) and the important work of J. A. T. Robinson (*Coming*) has since appeared.

[2] Cf. especially *Parables*, 1935: *Apostolic Preaching*, 1936. *History*, 1938: *Coming of Christ*, 1951: *Fourth Gospel*, 1953: *Studies* 1954. For a complete bibliography cf. *The Background of the New Testament and its Eschatology*, ed. Davies and Daube, 1956.

[3] I.e. Mtt. 12, 28 = Lk. 11, 20. Mk. 1, 14-15. Lk. 10, 23-24 = Mtt. 13, 16-17. Lk. 11, 32 = Mtt. 12, 41-42. Mtt. 11, 1-11 = Lk. 7, 18-30. Mtt. 11, 12 = Lk. 16, 16.

[4] Cf. Mk. 10, 31-45. Lk. 9, 51-62. 13, 22f. 14, 25-33. Mk. 8, 34. Mtt. 16, 24. Lk. 9, 23. Mtt. 10, 38 = Lk. 14, 27.

[5] Cf. Mk. 14, 58. Jn. 2, 19. Mk. 13, 2. Mtt. 23, 37-38 = Lk. 13, 34-35. Lk. 19, 43-44. 21, 20. Mk. 13, 14-20. Lk. 13, 1-5.

[6] Cf. Mtt. 11, 23f. = Lk. 10, 13-14. Mtt. 10, 13 = Lk. 10, 12. Mtt. 12, 41-42 = Lk. 11, 31-32. Cf. *Parables*, chapter 3 (pp. 81ff.).

[7] Dodd maintains their authenticity: *Apostolic Preaching*, pp. 30ff.

[8] *Apostolic Preaching*, p. 72.

death-resurrection-exaltation on the one hand, and Parousia on the other.[1] The Parousia, that is to say, came to be understood as the last event in a chronological series [2] and the early church fell back into apocalypticism.[3]

Dodd's understanding of Paul's thought is greatly influenced by his conviction that Paul underwent considerable spiritual and psychological development [4] involving the 'transcending of a certain harsh dualism . . . very deeply rooted in the apocalyptic eschatology which moulded the *Weltanschauung* with which Paul began . . .' [5] Thus, initially Paul's faith was fitted into an apocalyptic framework (cf I Thess.1, 9 -10. II Thess. 2).[6] This persists in I Corinthians though there is a slight change of emphasis, for 'whereas in I Thessalonians it is distinctly exceptional for a Christian to die before the Advent, in I Corinthians he has to assure his readers that not all Christians will die. He himself, with others, will survive to the Advent (I Cor. 15, 51-52).[7] Thereafter 'the thought of the imminence of the Advent retires into the background'.[8] At the same time there is a 'growing emphasis on eternal life here and now in communion with Christ',[9] and in place of the early world denial (cf I Cor. 7) comes a positive evaluation of the world, of political institutions (Rom. 13, 1-10), of the instinctive goodness of the natural man (Rom. 2, 14-15) and of the family and marriage ties (Col. 3, 18f. Eph. 5, 21-33).

In the Fourth Gospel, Dodd finds the ultimate stage of the development traced in Paul, namely the re-interpretation, or transmutation of popular eschatology,[10] and thereby the return to the true intention of Jesus' teaching.[11]

---

[1] *Apostolic Preaching*, pp. 64ff.

[2] Whereas, according to Dodd, the true, original hope is in 'the impending verification of the Church's faith that the finished work of Christ has in itself absolute value'. *Apostolic Preaching*, p. 92.

[3] *Apostolic Preaching*, pp. 8off.

[4] Cf. *Studies*, pp. 8off. 108ff.

[5] Cf. *Studies*, p. 126.

[6] Cf. *Studies*, p. 109.

[7] Cf. *Studies*, p. 110.

[8] Cf. *Studies*, p. 111.

[9] Cf. *Studies*, p. 113.

[10] Cf. Dodd's comments on Jn. 14, 1-24 (*Fourth Gospel*, pp. 390ff.). Here (he argues) it is made clear that 'the true Parousia is to be found in the interchange of divine ἀγάπη, made possible through Christ's death and resurrection' (*op. cit.* p. 395).

[11] Cf. *Fourth Gospel*, p. 406.

Dodd maintains that apocalyptic language was used by Jesus only as a form in which to express eternal truths.[1] The myths concerning the 'beginning' and 'end' of history serve to give absoluteness to particular concepts: ('the myth of the last Judgement is a symbolic statement of the final resolution of the great conflict'[2]).

T. F. Glasson [3] has endeavoured to trace more fully the transition from Jesus' view to that of the early church. Briefly, his thesis is that the Parousia idea 'is certainly absent from the Old Testament, the most important source for the teaching of Jesus',[4] nor is it found in apocryphal literature,[5] and, in apocalyptic writings 'we find in most of them the Old Testament conception of an earthly king'.[6] The idea of a Parousia in Jesus' teaching would be out of place (he says) since Jesus regarded his own death as the gateway to a new epoch.[7] Even in the earliest days of the church there was no idea of Parousia.[8] But by the time of Paul, the idea had developed, through the influence of the Old Testament and apparently unfulfilled prophecies,[9] through the identification of Jesus with 'the Lord' which facilitated the transference of theophanic imagery to him,[10] and through the Anti-Christ legend, imported into Christianity and serving to give imminence to the expectation.[11]

---

[1] Cf. *Parables*, pp. 195ff.

[2] *History*, p. 170. N.B. In Dodd's later work, *Coming of Christ*, he links the final resolution with a real conclusion of human history, thus providing a not insignificant modification of his former views: see esp. pp. 26f.

[3] *The Second Advent*, 1945 (revised 1947).

[4] *Advent*, p. 13 ('Daniel being no exception', p. 14).

[5] *Advent*, p. 19.

[6] *Advent*, p. 20. Glasson find that 'the bulk of this literature is either silent' about, or denies, the idea of a descent of the Messiah in visible glory from heaven (p. 23). The exception, the similitudes of Enoch are 'unique in Jewish writings' and 'present marked differences from the eschatology of the N.T.' (p. 33). He thinks Charles and Otto mistaken in maintaining the dependence of N.T. writers on Enoch (pp. 41ff.): that the Similitudes depend on Daniel for Son of Man imagery and that Jesus most likely went to the same source: that the Similitudes should (with Bousset's support) be dated mid 1st century A.D.

[7] Cf. *Advent*, pp. 63ff.

[8] Cf. 'The Kerygma: is our version correct', in *H.J.* LI, 1952-3, where Glasson reconstructs the original five main points of the primitive kerygma, from which the Parousia is absent.

[9] Cf. *Advent*, pp. 159ff.

[10] Cf. *Advent*, pp. 162ff.

[11] Cf. *Advent*, pp. 180ff. Glasson maintains that alongside this false development, leading to Millenarianism and the Book of Revelation, we find the true understanding (i.e. true to Jesus' intention) developed in Paul's

Glasson finds confirmation that the Parousia is an early church idea in the absence of the theme in Jewish writings of the Christian era.[1]

J. A. T. Robinson [2] has also sought to probe the foundations of the Parousia hope since (he argues) it is lacking in traditional Jewish expectation [3] and in early Christian preaching and confessions.[4] His conclusion is that into the traditional Jewish eschatological pattern, Jesus brought the message that God was *now* performing a decisive act 'whose climax he described in such terms as the coming in power, whether of the Kingdom of God or of the Son of Man'.[5] This climax involved two interrelated themes, vindication and visitation. Concerning the former, he affirms that 'as far as Jesus' own words are concerned, there is nothing to suggest that he shared the expectation of a return in glory which the Church entertained and ascribed to him'.[6] Visitation [7], Robinson maintains, has three aspects [8] none of which refers to the Parousia. The themes of vindication and visitation 'meet in a point where the crisis brought by his ministry comes to its head . . .' [9]

In the early days of the church's life, certain aspects of the crisis spoken of by Jesus were given a chronological setting and thus received a temporal instead of a moral connotation.[10] The reason behind such a transition was, according to Robinson, the confusion of two divergent Christologies.[11] The earliest held that 'the Christ

---

later work (especially in Ephesians) and, supremely, in the Johannine literature, the Gospels and Epistles.

[1] What instances there are, he concludes (following Bousset) to be due to contact with Christian thought or to interpolation: cf. *Advent*, pp. 231f.

[2] Cf. *In the End, God . . .*, 1950: 'The Most Primitive Gospel of All?' in *J.T.S.* VII, 1956, pp. 177ff. *Jesus and His Coming*, 1957.

[3] Cf. *Coming*, p. 22.

[4] Cf. *Coming*, pp. 28ff.

[5] Cf. *Coming*, p. 39.

[6] *Coming*, p. 57.

[7] A theme familiar (says Robinson) to the Jews through the conviction that God would 'visit' his people: cf. *Coming*, pp. 59ff.

[8] Jesus speaks of a 'coming' which has already come and of a consequent crisis facing all whom he addresses: also of an immediately impending crisis for the Jewish nation: and of a coming to the disciples. cf. *Coming*, pp. 66ff.

[9] *Coming*, p. 77.

[10] This shift of emphasis, Robinson says, is comparable to the transition from prophetic (cf. Jesus) to apocalyptic (cf. the church) eschatology. Cf. *Coming*, pp. 94ff.

[11] Cf. *Coming*, pp. 140ff. 'The Most Primitive Gospel of All?' in *J.T.S.* VII, 1956, pp. 177ff.

will come (he has not yet!), and will be Jesus' (cf Acts 3): the later Christology affirmed that 'Christ has come' (cf Acts 2). The latter properly represents Jesus' thought as he contemplated his passion and exaltation in advance. The two Christologies were never really reconciled in the church, with the result that the twin affirmations Christ *has come*, and Christ *will come*, were held. It is in the Fourth Gospel, according to Robinson, that the necessary synthesis is achieved and the Parousia is given its proper meaning as 'the mutual indwelling of Jesus and the disciples in love, which is the essence of the Parousia.'[1]

In an earlier work,[2] Robinson had already shown how, in his view, the myth of the Parousia was to be re-interpreted. He wrote, 'the idea of the Second Advent in the New Testament stands for the conviction that if the events of the Incarnation have the eschatological character asserted of them, then history MUST come to a close . . . . . It also represents the inescapable conviction that the end of God's purpose, however clearly embodied in the Incarnation, has NOT YET come in the most final sense possible'.[3] 'And yet the purpose of the eschatological myth is not simply or primarily to draw out the implications of what WILL BE. It is first of all a description of what IS . . . . .'[4]

In our criticism of Realised Eschatology we shall endeavour to discuss separately the four main areas of concern, the Synoptic evidence, the earliest Christian preaching, Paul's epistles and the Fourth Gospel.

In the Synoptic gospels there are two main areas where Dodd differentiates between Jesus' teaching and the embellishment of the early church. The first concerns the Parables. These have an individual stamp which (Dodd says) 'encourages us to believe that they belong to the most original and authentic part of the tradition'.[5]

---

[1] *Coming*, p. 178.
[2] *In the End, God* . . ., 1950.
[3] Cf. *In the End, God* . . ., p. 58.
[4] Cf. *In the End, God* . . ., p. 64. There is an interesting convergence in this matter of Protestant and Roman Catholic theology; cf. further below, p. 64.
[5] *History*, p. 89. Cf. Jeremias, *Parables*, p. 10. The *a priori* in Dodd's methodology is here apparent. Morgenthaler, *Kommendes Reich*, p. 88 writes, 'Er setzt hier offenbar voraus, dass im Menschen eine apriorische Urteilskraft vorhanden ist, die ihm die Möglichkeit gibt, innerhalb der evangelischen Tradition zwischen mehr oder weniger charakteristischen und echten Bestandteilen zu unterscheiden.'

Dodd, accepting that they were not intended as allegories [1]
affirms that they 'called to decision' by 'presenting one comparison
clearly'.[2] Mk. 4, 11-12 is, therefore, understood as the embarrassment solution of the early church [3] following the loss of the original
Sitz im Leben and of their original meaning. Dodd, however, appears
to be tied too closely to the term 'parable', whereas the background
meaning of παραβολή, as has been shown,[4] suggests that the required
decision could be evoked through the presentation of a problem,
riddle or mystery—here, the 'mystery of the Kingdom of God'.[5]
In this way, the parables can be seen to share in the equivocal
character of the entire ministry and teaching of Jesus,[6] and, precisely
because of their non-transparent quality, to have been especially
suited to become Jesus' teaching method, inviting and allowing a
free response to himself.[7]

Dodd claims to rediscover the original *Sitz im Leben* and to
use this as the key in determining the parables' true meaning.[8] He
does this in two ways. First, he finds the main theme of Jesus'
teaching from 'clear and unambiguous passages'—but these (which
we must discuss in a moment) are, actually, amongst the most
difficult and disputed in the New Testament. Secondly, he determ-
ines the meaning of the parables in the light of these 'clear' passages

---

[1] Jülicher's thesis, *Die Gleichnisreden Jesu*, 1899. His exclusiveness, however, has been modified by many; cf. Cadoux, *Parables*, pp. 50ff. Oesterley,
Parables, pp. 12ff. Jeremias, *Parables*, p. 16. Black, 'The Parables as Allegory',
in *B.J.R.L.* XLII, 1960. As A. H. M.'Neile said, 'The principal object in the
foreground of a picture is not the only object visible' (quoted by A. Walls, in
the *T.S.F.* Bulletin XXXII, 1962, p. 12).

[2] *Parables*, p. 22.

[3] Similarly Cadoux, *Parables*, p. 15. Smith, *Parables*, p. 28. Guy, *Last
Things*, pp. 24f. Boobyer, in *E.T.* LXII, 1950, pp. 131ff. Jeremias, *Parables*,
pp. 11f. concludes that the saying, though authentic, is wrongly applied to
the parables.

[4] Cf. Cranfield, 'Mark iv; 1-34' in *S.J.T.* IV, 1951, pp. 398ff. and V, 1952,
pp. 49ff. (with bibliography).

[5] Cf. Jeremias, *Parables*, p. 16.

[6] 'ἐν παραβολαῖς τὰ πάντα γίνεται', Mk. 4, 11.

[7] Cf. Torrance, in *Essays in Christology*, pp. 13ff. Cranfield, *Mark*, pp.
152ff. Torrance, 'A Study in N.T. communication', in *S.J.T.* III, 1950,
pp. 298ff. (Here, following Wallace in *S.J.T.* II, 1949, pp. 13ff., Torrance
writes, 'Jesus deliberately concealed the Word in the parable lest men
against their will should be forced to acknowledge the Kingdom, and yet He
allowed them enough light to convict them and to convince them.').

[8] Cf. *Parables*, pp. 26ff.

and *then* posits what their *Sitz im Leben* must have been [1]—but this is, of course, a circular method and the reverse of the procedure proposed! [2] Had the parables been so dependent upon their context for their true meaning as Dodd suggests, one might ask whether it is likely that this setting would quickly or lightly be forgotten. It is at least possible that their key is to be found not in any particular context but in their general relationship to the person and work of Christ. [3]

The second area of concern in the Synoptic material is apocalyptic. Some deny the presence of apocalyptic language and ideas in Jesus' message. [4] Others argue that Jesus used apocalyptic only as the *form* of his message. [5] The former contention can hardly be sustained except with the aid of *a priori* distinctions between a non-apocalyptic Jesus and an apocalyptic early church. [6] The other argument is also difficult; the use of the title Son of Man, for instance, suggests that not only is the term taken from apocalyptic [7] but also that it is being understood in terms of its meaning in apocalyptic tradition. [8] Besides, if Jesus used apocalyptic only as the form of his teaching, he clearly (on Dodd's thesis) failed to make this apparent to his hearers amongst whom the impression was created that this teaching actually embraced some of the ideas of apocalyptic.

---

[1] Cf. *Parables*, ch. 2 for the meaning: chs. 3-6 for the *Sitz im Leben*.

[2] Jeremias' method is ostensibly opposite: first 'Return to Jesus from the Primitive Church' (*Parables*, pp. 20-88), then, 'Message of the Parables' (*Parables*, pp. 89ff). Yet, in fact, here too the message of the parables is the guiding principle in the first section.

[3] Cf. Morgenthaler, 'Formgeschichte und Gleichnisauslegung', in *T.Z.* VI, 1950, pp. 1ff. contrast Jeremias, *Parables*, pp. 20f.

[4] Cf. Glasson, *Advent*, pp. 63ff. Bowman, *Intention*, pp. 51ff. Robinson, *Coming*, pp. 83f. Goguel, *Birth*, pp. 271ff.

[5] Cf. Dodd, *History*, p. 135. Guy, *Last Things*, pp. 63ff. Holmes-Gore 'The Ascension and the Apocalyptic Hope', in *Theology*, XXXII, 1936, pp. 356ff. ('even the most apocalyptic of Christ's sayings should be interpreted in a spiritual sense', he writes). It is interesting to note that Bultmann, who follows Wrede in his scepticism, follows Schweitzer in interpreting Jesus as strongly influenced by apocalypticism, whereas Dodd, who follows Schweitzer in his non-scepticism, follows Wrede in interpreting Jesus as not influenced by apocalypticism: cf. Bowman, 'From Schweitzer to Bultman', in *T.T.* XI, 1954, pp. 160ff.

[6] The same sort of distinction pressed by Schweitzer, but now in the opposite direction.

[7] Whether from Daniel or Enoch is for the moment immaterial.

[8] Cf. Cullmann, *Christology*, pp. 155f. Taylor, *Names*, pp. 25ff.

The demythologizing involved in realised eschatology is here to the fore.[1] Of course, the problem of recognising what is only picture language has long been felt,[2] and it is questionable whether every item in apocalyptic was ever taken literally.[3] But the distinction between imagery and literal truth is, surely, abandoned where (as in Realised Eschatology) all futurist eschatology is regarded as myth. This demythologizing, distinct from Bultmann's, is in danger of becoming Docetic: as Morgenthaler [4] writes, 'All die Argumente, die er (Dodd) gegen die futurische Eschatologie ins Feld führt, müssen sich schliesslich gegen seine realisierte Eschatologie wenden.'

Behind Realised Eschatology is an apologetic motif. Schweitzer maintained that Jesus was simply mistaken in his expectation of an imminent Parousia. Dodd accepts that the New Testament reflects such an imminent expectation and mistake, but transfers the onus of error onto the early church and safeguards Jesus from becoming an apocalyptic *Schwärmer*. His thesis, therefore, presupposes a cleavage between the early church and Jesus as great as that affirmed on Schweitzer's view, yet the antithesis may be no more necessary or correct than in Schweitzer's case.[5]

Fundamental in Dodd's thesis is his exegesis of the so-called 'clear and unambiguous' passages. A brief review of these will suffice to show how little they support Dodd's view:

i. Mtt. 12, 28 = Lk. 11, 20 [6]. Anticipating later discussion [7], we suggest that φθάνειν points to a real *yet proleptic* presence of the

---

[1] Demythologizing is intentional: cf. Dodd, *History*, p. 170, Glasson, *Advent*, p. 236. Robinson, *In the End, God* . . ., pp. 33ff.

[2] Cf. Cranfield, *Mark*, pp. 19f. Wilder, 'Eschatological imagery and earthly circumstance', in *N.T.S.* V, 1958, pp. 229ff.

[3] Leckie, *World to Come*, pp. 17ff. goes too far, cf. Cadoux, *Historic Mission*, pp. 340ff. Fritsch, in *T.T.* X, 1953, pp. 357ff.

[4] *Kommendes Reich*, p. 91.

[5] Bowman, in *T.T.* XI, 1954, pp. 16off. accepts McCown's remarks (concerning Schweitzer, in *The Search for the Real Jesus*, p. 252) 'Progress toward the truth is not made by the conflict between two (often confusedly opposed) alternatives, such as supernatural or rational, mythical or historical, eschatological or non-eschatological. His whole argument is based upon the "either/or" fallacy, the "fallacy of antithesis" or "abstraction" or "misplaced concreteness" (p. 169). The same could, surely, be said of Dodd.

[6] Cf. Dodd, *Parables*, pp. 43ff. *Apostolic Preaching*, p. 32. *History* p. 96. Glasson, *Advent*, p. 107. Robinson (*Coming*) has no mention.

[7] Cf. below, p. 167.

Kingdom in Jesus' exorcisms.[1] Werner [2] rightly maintains that the saying is difficult and must be interpreted by 'non-ambiguous' passages.

ii. Mk. 1, 14-15.[3] Again anticipating,[4] we suggest that ἤγγικεν here, parallel to πεπλήρωται, points to a real but proleptic presence of the Kingdom in the person and work of Christ.

iii. Lk. 10, 23-24 = Mtt. 13, 16-17.[5] The 'things' (ἅ) in question are Jesus' words and works. The Kingdom *is* present [6] but in this ambiguous, and therefore not final, manner.

iv. Lk. 11, 31-32 = Mtt. 12, 41-42.[7] Whilst the presence of the eschatological expectation in the person of Jesus is affirmed here, the possibility of further future fulfilment is not excluded. Indeed the future judgement is referred to in the future tense ἀναστήσονται and ἐγερθήσεται. Glasson [8] tries to evade the significance of these futures, but Kümmel [9] points out that a translation without a future reference would contradict the usage of κρίσις in the phrase ἡμέρα κρίσεως, and Klostermann [10] notes that 'will rise up' is NOT a Semitism for 'rising up in accusation' but definitely refers to the resurrection of the last day. The passage, far from denying a future final judgement, rather affirms it.[11]

v. Mtt. 11, 1-11 = Lk. 7, 18-30.[12] Whilst the presence of the Kingdom is here affirmed, it is directly related to Jesus' words and works (Mtt. 11, 5) and its presence is apparently ambiguous:[13] it remains, therefore, a prolepsis of a final, unambiguous manifestation.

---

[1] Cf. Michaelis, *Matthäus*, ad loc. Flückiger, *Ursprung*, p. 95. Morgenthaler, *Kommendes Reich*, p. 44. Manson, in *Eschatology*, p. 10.

[2] *Formation*, p. 50.

[3] Cf. Dodd, *Parables*, p. 44.

[4] Cf. below, pp. 166ff.

[5] Cf. Dodd, *Parables*, p. 46. Glasson, *Advent*, p. 115. Robinson, *Coming*, p. 64.

[6] Morgenthaler, *Kommendes Reich*, pp. 46f. denies a reference here to the Kingdom: contrast, rightly, Dodd, *Parables*, p. 46.

[7] Cf. Dodd, *Parables*, p. 47. Glasson, *Advent*, p. 108.

[8] Cf. *Advent*, p. 128 (following Wellhausen, McNeile and others). Contrast Robinson, *Coming*, p. 37, n. 1 who admits Glasson's failure here.

[9] *Promise*, p. 44, n. 84 (cf. also pp. 36ff.)

[10] *Matthäus*, ad loc.

[11] Cf. Kümmel. *Promise*, p. 44. Michaelis, *Matthäus*, ad loc. Morgenthaler, *Kommendes Reich*, p. 47.

[12] Cf. Dodd, *Parables*, p. 47.

[13] Cf. Kümmel, *Promise*, p. 111. Schniewind, *Matthäus*, ad loc.

vi. Mtt. 11, 12 = Lk. 16, 16.[1] The verb βιάζεται is difficult. Most probably it should be translated with a passive sense [2] and *in malam partem*.[3] The meaning then must be that in some sense the Kingdom of God is present (as it was *not* before Jesus' ministry), yet present in a way which allows it to be attacked. The ἕως ἄρτι sets a limit to this and contrasts the presence of the kingdom *now* with a presence yet to be realised ἐν δυνάμει.[4]

We find, therefore, in these passages a 'realised eschatology' which is a) directly related to the person and work of Christ and not affirmed in any abstract or universal sense: and b) hidden and ambiguous, pointing forward to a yet future fulfilment of the old expectation of a manifest, universal, unequivocal presence. These passages can hardly stand as the foundation of Realised Eschatology.

The second main area of concern is the earliest Christian preaching. Dodd reconstructs the kerygma from Acts 1-11, counting the Parousia among the five major components. But he interprets this from the standpoint of Mk. 1, 14f. and dismisses its character as a future historical event. However, the ultimate nature of the Parousia as a future event cannot, consistently, be demythologized without also bringing into question the nature and historicity of the past events on which the speeches of Acts lay great weight.[5]

Glasson [6] omits the Parousia from his reconstruction of the primitive kerygma, excising the two references in Acts on the basis of numerical inferiority. This methodology, however, is open to

---

[1] Dodd, *Parables*, p. 48. Glasson, *Advent*, p. 141. Robinson, *Coming* p. 41. Dodd, in the forward to his 3rd edition of *Parables* admits that the passage is not specially satisfactory for his thesis.

[2] Cf. Schrenk, in *T.W.N.T.* I, pp. 611f. Kümmel, *Promise*, p. 122, n. 67.

[3] Cf. Schrenk, in *T.W.N.T.* I, pp. 611f. Kümmel, *Promise*, p. 122. Cullmann, *State*, p. 20. *Early Church*, p. 197. Michaelis, *Matthäus*, I, *ad loc.* Schlatter, *Matthäus*, *ad loc.* Torrance, *When Christ comes*, pp. 117f. thinks that both active and passive can stand, and Klostermann, *Matthäus*, *ad loc.*, that both good and bad senses can.

[4] Cf. Kümmel, *Promise*, p. 124. Morgenthaler, *Kommendes Reich*, pp. 46ff. Grässer, *Problem*, pp. 180f. holds that this forward look is present in Matthew but removed by Luke.

[5] Cf. Cadbury, in *Background of the N.T.* pp. 300ff. Kümmel, in *N.T.S.* V, 1959, pp. 113ff. Morgenthaler, *Kommendes Reich*, pp. 91ff.

[6] *Advent*, pp. 154ff. and in *H.J.* LI, 1952-3, pp. 129ff.

serious criticism.[1] According to Glasson [2] the Parousia hope arose through the application to Jesus of certain Old Testament imagery referring to JHWH, on the basis of the conviction that 'Jesus is Lord'. But even Robinson (who accepts Glasson's thesis in so many particulars) cannot find here a suitable explanation, since the Gospels speak of a Parousia of the Son of Man, rather than of the Lord.[3] Besides, there is a qualitative distinction between recognising that the early church increasingly applied Old Testament passages to the risen Lord and supposing that, by the application of certain passages to him, the church created for itself a hope foreign to Jesus' teaching.

Robinson finds both Acts 3, 20 and 10, 42 unconvincing.[4] In Acts 10, 42 it is said that Jesus is ὡρισμένος, and Robinson says 'there is no suggestion that he will judge only at some second coming, no mention of which in fact is made'.[5] However, whilst the Old Testament knows of interim judgements in history,[6] one of its firm expectations was that God would ultimately exercise his judgement (either directly or through a mediator) at the great and final assize.[7] The reference to Jesus as judge-appointed of the living and the dead was, surely, intended to convey this idea of a final epiphany in judgement.[8] Acts 3, 20, Robinson argues,[9] does not contain a reference to Jesus' Parousia but to his status as Messiah-elect. Here we meet Robinson's answer to the question 'how did the Parousia hope arise?': he says it was through the confusion of the primitive Christology of Acts 3, 12-26 with the later Christology

---

[1] Glasson, by analysis (*Advent*, pp. 154ff.) finds 5 points which occur in every speech: but whether these 5 alone formed the original kerygma cannot be determined by his analysis alone (Cadbury, in *Background of the N.T.* p. 317 points out that the speeches are not necessarily typical or comprehensive . . .) Besides, the analysis says nothing about the historicity of articles which do not feature in every speech. The exaltation of Christ (Acts 2, 33. 3, 13. 5, 31) and the call to repentance (Acts 2, 38. 3, 19. 5, 31) are each only mentioned 3 times, but Glasson does not question their place.

[2] *Advent*, pp. 157ff.

[3] *Coming*, p. 41.

[4] Cf. *Coming*, pp. 28ff.

[5] *Coming*, p. 28.

[6] Cf. above, chapter 2. Peake, *Problem of Suffering in the O.T.* pp. 1ff. Bentzen, *Introduction to the O.T.* pp. 162f.

[7] Cf. above, chapter 2.

[8] Cf. Dibelius, *Studies*, p. 56. Jackson and Lake, *Acts, ad loc.* cf. also I Peter 4, 5. II Tim. 4, 1. Barnabas 7, 2. II Clem. 1, 1. etc.

[9] Cf. *Coming*, pp. 153f. and in *J.T.S.* VII, 1956, pp. 177ff.

of Acts 2. But we make here two criticisms of this. First, Acts 3, 12-20 does *not* contain a Messiah-elect Christology. During the narrative (3, 13-15) it is said that the Servant, the Holy and Righteous One, the Prince of Life *has* come, *has* died and risen and now works (v. 16). Verse 18 might contain, as Robinson holds [1] a Lukan formulation, but the idea it expresses is present already in vv. 13ff. Robinson supports his dismissal of v. 18 on the grounds that 'if we are to accept the words ... as an integral part of the original speech then it is difficult on any reconstruction to find in it a consistent theology'.[2] This is no justification for excising the verse and appears, anyway, to be unfounded—on the basis of the events of Christ's life, death etc. (summed up in v. 18) comes the call to repentance (vv. 22-26). Secondly, the relation of Acts 2 to Acts 3 must be questioned. Both contain an emphasis on fulfilled events (2, 3ff. 3, 18), on the present as the time of repentance (2, 37-40.3, 21-26), and the future aspect of salvation-history (though not explicit in Acts 2—(contrast 3, 20-21)—it is implicit in the call of vv. 39-40).[3] It would indeed be surprising if this supposed primitive Christology should so completely drop out of the tradition and yet be responsible for such far reaching and erroneous an understanding of the future.

Even if these two passages are allowed to stand as references to the Parousia [4] it remains true that early preaching, in general, 'was concerned with events which had already happened and of which the Apostles were witnesses'.[5] This, however, does not mean that the Parousia hope did not form an integral part of the earliest Christian faith. As 'conversion preaching' [6] these speeches would not be the context in which to find teaching concerning the Parousia. The conviction that the Parousia is to come is itself the mainspring of mission and lies *behind* the conversion preaching of Acts.

---

[1] Cf. in *J.T.S.* VII, 1956, p. 183. This is accepted by Jackson and Lake, *Acts*, p. 37. Contrast Bruce, *Acts, ad loc* 2, 23.

[2] *J.T.S.* VII, 1956, p. 183.

[3] The imagery is similar in some respects: cf. 2, 39 with 3, 24; 26. and 2, 40 with 3, 23.

[4] Cf. Bruce, *Acts, ad loc.* Jackson and Lake, *Acts, ad loc.* Dibelius, *Studies*, p. 56. All agree, with varying definiteness, that some idea of a Parousia is contained in one or both verses.

[5] Glasson, *Advent*, p. 155.

[6] Cf. B. Reicke, 'A synopsis of Early Christian Preaching', in *The Fruit of the Vine*, ed. Fridrichsen, esp. pp. 136ff.

The third main area of interest is Paul's eschatology. Dodd's hypothesis of a development in Paul's eschatological ideas may be criticised on general grounds. The dating of the Epistles, so important for Dodd's thesis, is open to dispute.[1] The psychological reconstruction of Paul's personality is extremely questionable.[2] The theory of a second conversion, which is said to have accomplished what the first could not, is also doubtful.[3] The idea of such radical development appears inherently improbable.[4]

Anticipating the exegetical discussion which concerns us later, we suggest that beneath the surface of Paul's letters, which changes according to the needs and circumstances being addressed, there is a constant and consistent eschatological framework in which the past, dominated by the Cross and Resurrection, the present, dominated by the Spirit, and the future, dominated by the Parousia, all have their necessary place. Taken alone, Realised Eschatology must give a one-sided and incomplete picture of Paul's thought.[5]

The fourth area of concern is the Fourth Gospel. Here, according to Dodd [6] is found the full return to Jesus' original intention.

---

[1] This matter is clearly vital for Dodd. He rightly allows 20 pages to argue for a late date for the Captivity Epistles. Yet in the matter of Galations — although recognising that 'the date of Galations is greatly disputed' (*Studies*, p. 85) — he is content to leave the question after a brief mention, concluding (following Burton) that it dates from c. 54-57.

[2] Cf. *Studies*, pp. 67ff. Deissmann, *Paul*, pp. 55ff. does not offer anything like the same picture, counting the remarkable tensions in Paul as his strength and greatness: similarly McNeile, *Paul*, pp. 2ff.

[3] Paul refers to the Damascus road incident (Gal. 1, 15) in a passage where important events bearing on his apostleship are being enumerated, yet does not mention the second 'really significant' experience save in a passing reference, II Cor. 12, 9!

[4] According to Gal. 1, 17-18; 21. 2, 1., Paul spent some 15 or 16 years (cf. Dibelius, *Paul*, p. 58) working in Syria and Cilicia before his missionary journeyings began and before any of his epistles were written. It seems intrinsically unlikely that we should find any radical development in Paul's thought in the letters dating from 'the last fifteen years of his working life' (Dibelius, *Paul*, p. 59). Dibelius concludes, 'Except for changes in the emphasis of certain particular doctrines, all the attempts of scholars to distinguish between a doctrinal system that was as yet undeveloped — in the earliest letters that we have (to Thessalonica) — and that of the four principal letters . . . have broken down' (*Paul*, p. 60). Contrast with Dodd, Barclay, *Mind*, p. 218. Davies, *Rabbinic Judaism*, pp. 286ff.

[5] Cf. Barrett, in *S.J.T.* VI, 1953, p. 145. Ladd, in *E.T.* XLVIII, 1956, pp. 268ff. Hunter, *Interpreting Paul's Gospel*, pp. 52f.

[6] Cf. *Apostolic Preaching*, pp. 155f. *Fourth Gospel, passim*. Glasson *Advent*, pp. 210ff. Robinson, *Coming*, p. 178.

The development is similar to that posited by Schweitzer, but this is now understood as a move nearer to Jesus rather than away from him. Exegetical discussion again concerns us later,[1] but here there are certain general matters which must be raised. Many scholars maintain that the historicity of the Fourth Gospel must be taken very seriously [2] and that the old antithesis 'Synoptics or John' is wholly inadequate.[3] The Johannine emphasis on the present is not unique (for it is by no means absent from the Synoptics [4]), nor is it, necessarily, exclusive. It is understandable in terms of the writer's intention.[5] Further, the Parousia is not so easily eliminated from the Fourth Gospel as Dodd suggests.[6] Certainly the Fourth Gospel recognises that with Jesus' past appearance came the End —and with it Judgement,[7] the Resurrection,[8] condemnation and blessing.[9] There are also passages where the present and future aspects of the End almost coincide [10] and where the two tenses must qualify each other: the hour is not wholly future, it is also *now*: but neither is it wholly present, it is *to come*. Again, there are sayings where the future aspects of the End are clearly expressed— the actual final judgement,[11] the actual final resurrection of the dead [12] and the actual Parousia of Jesus at the End.[13] The mystical

---

[1] Cf. below, pp. 157ff.

[2] Cf. Westcott, *John*, pp. liiiff. Barrett, *John*, p. 117. Lightfoot, *John*, p. 30. Strachan, *Fourth Gospel*, p. 18.

[3] Cf. Howard, *Fourth Gospel*, pp. 19ff. 128 f. Riesenfeld, *Gospel Tradition*. Strachan, *Fourth Gospel*, pp. 18f.

[4] Cf. Mk. 1, 15. 2, 18-22. 8, 34f. 9, 38f. 10, 42f. 13, 5ff. etc. Moule. 'The Individualism of the Fourth Gospel', in *N.T.* V, 1962, pp. 171ff.

[5] Dodd and others (including Barrett, *John*, p. 115) conclude that the gospel was in part prompted by the Parousia delay and its consequences. But the reason given in 20, 30-31 is surely adequate—'to encourage the readers to hold fast their belief' (Tasker, *John*, p. 28). If the gospel had in mind certain false ideas, and especially gnosticism (cf. Barrett, *John*, pp. 31ff. 114f.) then its emphases are understandable: in combatting gnosticism, the writer does not eliminate futurist eschatology, but he emphasises present faith union with Christ—faith as union rather than gnosis, effectual through the Spirit (cf. Weber, *Eschatologie und Mystik*, pp. 168ff. and Howard, *Christianity*, p. 120).

[6] *Apostolic Preaching*, p. 151. *Fourth Gospel*, esp. pp. 390ff.

[7] Cf. Jn. 3, 18. 9, 39. 12, 47. 5, 22. 12, 28.

[8] Cf. Jn. 5, 24. 6, 47. 11, 25.

[9] Cf. Jn. 5, 24. 6, 11; 40; 51. 3, 36. 12, 31. 16, 11.

[10] Cf. Jn. 4, 23. 5, 25. where the 'clash and paradox of tense characteristic of the N.T.' (Barrett, *John*, p. 56) is to be seen.

[11] Cf. Jn. 12, 48. 5, 29.

[12] Cf. Jn. 5, 29. 6, 40. 11, 24.

[13] Cf. Jn. 14, 2-3. 17, 24. chapter 21.

present aspect of salvation is but 'die Vorausnahme der Zukunft Gottes'.[1] The present mystical appropriation of the present reality of salvation is set forth in the Fourth Gospel within the framework of eschatology, and the clearly ambiguous usage of e.g. ἀνίστημι, ὁ ἄρτος τῆς ζωῆς, τετέλεσται, serves to emphasise this.[2] 'Christ as a figure of history belongs to the past and to the present. He came forth from God, sent by him. He has gone back to the Father. The Johannine view of revelation demands that he should have a future if the historical revelation is to be fulfilled. That is why St. John has not given up his expectation of a consummation.'[3]

Realised Eschatology rightly recognises that the New Testament emphatically declares that the Kingdom of God has come and is not 'wholly futurist'.[4] However, this 'realisation' is connected in the New Testament directly with the person and work of Christ and therefore with the lowliness and hiddenness characteristic of his ministry. It therefore carries the promise of future fulfilment, indeed demands future fulfilment. The pre-Christian hope centered upon an awaited universal, unambiguous manifestation of God's rule, and the coming of God's kingdom in Jesus' incarnate life does not exclude such a future, unambiguous coming, but rather confirms it as an object of hope.[5] The present is evaluated falsely if it is seen only in the light of the past event (Incarnation) and not also in the light of the future End. Realised Eschatology can 'speak no word of teleological hope to those now grappling with the historical dilemmas of our time.'[6] The future for which Realised Eschatology looks [7] misses entirely the historical particularity of

---

[1] Weber, *Eschatologie und Mystik*, p. 196.

[2] Cf. Cullmann, in *T.Z.* IV, 1948, pp. 360ff.

[3] Howard, *Christianity*, p. 212. Cf. also Ladd, in *E.T.* LXVIII, 1956-7, pp. 270ff. Kümmel, in *T.B.* XV, 1936, pp. 225ff. Meinertz, *Theologie*, II, pp. 280ff. Körner, in *Ev. T.* 1954, pp. 171ff. Stählin, in *Z.N.W.* XXXIII, 1944, pp. 225ff. Strachan, *Fourth Gospel*, pp. 13f. Barrett, *John*, pp. 56ff. Wood, *Jesus*, p. 185.

[4] Cf. Kümmel, *Promise*, pp. 105ff. Morgenthaler, *Kommendes Reich*, pp. 58ff. Cullmann, *Early Church*, p. 115. Rust, in *T.T.* X, 1953, pp. 327ff. Bruce, in *L.Q.H.R.* 1958, pp. 99ff.

[5] Cf. Cranfield, in *Essays in Christology*, p. 87.

[6] Fison, *Hope*, p. 65.

[7] Dodd, *Coming*, p. 26 says, 'When in due course history ends, and the human race perishes from this planet, it will encounter God . . . This is how I understand the mysterious language of the Gospels about the final coming of the Son of Man.' Glasson, *Advent*, pp. 232f. thinks man may even 'look for a world-wide triumph of the Gospel' and suggests that 'man may ulti-

the Parousia in the New Testament, a particularity which is strictly parallel to that attaching to the Incarnation.[1] The difference between the two 'comings' is not that the first involved a coming onto the plane of history whilst the second does not, nor that the first involved the coming of the Son of Man whilst the second does not, but rather that whereas the first involved the coming of Jesus Son of Man in hiddenness, the second will consist of his coming in glory. It appears impossible to remove this particularity without misinterpreting the New Testament hope.[2] With the abandonment of such a hope comes the inevitable over-evaluation of the institutions of the present which is specially marked in Roman-Catholicism[3] but is not the prerogative of that church.[4] Realised Eschatology represents the swing of the pendulum from Schweitzer's extreme view, but it is doubtful whether the New Testament can be interpreted adequately at this extreme any more than it was at the opposite.

An appended note on Dodd's interpretation of the parables (cf. above pp. 53ff.) Dodd differentiates into two main blocks: parables of crisis (*Parables*, pp. 154ff) and parables of growth (*Parables*, pp. 175ff.). Concerning these we make the following brief comments:

1. Mtt. 24, 45-51 (= Lk. 12, 42-46). Cf. Dodd, *Parables*, p. 158: Jeremias *Parables*, pp. 45f. Both see the original as a warning to the religious leaders of the time which has been re-interpreted (particularly by Luke) in terms of the Apostles and the Parousia hope. But, though 'servants' is a familiar designation (through the O.T.) of Israel's leaders, it appears from Mk. 10, 44 (cf. Mtt. 10, 24. Jn. 15, 15) that Jesus could refer to his disciples as δοῦλοι. Further, the picture of the return of the 'lord' is certainly painted in terms

---

mately be able to renew and wind up the universe . . .' (In *Appearing*, p. 191, he is willing to allow the possibility of a consummation of history 'by some supreme manifestation of the presence and power of Christ.')

[1] Acts 1, 11 is a good example of this particularity: 'this same Jesus' stresses the Christological particularity: 'shall so come in like manner as ye beheld him going into heaven' emphasises the particularity of the context.

[2] Cf. e.g. Vidler, *Essays in Liberality*, p. 35.

[3] The Vatican Council of 29th July, 1944, decided to remove the dogma of a physical return of Christ into the world from that which can with certainty be taught: cf. the report by Werner, in *S.T.U.* 1944, pp. 117f.

[4] Cf. Robinson, *Coming*, p. 15. Fison, *Hope*, p. 65 speaking of 'catholically minded incarnationists' writes that 'their thinking centres round a community conceived of as organised on an organic rather than a dialectical pattern. This leads at times to a virtual deification of the church and to a transubstantiation of its earthly realities into realities of grace. For such an outlook lip-service to a traditional future eschatology may be genuine in so far as individual hopes of immortality are concerned, but it can hardly have any meaning in the biblical sense for any corporate hope either for the world or for the church.'

of a final judgement, resulting in rewards and punishments: Jesus could hardly have expected that such a picture would be understood only as framework.

2. Mk. 13, 33-37 (= Lk. 12, 35-38). Cf. Dodd, *Parables*, pp. 160f. Jeremias, *Parables*, pp. 43f. Both maintain that it is a parable of crisis which may conceal a Messianic utterance of Jesus but has been variously interpreted by the early church in terms of the Parousia. Again, however, the imagery is of one who first goes away and then returns, and this is integral to the call to watchfulness. Had the crisis not been the impending Parousia, it is difficult to see why this particular 'framework' has been utilised (the prophets have, for example, other imagery in their crisis preaching: cf. Amos 3, 1ff.).

3. Mtt. 24, 43-44 (= Lk. 12, 39-40). Cf. Dodd, *Parables*, pp. 167f.: Glasson, *Advent*, p. 95: Robinson, *Coming*, p. 113: Jeremias, *Parables*, pp. 93f. Jeremias says 'the proclamation of the coming catastrophe became a direction concerning conduct in view of the delayed Parousia' (*op. cit.* p. 41). Only Jeremias offers support for this conclusion (which is accepted by Robinson, *Coming*, p. 113 n. 2) (Glasson quotes a suggestion of Harnack, but appears to reject it). Jeremias objects that 'thief' in every other N.T. usage (I Thess. 5, 2; 4. II Pet. 3, 10. Rev. 3, 3. 16, 15) is a picture of imminent catastrophe: so the parable, he argues, must have been addressed to the crowd concerning the crisis of Jesus' presence. But the parable is equally suited, even where 'thief' is given Jeremias' meaning (which it does not necessarily have to bear!), to the disciples. The charge is to watchfulness in order that no thief will appear at all: though the Son of Man come, it would not be as a thief if they watch (Rev. 3, 3 supports this understanding).

4. Mtt. 25, 1-12. Cf. Dodd, *Parables*, p. 172: Glasson, *Advent*, p. 93: Robinson, *Coming*, p. 69: Jeremias, *Parables*, pp. 41f. Jeremias says that the clue is in v. 5 χρονίζοντος δὲ τοῦ νυμφίου which was originally unstressed. However, the delay *remains* unstressed! He also argues that the 'allegorical representation of the Messiah as a bridegroom is completely foreign to the whole of the O.T.', and he finds only one late Rabbinic example. However, as Meinertz (in *Synoptischen Studien für A. Wikenhauser*, pp. 94ff.) rightly notes, the O.T. often sees the relation of JHWH to Israel as that of groom to bride (cf. Ezek. 16, 7. Hos. 1-3. Is. 65, 2. Ps. 45, 3), and it would not be surprising therefore to find Jesus using such a picture of the Parousia of the Son of Man.

These are the parables of crisis. The parables of growth are seen in a similar light and originally (it is said) represented Jesus' ministry as 'the climax of a long process which prepared the way for it' (Dodd, *Parables*, p. 180).

1. Mk. 4, 26-29. Cf. Dodd, *Parables*, pp. 175f.: Jeremias, *Parables*, pp. 91f. But the parable is not about growth! It is a comparison of the secret beginning with the certain, glorious harvest (cf. Kümmel, *Promise*, pp. 128f. Cranfield, *Mark*, pp. 169f. Schniewind, *Markus*, p. 47).

2. Mk. 4, 2-8 (cf. Mtt. 13, 3-9=Lk. 8, 5-8). cf. Dodd, *Parables*, pp. 180f. Jeremias, *Parables*, p. 92. For Jeremias, this is an assurance that 'out of nothing, in spite of apparent neglect, undeterred by failure, God is bringing in His Kingdom'. But it may well be (with Hunter, *Mark, ad loc*: Cranfield, *Mark, ad loc*: Klostermann, *Mark, ad loc*) that the emphasis is on 'hearing' and not at all on growth.

3. Mtt. 13, 24-30. Cf. Dodd, *Parables*, pp. 183f. Jeremias, *Parables*, p. 155. Whereas Dodd suggests that the parable originally answered the disciples' question about the Baptist's coming, Jeremias rightly regards it as a parable

of the consummation (similarly Kümmel, *Promise*, p. 134). Clearly appropriate to the early church's life, it may well be that the disciples expressed doubts about their fellows (cf. Schlatter, *Mark, ad loc*) (cf. Lk. 9, 49) and the parable answers by contrasting present ambiguity with future unveiling and disclosure.

4. Mtt. 13, 47-50. Cf. Dodd, *Parables*, pp. 187f. Jeremias, *Parables*, pp. 155f. Dodd (cf., too, Robinson, *Coming*, p. 37, n. 2) sees Matthew's interpretation, vv. 49-50, as secondary, the original being a reference to the mission and men's self-judgement according to their reaction to Jesus. But Matthew's 'interpretation' is more likely to be correct: on Dodd's view the fish should be described as themselves jumping back into the sea or into the vessels! The points of contact with the metaphor of Mk. 1, 17 are actually very slight.

5. Mk. 4, 30-32 (Mtt. 13, 31-32 = Lk. 13, 18-19). Cf. Dodd, *Parables*, pp. 189f. Jeremias, *Parables*, p. 90. Many (e.g. Kümmel, *Promise*, pp. 129f. Cranfield, *Mark*, p. 169) refute Dodd's view that Luke's form or Matthew's apparent conflation overrule the emphasis in Mark—which clearly stresses the littleness of the mustard seed. The point is surely, the contrast rather than the process of growth.

6. Mtt. 13, 33 (= Lk. 13, 20-21). Cf. Dodd, *Parables*, p. 191: Jeremias, *Parables*, p. 90. Dodd argues that the stress is on the influence of the leaven— a picture of Jesus' obscure work. Kümmel (*Promise*, p. 132 and cf. n. 99 for other authorities) argues that there are two events, one small and insignificant, the other manifest and large, and that the emphasis is on contrast (similarly Jeremias).

Neither the parables of crisis, nor the so-called parables of growth, necessarily exclude the Parousia theme: much rather do they point to the Parousia, in a number of cases.

CHAPTER FIVE

CONTINENTAL DEMYTHOLOGIZING

Bultmann's programme of demythologizing, proposed during the second world war in an essay, *Neues Testament und Mythologie* (1941) was confined to the continent for some years but is now a central issue throughout theological discussion.[1] His connection with Consistent Eschatology is interesting, for although markedly distinct[2] 'nonetheless, the influence of Weiss and Schweitzer is strong upon Bultmann; for him Jesus is as thoroughly eschatological in his views of the kingdom of God and its coming as for them'.[3] The affinity with Dodd's Realised Eschatology is well expressed by Morgenthaler:[4] 'Bultmann geht auf demselben Wege, den Dodd schon ein Stück weit gegangen ist, noch einen Schritt weiter ... Dodd legt in seiner realisierten Eschatologie einen Entmythologisierungsversuch vor, der mit dem Entmythologisierungsversuch Bultmanns darin übereinstimmt, dass er nicht auf die hergebrachte Weise auf der Ebene der Subtraktion bleiben will, sondern sich als Aufgabe eine Interpretation des Mythos gestellt hat ...'

Bultmann maintains that the early church, conscious of an encounter with God through Jesus Christ, sought to express the significance of this for itself and the world. But in doing so it partly failed to penetrate to the full significance and also it expressed

---

[1] Bartsch, in *Kerygma*, I. p. vii, writes, 'No single work which has appeared in the field of N.T. scholarship during the war years has evoked such a lively discussion. An increasing number of translations, contributions and criticisms are appearing in this country: cf. esp. Bultmann, *Theology of the N.T.* I and II (1952 and 1955): *Essays*, (1955): *History and Eschatology* (Gifford Lectures, 1957): Bartsch (ed.) *Kerygma and Myth* I (1953), II (1962): Henderson, *Myth in the N.T.* (1952): Gogarten, *Demythologizing* (1965): Miegge, *Gospel and Myth* (1960): MacQuarrie, *An Existentialist Theology* (1955): *The Scope of Demythologizing* (1960): Malevez, *The Christian Message and Myth* (1958): Bornkamm, *Jesus of Nazareth* (1960): Cairns, *A Gospel without Myth?* (1960): Robinson, *The Problem of History in Mark* (1957): *A New Quest of the Historical Jesus* (1959). For an outline of this Bultmann epoch and the post-Bultmann view of the 'historical Jesus' the last mentioned book is informative.

[2] Cf. Turner, *Pattern*, p. 23.

[3] Bowman, 'From Schweitzer to Bultmann', in *T.T.* XI, 1954, p. 168.

[4] *Kommendes Reich*, p. 94.

itself in terms which can no longer be meaningful for us.[1] The
Parousia idea, Bultmann argues, is an example of the former kind.
The early church has not properly understood the significance
of its encounter: 'history did not come to an end, and, as every
schoolboy knows, it will continue to run its course. Even if we
believe that the world as we know it will come to an end in time,
we expect the end to take the form of a natural catastrophe,
not of a mythical event such as the New Testament expects'.[2]
Eschatology in general, however, he holds to be an example of the
latter kind. Here, 'Christ as the eschatological event' is a concept
which can be and must be demythologized. What its precise
truth is, and how this can best be expressed are problems to be
dealt with, but the main point is (Bultmann contends) that there
is something valid to be re-interpreted.[3]

Our criticism of this thesis must be concerned firstly with Bultmann's methodology, in order to lay the foundation for differences
in exegesis which will concern us in later chapters: and then we
shall venture some general remarks concerning his programme of
demythologizing and its meaning for eschatology.

Characteristic of Bultmann and many of his followers is a radical
scepticism concerning the data of the New Testament. The old
antithesis between the Jesus of history and the Christ of faith is
ostensibly rejected by the acknowledgement that history and interpretation, event and meaning must go together, and that purely
objective history is impossible.[4] The New Testament gives us, to be
sure, the kerygma of the early church: a proclamation not only that
'Jesus died' (event) but also 'that he died for our sins and rose
again for our justification' (interpretation).[5] Bornkamm rightly
declares,[6] 'Wir besitzen keinen einzigen Jesusspruch und keine
einzige Jesusgeschichte, die nicht — und seien sie noch so unanfecht-
bar echt — zugleich das Bekenntnis der glaubenden Gemeinde

---

[1] Cf. in *Kerygma*, p. 16.
[2] Cf. in *Kerygma*, p. 5.
[3] Cf. 'History and Eschatology' in *N.T.S.* 1954, pp. 5ff. *History and
Eschatology, passim.*
[4] Cf. Gogarten, 'Theologie und Geschichte' in *Z.T.K.* L, 1953, p. 349.
Robinson, *New Quest*, pp. 77f. Gogarten, *Demythologizing*, pp. 25f. Bornkamm,
Jesus, pp. 11f.
[5] Cf. Henderson, *Myth*, p. 42.
[6] *Jesus*, p. 12.

enthalten oder mindestens darin eingebettet sind. Das macht die Suche nach den blossen Fakten der Geschichte schwierig und weithin aussichtslos.' From this recognition, two questions arise. The first is, are there any bare facts behind this kerygma? Bultmann anticipated this question,[1] realising that 'Christianity without Christ' *is* conceivable.[2] He claims to preserve (as he says, *unlike* the liberal theologies before him) a core of bare facts, but many critics [3] feel that he does so rather uncertainly. Miegge, for example, writes, 'It is necessary to affirm, much more strongly than Bultmann finds himself able to do, the truth and objective reality of the historical and supra-historical event which is summed up in the name Jesus Christ, the Crucified and Risen One: Christian faith stands or falls with the objective truth of these events.' [4] The danger of allowing historical theology to become mere religious psychology is a very serious one [5] and the 'post-Bultmann school' strives to avoid it.[6]

The second question which arises is, what reliance can be placed upon the early church's witness to Jesus Christ as we find this in the New Testament? As Bultmann has shown,[7] the units of tradition in the early church proclamation seem, generally, to have served some practical purpose in the church's life: but this discovery alone should not lead to scepticism regarding the historical veracity of the pericopae.[8] Often it is claimed that form criticism supports this scepticism, but this is not so. Conzelmann [9] for instance, argues that Mk. 1, 16-20 is 'altogether non-historical, but rather-ideal: the central word "I will make you fishers . . ." is a call

---

[1] In *Kerygma*, p. 22.

[2] Cf. 'There are people who will say that this whole account is a lie, but a thing isn't necessarily a lie even if it didn't necessarily happen' (Steinbeck, *Sweet Thursday*, Pan ed. p. 47). Which is what Knox, for example (in *Jesus, Lord and Christ*, pp. 258ff) is saying in a theologically respectable form.

[3] Cf. Thielicke, in *Kerygma*, pp. 138ff. esp. 147f. Schniewind, in *Kerygma*, pp. 66f. Malevez, *Christian Message*, pp. 71f (who tries to see a real objectivity in Bultmann's thought, though Miegge, *Gospel*, pp. 134f., thinks without success.).

[4] *Gospel*, p. 136.

[5] Cf. Butterfield, *Christianity and History*, pp. 128f. Cairns, *Gospel*, pp. 213f.

[6] Cf. Bornkamm, *Jesus*, pp. 18f. Conzelmann, in *Z.T.K.* LVI, 1959, pp. 2ff. Fuchs, in *Z.T.K.* LIII, 1956, pp. 210ff. Käsemann, in *Z.T.K.* LI, 1954, pp. 125ff.

[7] Cf. esp. *Geschichte* (1921): *Primitive Christianity* (E.T. 1956).

[8] Cf. Manson, in *Background of the N.T.* pp. 212ff.

[9] 'Die formgeschichtliche Methode', in *S.t.U.* III, 1959, pp. 54ff.

addressed to the present reader'. Of Mk. 15, 34 he says, it is 'originally a *Gemeinde* saying reflecting a particular theological motif. . .' [1]
But form criticism cannot make such judgements.

The historical veracity of the tradition *must be* probed. Form
criticism only rules out the possibility of reconstructing a biography.[2] But concerning the criteria which might be employed on
the task, two points are vital. First, the criteria must accord with
what can be learnt from the gospel records themselves and from
elsewhere, of the composition and character of the early community,
of its understanding of history and its attitude towards its task
of preaching and witnessing. On this basis, many would conclude
that considerable historical reliability can be attached to the
gospel narratives in general. Cranfield,[3] for instance, offers six
arguments which he holds 'would seem to justify us in rejecting
the radical scepticism of Bultmann and in believing that a substantially reliable picture of the historical Jesus was preserved in
the sources available to Mark'.[4] Secondly, the criteria should not
presuppose a breach between Jesus himself and the early church
witness to him. Such a presupposition would mean an acceptance of
the old antithesis between the Jesus of history and the Christ of
faith. Cullmann rightly criticises Bultmann's methodology on this
account. He agrees with Bultmann that 'all that contradicts the
theology of the early church can be assumed to be authentic to
Jesus' (else why should it have been preserved?).[5] But, as he says,
the opposite principle does not necessarily apply, namely 'that
all that corresponds to the theology of the early church is foreign
to the Jesus of history'.[6] The reverence for Jesus' words and
deeds (presupposed by the retention of pericopae which may well
have occasioned difficulty or embarrassment) must suggest that in
general we can expect to find that the early church has taken pains
in fashioning its thinking and teaching on words and deeds of
Jesus himself.

---

[1] Similarly Ackermann, *Jesus*, pp. 143ff.

[2] Yet Sjöberg's conclusion (*verborgene Menschensohn*, p. 216) that everyone
agrees there is no biographical interest behind the N.T. witness, surely goes
too far (as Wood, *Jesus*, pp. 148f. points out).

[3] Cf. *Mark*, pp. 16f.

[4] Cf. Manson, *Jesus*, pp. 20f. Manson, in *Background of the N.T.* pp. 211ff.
Cullmann, 'Out of season remarks', pp. 131ff.

[5] Cf. Cullmann, 'Out of season, remarks', pp. 131ff.

[6] Cf. Cullmann, 'Out of season remarks', pp. 131ff. and in *T.L.* I Jahrgang
83, 1958.

Bultmann and his followers build much upon a supposed discontinuity of thought not only between Jesus and the early church as a whole, but between particular elements in the early church itself. The old antitheses 'Jesus or Paul', 'Paul or John', 'John or the Synoptics' are again raised. Even within the Synoptics a cleavage is said to exist between Matthew and Mark on the one hand and Luke on the other.[1] In this way the New Testament is subjected to severe fragmentation and any unity of witness within the early church is discountenanced. Yet the profession of faith in the person Jesus Christ, the acceptance of the 'tradition', involved the several communities, whatever their differences, in 'one body, and one spirit . . . one hope of . . . calling; one Lord, one faith, one baptism . . .' (Eph. 4, 4). Whether this unity of faith involved also a unity of witness or not, the *possibility* of such unity ought not to be excluded by any method of interpreting the several elements in the New Testament. Besides, as Bosch [2] points out, it is difficult to suppose that the gospel compilers reflected *so* carefully over each phrase, or sought to express their individualistic characteristics *so* emphatically as adherents of radical redactional criticism suggest.

These criticisms have been made here in order to serve as a basis for later exegetical discussion. We turn now to some general criticisms of Bultmann's programme of demythologizing in order to justify rejecting the concept of a demythologized Parousia. We have already mentioned the problem of understanding and interpreting picture language. Bultmann's concern is much wider than this: for he defines as 'myth' requiring re-interpretation most of the New Testament proclamation.[3] As Henderson says, 'it is fair to say that Bultmann groups together a number of not particularly homogeneous elements under the heading of the mythological. The category

---

[1] Cf. Robinson, *Problem*: Marxsen, *Der Evangelist Markus*: Bornkamm 'Enderwartung und Kirche': Bornkamm, Held and Barth, *Überlieferung und Auslegung im Matthäusevangelium*: Lohse, 'Lukas als Theologe der Heilsgeschichte', in *Ev. T.* XIV, 1954, pp. 256ff. Grässer, *Problem*: Lohse, 'Zur N.T.'lichen Eschatologie', in *V.F.* 1956 (Jahresbericht 1953-55) pp. 184ff. Conzelmann, 'Gegenwart und Zukunft in der synoptischen Tradition', in *Z.T.K.* LIV-LV, 1957-8, pp. 277ff. *Mitte*.

[2] *Heidenmission*, p. 14 n. 14. Wood, *Jesus*, p. 61, rightly speaks of 'those elements which the distinctive temperaments of the Evangelists led them to emphasise . . .', but this complementariness does not amount to a presupposition of cleavage.

[3] Bultmann, in *Kerygma*, p. 16, finds two categories of mythical imagery in the early church witness: the one drawn from Jewish apocalyptic, the other from Gnosticism.

covers the account of the miracles of Jesus, descriptions of his person as the pre-existent Son of God, of his work as atoning for the sins of mankind, of the Holy Spirit as a quasi-natural power communicated to us through the sacraments'.[1] It is questionable whether the term 'myth' is well used in this sense. More seriously, Bultmann maintains that the subject of New Testament myth is man, and the purpose of myth is 'to express man's understanding of himself in the world in which he lives.' [2] But it is certainly possible to argue that the New Testament seeks to give expression not to what is being felt and experienced in the heart or mind of its writers, but to an actual encounter of God with man and to the history of this divine action.[3] In other words, all that Bultmann calls myth in the New Testament is primarily to be understood not cosmologically, nor anthropologically, but theologically. Of course, the theological proclamation has cosmological and anthropological significance: but this is secondary.[4] Notwithstanding some pictorial expression, some 'mythical' imagery, the *content* of the N.T. is not mythical in Bultmann's sense.[5] 'Myth' understood as an expression of human self-consciousness in historical or quasi-historical terms is 'not native to the Bible or to the N.T.' [6]

The question remains how far the New Testament proclamation requires to be re-interpreted. This problem is by no means new nor the concern of Bultmann only.[7] As MacQuarrie writes,[8] much religious language becomes, over the course of time, debased and esoteric, and 'the Christian vocabulary stands in continual need of being re-interpreted if it is to remain meaningful.' To employ contemporary modes of thought and forms of language is ever the preacher's duty—and therefore the dogmatician's too. But this could involve demythologizing only if the subject of the N.T. were

---

[1] *Myth*, p. 46.

[2] In *Kerygma*, p. 10.

[3] Cf. Barth, *Ein Versuch*, pp. 32f. Miegge, *Gospel*, pp. 98f. Wright in, *Biblical Authority*, p. 224. Cairns, *Gospel*, pp. 100ff.

[4] Contrast Bultmann, in *Kerygma*, p. 16. 'What is demythologizing' in *The Listener*, 5th Feb. 1953. p. 217. Brandon, 'Myth and the Gospel', in *H.J.* LI, 1952-3, pp. 121ff.

[5] Cf. Stählin, in *T.W.N.T.* IV, pp. 771ff.

[6] Miegge, *Gospel*, p. 106. Cf. Barrett, 'Myth in the N.T.' in *E.T.* LXVIII, 1956, pp. 345ff. and 359ff.

[7] Cf. Munz, *Problems of Religious Knowledge*, p. 182.

[8] 'Existentialism and the Christian vocabulary', in *L.Q.H.R.* 1961, pp. 250ff. cf. Schniewind, in *Kerygma*, pp. 87f.

man and his self-understanding, and this we doubt. It could mean re-mythologizing,[1] but then the question would need to be asked, whether the language of twentieth century existentialism is the best form for the Biblical proclamation.

This is a most important question, being related to the whole problem of the bearing of philosophy upon theology. Bultmann, of course, lays worth upon what we shall call 'preliminary philosophy'. The phenomenon of our existence as thinking beings means that we inevitably come to the New Testament, as to anything, with pre-conceived ideas. The question is, what status should be given to these inevitable thoughts. Here a deep cleavage exists between much Protestant thought and Roman Catholic theology, and it is not surprising to find, on the one hand, Malevez [2] agreeing with Bultmann that though a certain correction of these preliminary thoughts must be expected, the principle that hermeneutics is dependent on some preliminary philosophy is sound: and on the other hand, Barth arguing against such a *Vorverständnis*,[3] maintaining that the possibility of knowing God occurs in the act of God revealing himself to us, thereby showing that God's word is fundamentally alien to man's thought. Hence, Barth holds, Biblical hermeneutics is not just the application of a general hermeneutic principle, but is unique.[4] Bultmann's arguments [5] against this position seem to be ineffective. Barth's hermeneutics are bound to appear 'only arbitrary assertions' [6] for Barth is concerned primarily to repeat the proclamation of God's activity as this is testified in the Bible and is prepared to find his hermeneutic principles only as given in the commitment to this proclamation.[7]

The homiletic expedient of using current concepts clearly needs to be considered seriously. But if the New Testament *is* concerned to confess and proclaim a divine activity (if the New Testament 'myths' *are* theological) then such contemporary concepts should

---

[1] The principle of analogy underlying the use of mythological language is, surely, indispensable (as Bultmann admits, in *Kerygma*, p. 44), Bultmann's language being no less analogical than the 'less sophisticated language of the Bible' (Owen, in *S.J.T.* XIV, 1961, p. 197. Cf. Lohmeyer, in *Kerygma*, pp. 126ff. Wright, in *Biblical Authority*, p. 224).

[2] *Christian Message*, pp. 170f. 183f. 190.

[3] Cf. *Ein Versuch, passim.*

[4] Cf. Malevez, *Christian Message*, pp. 170ff.

[5] Cf. *Essays*, pp. 259ff.

[6] *Essays*, p. 261.

[7] Cf. also Barth, *C.D.* III/2, p. 534.

only subserve this proclamation and 'have no right to pontificate' over the subject matter.[1] This means that no one particular philosophical language and thought form should be elevated to the position of sole interpretative medium for whilst one thought form could subserve the proclamation here and now it might not tomorrow or in another place.[2] Whether or not the particular philosophy of existentialism is as vital an interpretative medium to-day as Bultmann would suggest it is, is open to dispute: doubtless the technical terminology of existentialism is more difficult for many to grasp and understand than the more naive language of the New Testament.[3]

Another very serious question which must be asked is, whether Jesus' life as historical event is properly or adequately evaluated by Bultmann. If the thesis 'God was in Christ reconciling the world to himself' (II Cor. 5, 19) is a valid affirmation of the significance of Jesus' life, then although this 'once for all' [4] event must be contemporised if it is to have full significance 'for me' [5] the historical particularity and self-sufficiency of the Christ-event must never be abandoned in favour of this contemporising which it demands and facilitates. The historical particularity of the Christ event is presented in the New Testament as meaningful for the past and for the future, as well as for each 'now', for in his encounter with man, Jesus Christ reveals himself to be the One who was and who will be, as the 'pre-existent Son of God' and as the 'Judge of the End time'. In that encounter is given impetus and authority to refer God's activity in Christ both backwards into the past, involving some idea of creation, and forwards into the future, involving some idea of a Parousia. Whatever imagery and vocabulary we choose to express and elucidate this significance, the concept of a salvation-history is contained and imparted in the central event of revelation, the once-for-all event of the Incarnation of Jesus Christ.[6]

At this point the problem of time in the New Testament is raised.[7] Bultmann has no wish to return to the idea of 'timeless

---

[1] Lohmeyer, in *Kerygma*, p. 133.

[2] Cf. Barth, *Ein Versuch*: Malevez, *Christian Message*, p. 198.

[3] Cf. Miegge, *Gospel*, p. 134. Schniewind, in *Kerygma*, pp. 89f.

[4] Rom. 6, 10. Heb. 9, 12. 9, 28. etc.

[5] Cf. Barth, *C.D.* III/2, p. 447.

[6] This is, of course, what Cullmann maintains in *Christ and Time*. Many, in various categories, seek to affirm the same—cf. for example Brunner, *Das Ewige*, esp. pp. 35ff.

[7] Cf. above, chapter 2, p. 17 n. 1 concerning the O.T. view.

truths' (though some think he does in effect do so[1]): but he maintains that futurity is simply a phenomenon of existence and claims
that to hold to a particular hope concerning the content of the
future is to seek to emancipate oneself from the essential conditions
of human life, and is therefore sin. There can, therefore, be no
Christian teleology. Time, he says, is a phenomenon which involves
a future as much as a past: but about this future, nothing more
can be said than that occasion will be given in it, through the word
of preaching, for further encounter with God in Christ.[2] Eschatology,
on this view, if not made positively timeless is certainly de-tempo-
ralised. It is a definition of the quality of the Christ-event and
man's participation in it. Let Bultmann speak for himself: 'The
New Testament understanding of the history of Jesus as eschatological event is not rightly conceived either in the conception of
Jesus as the centre of history, or in sacramentalism. Both are
solutions of the embarrassment into which the Christian community
was brought by the non-appearance of the Parousia. The true
solution of the problem lies in the thought of Paul and John, namely,
as the idea that Christ is the ever present, or ever-becoming event
(i.e. the eschatological event): the "now" gets its eschatological
character by the encounter with Christ or with the Word which
proclaims Him, because in this encounter with Him the world and
its history comes to its end and the believer becomes free from the
world in becoming a new creature'.[3] We venture to suggest that
this does not do justice to the New Testament understanding of
time, or to its understanding of the Christ-event, or to its evaluation
of the present age. We consider these three areas in turn.

Much recent discussion [4] stresses that the New Testament view of
time involves the recognition that futurity is *not* simply a phenomenon of existence but is also God's time, time and occasion for divine
action: it is subject to the Lordship of Christ. This is far from
saying that Christ is subject to the sovereignty of time as men are,
knowing no other possibility of existence except one in which there
is a past into which each present passes and a future which ever

---

[1] E.g. Kümmel, in *V.F.* 1947-8, pp. 75ff. and cf. Fuchs' answer in *Ev. T.*
1949, pp. 447ff.

[2] Cf. *History and Eschatology*, pp. 149ff.

[3] 'History and Eschatology' in *N.T.S.* 1954, pp. 5f. cf. Conzelmann, in
Z.T.K. LIV-LV, 1957-9, pp. 277ff.

[4] Cf. esp. Cullmann, *Christ and Time*: Marsh, *Fulness of Time*: Minear in
S.J.T. VI, 1953, pp. 337ff. Barth, *C.D.* III/2, pp. 437ff. Rust, in *T.T.* X, 1953,

anew becomes present: but it does mean that God, in his encounter with the world does not ignore man's time frame-work. God allows succession and chronology to be really involved, and so he creates a salvation-history. To be sure, the relation of past to present and of present to future with God and his salvation history is not simple: but the complexity is not such as to diminish the reality of past and future in salvation-history. 'What is past, so far from perishing, lives on in every new present, though the past-ness of the past, like the futurity of the future is not in the least impaired. The *kairoi* taken together stand under some decisive "beginning" (ἀρχή) where an "age" (αἰών) is inaugurated and move towards an "end" (ἔσχατον) where the content of the age is rounded off and established in its completeness or fulfilment as something eloquent of the glory of God'.[1]

Secondly, the revelation of God in Jesus is regarded in the New Testament as informative and authoritative for past and future revelation. Not only is Israel's history understood by reference to him,[2] but creation and therefore the entire sweep of past history is illuminated by reference to him.[3] Although Luke and Matthew tend to emphasise this backward reference more, Mark does not by any means altogether neglect it.[4] Similarly the New Testament writers (in varying degrees) read off from this central Christ-event, a real future significance. The present relationship of the believer to Christ is 'in hope',[5] hope not simply that the relationship will continue (through constant renewal of a divine encounter), but hope that the provisional nature of the relationship ('in faith') is *really only* provisional, being bounded by the awaited future revelation of Christ in glory. Without holding this event as an object of

---

pp. 327ff: Minear, in *Interpretation*, V, 1951, pp. 27ff. Dillistone, in *S.J.T.* VI, 1953, pp. 156ff.

[1] Whitehouse, in *Eschatology*, p. 74. Cf. similarly Barth, *C.D.* III/2, pp. 464f. 485f. On the whole question of the future aspects of salvation-history cf. further, Thurneysen, 'Christus und seine Zukunft', in, *Zwischen den Zeiten*, 1931, pp. 18ff. Wright, in *Biblical Authority*, p. 224. Körner, in *Ev. T.* 1954, pp. 177ff. Wendland, *Die Eschatologie des Reiches Gottes bei Jesus*, pp. 27ff. 240ff. Althaus, *Letzten Dinge*, pp. 28ff. Künneth, *Theologie der Auferstehung*, pp. 218ff. Rich, *Die Bedeutung*, pp. 4ff. Delling, *Zeitverständnis*; Fuchs, in *Ev. T.* 1949, pp. 447f., etc.

[2] Cf. e.g. Acts 2, 14ff. 7, 2ff.

[3] Cf. Col. 1, 16. Heb. 1, 2. Jn. 1, 1ff.

[4] Cf. Mk. 1, 2f. Robinson, *Problem*, pp. 22ff.

[5] Cf. e.g. Rom. 5, 2. 8, 24. Eph. 1, 18.

hope, the full significance of the Christ-event has not been drawn.[1]

Thirdly, is it not true to say that what the New Testament regards as characteristic of the present epoch is not simply that in it men are 'brought face to face with the last things in crucial decision' [2]—the aspect Bultmann is so anxious to emphasise—but that man is for the moment given time and occasion for a response of free decision to the *Eschaton*, inasmuch as it encounters him as yet only in a mystery, veiled? He, the *Eschatos*, invites men to participate in a real past and to anticipate a real future consummation. Hence each present encounter with Christ has a reference backwards and one forwards, by which the present is qualified. Demythologized eschatology appears to lead to a docetic view of time, to a docetic view of the work of Christ, and therefore to a docetic view of the present.[3] The faith which witnesses to us in the New Testament, and without which the Christ-event would remain unknown to us, presents us with other objective historical events on the same level as that central one and in fact posited by it: it recognises that the 'decisive action wrought by God within history at a particular centre in some sense accompanies history and bears decisively on all the process of historical connexions by which the cosmos moves to its consummation.' [4]

The faith which the New Testament seeks from us is not simply an openness to encounter but commitment to certain divine events in history and their significance. In this commitment is given the will to acknowledge that the events, being divine events for man's salvation, have an objective, independent status and meaning quite apart from man. That is to say, the Cross did not acquire its saving significance only at the moment when later the disciples began to believe that it held such meaning and possibility for them; but, rather, in the economy of God, the Cross held that significance in the relationship of God to the world both before and independently of the disciples' faith. The New Testament writers are surely not

---

[1] Cf. Schniewind, in *Kerygma*, p. 81f. *Nachgelassene Reden*, pp. 38ff.

[2] Whitehouse, in *Eschatology*, p. 70.

[3] Wright, in *Biblical Authority*, p. 224. arguing that the Christian cannot set aside the Biblical view of time, says, 'without it one has no means of interpreting the meaning of history, other than as the secular order in which he lives provides it, and he must live without hope in the future which will redeem the present by the power of the God who is the directing Lord of time.'

[4] Whitehouse, in *Eschatology*, p. 70.

concerned only to confess their own faith and so to arouse ours, but to relate the events, centring on Jesus and reaching backwards and forwards throughout the whole sweep of history, on the basis of which the present is what it is and faith is made possible.

Bultmann undoubtedly emphasises matters of considerable import. His programme is prompted by an evangelical motive.[1] The present time *is* a period of opportunity calling forth faith—as a dialectic between self and self-abandonment in commitment. This is demanded by the preaching of God's encounter with man in Jesus Christ. Without such commitment to the gospel, the historical life and death of Jesus can never appear more than the tragic story of a good man. Doubtless, too, there *is* a pastoral requirement to proclaim all this in language which our contemporaries can understand, and it may well be that some to-day will understand the language of existentialist philosophy and that this terminology can be used for apologetic purposes.

At the same time, Bultmann 'in his eagerness to tear away the mythological coverings which hide the truth'[2] appears to give insufficient emphasis to a further dialectic which faith must notice, namely the dialectic between the 'now' of faith and the 'not yet' of hope, between the 'now' of 'seeing through a glass, darkly' and the 'then' of 'seeing face to face' (I Cor. 13, 12). It is the very dialectic in which faith is itself caught up, which is to be replaced one day by the certainty of fulfilment and possession, a certainty towards which faith, because of its dialectical nature, strains forward in constant hope.

Further, in his desire to present the significance of the gospel in a contemporary form,[3] Bultmann appears to abandon what is, surely, the conviction of the New Testament writers, namely that the gospel calls men to the decision not only to authentic existence understood and appropriated in 'existentiell' moments of life, but to acknowledge the sovereign saving acts which God has accomplished in the historical life, death and resurrection of Jesus Christ. Therefore, however ontic faith must be, it is in the first place, noetic: a confession of the truth of the situation which has arisen through the salvation-history of God in Christ 'reconciling the world unto himself'.

---

[1] Cf. in *Kerygma*, p. 3.
[2] Woods, *Theological Explanation*, p. 209.
[3] Cf. *Essays*, pp. 236 ff.

Commitment to the particularity of God's work in history in the person of Jesus Christ involves recognition of a real salvation-history which is directly related to Christ,[1] so that past and future outreaches, even the beginning and end themselves, centre upon him. The phenomenon of faith itself authenticates the hope of a future unambiguous revelation of the End, for such hope is inescapably bound up in the recognition that the End has occurred in a particular (and therefore equivocal, ambiguous) historical event. Hope, and particularly hope in the Parousia of Jesus Christ, is presupposed by faith.

---

[1] So that Cullmann, for instance, speaks of this salvation-history as the 'Christ-line' (*Time*, pp. 107ff.).

CHAPTER SIX

SALVATION-HISTORY AND THE PAROUSIA
IN THE NEW TESTAMENT

The interpretations of New Testament eschatology which we have now reviewed have been questioned on grounds of methodology and of theology. It is difficult, we maintain, without expressly *re*-interpreting the New Testament message, to evade the conclusion that the New Testament as a whole works with the concept of a salvation-history of which the Parousia is an integral part: and without resorting to a dubious methodology, it is difficult to account for the specifically future phase of this total salvation-history by referring it to the early church alone, or to one particular line of thought current within the early church. All three theses reviewed here abandon or call in question the reality of salvation-history and its overall pattern. Schweitzer abandons the reality of salvation-history for the idea of mystic communion and the inspiration of Jesus' example. Bultmann substitutes for the idea of a salvation-history the idea of a new 'self-knowledge', a new 'gnosis'. Dodd, in less radical fashion, imperils the reality of the total salvation-history by his re-interpretation of the idea of the End.

On the other hand, many scholars regard the concept of salvation-history as fundamental to the New Testament.[1] We give now a brief account of the arguments in support of this view—which will serve as a postscript to the arguments already reviewed and as an introduction to our examination later of the view of those who regard the Parousia hope itself as an integral part of the New Testament message, but find the apparent insistence on its imminence problematical.

The abandonment of a salvation-historical understanding of the gospel goes back to the earliest days of the church. Both

---

[1] From the very many we mention Cullmann, *Time*: *Christology*: *Heil als Geschichte*: Filson, *The N.T. against its environment*: Richardson, *Introduction*: Taylor, *Names*: *Life and Ministry*: Stauffer, *Jesus*: Manson, *Jesus*: Roberts, *Kingdom of God*.

Ebionism and Docetism shrank from the belief that the Divine could actually come into history, into the particularity of history in the form of an individual person: and so, in their opposite ways, they evacuated the life of Jesus of its saving quality.[1] It is clear why Docetism should have been congenial to the Gnostics, for though fundamentally a Christological concept, it is acceptable only where salvation is thought of as mystical enlightenment (γνῶσις) where 'the concrete is resolved into the abstract' and 'redemption is a deliverance from the material world, which is regarded as intrinsically evil',[2] and where the cosmic dimension of salvation is exchanged for individual concern for present communion with the divine and a safe destiny.[3] The mysteries, too, intending to impart salvation through knowledge and emancipation from the fetters of human existence, had no place for a salvation-history. The struggle to affirm a real salvation-history continued through the Trinitarian debates [4] and the Christological controversies.[5]

Salvation-history and the Old Testament:

We have already seen [6] that the concept of salvation-history is quite fundamental to the Old Testament. The Creation narratives are clearly written from the standpoint that they prepare for and make possible a salvation-history.[7] The Covenant is regarded as God's manifestation of his concern for the furtunes of Israel, and this concern is seen to accompany Israel's history [8] and, ultimately, to have a universal outreach.[9] The Old Testament resolutely refuses to look upon history (even the history of other nations) divorced from the relation it bears to salvation, or upon salvation outside

---

[1] Cf. Cullman, *Time*, pp. 127ff.

[2] Scott, 'Gnosticism', in *E.R.E.* VI, pp. 233f.: cf. Gal. 4, 4. Rom. 1, 3. 9, 5. Heb. 2, 14. I Jn. 1, 1-3. 4, 1-3. 2, 22. II Jn. 7. Col. 1, 9-22. 1, 26-27. 2, 3. 2, 8-9. 3, 10; 16. Ignatius Eph. 7, 18. Smyrna chs 1-6. Polycarp Phil. 7, 1-2. Irenaeus ad. Haer. III: 3, 4. Justin Dial. 35.

[3] Cf. Gardner, 'Mysteries', in *E.R.E.* IX, p. 81.

[4] Cf. Kelly, *Doctrine*, pp. 223ff., esp. p. 233.

[5] Cf. Kelly, *Doctrine*, pp. 263ff.: Bethune-Baker, *Introduction*, pp. 249ff.: Prestige, *Fathers*, pp. 94ff.

[6] Cf. above chapter 2, pp. 7ff. Anderson, *Introduction*, p. 237.

[7] Cf. Barth, *C.D.* III/1, pp. 63ff.: Whitehouse, in *Essays in Christology*, pp. 115ff.: also Ps. 119, 89-90. I Chron. 29, 11. Is. 48, 12.

[8] Cf. Ex. 33, 16. 19, 9. 33, 12-23.

[9] Cf. Jer. 16, 19. Ps. 22, 7. Zech. 8, 22. Zeph. 3, 10. Is. 11, 10. 30, 23f. 65, 20-25. Dan. 7, 27, etc.

of its historical context. The significance of this for the understanding of the New Testament is obvious.[1]

Salvation-history and the New Testament:

Evidence that the *early church* understood its faith and life in terms of a salvation-history is found in the earliest preaching and the earliest confessions of faith. The early speeches of Acts [2] reveal a major emphasis upon past events, supremely the death and resurrection of Jesus [3] of which the disciples are witnesses [4] and which form the fulfilment of the promises contained in past salvation-history.[5] The significance of this fulfilment is applied to the present [6] and to the future,[7] and it is evident that such preaching cannot be understood apart from its salvation-historical context.

The shortest credal confession, 'Jesus is Lord' (κύριος ᾿Ιησοῦς) [8] and the expanded summaries of faith [9] presuppose the idea of salvation-history. Faith is based on the fulfilment of God's promises in Christ, culminating in his present Lordship.[10] It is not fortuitous

---

[1] One need only note the extensive use of the O.T. (cf. the N.T. Nestle ed., P.W.B. 1952, pp. 658ff.) its imagery and language: and the place of Temple and synagogue worship (Lk. 4, 16, Acts 3, 1. 9, 20. 13, 5. 13, 14. 14, 1. 17, 1. 18, 4. 19, 8) in early christian life.

[2] Cf. Acts 2, 14-36; 38-41. 3, 12-26. 4, 8-12. 5, 29-32. 7, 2-53. 8, 31-36. 10, 35-43. 13, 17-41. Whilst Dibelius, *Studies*, pp. 138ff., Cadbury, *Luke-Acts*, pp. 187ff., Haenchen, *Apostelgeschichte*, pp. 96f. and others regard these speeches as unauthentic, there is much to be said in favour of their authenticity — cf. Knox, *Acts*, pp. 9ff., Dodd, *Apostolic Preaching*, pp. 20ff., Bruce, *Acts, ad loc* — or at least the authenticity of ideas if not also of form — cf. Erhardt, 'The construction and purpose of the Acts of the Apostles', in *S.T.* XII, 1958, pp. 45ff.

[3] Cf. Acts 2, 22-23, 3, 13-14; 15. 4, 10. 5, 30; 31. 7, 53. (8, 35). 10, 37-39; 40-41. 13, 27-29; 30. Cf. Evans, 'Kerygma', in *J.T.S.* (NS) 1956, pp. 25ff.

[4] Cf. Acts 2, 32. 3, 15. 5, 32. 10, 39; 41. 13, 31.

[5] Cf. Acts 2, 16-21. 3, 12; 18; 22-26. 4, 11.? 5, 30. 7, 2-47; 52. 8, 32f. 10, 43. 13, 17-23; 27; 32-37.

[6] Jesus reigns and works (2, 33-36, 3, 21. 4, 10. 5, 31. 10,37): the Spirit is given (2, 16-21. 5, 32): therefore repent and believe! (2, 38-41. 3, 19. 5, 31. ?7, 51. (8, 37). 10, 43. 13, 40).

[7] Jesus will judge (3, 20f. 10, 42): salvation will come (4, 12. 5, 31. 10, 43. 13, 38).

[8] Cf. Acts 11, 17. Rom. 10,9. I Cor. 12, 3. Phil. 2, 11. Col. 2, 6. Arndt-Gingrich, *Lexicon*, for biographical detail, cf. Foerster, *T.W.N.T.* IIII, pp. 1038ff.: O'Neill, 'The use of κύριος in the Book of Acts', in *S.J.T.* VIII, 1955, pp. 155ff.: Cullmann, *Confessions*; Kelly, *Doctrines*, pp. 459ff: Cullmann, *Worship*, pp. 12ff.: Bultmann, *Theology* I, pp. 51 and 121ff.

[9] Cf. I Pet. 3, 18-22. Phil. 2, 6-11. I Cor. 15, 3f. II Cor. 4, 5.

[10] Cf. Cullmann, *Confessions*, p. 58.

that the future phase of salvation-history is not immediately brought into the credal confessions,[1] for the Parousia hope is not the basis of faith but faith's necessary corollary and is expressed initially in prayer. Other early tradition can be detected in sections of catechetical instruction:[2] ethical behaviour is enjoined here both on the basis of the past acts of God in Christ[3] and also with a view to the fulfilment of the Christian eschatological hope,[4] and so must be seen it its relation to the entire salvation-history. Christian hope is expressed in such obedience, and also in the prayer μαραvα θα.[5] The connection of this prayer in Did. 10, 6 with the eucharistic liturgy[6] is important, for here μαραvα θα must share the salvation-historical character of that meal. Hence Cullmann[7] writes, 'This ancient prayer . . . . points at the same time backwards to Christ's appearance on the day of his resurrection, to his present appearance at the common meal of the community and forwards to his appearance at the End, which is often represented by the picture of a Messianic meal'. It seems, therefore, that the concept of a salvation-history runs through the early church's preaching, teaching, worship and prayer.

The salvation-historical significance of *Paul's teaching* is under-evaluated by Schweitzer,[8] by Dodd[9] and by Bultmann,[10]whereas many find in the idea of salvation-history the context for his entire teaching.[11]Paul appears to regard the present as a time in

---

[1] Cullmann, *Confessions*, pp. 58f., finds it first in II Tim. 4, 1. Robinson, *Coming*, p. 33, n.1, regards this as hardly a credal formula. For its occurrence in the Apostolic Fathers and later, cf. Kelly, *Creeds*, chapter 3 and *Doctrines*, pp. 462ff.

[2] Cf. I Thess. 2, 13. 4, 1-8. II Thess. 2, 15; 36. etc.

[3] Cf. I Thess. 5, 9-11. Rom. 12, 1ff. etc.

[4] Cf. I Pet. 4, 7. Rom. 13, 12. etc. Dodd in *N.T. Essays*.

[5] Though I Cor. 16, 22 is neutral, the translated form in Rev. 22, 20 is clearly a prayer. Cf. Cullmann, *Worship*, p. 13: Kuhn, in *T.W.N.T.* III, pp. 500f.

[6] If the connection is right — cf. Dix, *Shape of Liturgy*, pp. 90ff.

[7] *Worship*, p. 14.

[8] In the claim that Paul saw the present in an immediate relationship to the imminently awaited Parousia, and therefore ignored a real time element (cf. recently Vielhauer, 'Zur Paulinismus der Apostelgeschichte', in *Ev.T.* X, 1950-51, pp. 1ff.).

[9] In the thesis that Paul abandoned eventually any specific hope in the Parousia (cf. above pp. 50f.).

[10] In his interpretation of hope in Paul in terms of an openness to the future ('The openness of Christian existence is never-ending' — *Primitive Christianity*, p. 208. cf. further, *Theology* I, pp. 190ff.: *Primitive Christianity*, pp. 185ff.)

[11] Cf. Munck, *Paul*: Davies, *Rabbinic Judaism*: Cullmann, *Heil als Geschichte*

which the new aeon has begun [1] though the old continues. [2] The tension between the past acts on which faith rests and the future phase of salvation-history towards which hope strains, is a strictly temporal tension between a 'then' in the past and a 'then' in the future (e.g. II Cor. 1, 10). Between these two points stands the present characterised by mission [3] and the presence of the Spirit.[4] The present tension is interpreted by Bultmann as one between *Weltlich* and *Entweltlich*, but the expressions of the tension are so full of temporal terms ('waiting', 'day', 'now', 'then' 'inherit') that such a re-interpretation is hardly justified.[5] Further, the present is not a mere phenomenon, nor simply a haphazard continuum, but has a definite content and progression fore-ordained and divinely directed.[6] To be true to Paul, we can neither say that salvation is simply personal encounter or understanding, nor that history is a mere phenomenon, but that salvation is fully historical and that history is entirely embraced by the intention of salvation.

The assessment of *Luke* as theologian and historian is a foremost problem to-day.[7] Conzelmann,[8] particularly, maintains that Luke departs from early eschatology and, under the pressure of the Parousia delay, alters the tradition in favour of his own historicising.[9] But this thesis both diminishes the centrality of a salvation-history concept in the thought of Paul and of the earliest community

---

and many older works, e.g. Nock, *Paul*: Stewart, *A Man in Christ*: Kennedy, *Last Things*, etc.

[1] Cf. e.g. Col. 1, 12f. II Cor. 5, 14f. Gal. 6, 14f.

[2] Men continue to die (I Cor. 11, 30. I Thess. 4, 13f.) and continue to sin (I Cor. 1, 11f. 5, 1ff.) because evil still works in the world (II Cor. 2, 11. Gal. 4, 8) and men still need to be admonished and encouraged to obedient behaviour (Gal. 5, 4. 6, 6. Rom. 12, 1ff. etc.).

[3] Hence Paul is anxious to further the mission (I Cor. 9, 23. II Cor. 10, 16. Rom. 15, 19ff.) and in no way hinder the progress of the gospel (I Cor. 9, 13. II Cor. 6, 3-4).

[4] Cf. II Cor. 1, 22. 5, 5. Eph. 1, 14. Rom. 8, 23. etc.

[5] Such a tension would be accessible to human reason, whereas for Paul it is a mystery which must be revealed — Rom. 11, 25; 33.

[6] Cf. Phil. 1, 12f. Rom. 9-11 (Cullmann, *Time*, pp. 163ff. Sanday and Headlam, *Romans, ad loc*) II Thess. 2, 6ff. Col. 1, 22-29. Rom. 11, 13. I Cor. 9, 16.

[7] Cf. Barrett, *Luke the Historian* for an introduction and an indication of the place this problem holds to-day.

[8] *Mitte, passim*: cf. also Grässer, *Problem*: Haenchen, *Apostelgeschichte*, pp. 90ff. Käsemann, in *Z.T.K.* IL, 1952, pp. 272ff. and in *Z.T.K.* LI, 1954, pp. 125ff. Vielhauer, in *Ev. T.* 1952, pp. 1ff.

[9] *Mitte*, p. 81.

(discussed already) and also exaggerates any distinctive emphasis in Luke. The following examples support this latter contention:

i. It is said that Luke treats John the Baptist no longer as the eschatological forerunner,[1] but only as a prophet of the Old Israel.[2] However, it is noteworthy that Mk. 1, 6 (= Mtt. 3, 4) — a description which places the Baptist firmly within the epoch of the prophets —is omitted by Luke. Conzelmann argues[3] that Lk. 3, 10ff. is typically Lukan since the judgement is no longer 'near': it is, however, important to notice that Luke has retained the original (? Q) connection with 3, 9 (cf Mtt. 3, 10) so that Lk. 3, 10-14 appear to be only an expansion of the demand of v. 8 in the light of the imminent judgement, v. 9. Further, the ἀπὸ τότε of Lk. 16, 16 is probably only a stylistic alteration, not necessarily intending a meaning distinct from Matthew's ἕως ἄρτι (Mtt. 11, 12).[4]

ii. Luke is said to have written the first 'life of Jesus'.[5] However, Mtt. 1-2, though betraying different motifs, has a similar emphasis on the 'historical Jesus' and even Mark appears to be interested in the objective, historical events of Jesus' life.[6] Further, if the Lukan prologue is to be taken seriously, it appears that others had already shown the same interest,[7] and also that Luke's concern was not simply an historical, but also a pastoral one (cf 1, 4).

iii. Luke is said to be especially concerned with the present as an epoch rather than a *Zwischenzeit*.[8] To be sure, his special parables stress the character of Christian behaviour,[9] but this concern represents rather an emphasis than a special theological standpoint.

---

[1] Cf. Mk. 1, 4. Mtt. 3, 2. 4, 17.

[2] Cf. Lk. 1. 9, 28-36. 3, 15. 3, 10-14. 9.9, 16, 16. Conzelmann, *Mitte*, pp. 86, 95; Grässer, *Problem*, pp. 180f.: Haenchen, *Apostelgeschichte*, p. 89.

[3] *Mitte*, pp. 86f.

[4] Cf. under Mk. 14, 62 below, pp. 139f. Contrast Grässer, *Problem*, p. 182.

[5] Cf. Conzelmann, *Mitte*, pp. 124ff.: Käsemann, in *Z.T.K.* LI, 1954, pp. 125ff. and Haenchen, *Apostelgeschichte*, p. 88, n. 3.

[6] Cf. Robinson, *Problem*, passim: Moule, in *N.T. Essays*, pp. 165ff. Leaney, *Luke, ad. loc.* 1, 4.

[7] Lohse, 'Lukas als Theologe der Heilsgeschichte', in *Ev.T.* XIV, 1954, pp. 256ff. argues that the πολλοὶ of 1, 1 cannot be taken literally, referring actually (he says) to Mark and 'Q' only. Perhaps, however, the 'many' should be treated more seriously (cf. Barrett, *Luke the Historian*, p. 21): in any case, Luke means that he is *not* the first to be occupied with such a narrative.

[8] Conzelmann, *Mitte*, pp. 181ff.

[9] Cf. 10, 29-37. 13, 6-9, 15, 11-32. 18, 9-14. 16, 19-31. 18, 1-8. 12, 13-21. 16, 1-13.

Mark is by no means *un*concerned about the ethical aspect of faith in Jesus Christ.[1]

iv. It is alleged that Luke no longer has the note of urgency so characteristic of the earliest church.[2] This, however, cannot be maintained consistently,[3] and, if Lk. 13, 6-9 is actually Luke's alternative to Mk. 11, 12 ff.,[4] it is interesting that he has preferred a parable in which urgency is the key-note.

v. The redactional-critical method appears to encourage exaggerated emphases. An example may suffice here to establish the point. Conzelmann [5] finds throughout Lk. 21 a conscious alteration of Mk. 13.[6] An analysis suggests that Conzelmann has made more of the differences than should be allowed:

Lk. 21, 7 is said, by the shift of setting to eliminate the eschatological significance of the Temple's destruction. Yet the connection remains in Lk. 21, 5-6, and the question in v. 7 is a question of the date of the Temple's destruction, to which an answer is given in terms of the End itself (vv. 8ff.).

Lk. 21, 8 is said to reject a near expectation. Certainly Luke adds ὁ καιρὸς ἤγγικεν but this is exactly parallel to the false claims ('Εγώ εἰμι) which Mk. 13, 6 warns will be made. The words 'the end is not yet' (Mk. 13, 7) and 'these things are the beginning of travail' (Mk. 13, 8) are clearly intended to discourage a *false Naherwartung*, and to encourage watchfulness.

Lk. 21, 9 similarly: but Mark's ἀλλ' οὔπω τὸ τέλος gives the same sense as Luke's ἀλλ' οὐκ εὐθέως τὸ τέλος, and Luke, far from eliminating an imminent hope by his use of πρῶτον, is more precisely temporal in his expression than Mark with δεῖ γενέσθαι.

Lk. 21, 12 is said to emphasise universal proclamation as the chief factor in the present. But Mk. 13, 10 is entirely parallel (cf. the temporal πρῶτον and the divine constraint in δεῖ). Many question the authenticity of Mk. 13, 10 [7] but the main grounds for this

---

[1] Cf. Mk. 3, 35. 7, 6ff. 9, 35. 10,5f.

[2] Cf. Conzelmann, *Mitte*, p. 129; Cadbury, *Luke-Acts*, p. 292; Grässer, *Problem*, pp. 178ff.

[3] Cf. Cadbury, *Luke-Acts*, p. 292. The two references, Lk. 13, 6-9 and Lk. 18, 8 (ἐν τάχει) are highly significant.

[4] Leaney, *Luke*, ad loc.

[5] *Mitte*, pp. 107ff.

[6] Conzelmann regards Mk. 13 as Luke's source; contrast Beasley-Murray, *Future*, p. 226.

[7] Cf. Jeremias, in *T.B.* XX, 1941, p. 217: Klostermann, *Markus, ad loc*:

appear unsound.[1] Conzelmann further claims that Lk. 21, 12 presents a definite pattern, persecution being seen as the preface to the final end. But in Mk. 13, 10 and 13, 13 a similar conviction appears: persecution and witness form a period prior to the end itself.

Lk. 21, 19 is said to emphasise ὑπομονή as the climax and to show that Luke was thinking in terms of a *long duration* of the church. Yet the expression 'he that endureth to the end . . .' (Mk. 13, 13) seems to carry a similar emphasis.

Lk. 21, 6 and 18 are said to emphasise God's providence. However, the same emphasis occurs in Mk. 13, 12-13 too.

Lk. 21, 20f. is said by Conzelmann to correct Markan ideas about the Temple destruction and the fall of Jerusalem by historicising these events and removing their eschatological connection and character. Yet Lk. 21, 22 shows that Luke regarded the fall of Jerusalem as the fulfilment of prophecy, and thus to have a salvation-historical context. Verse 25, which refers to the cosmic signs which herald the end, follows (as in Mk. 13, 24f. also) without any discontinuity the mention of the fall of Jerusalem and the mission to the Gentiles, so that the entire section (vv. 20-26) is seen as 'signs' of the End.

Lk. 21, 25-28 is said, by Conzelmann, to push the Parousia into the background. Yet there is no significant change from the pattern of Mark 13. Both gospels introduce the section as a phase chronolo-

---

Conzelmann, *Mitte*, p. 108: Grässer, *Problem*, p. 5, pp. 159f. Kümmel, *Promise*, pp. 84f.

[1] The grounds are a) that the verse interrupts the continuity between vv. 9 and 11: but this might only mean that an authentic saying has been inserted by an editor (cf. Cranfield, *Mark*, pp. 399f.) b) that the idea is foreign to Jesus: however, the idea of a universal mission goes back to the O.T. (cf. Bosch, *Heidenmission*, pp. 17ff.: Cullmann, in *E.M.* 1941, pp. 98ff.), is found in Judaism (cf. Ps. Sol. 11, 1; 8. 17, 43. etc.) and was to some degree accepted by the Pharisees of Jesus' day (Beasley-Murray, *Future*, pp. 194f. asks 'was Jesus more narrow?'). Jesus' restriction of his ministry to the Jews can be understood as provisional (cf. Bosch, *Heidenmission*, pp. 76f.) Taylor, *Mark, ad loc.* thinks that the Gentile mission problems could not have arisen in the early church if this verse (Mk. 13, 10) had been known as a word of Jesus: but Cranfield, *Mark, ad loc.* and Schniewind, *Markus, ad loc.* point out that the real problem of Gentile mission was not whether or not there should be such a venture, but whether or not the heathen converts should go through the stage of being Jews. (If the reading of ℵ in Acts 2, 5 were to be preferred, it would appear that Gentiles were included from the first: but see Haenchen, *Apostelgeschichte*, p. 135, n. 9 and Barth, *C.D.* III/4, p. 322).

gically subsequent to the 'tribulation' and mission (Mk. 13, 24, Lk. 21, 24-25). Both refer to cosmic events (Lk. 21, 26 adds tribulations on earth, but these are assumed as continuing to the End in Mk. 13, 20; 22). Lk. 21, 28 cannot mean that the Parousia itself is still only near, since it is already spoken of in v. 27: it is probable that v. 28 refers to that aspect of the Parousia which is spoken of in Mk. 13, 27, so that Luke is right in saying that when these things begin to happen 'our redemption draws nigh'. Lk. 21, 29-31 is said to historicise eschatology further by asserting that only during the final cosmic stage is the Kingdom of heaven 'nigh'. The sense, however, is exactly parallel to that of Mk. 13, 28-29.

We suggest, therefore, that Luke's emphases are only emphases and not the result of a quite different or new standpoint. These emphases do not prove that Luke's central concern was the Parousia delay or that he felt it necessary to reformulate earlier hopes,[1] for he shares his salvation-historical standpoint, as we have seen, with the early church and Paul—and, as we shall now suggest, with *John*.

Bultmann [2] regards the primitive eschatology as demythologized by the Fourth Gospel. But the basis of the gospel appears to be still the life of Jesus understood as historical phenomenon,[3] and we may notice the frequent temporal connections throughout and the geographical data.[4] John does not attempt a separation of Jesus' significance for salvation from the historical particularity of his life, death and resurrection. The Prologue is condensed salvation-history, drawing out the significance of the 'Word made flesh' in its backward reference through Covenant history in its narrow sense into the general history of creation and pre-creation. Similarly the

---

[1] A good case can be made out for other aims and pressures behind Luke's composition: cf. Dibelius, *Studies*, pp. 146ff.: Ehrhardt, in *S.T.* XII, 1958, pp. 45ff.: Leaney, *Luke*, pp. 5ff.: and most recently O'Neill, *Theology of Acts*, p. 168.

[2] Cf. *Johannes, passim*: *Theology*, II, pp. 3ff.

[3] Bultmann, *Theology*, II, p. 8, maintains that the history-of-salvation perspective as a whole is lacking in John. But it is fair to notice that John gives us his theological views only in the form of a life of Jesus and it is arguable that this historical life meant, to John, much more than a mere symbol or paedagogic tool.

[4] Cf. temporal data in Jn. 1, 29; 35; 43. 2, 1; 12. 3, 22. 4, 43. 5, 1; 9. 6, 1; 22. etc. and geographical data in Jn. 1, 28; 43. 2, 1; 12. 3, 22. 4, 3; 43; 46. 5, 1; 2. 6, 1. etc.

conclusion of the gospel [1] looks to the future, to the mission arising from Jesus' own mission (20, 21f.) and, perhaps, hinting at the final End (20, 31). The *past* phases of salvation-history are emphasised in chapters 1-12 apparently because the theme throughout is the demand for faith. In chapters 13f. it is the believing community which is addressed and the hope centred upon the future phases of salvation-history becomes more prominent.[2] The centrality of the concept of salvation-history in the Fourth Gospel is well brought out in its treatment of the Sacraments. In both baptism and the last supper the tokens of the presence of the risen Lord with his community point back to his historical life, and forward to his final coming.[3]

It is hardly necessary to examine the remaining New Testament evidence,[4] and we conclude with the following résumé. Salvation-

---

[1] I.e. chapter 20. Chapter 21 we take to be a secondary addition (cf. Barrett, *John*, p. 479).

[2] Cf. further below, pp. 212f.

[3] Baptismal imagery runs throughout (1, 19-34. 3, 1-21. 3, 22-36. 5, 1-19. 9, 1-39. 13, 1-20. 19, 34) and so connects the sacrament with the whole course of Jesus' Life. The theme runs backwards (to John the Baptist, 1, 19f. and to Moses, 3, 14) and forward to the consummation at the End (3, 5. 3, 13-14). Eucharistic imagery also runs throughout (2, 1-11. 4, 1-30. 6, 1-13. 6, 26-65. 13, 21f. 19, 34. 21, 5-14). The theme again runs backward (to the manna of the old Covenant, 6, 41-51: to the Passover meal as proto type of the Crucifixion, 13, 1. 18, 28) and forward to the pouring out of the Spirit and the Messianic meal (4, 14. 4, 24) (cf. Cullmann, *Worship*, pp. 37ff.).

[4] In the Pastorals, the right order emphasised (cf. I Tim. 1, 3-4. 3, 1ff. 4, 1f. II Tim. 1, 13. 2, 2. 3, 1f. 4, 3. Titus 1, 5f. 2, 1f. etc.) is understood as right evaluation of the salvation-history as it centres on Jesus — the fulfiller of the old promises (I Tim. 1, 15. 2, 5. 3, 16. 4, 10. 6, 13-14. II Tim. 1, 9f. 2, 8-9. Titus, 1, 1-3. 2, 11. 3, 7), the present Lord (I Tim. 1, 12. 6, 14-15) and the one who will come at the End (I Tim. 4, 10. 6, 14-15. II Tim. 1, 18. 4,1. Titus 2, 13. 3, 7). The divine ordering of this history is attested (I Tim. 2, 6. II Tim. 1, 9).

In the Catholic Epistles Jesus' life and work are presented as the fulfilment of prophecy (I Pet. 1, 10-11, 2, 24. 3, 18f. II Pet. 1, 19f. 2, 5f. 3, 2f. Jude 5f.). It is from this standpoint that the present and future are viewed. In the future, the salvation-history line reaches out to the Parousia (James 5, 7-8. I Pet. 1, 8; 13. 4,7. II Pet. 3, 8f. I Jn. 2, 28.) The present is a period of patient waiting and obedience (James 1, 3f. 5, 7-11. I Pet. 3, 14. 4, 7f. II Pet. 1, 10. 3, 9) and of mission through the Spirit (I Pet. 1, 12. I Jn. 1, 20. 4, 2-3). Hebrews opens with a salvation-history summary (1, 1-4). In 2, 1-4 and 9-11 (also 12,2. 13,8) we find further summaries.The present period is one in which men are called to pay 'earnest heed' to the gospel proclamation (2, 1) and is therefore regarded as a merciful provision (11, 39). In the Book of Revelation the assurance of Jesus' return (1, 6. 3, 3; 12. 19, 11f. 22, 7; 20) is based on the Covenant of God with man. The line of salvation-history

history is a basic conception of the entire New Testament. From the centre, Jesus Christ, the line of salvation-history runs backwards through the covenant to creation and beyond, and forwards through the church and its mission to the Parousia and beyond. That God gives to certain events special significance is a 'mystery' (Rev. 10, 7) not obvious to human understanding but requiring to be revealed.[1] So that such revelation is an integral part of salvation-history, making faith (the confession of past phases of salvation-history) possible and with it the corollary, hope (in future phases of salvation-history yet to be unfolded).

There are numerous indications that Jesus himself held firmly to the concept of salvation-history which we have traced in Old and New Testaments. His submission to John's baptism is instructive, for the Baptist's work is orientated about the salvation-history expectation of Elijah prior to Messiah's appearing.[2] The Baptist's preaching, too, μετανοίας εἰς ἄφεσιν ἁμαρτιῶν (Mk. 1, 4) can only be understood by reference to the Old Testament.[3] Jesus' submission to John's baptism indicates sympathy with his salvation-history standpoint. Jesus' own preaching is likewise based upon the concept of salvation-history. The summary, Mk. 1, 15, is very probably an editorial compilation, but there is no reason to suppose that Mark or his source has misrepresented the substance of Jesus' message,[4] and the terminology is charged with the concept of

---

extends backwards (so cf. 13, 8. 5, 5-6, 15, 3). The present period is one in which the gospel is proclaimed (6, 11. 7, 3f. 14, 6. 22, 17) calling forth faith and repentance (1, 3. 2, 1-3, 22) and there is a withholding of the End until the gospel has been fully proclaimed (6, 10 7, 3f. 8, 1), whilst the faithful long for the End (3, 10. 6, 10. 22, 20) and the interim judgements and 'comings' take their course (3, 20. 9, 5ff. 12, 6).

[1] Cf. I Cor. 2, 10. Lk. 10, 21. Gal. 1, 16. Eph. 3, 5. Warfield, *The Inspiration and Authority of the Bible*, p. 80.

[2] Cf. Mal. 4, 5. John's dress and diet were modelled, clearly, on Elijah's (II Kings 1, 8). The Synoptists agree in prefacing John's work with words of prophecy relating to the expected salvation, Mtt. 3, 3. Mk. 1, 2-3. Lk. 3, 4-6. Cf. Mal. 3, 1. Is. 40, 3-5. Cf. also Jn. 1, 23. Is. 40, 3.

[3] Cf. Grundmann, in *T.W.N.T.* I, pp. 305ff. Behm and Wurthwein, in *T.W.N.T.* IV, pp. 947ff. Cranfield, *Mark*, pp. 44ff. Luke emphasises this context (cf. 1, 5-25, 1, 39-80. 3, 1-20), but cf. also Mtt. 3, 1-16. Mk. 1, 2-8. Jn. 1, 6-37. Robinson, *Problem*, pp. 22f.

[4] Sharman, *Son of Man*, pp. 99f. contends this, but Kümmel, *Promise*, p. 25, n. 18 shows his arguments to be inadequate. Rawlinson, *Mark*, p. 13 says 'Mark's sentence . . . does admirably sum up the essence of our Lord's primary message.'

salvation-history (πεπλήρωται ὁ καιρὸς [1] and ἤγγικεν ἡ βασιλεία τοῦ θεοῦ).[2] The terms which Jesus used of himself or apparently accepted from others [3] are all understandable only in terms of the Old Testament and its pattern of salvation-history. It is reasonable to suppose, therefore, that Jesus saw his role as fulfilling the expectation to which past stages of salvation-history and successive experiences of Covenant relationship looked in hope. Further, his own death and resurrection are seen as divinely ordained [4] and to have 'prophetic' significance: that is, they cannot be understood apart from their place in salvation-history.[5] The mission of the church is viewed, most probably, as a significant stage in the ongoing salvation-history.[6] The fall of Jerusalem is seen from the same standpoint—not from some other (secular) position.[7] And the Parousia is similarly understood. Although the End event is to be of a different texture from the events prior to it,[8] it will be a real presence of Christ in the context of history and the total cosmic structure—i.e. it is a further phase in salvation-history.[9]

---

[1]. Cf. Cranfield, *Mark*, p. 63. Marsh, in *T.W.B.* pp. 258ff. Barth, *C.D.* III/2, pp. 457ff.

[2] Cf. Schniewind, *Markus*, p. 16.

[3] Cf. above chapter 3, pp. 42ff.

[4] Mk. 8, 31. 9, 31. 10, 33 par. cf. Grundmann in *T.W.N.T.* II, pp. 21ff.

[5] Cf. Lk. 13, 32f. Mk. 14, 3-9. 14, 22-31.

[6] Cf. further below, pp. 95ff.

[7] It is not sufficient to see it as merely the outcome of political events (Beasley-Murray, *Future*, p. 199 mentions the view of V. G. Sinklovitch that Jesus forecast its doom from this standpoint *alone*).

[8] Cf. e.g. Lk. 17, 24 par.

[9] Cf. Cullmann, *Early Church*, p. 144: *Time*, pp. 60f., 109. Barth, *C.D.* III/2, pp. 447ff. 464f.

CHAPTER SEVEN

THE NEW TESTAMENT INSISTENCE ON THE IMMINENCE OF THE PAROUSIA

In this chapter we pass from the conclusion that Jesus and the early church appear to have awaited an actual Parousia of the Son of Man to the fact that this expectation appears to be coupled with an insistence on its imminence.[1] The imminent character of New Testament hope has long been regarded as a problem,[2] and a variety of solutions have been proposed. These we now discuss.[3]

1. Ostensibly the simplest answer to the problem is to accept that Jesus taught that the Parousia was imminent, and to confess that this hope proved to be mistaken. This view is, therefore, akin to the Consistent Eschatology of Schweitzer, except that the error now is confined to the *nearness* of the expectation, not involving the expectation itself. The thesis has a variety of particular forms. Some hold that, though mistaken, Jesus' imminent hope formed an integral part of his teaching and attitude.[4] Others suggest that whilst he was mistaken, his apparently delimited expectation was only peripheral to his more generally based hope.[5] Some understand Jesus' imminent expectation in the light of Mk.

---

[1] Cf. Mk. 9,1 = Mtt. 16, 28. Lk. 9, 27. Mk. 13, 30 = Mtt. 24, 34. Lk. 21, 32. Mk. 14, 62 = Mtt. 26, 64. Lk. 22, 69. Mtt. 10, 23.

[2] Cf. Muirhead, 'Eschatology' in *H.D.C.G.* pp. 525ff. Scott, *Tributaries*, p. 181. Branscomb, *Mark*, p. 159.

[3] The divisions must be somewhat artificial for there will be frequent overlapping: but they are useful for our discussion.

[4] Cf. Loisy, *Synoptiques*, I, p. 247. Nicklin, *Gleanings*, pp. 436f. Easton, *Christ in the Gospels*, p. 163. Mackinnon, *Historic Jesus*, pp. 206f. Turner, in *A New Commentary*, p. 104. Guignebert, *Jesus*, p. 346. Lowrie, *Mark*, p. 316. Ackermann, *Jesus*, pp. 143f. Manson, *Teaching*, pp. 277ff. Barrett, *H.S.G.T.* pp. 157ff. 'N.T. Eschatology', in *S.J.T.* VI, 1953, pp. 163ff. pp. 225ff. Owen, 'The Parousia of Christ in the Synoptic Gospels', in *S.J.T.* XII, 1959, pp. 171ff.

[5] Cf. Cullmann, *Time*, p. 88, 149: *Early Church*, pp. 141ff.: 'Eschatologie und Mission' in *E.M.* 1941, pp. 98ff.: 'Die Hoffnung der Kirche auf die Wiederkunft Christi', in *V.s.P.* 1942, pp. 27ff.: 'N.T. Eschatologie und die Entstehung des Dogmas', in *K.r.S.* 1942, pp. 161ff.: 'Die Wahrheit von der Parousieverzögerung', in *T.Z.* 1947, pp. 177ff., 428ff.: Michaelis, *Verheissung, passim*.

13, 32 and maintain that this confession must modify all Jesus'
prophetic utterances.[1] Akin to this is the suggestion that Jesus
began during his lifetime to remove the element of imminence (so
typical, it is said, of apocalyptic) from his hope for the future.[2]
And a further suggestion is that since Jesus anticipated at least
a slight interval between his resurrection and the Parousia, his
occasional insistence on the nearness is of no consequence, for the
principle of an interval (of whatever duration) is established.[3]

This thesis is propounded often with considerable hesitancy,[4]
since it is recognised that to attribute to Jesus errancy can create
(and sometimes has created) great distress.[5] Nevertheless, it is
suggested, errancy formed an essential feature of Jesus' true
humanity.[6] Not all who find this thesis unsatisfactory are motivated
simply by a desire to preserve Jesus from the charge of fallibility—
the thesis, in fact, contains a number of difficulties both exegetical
and theological. Here we wish only to select certain important
issues in order to facilitate a re-examination of the passages where
an imminent Parousia appears to be foretold.

One of the primary theological questions is the exact nature
of Jesus' fallible humanity. Manson [7] cites as parallel examples of
error Jesus' medical diagnosis in certain cases, and his views on

---

[1] Cf. Michaelis, *Verheissung*, pp. 45f.: Hadorn, *Zukunft und Hoffnung*,
pp. 124f.: Titius, *Jesu Lehre*, pp. 147f.: Lake, *Introduction*, p. 32.

[2] Cf. Taylor, *Life and Ministry*, pp. 76f. Nairne, *Epistle of Priesthood*,
p. 207: Baldensperger, *Selbstbewusstsein Jesu*, pp. 254f. contrast Wendt,
Lehre Jesu, pp. 307f.

[3] Cf. Beasley-Murray, *Future*, pp. 191ff. Kümmel, *Promise*, pp. 64ff. 141ff.
Flew, *Church*, pp. 23ff. Michaelis, *Verheissung*, pp. 18f. Morgenthaler,
Kommendes Reich, pp. 68ff.

[4] Cf. Barrett, *H.S.G.T.*, p. 159. Beasley-Murray, *Future*, pp. 183f. Turner,
in *A New Commentary*, p. 104. contrast Mackinnon, *Historic Jesus*, p. 206.

[5] William Temple, in a letter dated 1913 to Ronald Knox wrote, 'Anyhow
I think our Lord definitely rejected the apocalyptic idea of Messiahship. And
if I thought He expected an immediate catastrophe other than His own
Death and Resurrection, I *think* I should have to renounce Christianity'
(Iremonger, *William Temple*). Cadbury, *Luke-Acts*, p. 283 notes that the
idea of errancy is 'abhorrent' to some. Beasley-Murray, *Future*, p. 183,
reminds us that 'on this ground Sidgwick felt compelled to abandon Christian
faith. Christian believers shrink from admitting that their Lord was mistaken in a major item of his preaching . . .'

[6] Cf. Baldensperger, *Selbstbewusstsein*, p. 148. Nicklin, *Gleanings*, pp. 348f.
Turner, in *A New Commentary*, p. 100. Nairne, *The Faith of the N.T.* pp. 26,
29. Manson, *Teaching*, p. 282. Owen in *S.J.T.* XII, 1959, pp. 184f. Gore,
Dissertations, pp. 94f. Taylor, *Mark*, p. 523.

[7] Cf. *Teaching*, pp. 282f. *Sayings*, p. 37. Quote from *Teaching*, p. 283.

literary criticism, and says 'the unfulfilled prediction of the early
Parousia may well be a similar case . . .' Unfortunately, the character of these examples makes them of little value, for they are both
details of technical knowledge rather than of religious conviction,
and errors of the former kind must, surely, carry a different significance from errors of the latter.[1] Further, Jesus appears never to
base his standpoint upon an errant diagnosis or literary judgement,[2]
whereas in the case of the passages in question the temporal aspect
(however this is evaluated) is fundamental to the whole assertion.[3]
As a matter of methodology, too, it is difficult to see why if the
clauses 'ye shall see', 'there be some of them standing here', can
be dismissed as based on a miscalculation, the other clauses 'The
Son of Man coming' and 'the Kingdom of God come . . .' should be
allowed to stand, for on what grounds may the distinction be made?
Manson [4] makes the distinction on the grounds that '. . . the belief
in the nearness of the Day of the Lord is not one of the unique
features in the eschatology of Jesus, but a belief which, like the
belief in demons or the Davidic authorship of the Psalter, was the
common property of his generation.' On the other hand, others too
expected a coming of the Son of Man!—this too was 'common
property'.

In this respect the consistency of Consistent Eschatology appears
to be more logical: and, to be sure, many who approach the problem
of imminence along these lines conclude by interpreting the
'Kingdom of God' in an 'old liberal sense',[5] and evacuate the

---

[1] Cf. Stebbing, *A Modern Introduction to Logic*, pp. 16ff. Lawton, *Conflict in Christology*, pp. 44f.

[2] Cf. Rawlinson, *Mark*, p. 173. Even in Mk. 12, 35f. the argument hinges on whether or not Jesus' dissatisfaction with contemporary Messianic views was justified (Taylor, *Mark*, p. 492. Although he says 'the argument based on the quotation fails if David is not the speaker,' he rightly adds, modifying this, 'the value of the saying is not thereby destroyed, since its main im-portance is the light it throws on the manner in which Jesus interpreted Messiahship'.) Concerning Jesus' views on demons cf. Taylor, *Mark*, p. 239.

[3] The saying Mk. 9, 1 for instance is—in 1st century Judaism—a platitude, if its essence is simply 'some . . . will see the Kingdom of God come with power', and not 'some of them that stand here . . .'

[4] Cf. *Teaching*, p. 283.

[5] Our justification for this phrase is Hunter's statement (in *Interpreting the N.T.* 1900-1950, p. 125) that at the beginning of the century 'we inter-preted the Kingdom of God, in some Kantian form of a "republic under the moral law" or as a Christian social reformer's paradise on earth . . .')

Parousia hope of all significance [1]—though this is certainly not true of all.[2]

This thesis must also be questioned on the ground that it tends to overemphasise the skill and religious insight of the primitive Christian community in contrast to that of its Lord.[3] This must not be pressed, since it could be argued that the new situation following the resurrection of Christ led to such insight.[4] At the same time, there is some point in Cullmann's suggestion that if Jesus had so confidently expected an early Parousia, then the early church would surely have abandoned its allegiance to him after the 'cardinal error' had been exposed'.[5]

Those who hold that Jesus, absorbed with his imminent hope in the End, anticipated no appreciable interval at all between his resurrection and Parousia—that he did not in fact differentiate between them [6]—are faced with the problem that certain of Jesus' words and works are interpreted by many [7] as preparing for and anticipating a new community, a church. We note, particularly, Dr. Barrett's thesis that Jesus 'did not prophesy the existence of a Spirit-filled community, because he did not foresee an interval

---

[1] Cf. Orr, 'Kingdom of God', in *H.D.B.* II, pp. 849ff. Du Bose, *Gospel*, pp. 63ff. Savage, *The Gospel of the Kingdom*, pp. 27ff. Burkitt, *Sources*, pp. 56ff. Easton, *Christ in the Gospels*, pp. 159f. Streeter, in *Oxford Studies*, pp. 425ff. Lowrie, *Mark*, pp. 315f.

[2] Cf. Cullmann, *Early Church*, p. 147. Michaelis, *Verheissung*, *passim*. Manson, *Teaching*, pp. 244ff. Beasley-Murray, *Future*, p. 204. Barrett, *Yesterday, to-day and for ever*, *passim*. Owen, in *S.J.T.* XII, 1959, pp. 171ff.

[3] Cf. Nairne, *Epistle of Priesthood*, p. 207. Easton, *Christ in the Gospels*, pp. 159f.

[4] Cf. Easton, *Christ in the Gospels*, pp. 196f. With reference to a different event, Brandon (*Fall of Jerusalem*, esp. pp. 185ff.) wants to speak of the 'rebirth of Christianity'.

[5] *T.Z.* III, 1947, pp. 177f. cf. Manson, *Jesus*, p. 149.

[6] Cf. esp. Barrett, *H.S.G.T.* (It is strange that Beasly-Murray, *Future*, pp. 191ff. in discussing 'The Provision for a period between the Resurrection and the Parousia' does not mention this work).

[7] Cf. esp. Flew, *Church*, pp. 41ff. Beasley-Murray, *Future*, pp. 191f. Gloege, *Reich Gottes und Kirche*, *passim*. Roberts, *Kingdom of God*, pp. 38ff. Wendland, *Eschatologie*, pp. 146ff. Schmidt, in *T.W.N.T.* III pp. 525ff. *Die Kirche des Urchristentums*, pp. 258ff. Manson, 'The N.T. Basis of the Doctrine of the Church', in *J.E.H.* I, 1950, pp. 1ff. Walter, *Kommen*, pp. 41ff. Oepke, 'Der Herrenspruch über die Kirche, Mtt. 16, 17-19' in *S.T.* II, 1948-50, pp. 110ff. Dahl, 'The Parables of Growth', in *S.T.* V, 1952, pp. 132ff. *Das Volk Gottes*. Cullmann, *Early Church*, pp. 105ff. Quinn, 'The Kingdom of God and the Church in the Synoptic Gospels', in *Scripture* IV, 1949-51, pp. 237ff. Behm, in *T.W.N.T.* II, pp. 132ff.

between the period of humiliation and that of complete and final glorification'.[1] Barrett's criticism of Flew's thesis is especially important [2] and is itself, we suggest, open to some question. His first criticism is that since Christ's death is fundamental to the existence of the new community 'it seems undesirable to say that the foundation of the Church took place before the death and resurrection of Jesus'.[3] This, however, (as Barrett notes) is a point stressed by Johnston [4] which does not rule out the possibility that Jesus regarded the disciples as 'potentially the Church'.

Acknowledging this possibility, Barrett maintains that he can find no evidence for assuming this anticipated community would not be the glorified Church 'in heaven with God'.[5] Here, however, the problem of Jesus' ethical teaching is raised in an acute form. Dr. Barrett argues that 'the "absolute" ethical teaching of Jesus would be entirely appropriate to such an Israel, in the day when heaven and earth had vanished and with them the Law of Moses'.[6] Yet it is impossible to overlook the connection of much of Jesus' ethical demand with earthly circumstances,[7] and the ordinary conditions of human life appear to be in mind. Barrett bids us compare Mtt. 5, 18 with Mk. 13, 31: [8] on the other hand, we may compare Mtt. 19, 3ff. with its directive concerning marriage and divorce, with Mtt. 22, 30 where 'in the resurrection' such regulations are expressly said to be inappropriate.[9]

Barrett argues that if Jesus had anticipated the existence of

---

[1] *H.S.G.T.* p. 160. Similarly (either wholly or partially) Johnston, *Church*, pp. 46ff. Kümmel, *Kirchenbegriff*, pp. 27ff. *Promise*, pp. 138f. (and authorities cited p. 139, n. 123). Ackermann, *Jesus*, pp. 119ff.

[2] Cf. *H.S.G.T.* pp. 137-9.

[3] *H.S.G.T.* p. 137.

[4] *Church*, pp. 50-56.

[5] Cf. *H.S.G.T.* p. 137. Barrett admits Flew's argument (*Church*, p. 25) that Jesus could foresee an 'enduring organism' without planning for it.

[6] *H.S.G.T.* p. 138.

[7] Cf. Mk. 10, 5-12. Mtt. 5, 22f. 5, 33f. 6, 1f. 18, 15f. etc. Wilder, *Eschatology and Ethics*, p. 160 says Jesus' ethic 'is not primarily an ethic for the relations and conduct of the future transcendental Kingdom'.

[8] *H.S.G.T.* p. 138, n. 3.

[9] Not all who agree with the thesis concerning Jesus' imminent expectation would describe Jesus' ethic as 'interim': cf. Easton, *Christ and the Gospels*, p. 176: Lowrie, *Mark*, pp. 320f. Many think his ethics presuppose an interval after resurrection and prior to the Parousia — cf. Windisch, *Bergpredigt*, pp. 13f. Wilder, *Eschatology and Ethics*, pp. 37ff. Sevenster, *Ethiek en Eschatologie in de Synoptische Evangelien*, Fison, *Hope*, pp. 68f.

a church he would have spoken of the forthcoming Spirit by whom it would be established.[1] Flew's explanation [2] about the lack of teaching in the Synoptics is rightly rejected by Barrett.[3] At the same time any argument from the Synoptic 'silence' must be open to question and Barrett's own answer to the problem is not wholly satisfactory. He maintains that 'it is easy to understand why Jesus did not foretell the gift of the Spirit to the Church. There was no occasion for him to do so. The period of humiliation and obscurity of the Messiah was to continue until its climax and the day of final glorification. In the former period, the general gift of the Spirit was inappropriate ... in the latter period it was not a sufficiently significant feature of the eschatological hope to be mentioned'.[4] The second part of this argument could, however, be applied also to Jesus' absolute ethical demand. If Jesus saw fit to give ethical instruction though foreseeing only 'the reign of the saints in heaven', it is not enough to say that he refrained from teaching about the Spirit because the Spirit was insignificant in that heavenly life: conversely, if the ethical teaching had in mind a continuing earthly life of the new community it might be necessary to find some reason for the lack of instruction about the Spirit other than that offered by Barrett.

This problem of the Spirit notwithstanding, there remain hints that Jesus *did* anticipate a future missionary activity and therefore in some sense a church. There is the calling of the Twelve (Mk. 3, 13f. par) who are to 'be with him' and to be 'sent forth'.[5] Barrett holds [6] that 'the "word of God", the "Gospel", the mission of the disciples belong to the period before the crucifixion.' But it is significant that the only fulfilment of the purpose of the Twelve's calling prior to the crucifixion could only be the brief preaching tour (Mk 6, 7ff. par) and this *precedes* the phase of Jesus' ministry during which he appears to have concentrated on teaching his disciples.[7] If Jesus had not had in mind further, much more extensive

---

[1] Cf. *H.S.G.T.*, p. 139.

[2] Cf. *Church*, p. 70.

[3] Cf. *H.S.G.T.*, p. 142.

[4] Cf. *H.S.G.T.* p. 160.

[5] Both Mtt. 10, 1ff. and Lk. 6, 12ff. assert that the Twelve are 'Apostles': Cf. Rengstorf, in *T.W.N.T.* I, pp. 397ff.

[6] Cf. *H.S.G.T.*, p. 138.

[7] Cf. Mk. 6, 30f. 7, 24. 9, 30-31. 10, 32. Johnston, *Church*, p. 54, holds that the initial mission occurred whilst Jesus' early optimism lasted. Cf. Taylor, *Life and Ministry*, pp. 134ff.

preaching by the disciples, it is difficult to understand why *after* this short tour he should have laid such emphasis on training them. We notice also such references as Mk. 13, 10 and 14, 9, which must be discussed at a later stage,[1] but which most probably support the conclusion that Jesus anticipated a missionary activity during the interval between his resurrection and the final consummation.

This leads to a consideration of the suggestion that since Jesus expected *some* interval, the *length* of that interval is secondary, and that a miscalculation on Jesus' part here is insignificant.[2] This solution encounters the difficulty that, of the passages in the Synoptics which pose the problem of an imminent expectation most acutely, three (Mk. 9, 1. Mk. 13, 30 and Mtt. 10, 23) are introduced by the clause αμην λεγω υμιν. The serious significance of this introductory clause has sometimes been recognised,[3] but often overlooked.[4] In the Old Testament and Judaism αμην (אמן) denoted absolute certainty. Schlier writes, 'In allen Fällen ist das אמן die Anerkennung eines Wortes, das "feststeht", und dessen Festigkeit für mich und dann überhaupt in dieser Anerkennung verpflichtend wird. So heisst אמן: *es steht fest und es gilt.*'[5] This same force is retained in the New Testament.[6] The word has, actually, added emphasis since it is found here only in connection with sayings of Jesus, giving 'emphasis and solemnity to that which follows'.[7] Two very far-reaching questions arise from this consideration. The first is, if Jesus was mistaken in an assertion so solemnly introduced and emphatically affirmed, what reliance, if any, can or ought to be placed on words not so introduced?

The second is, if Jesus knew himself to be limited in his knowledge of the Parousia's date,[8] or if he was not sure about his knowledge here, was it not arrogance or lack of humility to make such solemn affirmations that it would come within his own generation? This

---

[1] Cf. below, pp. 202ff.

[2] Cf. authorities cited above 93, n. 3. Cf. also the suggestion that since Jesus' imminent hope was basically theological, the occasional delimitation of his hope is of no import — authorities cited above 92, n. 5.

[3] Cf. Beasley-Murray, *Future*, p. 186. Nicklin, *Gleanings*, p. 346.

[4] Cf. Manson, *Teaching*, pp. 277ff. Cullmann, *Early Church*, p. 152.

[5] In *T.W.N.T.* I, p. 339.

[6] Cf. Martin-Achard in *Vocabulary, ad loc*: Blackman, in *T.W.B.* p. 18: Carrington, *Mark*, p. 188. Manson, *Teaching*, pp. 105ff. Cranfield, *Mark*, pp. 139f.

[7] Taylor, *Mark*, p. 242.

[8] Cf. the argument of the authorities cited above, pp. 92f.

difficulty could be eased if Mk. 13, 32 could be shown to be unauthentic as many claim.[1] But the saying may well be genuine:
as a piece of Christian apologetic [2] it is unnecessarily offensive [3]
and quickly proved difficult: [4] and the inclusion of the phrase
οὐδὲ οἱ ἄγγελοι would appear unnecessary.[5] Or the difficulty might
be slightly eased if Mk. 13, 32 were only a relative affirmation of
ignorance meaning that though the Parousia would come within
the contemporary generation, Jesus was not certain of its *exact*
date.[6] Beasley-Murray arguing for this view, holds that if 'Day'
and 'Hour' here referred to the 'Day of the Lord' rather than to a
'narrower limitation of time over against a broader period' then
'strictly speaking such an assertion ought to mean that Jesus knew
nothing of the Day itself, i.e. of its nature, an impossible view in
face of the rest of his teaching'.[7] But surely, the meaning 'No
one, not even the angels in heaven, neither the Son knows anything
concerning the *nature* of the Day of the Lord' is so obviously an
exaggeration that the limitation of ignorance to a certain aspect of
the 'Day' is self-evident. And the particular aspect in the context
is 'when' it is to come. Since there is no compelling reason to
understand 'that day or that hour' as precise temporal terms, it is
natural to take them, following the Old Testament background [8] as

---

[1] Beasley-Murray, *Mark* 13, pp. 105f. reviews the ancient and modern
'revulsion against the text'. Cf. further below, pp. 193ff.

[2] Cf. Loisy, *Marc ad Loc.* Grässer, *Problem*, p. 82. Bousset, *Kyrios Christos*,
pp. 43f.

[3] Schniewind, *Markus, ad loc.* rightly notes that the line of argument
adopted in II Peter 3, 5ff. was always available and inoffensive. Cf.
further Lohmeyer, *Markus, ad loc*: Cadoux, *Historic Mission*, p. 33. Taylor,
Mark, ad loc.

[4] Luke appears to find the saying difficult. Grässer, *Problem*, p. 82 argues
that Luke omits because of his special *Heilsgeschichte* and because Acts 1, 7
suffices. But Luke's supposed programme of salvation-history would not
make Mk. 13, 32 necessarily inappropriate, and it remains true that Acts 1, 7
is less offensive. Further, indications of the trouble caused by Mk. 13, 32 are
suggested by the variants of Mtt. 24, 36 (οὐδὲ ὁ υἱός omitted by ℵ ᶜᵃ, W, f1,
700, 565): Taylor, *Mark*, pp. 522f. cites the evasions offered by Ambrose,
Cyril of Alexandria, and Basil.

[5] Cf. Kümmel, *Promise*, p. 42 who maintains this against Dalman, *Words*,
p. 194 and Bultmann, *Geschichte*, p. 130 (who suggest that 'neither the Son
but the Father' is a Christian addition).

[6] Cf. Nicklin, *Gleanings*, p. 347. Guignebert, *Jesus*, p. 346. Lake, *Introduction*, p. 32. Beasley-Murray, *Future*, pp. 261f. *Mk.* 13, pp. 107f.

[7] *Mk.* 13, pp. 107f.

[8] Cf. von Rad, in *T.W.N.T.* II, pp. 947ff.

references to the Last Judgement and the Parousia.[1] Beasley-Murray's case would be helped if the demonstrative adjective were missing: indeed, his argument allows it to lapse when he says, 'If at the present time one were asked, "Have you any idea when war will next break out in Europe?" and the reply were given, "I do not know the day or hour" . . .' [2]—whereas the point is that '*that* day' carries Old Testament overtones which '*the* day' in modern usage does not.[3]

To reconcile Mk. 13, 30—understood as mistaken—with Mk. 13, 32 is therefore an acute problem.[4] It is a dogmatic point which we cannot discuss here, but it is important to notice that the real issue is much more crucial than the advocates of this solution sometimes suggest: [5] a simple recognition of Jesus' ignorance does not answer the question when seen in this form.

2. Another possible answer to the problem of the apparently unfulfilled predictions of an imminent Parousia is to say that the time element in the sayings has no special temporal significance, but has only a pastoral or epistemological basis. This view has been held over a considerable period and has a number of advocates today.[6] In its demythologization of the temporal element in the Parousia expectation this answer leans towards Bultmann's metho-

---

[1] Cf. Taylor, *Mark*, pp. 522f. following Lohmeyer (*Markus*, p. 283) ' "Jener Tag" ist bekantlich der Tag des letzten Gerichtes'; similarly Cranfield, *Mark*, pp. 410f.

[2] *Mk.* 13, p. 108.

[3] Feuillet, in *R.B.* LVI, 1949, p. 87 thinks 'that day' refers to the Fall of Jerusalem. Glasson, *Advent*, pp. 97f. thinks it 'may have been an answer to a question about the end of the world or the last day', though 'in itself the phrase "that day or that hour" tells us nothing'. Against both, the O.T. background is decisive. We may also note, with Kümmel, *Promise*, pp. 36f. that 'Jesus uses this term (ἡ ἡμέρα, ἡ ἡμέρα ἐκείνη) invariably for the end of time in the future'. Cf. Lk. 10, 12. Mtt. 10, 15. Mk. 14, 25. Lk. 17, 26. Mtt. 25, 13 (In Lk. 17, 31 Glasson, *Advent*, p. 98 says 'that day' *is* used of the fall of Jerusalem: but against him rightly Kümmel, *Promise*, p. 38, n. 62).

[4] Kümmel, *Promise*, pp. 149f. accepts this and says 'we cannot know how to strike a balance between these two series of assertions.'

[5] Cf. Beasley-Murray, *Future*, pp. 183ff. *Mk.* 13, pp. 99f. Owen, in *S.J.T.* XII, 1959, pp. 171ff. Manson, *Teaching*, p. 282.

[6] Cf. Titius, *Reich Gottes*, pp. 147ff. Schmaus, *Dogmatik*, pp. 29ff. Graham, *Christ of Catholicism*, p. 299. Levertoff, 'Eschatological teaching in the gospels', in *Theology*, XXXII, 1936, pp. 339f. Oepke, in *S.T.* II, 1948-50, pp. 110ff. Rawlinson, *Mark*, p. 180. Fison, *Hope*, pp. 29ff. and partially Beasley-Murray, *Future*, p. 150f. Guy, *Prophecy*, p. 59. Wilder, *Eschatology and Ethics*, p. 188. Kümmel, *Promise*, pp. 150f.

dological programme, though clearly it aims at something much less radical for it still regards the Parousia as something temporally future—an End towards which Christian hope can be directed.[1]

Again the answer appears to be simple and inoffensive: yet there are real difficulties. The argument is that the 'prophetic perspective' which Jesus shared meant that 'time telescoped itself in his vision of the approaching battle of light and darkness'.[2] Events near and far were seen as peaks standing out one behind the other whilst the plains in between could not be discerned.[3] Beasley-Murray [4] claims that 'every Old Testament prophet', due to the 'intensity and certainty of prophetic convictions invariably express themselves in terms of a speedy fulfilment.' However, as we have already suggested,[5] even where this is most marked in apocalyptic literature, a temporal nearness is subordinated to a theological conviction: the chronological calculations served a pastoral end. Are we then to say that Jesus followed, out of pastoral expediency, the apocalyptic pastoral method: that he spoke of the Parousia as coming within the life-time of his contemporaries in order to encourage hope and incite watchfulness? [6] But as a pastoral expedient the procedure is quite unsatisfactory for it could lead to false optimism and so to disillusionment: [7] and, unless the forecast of an early Parousia proved correct, would necessarily create difficulties for the second generation.[8] Besides, it is questionable how far the solemn asseveration αμην λέγω ὑμῖν could be justified on the grounds of expediency, particularly when the pastoral intention could apparently be met perfectly adequately by calls to watchfulness which do not speak of an End coming within a delimited time.[9]

---

[1] Cf. esp. Graham, *Christ of Catholicism*, p. 297. Fison, *Hope*, p. 70.

[2] Levertoff, in *Theology*, XXXII, 1936, p. 339.

[3] Cf. Schmaus, *Dogmatik*, pp. 29f. following Billot, *La Parusie*: Beasley-Murray, *Future*, p. 204 gives another simile.

[4] Cf. *Future*, pp. 170, 186f.   [5] Cf. above, pp. 21f.

[6] Cf. Beasley-Murray, *Future*, p. 189. Oepke, in *S.T.* II, 1948-50, pp. 110f. Titius, *Reich Gottes*, pp. 147f. Michaelis, *Verheissung*, pp. 5f. 17f. Michel, in *Z.s.T.* 1932, pp. 645ff.

[7] Continual distress and disappointment has been caused down the ages because of erroneous calculations of this sort: cf. Glasson, *Appearing*, pp. 44f.

[8] Althaus, *Letzten Dinge*, pp. 275f. followed by Beasley-Murray, *Future*, p. 190, says that the early imminent hope should continually drive the church to preparedness: but it is just not true that a call to preparedness *on the basis of an open possibility* cannot achieve what a temporally delimited hope alone can.

[9] Cf. Mtt. 25, 13. 24, 42f. Mk. 13, 33f. par. Lk. 12, 35-40. etc.

Or are we, on the other hand, to say that the 'prophetic per-spective' was epistemologically inevitable?[1] If this were so, then the problem posed by Mk. 13, 32 would be even more acute since this saying recognises an epistemological limitation which, it would then be said, Jesus solemnly transgressed. This answer also makes insufficient allowance for a unique *sui generis* element in Jesus' thought and teaching. The inability of scholars, despite intense effort[2] to fit Jesus into one mould or another surely suggests not only that our methodology is sometimes difficult to handle, some-times wrong, but also that the man Christ Jesus *did not* exactly conform to a pre-cast mould[3] but enjoyed a certain freedom over against past and contemporary thoughts and was not entirely bound to the epistemological paths laid out by his forbears and fellows. If he *was* so bound, then it is at least more consistent, with Bult-mann, to demythologize not only the temporal framework but also the concept of the Parousia, rather than to leave off where this answer does.[4]

3. The third answer to the problem of the insistence on nearness is to say that Jesus spoke of certain events as about to occur, at least within the life-time of his contemporaries, but that he did not include amongst them the Parousia. The early church sometimes wrongly interpreted those imminent sayings as referring to the Parousia. The events which Jesus expected imminently, it is said, were the fall of Jerusalem and the destruction of the Temple,[5] the

---

[1] Cf. Rawlinson, *Mark*, p. 180. Beasley-Murray, *Future*, p. 186. p. 170. Owen, in *S.J.T.* XII, 1959, pp. 171ff. Levertoff, in *Theology*, XXXII, 1936, pp. 339f.

[2] Cf. Jesus in the mould of the non-apocalyptist (Wrede, Dodd): in the mould of Orthodox Judaism (Klausner): in the mould of the apocalyptist (Weiss, Schweitzer): in the mould of the liberal religious teacher (Harnack, Middleton-Murray, etc.): in the mould of the Essenes (recently Allegro): in the mould of the Zealot (R. Eisler), and in the mould of the existentialist (Bultmann).

[3] Cf. Bornkamm, *Jesus*, pp. 56f. Wilder, *Eschstology and Ethics*, pp. 147ff. Flew, *Perfection*, p. 35. Johnston, *Church*, p. 55. Borchert, *Original Jesus*, p. 328.

[4] Fison, *Hope*, pp. 125ff. interprets the N.T. perspective slightly differ-ently: he warns against abandoning 'Jesus' time' for an abstract philoso-phical truth, maintaining that lover's time, and so the key to the Parousia's nearness, is understood only in present encounter with Christ.

[5] Cf. Schmaus, *Dogmatik*, pp. 35ff. Nairne, *Epistle of Priesthood*, p. 206. Muirhead, 'Eschatology', in *H.D.C.G.* pp. 525ff. Lagrange *Marc*, p. 325. Graham, *Christ of Catholicism*, pp. 299f. Levertoff and Goudge, in *New Commentary*, p. 194. Swift, in *New Bible Commentary*, p. 823. Brown, 'Parou-

Resurrection and Ascension,[1] Pentecost,[2] and the church's growth and missionary work.[3] Most advocates of this view do not confine themselves to only one of the events listed but think that Jesus probably had in mind in his prophecies two or more of them. This view is parallel to Realised Eschatology,[4] the main difference being that the early church, on this view, is said to have attributed to Jesus only an *imminent* Parousia hope, not the Parousia hope itself.[5]

One immediate methodological difficulty which this view encounters is that it exists only on the basis of that presupposition of cleavage between Jesus and the earliest community which we have already criticised.[6] Whereas the first solution discussed in this chapter appeared to overestimate the early church's religious insight, this answer surely implies that the early church was rather too stupid![7] But the methodological difficulty arises because of a problem in exegesis. Mk. 9, 1, for instance, *in its present context,*

---

sia', in *H.D.B.* III, pp. 647ff. Feuillet, in *R.S.R.* XXXV, 1947, pp. 303ff. XXXVI, 1948, pp. 544ff. in *N.R.T.* LXXI, 1949, pp. 701ff. 806ff. in *R.B.* LVI, 1949, pp. 61ff. 360ff. LVII, 1950, pp. 43ff. 180ff. *Introduction à la Bible*; Major, *Reminiscences*, pp. 44f. Gould, *Mark*, on Mk. 13, 26. Plummer, *Matthew*, p. 338. Jones, in *Scripture*, IV, 1949-51, pp. 222f. 264ff. Walter, *Kommen*, p. 96.

[1] Cf. Muirhead, 'Eschatology', in *H.D.C.G.* pp. 525f. Gore, *Belief in Christ*, pp. 136ff. Graham, *Christ of Catholicism*, pp. 299f. Major, *Reminiscences*, pp. 44f. Hunter, *Mark*, p. 91. Stonehouse, *Matthew and Mark*, pp. 112f. Holmes-Gore, 'The Ascension and the Apocalyptic Hope' in *Theology*, XXXII, 1936, pp. 356ff.

[2] Cf. Gore, *Belief in Christ*, pp. 136ff. Levertoff and Goudge, in *New Commentary*, p. 194. Swift, in *New Bible Commentary*, p. 823. Scott, *Tributaries*, p. 56. Headlam, *Life and Teaching*, pp. 260ff. Sanday, *Life of Christ*, pp. 117f. Hunter, *Mark*, p. 91. *Design for Life*, pp. 103f. Prideaux, 'The Second Coming of Christ', in *E.T.* LXI, 1949-50, pp. 240f.

[3] Cf. Richardson, *Theology*, p. 87. Graham, *Christ of Catholicism*, pp. 299f. Feuillet (cf. note 5 previous page). Stonehouse, *Matthew and Mark*, p. 240. Jones, in *Scripture*, IV, 1949-51, pp. 222f. 264f.

[4] Especially as this is presented in a modified form—cf. Dodd, *Coming of Christ*, pp. 26f. Glasson, *Appearing*, p. 191.

[5] Though many who interpret the imminent references in this way do, in fact, dissolve the Parousia hope altogether: cf. Feuillet, (articles cited note 5 previous page): Jones, in *Scripture*, IV, 1949-51, pp. 264f. Holmes-Gore, in *Theology*, XXXII, 1936, pp. 356ff. Prideaux, in *E.T.* LXI, 1949-50, pp. 240f.

[6] Cf. above, p. 40.

[7] MacCulloch, 'Eschatology and the Gospels', in *E.R.E.V.* pp. 381ff. quotes with approval Matthew Arnold's maxim, 'Jesus above the heads of his reporters': cf. similarly Streeter, in *Oxford Studies*, p. 433, who says it is a case of a 'great man misunderstood'.

can hardly be taken as a prediction of the fall of Jerusalem.[1] So
the context is said to be due to the Evangelist's misunderstanding.
This exegetical difficulty, however, is not easily resolved for the
real problem is that the texts are essentially Christocentric and
revelational in character and are being (on this proposed solution)
treated as non-Christocentric and non-revelational.

Both aspects of this criticism require some expansion. We take
it as axiomatic that the Kingdom of God and the person of Jesus are
so integrally bound together as to be inseparable.[2] This is acknowledged by very many scholars to-day and is highly significant for
our problem [3] for it suggests that just as the Kingdom of God in
its realised aspect is inseparable from the person of Jesus Christ
so also in its future aspect it cannot be divorced from him.[4] Fison [5]
rightly remarks, 'we are apt to-day to recognise the practical
identity of the coming of Jesus in the past with the coming of
the Kingdom of God, but we are strangely loath to commit our-
selves to a similar identity in the future. Yet there is no getting
away from the latter if we accept the former.' If we recognise this,
we shall be careful to see that the concept of the Son of Man coming
in clouds with great glory and the concept of the Kingdom of God
come with power both have a strictly Christocentric interpretation.
It is such a Christocentric interpretation which is lacking in the
'solution' under discussion. To be sure, the fall of Jerusalem is

---

[1] Chiefly because a) the downfall of Jerusalem is never spoken of as
'coming of the Kingdom of God' (cf. Mk. 2, 22 par. 11, 15f. par. Lk. 13,
1ff. Mk. 12, 9 par. Lk. 19, 41-44, 23, 28f.) and b) other references to 'the
coming of the Kingdom' cannot support such an identification (cf. Lk. 11, 2
par. 13, 28f par. Mk. 14, 25 par). Cranfield, *Mark*, p. 287: Lowrie, *Mark*,
p. 315: Guignebert, *Jesus*, pp. 333f.: Kümmel, *Promise*, pp. 26f. Manson,
Teaching, pp. 279ff. oppose the idea.

[2] Origen's term αὐτοβασιλεία (Migne, *P.G.* xiii, 1197) remains the most
convenient short-hand account of the relationship of the Kingdom to Jesus'
person and work.

[3] Cf. Feine, *Theologie*, p. 99. Kümmel, *Promise*, pp. 105f. Cranfield *Mark*,
p. 66. Flew, *Perfection*, p. 35. Preiss, *Life in Christ*, p. 68. Schmidt, in *T.W.N.T*
I, p. 591. Borchert, *Original Jesus*, p. 359. Cullmann, *Early Church*, pp. 115f.
Contrast, Sharman, *Son of Man*, pp. 89f. Johnson, *Mark*, p. 153. Morgenthaler, *Kommendes Reich*, pp. 35ff.

[4] Cf.? Matthew's interpretation of Mk. 9, 1 in Mtt. 16, 28 (Kümmel,
Promise, p. 27): cf. also the prayer 'Thy kingdom come' (Mtt. 6, 10 = Lk.
11, 2) with the early church prayer μαρανα Θα (I Cor. 16, 22, Rev. 22, 20,
Did. 10, 6): Heb. 13, 8 and Acts 1, 11 may also be noted.

[5] *Hope*, p. 138. Cf. also Forsyth, *Person and Place of Jesus Christ* p. 122.
Borchert, *Original Jesus*, p. 374.

rightly understood as a signal manifestation of God's sovereignty in Christ exercised in judgement upon recalcitrant Israel,[1] but it is not *specifically* Christocentric. The Spirit certainly is Christ's *alter ego*,[2] but hardly 'in great power and glory': and it *is* Christ's *ALTER ego*, not the Son of Man in his historical particularity. The Church may indeed be regarded as the body of Christ,[3] but it is not Christ himself, being actually subjected to him: it is not the Kingdom but 'expects the Kingdom and preaches the gospel of the Kingdom'.[4] If the Kingdom of God come with power is to be interpreted Christocentrically, it is impossible to see how it has come in any or all of these events—though they may point as signs to that coming of the Kingdom which is yet to occur.

Only the resurrection of Christ bears the directly Christocentric character required: but this event is subject to the second criticism raised against this solution, namely that certain sayings are interpreted in a way which diminishes, if not ignores, an essential contrast between concealment and revelation. At least as they stand, Mk. 9, 1 and 14, 62 speak of a *visible manifestation* of the Kingdom of God and of the Son of Man, and this in both instances is contrasted with the hiddenness of the Kingdom and of the Son of Man in the ministry of Jesus.[5] It is this *manifestation* of the sovereignty of God in the triumphant revelation of the Son of Man in glory and power which alone can fulfil the expectation of the New Testament. The resurrection appearances were witnessed, to be sure, by the disciples: yet the resurrection was no open, universal manifestation and must therefore be distinguished sharply from the Parousia. It seems that verbs of *seeing* are often used in the New Testament in connection with sayings relating to the future coming of the

---

[1] Cf. Taylor, *Mark*, p. 501. Beasley-Murray, *Mark*. 13, p. 22. Goguel, *Life*, p. 403.

[2] Jn. 14, 16f. 14, 26f. 15, 26f. 16, 7f. 16, 14.

[3] Col. 1, 18. 3, 15. Eph. 1, 23. 4, 4. 4, 12f. 5, 30. I Cor. 10, 17. 12, 12. 12, 27. Rom. 12,5.

[4] Cf. Visser 'T Hooft, *Renewal*, p. 37. Johnston, *Church*, p. 57. Gloege, *Reich Gottes und Kirche*, p. 259. Schmidt, in *T.W.N.T.* III, pp. 522f. As has been pointed out (e.g. by Rawlinson, *Essays*, p. 212) the identification of church with Kingdom does not occur prior to Augustine.

[5] Cf. Mk. 8, 38 and its contrast (Kümmel, *Promise*, p. 27, n. 44). Mk. 14, 62 was spoken in circumstances of the utmost veiledness. There seems to be no justification for Taylor's interpretation (*Mark*. p. 568) of ὄψεσθε κτλ, as Kümmel (*Promise*, pp. 49f.) shows.

Kingdom and of the Son of Man.[1] At the eschatological consummation 'wird . . . die Offenbarung eine vollendete und unmittel-
bare sein'.[2] We notice also the connection of this future act of
revelation with 'glory' (δόξα)[3]—that essential attribute of God
which was veiled in Jesus' earthly ministry.[4] It is this 'glory' which
will appear in the final coming of the Son of Man so that his true
nature and the true significance of his earthly ministry will be
made unmistakably clear. In certain references to the Parousia
'clouds' (νεφέλη) are mentioned [5]—an Old Testament symbol for
God's self-revelation (as also of his 'otherness').[6]

We take it therefore that the *revelational character* of the
coming of the Kingdom 'in power' (and of the Son of Man 'in glory')
is quite fundamental to the expectation. This does not, of course,
mean that *every* instance of a prophecy using the verb 'to see'
necessarily is a prophecy of the End.[7] It does, however, mean that
events of an ambiguous nature, events visible only to faith, cannot
be said to be fulfilments of a specific Parousia hope. As Richardson
writes, 'There is . . . a difference between the revelation that will
be made at Christ's Parousia and the revelation that has been
given in history. At the Parousia the revelation will be a "sight"
revelation as contrasted with a "faith" revelation that is given
in history.' [8]

In view of the difficulties attaching to all of the proposed solutions which we have examined in this chapter it is hard to resist

---

[1] Mk. 9, 1 ἴδωσιν: Mk. 13, 26 ὄψονται: Mk. 14, 62 ὄψεσθε: Mtt. 24, 33 ἴδητε:
Mtt. 26, 64 ὄψεσθε: Mtt. 23, 39 ἴδητε: Mtt. 16, 28 ἴδωσιν: Mtt. 24, 30 φανήσεται,
ὄψονται: Lk. 13, 35 ἴδητε: Lk. 21, 27 ὄψονται: Lk. 17, 22 ἰδεῖν, ὄψεσθε: Lk.
9, 27 ἴδωσιν: Lk. 21, 31 ἴδητε: cf. also Jn. 17, 36. 16, 16. 19, 22. Heb. 12, 14.
I Jn. 3, 2. Acts 1, 11. Mtt. 10, 26. Lk. 17, 30. Rom. 8, 18. I Cor. 3, 13. Rom. 2,
5. II Thess. 1, 7. I Pet. 1, 5. 1, 7. 4, 13. 5, 4. Col. 3, 4. Mtt. 24, 30. Lk. 19, 11.
I Jn. 2, 28. Heb. 9, 28. I Tim. 6, 14. II Tim. 4, 1. Titus 2, 13.

[2] Michaelis, in *T.W.N.T.* V, p. 366.

[3] Cf. Mtt. 16, 27. 19, 28. 25, 31. Mk. 8, 38. 10, 37. 13, 26. Lk. 9, 26. 21, 27
(also Rom. 5, 2. 8, 18. 9, 23. I Cor. 2, 7. Col. 3, 4 etc.) Kittel, in *T.W.N.T.*
II, p. 252.

[4] Cf. Phil. 2, 6. Jn. 1, 14 ('we beheld' is the testimony of faith: cf. Barrett,
John, pp. 138f.).

[5] Cf. Mtt. 24, 30 par. 26, 64 par. Acts 1, 11. I Thess. 4, 17. Rev. 1, 7.14, 14.

[6] Cf. Oepke, in *T.W.N.T.* IV, pp. 908ff.

[7] This is the mistake made by Lohmeyer, *Galiläa und Jerusalem,* pp. 10ff.
and Lightfoot, *Locality and Doctrine*, pp. 66ff. Contrast, Stonehouse, *Matthew and Mark*, pp. 183ff. Kümmel, *Promise*, p. 66. Evans, 'I will go before
you into Galilee', in *J.T.S.* V, 1954, pp. 3ff.

[8] *Introduction*, p. 55.

the conclusion that there are sayings which speak of the Parousia and which speak of it as, in some sense, near: that there is no compelling reason to lead us to conclude that this is due only to a shift of context in the early church for the sayings in question must refer in whatever context they have to the visible manifestation of God's rule in the person and presence of Christ.

These proposed solutions to the problem posed by the New Testament insistence on the nearness of the Parousia have been discussed here only briefly partly because they are (as we have suggested) akin to the more consistent and radical interpretations of New Testament eschatology examined in chapters three, four and five, and partly because it is our purpose at this point only to suggest the inadequacy of these solutions and so to open up the possibility of a further examination of the material. We suggest that a renewed enquiry *is* justified and that, despite the confident assertions sometimes made that the question is now quite settled,[1] the problem remains to be given a satisfactory solution.

Our immediate aim will now be to attempt, through a re-examination of the relevant material, to answer four questions:

1. Did the early church delimit its expectation of the Parousia?

2. Did the early church think of the Parousia as in any sense near, and if so, in what sense?

3. Did Jesus delimit his expectation of the Parousia?

4. Did Jesus conceive of the Parousia as in any sense imminent, and if so, in what sense?

---

[1] Cf. for example the leader 'Advent Hope' in the *Methodist Recorder*, for Thursday November 30th, 1961.

CHAPTER EIGHT

DID THE EARLY CHURCH DELIMIT ITS EXPECTATION OF THE PAROUSIA?

In this chapter we seek an answer to the first of our four questions. Is there any evidence to determine that the early church as a whole expected the Parousia would certainly occur shortly, and definitely within its own generation? Since we cannot presuppose a united voice within the christian communities and the different elements within the New Testament, we begin by addressing the question to Paul; and because it is often argued [1] that here particularly Paul reveals a development of understanding, we examine the evidence chronologically.

I Thess. 4, 13-18

An analysis of the letter shows that 4, 13-18 is not the high peak but simply one paraenetic section amongst others.[2] It is not, however, unimportant.[3] Paul writes in order that the Thessalonians should not sorrow, ἵνα μὴ λυπῆσθε,[4] and the cause of their sorrow is clearly *not* disappointment over the non-arrival of the Parousia, as some scholars hold,[5] but rather anxiety over the question whether (and how) Christian dead would experience the first festive phase

---

[1] Cf. above, p. 50f.

[2] After thanks and explanation (1;2 — 3;13) Paul turns to particular themes through which he apparently hopes to build up the faith of the Thessalonian community. 4; 1-5 concerns sexual purity; 4; 9-12 encourages brotherly love; 4; 13-18 encourages hope; 5; 1-11 exhorts to watchfulness; 5; 12-22 discusses discipline and order. (This, against Neil, *Thessalonians*, p. 89, who says, 'This important passage (4; 13-18) . . . gives the epistle its characteristic note.')

[3] The clause οὐ θέλομεν δὲ ὑμᾶς ἀγνοεῖν suggests that the teaching which follows is of special significance; cf. Rom. 1, 13; 11, 25; I Cor. 10, 1; 12, 1; II Cor. 1, 8; cf. also Phil. 1, 12; Col. 2, 1.

[4] Haak, 'Exegetische dogmatische Studie zur Eschatologie I Thess. 4; 13-18, in *Z.s.T.* XV, 1938, pp. 544ff., rightly reminds us that the section is given with this end in view, and that exegesis should not overlook this nor import some other intention; similarly Rigaux, *Thessaloniciens*, p. 527.

[5] Cf. Héring, in *R.H.P.R.* XII, 1932 pp. 316ff.; Heard, *Introduction*, p. 186; Davies, *Rabbinic Judaism*, pp. 291f.; partially, Sparks, *Formation*, p. 33.

of the Parousia.[1] The conclusion is supported by the following considerations. Verse 13 expressly states that Paul will not have his converts ignorant 'concerning them that fall asleep' (κοιμηθέν-τας).[2] Clearly it is *Christians* who are in mind,[3] and the problem—if the answer given is not irrelevant!—is their status over against the status of living Christians at the moment of the Parousia.[4] Verse 15 compares οἱ ζῶντες οἱ περιλειπόμενοι with τοὺς κοιμηθέντας, the argument speaking about the fact that neither group will have advantage over the other. The mention of precedence shows that *this* was the problem, and not the fact that Christians died.[5]

The question remains whether ἡμεῖς in vv. 15 and 17 [6] indicates that Paul thought the Parousia would definitely occur within his own lifetime, as many contend.[7] There is considerable support for the suggestion that Paul is speaking not of a particular group (you

---

[1] Cf. Haak, in *Z.s.T.* XV, 1938, pp. 544ff., Cullmann, *Time*, pp. 240f.; Michaelis, in *Wikenhauser Festschrift*, pp. 116f.; Schmaus, *Dogmatik*, p. 40; Beasley-Murray, *Future*, pp. 232f.; Neil, *Thessalonians*, p. 99; Rigaux, *Thessaloniciens*, pp. 527f.

[2] The present κοιμηθέντας is to be preferred; cf. Rigaux, *Thessalinociens*, p. 529.

[3] For (a) the N.T. usage of κοιμῶ is almost uniformly of Christians (Acts 7, 60; I Cor. 15, 6; 8) or of believers under the old covenant (Mtt. 27, 52, Acts 13, 36;? II Peter 3, 4), and (b) v. 14 speaks of those asleep κοιμη-θέντας διὰ τοῦ 'Ιησοῦ (This punctuation seems best; cf. Rigaux, *Thessaloniciens*, p. 535; Frame, *Thessalonians*, p. 169).

[4] Clearly this problem would not be tackled in the course of missionary preaching, but later, when it arose in connection with the real situation of christians dying (cf. Moffatt, in *E.G.T.* p. 36; Rigaux, *Thessaloniciens*, p. 528). Some concern over a similar matter is seen in Bar. 11; 6f., II Esdras, 5, 41, 42, etc. Oepke, *Thessalonicher*, pp. 144ff. (an appended note, 'Die Parusie-Erwartung in den älteren Paulus-Briefen') argues that the problem could only arise where a delimited hope had been held out; but this overlooks the fact that death itself was not the problem causing anxiety but only brought to light the problem (which one could hardly expect to arise in abstraction).

[5] Those who argue that the early church was alarmed at the 'unexpected' death of Christians (cf. Moffatt, in *E.G.T.*, p. 40; Schweitzer, *Mysticism*, p. 92; Héring, in *R.H.P.R.* XII, 1932, pp. 316ff; Davies *Rabbinic Judaism*, p. 291) appear to overlook the fact that Stephen had already died (Acts 7, 60) and, according to Acts 8, 1, a 'great persecution' had arisen; cf. also Acts 9, 1.

[6] Cf. also I Cor. 15, 51.

[7] Cf. Deissmann, *Paul*, p. 217; Frame, *Thessalonians*, pp. 172f.; Milligan, *Thessalonians*, pp. 58f.; Hadorn, *Zukunft und Hoffnung*, p. 125 Michel, in *Z.s.T.* 1932, pp. 645ff.; Oepke, *Thessalonicher, ad loc*; Dodd, *Studies*, pp. 80ff.; 108ff.; Cullmann, *Time*, p. 88; *Early Church*, p. 152; Barclay, *Mind*, p. 134; Neil, *Thessalonians*, pp. 98f.; Rigaux, *Thessaloniciens*, pp. 225, 539f.; Albertz, *Botschaft*, II/1. pp. 203f.

Thessalonians and I, Paul), but of the Christian church in general; that Paul is not stating that he is certain he himself will be alive at the Parousia but only that some Christians will be.[1] We mention the following: first, the essential contrast being made is an impersonal one, between those alive at the Parousia and those dead; it is the *contrast* as such which is primary, not who comprises each group. Secondly, although Paul is not here speaking of the time of the Parousia's arrival, he does go on to discuss this in 5; 1-11, and there he affirms explicitly that the Parousia will come suddenly and all must watch (5, 2 ff.) and implies that 'we' (5; 9, 10) might either 'watch' (γρηγορῶμεν) or 'sleep' (καθεύδωμεν); i.e. the possibility seems to be held out that Paul and his readers might live to the Parousia but also that they might die prior to it.[2] Thirdly, the fact that in v. 15 and v. 17 'we' is expanded, ἡμεῖς οἱ ζῶντες οἱ περιλειπό-μενοι . . . εἰς τὴν παρουσίαν should probably be taken to imply that the actual composition of the group is being left open. Fourthly, it would appear unlikely that Paul's personal experiences should have led him to any confident expectation of life.[4] Finally, whilst it is usual to contrast I Thess. 4, 13ff. with the so-called changed perspective of II Cor. 5; 6-10, Phil. 1, 23, etc., it is noteworthy that II Cor. 5, 9 still reckons with the dual possibility, εἴτε ἐνδημοῦντες εἴτε ἐκδημοῦντες, and Phil. 1, 20 similarly. We therefore do not take ἡμεῖς as necessarily indicative of a delimited hope. As the expression of an *un*delimited hope it is the natural prelude to 5; 1-11 where Paul reminds his converts that since the date of the End is unknown, all are enjoined to watchful, obedient discipleship.[5]

II. Thess. 1, 5-12, 2, 1-15

It is frequently argued that here Paul teaches that the Parousia

---

[1] Cf. e.g. Chrysostom, Augustine, Theodoret (see Rigaux, *Thessaloniciens*, pp. 540f); Schmaus, *Dogmatik*, p. 40; Haak, in *Z.s.T.* XV, 1938, pp. 544ff.; Flückiger, *Ursprung*, p. 144. We may compare Jn. 1, 14 where ἐθεασάμεθα probably means 'we Christians . . .' and, according to Barrett (*John*, pp. 119, 138) does not include the author. (cf. also 'you' in Amos 2, 10, which cannot mean that the prophet thought those he was addressing were ever in Egypt.)

[2] This is said to be already familiar to the Thessalonians; 5, 1f.

[3] Cf. Flückiger, *Ursprung*, p. 144.

[4] Cf. Acts 8, 1, 9, 23f., II Cor. 11, 23f.

[5] Exactly similarly Mk. 13; 33-37 following v. 32, and II Peter 3, 11f., following vv. 8-10.

will arrive shortly.[1] However, far from affirming such a view, this letter distinctly emphasises that the 'end is not yet'.[2] Two passages in particular support this contention.

The first is II Thess. 2, 3, a reminiscence of Dan. 11, 36f., where Paul maintains that prior to the End there must be an upsurge of evil in unique form, involving Antichrist.[3] Clearly the point of the reference lies in the fact that such unique wickedness had not yet occurred. To be sure, Paul speaks (v. 7) of the 'mystery' of lawlessness already at work' τὸ γὰρ μυστήριον ἤδη ἐνεργεῖται τῆς ἀνομίας. Many [4] take this as a reference to Caligula, from which it follows that Paul expected the End to come very soon (once Claudius was removed and Nero came to power). But this identification is hardly likely since (a) Paul's present indicative ἐνεργεῖται does not mean that lawlessness has once occurred (which would require an aorist): [5] (b) Paul speaks of a 'mystery' μυστήριον, whereas if the reference were to Caligula he could easily have said 'lawlessness has been manifested': [6] (c) Paul would need an astounding foreknowledge to know that Nero would succeed Claudius [7] and that Nero would prove to be a ruler of unprecedented wickedness.[8] We must understand the relation between the future 'revelation of the man of sin' and the present 'working of the mystery of lawlessness' in some other way, and probably the clue lies in the terms

---

[1] Cf. Glasson, *Advent*, p. 183, pp. 193ff., (who regards the 'adoption' of the man of sin tradition into the primitive tradition as one of the causes of the delimited hope); Neil, *Thessalonians*, p. 177.; Frame, *Thessalonians*, p. 243; Milligan, *Thessalonians*, pp. 94f.

[2] Schweitzer, *Mysticism*, p. 42, regarded the non-immediate note of the letter as proof of its unauthenticity!

[3] The ref. in Dan. 11, 36f., is to Antiochus Ephiphanes; cf. Rigaux, *Thessaloniciens*, p. 658.

[4] Cf. Hölscher, in *T.B.* VI, 1933, p. 137; Glasson, *Advent*, p. 183 (following Andrews, in Peake's *Commentary* (unrevised ed.) ad loc).

[5] Cf. Blass-Debrunner, *Grammar*, p. 167, p. 171.

[6] So, in fact, Andrews, in Peake's *Commentary*, quoted by Glasson, *Advent*, p. 183, writes 'The mystery of lawlessness has already manifested itself in Caligula.'

[7] Though announced in A.D. 50 (when Nero was 13), the succession depended largely on his mother Agrippina's support (Claudius' fourth wife), and involved the supersession of Claudius' son Britannicus.

[8] Though influenced by Seneca, Nero was also influenced for the good by 'Burrus, prefect of the praetorian guard, an honest and virtuous soldier' (Cowan, in *H.D.B.* III, pp. 514f.). Cf. also the favourable judgements on his early years of rule given in Suet. Nero 10, 11. Tacitus, Ann, xii, 45. Neil, *Thessalonians*, pp. 167f., notices the problem.

ἀποκαλυφθῇ (v. 3) and μυστήριον (v. 7). In the period prior to the Parousia (cf 2, 8f.), wickedness is at work in hidden form.[1] That does not mean that wickedness does not ever become open and apparent, but rather that in general it works in a subtle way, only on occasions and in violent upsurges taking on an apparent form. Such a violent upsurge of evil, concentrated in the person of Antichrist, was expected prior to the End,[2] and Paul warns that since it has not yet occurred, it is absurd to suppose that 'the day of the Lord is present' (2, 2). We may notice that although Paul aligns himself with the expectation of an upsurge of evil in this form prior to the End, he does not conclude that the End would necessarily follow any lesser outbreak of violence, nor that violent outbreaks cannot often occur.[3]

The other passage is II Thess. 2, 6-7, the teaching concerning τὸ κατέχον and ὁ κατέχων. The general interpretation [4] sees τὸ κατέχον as the Roman state and ὁ κατέχων as Claudius the reigning emperor. It is pointed out in support that the neuter and masculine parallel the usage in Mk. 13; 14 where the allusion originally was to state power (neuter) represented by the emperor Antiochus (masculine): also that this view accords with Paul's high evaluation of the state.[5] However, this interpretation is very unlikely to be correct, and there are many reasons for accepting the suggestion [6] that Paul

---

[1] Cf. on μυστήριον in this sense, Robinson, *Ephesians*, pp. 234ff.; Moule, *Colossians*, pp. 8off.

[2] Cf. Dan. 11, 36ff, 9, 25ff., which idea emerges in Ps. Sol., Test. of the Twelve Patriarchs, etc. cf. also Ezek. 28, 2, Is. 14, 13-14. Rigaux, *Thessaloniciens*, pp. 259ff. (and authorities there cited).

[3] Every working of the 'mystery of lawlessness' will point to the final revelation of ὁ ἄνομος at the Parousia, but not every working — even violent — is to be seen as the immediate prelude to the removal of the restraint and the revelation of wickedness. Cf. Bornkamm, in *T.W.N.T.* IV, p. 830.)

[4] Which goes back to Tertullian (de Ress. 24; cf. also Apol. 32) and has 'since won the support of the great majority of ancient and modern scholars' (Milligan, *Thessalonians*, p. 101); cf. Glasson, *Advent*, p. 183; Hölscher, in *T.B.* VI, 1933 p. 137.; Lauk, *Thessalonicher, ad loc*; Oepke, *Thessalonicher, ad loc*, allows it as a possibility.

[5] Most refer to Rom. 13, 1-7; cf. Lauk, II *Thessalonicher, ad loc*; Milligan, *Thessalonians*, p. 101. Oepke (who thinks Paul may have in mind angelic powers working in the political institutions) thinks the evaluation is due partly to psychological causes, partly to experience (cf. Acts 13, 6f., 17, 6f.) and partly to Paul's sober realism; *Thessalonicher, ad loc*).

[6] Which goes back to Theodoret (Migne *P.G.* Vol. 82, 665A) and Theodore of Mopsuestia (Migne, *P.G.* Vol. 66, 936A), was held by Calvin (*Commentary on Thessalonians, ad loc*), and recently is advocated by Cullmann (first in

is actually referring to gospel proclamation. Thus (a) the identification of Claudius with ὁ κατέχων would mean that Paul placed a high evaluation on this emperor not *qua* emperor but in contrast to his predecessor Caligula and the untried Nero. But Stauffer [1] says of Claudius that he was 'an insignificant fool who was ruled by his wife of the moment': is it this weakling ruler whom Paul defines as 'he who restrains'? (b) on the other hand, if one speaks not of Claudius particularly, but simply of the Roman rule, then the specific ὁ κατέχων is difficult: [2] (c) the prevailing New Testament usage of κατέχω suggests *activity* [3] which is rather different from a restraining which arises from the passive fact of being alive and of thus hindering one's successor from ruling: (d) the evaluation of the state in terms of a power ordained of God, and therefore to be honoured [4] is not questioned,[5] nor do we doubt that Paul thinks of the state as something which often opposes itself to God's rule.[6] But it is, surely, unlikely that Paul would refer in the same passage to the state both as that which requires restraining and as that which does the restraining; Cullmann [7] rightly says that 'Paul would thereby have introduced into the eschatological conceptions a remarkable confusion': (e) gospel preaching is frequently referred to in the context, 1, 8; 1, 10; 2, 5; 2, 10; 2, 13. Paul was ever anxious to preach the gospel continually [8] and to do nothing to hinder the course of the gospel: [9] (f) ὁ κατέχων can satisfactorily be understood [10]

R.H.P.R. 1936, pp. 210ff.; later in *Time*, pp. 145ff.; *State*, p. 64, n. 7; in *Background of the N.T.*, pp. 418f.) and Munck, *Paul*, pp. 36ff.

[1] *Christ and the Caesars*, p. 138; cf. also Benecke, in *H.D.B.* I, pp. 446f.

[2] Hanse (in *T.W.N.T.* II, pp. 829f.) writes, 'die beliebte Deutung auf die Ordnung des römischen Reiches passt schlecht zu dem persönlichen ὁ κατέχων'. Without altogether underestimating the significance of the masculine and neuter (as Rigaux, *Thessaloniciens*, p. 275, appears to do) it could perhaps be said that the masculine is a reference to *any* personification of the state power (cf. Milligan, *Thessalonians*, p. 101).

[3] Cf. Arndt-Gingrich, *Lexicon*, p. 434. Hanse, in *T.W.N.T.* II, p. 829.

[4] Cf. Rom. 13, 1-17 (I Tim. 2, 2).

[5] Cf. Barth's comment (re Jn. 19, 11) 'The State, even in this "demonic" form, cannot help rendering the service it is meant to render'. (*State*, p. 17).

[6] Cf. Stauffer, *Theology*, p. 85.

[7] *Time*, p. 164.

[8] Cf. I Cor. 9, 23; II Cor. 10, 16; Rom. 15. 19ff., etc.

[9] Cf. I Cor. 9, 13; II Cor. 6, 3-4.

[10] With Cullmann, *Time*, pp. 145ff., *State*, p. 64, n. 7, etc.; Munck, *Paul*, pp. 36ff.

as a reference to Paul himself, or more probably [1] as a reference to 'the preacher' who gives actual form to the restraining force, τὸ κατέχον, namely the gospel itself.[2] We conclude, therefore, that Paul is here teaching that the Parousia *can* delay; and that this teaching is not a corrective for a delimited hope previously held, but is precisely the message which he had already preached at Thessalonica (cf 2, 5; 2, 15).

I Corinthians 7

Many scholars[3] maintain that this chapter betrays Paul's con-

---

[1] Because the view of Cullmann and Munck (which Rigaux, *Thessaloniciens*, p. 266, calls gratuitous) is supported by two considerations which are open to criticism; they are: —

a) Paul's lofty consciousness of mission (Cullmann, *Time*, p. 165; Munck, *Paul*, pp. 39f.) But Paul must have been aware that he was not *alone* in his missionary task; cf. I Cor. 3, 1-9 in which it is basic to the argument that both Paul and Apollos are 'ministers through whom ye believed'; also Acts 13, 2; where Paul *and* Barbanas are set aside for special work together; II Cor. 11, 23f, too, where Paul does not even hint that the mission to the Gentiles was altogether imperilled by the experiences which threatened his own life. The unique function of apostleship, whether to Jew or Gentiles, lay in witnessing (cf. Barrett, in *Studia Paulina*, pp. 18f.) But it is an exaggeration to suggest that Paul regarded *his* witness as decisive for the inbreak of the End. (It is interesting that Munck nowhere mentions I Cor. 15, 9; except p. 13, n. 2, as evidence that Paul was a persecutor; for although he declares in v. 10 that he laboured more than others, his self-assessment in v. 9 should be taken seriously.) b) Supporting the allusiveness of the so-called self designation, Cullmann (*Time*, pp. 156f.) refers to II Cor. 12, 2; — another self designation couched in the 3rd person. But this is an exception (contrast Rom. 1, 1; 11, 13; I Cor. 1, 1; 9, 1; II Cor. 1, 1; 11, 5; etc.) intended to point away from his own glorying. Rigaux (*Thessaloniciens*, p. 276, following Schmid, in *T.Q.*. CXXIV, 1949, p. 336 is right: 'Paul ne l'aurait pas dit secrètement, mais ouvertement.' (Though Rigaux's own objection (*Thessaloniciens*, p. 277), 'contre ceux qui identifient Paul aux κατέχων et font de la mort de Paul la condition de l'éclosion de la lutte eschatologique on est en droit de faire valoir que, dans ce cas, il y a une contradiction flagrante entre notre péricope et I Thess. 4; 13-18 où Paul exprime l'espoir d'être vivant à la parousie', will not stand on our interpretation of I Thess. 4, 13-18. Cf. too the despairing conclusion of Dibelius, *Thessalonicher*, p. 43; Neil, *Thessalonians*, pp. 165ff.)

[2] Cf. Hanse, in *T.W.N.T.* II, p. 830 (though Hanse does not identify ὸ κατέχων with 'the preacher'). Perhaps support for this interpretation can be drawn from the chain of events listed in Rom. 10, 13ff.; 'how can they believe in whom they have not heard?' is a reference to preaching as such; and 'how shall they hear without a preacher?' is a reference to the concrete form. It is when there is no longer 'a preacher' (i.e. when God decrees; cf. Blass-Debrunner, *Grammar*, p. 164) that the mission must cease and the End come.

[3] Cf. Dodd, *Studies*, pp. 180ff.; Robertson-Plummer, *I Corinthians*, p. 152; Lietzmann, *Korinther*, p. 29; Glasson, *Advent*, p. 139; Munck, *Paul*, p. 165.

viction that the Parousia would definitely arrive within a few years. Against this interpretation of the chapter we offer the following considerations:

Though the ethics expressed here are, to some extent, ascetic in character,[1] this asceticism should be evaluated with the special situation of the Corinthians in mind.[2] Not only was Corinth traditionally vicious [3] but within the Christian community there was division (1, 11), 'worldliness' (3, 2f.), especially sexual impurity (5, 1ff.) [4]

The relativity of the asceticism[5] suggests that it was motivated by Paul's concern for the well-being and faithfulness of his Corinthian converts, rather than by a conviction that the world would necessarily end within a few years. Paul is above all else concerned with the problem how Christians can best 'please the Lord' (v. 32) and he enumerates in fact three principles: first, do what will avoid sin: [6] secondly, do that to which God calls; [7] thirdly, do that which will not distract from discipleship.[8] This complex of world affirmation and of world denial, neither of which is absolutised,[9] certainly does not necessitate as its basis the expectation that the Parousia must come within a definite, short, period.[10]

Three particular expressions in vv. 26-31 are often taken to indicate a delimited expectation. The first τὴν ἐνεστῶσαν ἀνάγκην,

---

[1] Cf. esp. v. 1, v. 8, vv. 26-27, v. 40.

[2] Cf. Morris, I Corinthians, p. 106.

[3] Cf. Metzger. Journeys, p. 48.

[4] It is possible that Paul was seeking not only to counter laxity but also to counter an overstressed rigorism; 7, 1-2 look as though Paul acknowledges the thesis put to him by the Corinthians and then modifies it (καλὸν . . .διὰ δὲ . . .); cf. Goudge, I Corinthians, p. 52; Héring, I Corinthiens. p, 50.

[5] V. 1 is modified by v. 2; v. 8 by v. 9; vv. 26-27 by vv. 28f; v. 37 by v. 36; and v. 40 by v. 39.

[6] Cf. vv. 2, 5, 9, 36.

[7] Cf. vv. 7, 17f., 20, 21ff.

[8] Cf. vv. 19, 24, 32, 33-36.

[9] Cf. Cullmann, Time, pp. 212f. Earthly ties must be regarded as subservient to the demands of the Lord and his gospel (cf. Mtt. 10, 37) and the things which the world counts vital, recognised as transient (cf. similarly Rom. 12, 2; Phil. 4, 11).

[10] It is interesting that in Phil. 4, 11; (where, according to those who affirm a development in Paul's thought, we have his later ideas) contentment with his conditions is again stated. It appears quite possible that this contentment with what befalls one (and refusal to seek to change one's lot) is what Paul is commending in I Cor. 7, 7; 8. Such freedom from cares is encouraged in 7, 32-36 (cf. v. 28), and is the ground for a man to be as he is (v. 26) and not seek change.

is sometimes taken to denote pre-messianic woes (cf Lk. 21, 23); but even if we understand the phrase in this way, it does not need to mean that Paul believed the period of woes to be very short. There is, however, good reason to suggest that Paul had in mind here the distressing situation in Corinth [1] which complicated and jeopardized the formation of new relationships, and which could be of any imaginable duration, long or short.[2]

The second expression ὁ καιρὸς συνεσταλμένος ἐστίν need not simply mean that there is not much time left, for καιρὸς is neutral concerning its duration,[3] and the expression συνεσταλμένος [4] whilst clearly affirming that the Parousia is in some sense imminent, does not necessarily mean that Paul thought it must come within a delimited time.[5]

The third expression παράγει γὰρ τὸ σχῆμα τοῦ κόσμου τούτου is hardly a reference to the expected destruction and renewal of the world (cf Rom. 8, 19f.), for the present tense (cf also ἐνεστῶσαν ἀνάγκην)

---

[1] Roberton-Plummer *I Corinthians*, p. 152; Héring, *I Corinthiens*, p. 57; and Lietzmann, *Korinther*, pp. 33f.; all take ἀνάγκη in connection with ὁ καιρὸς συνεσταλμένος and interpret v. 26 of the messianic woes. But whilst Lk. 21, 23 uses ἀνάγκη in this connection, Mtt. 24, 21; 29 and Mk., 13, 19; 24, use rather Θλῖψις. Certainly Paul can use ἀνάγκη elsewhere of distress not *directly* connected with the End, cf. Rom. 13, 5; II Cor. 6, 4; 9, 7; 12, 10; I Thess. 3, 7 (Arndt-Gingrich, *Lexicon*, give only I Cor. 7, 26 as meaning 'the distress in the last days,' apart from Lk. 21, 23) (cf. also III Macc. 1, 16 for the phrase 'present distress' where there is no direct connection with messianic woes). Significantly Paul uses ἀνάγκη in 7, 37 where he suggests that the present distress of v. 26 might not affect all the Corinthians. The chief objection to interpreting the expression in terms of the local Corinthian trouble is that vv. 29-31 speak certainly of the 'End'; but the clear break in v. 29 (τοῦτο δέ φημι, 'indiquant sans doute qu'il s'agit d'une révélation nouvelle'; Héring, *I Corinthiens*, p. 57) makes this objection weak. It may well be that the two ideas should be taken together, and that Paul saw in the distress in Corinth one aspect of those woes which precede the Parousia.

[2] It is unlikely that τῇ σαρκὶ in v. 28 refers to the sort of situation envisaged in Mk. 13, 17 par., but that Paul rather had in mind the 'outward cares of living'; Bultmann, *Theology*, I, p. 233; Lietzmann, *Korinther*, p. 34.

[3] Delling, in *T.W.N.T.* III, p. 463, calls καιρός 'der entscheidende Zeitpunkt' (cf. Cullmann, *Time*, p. 39); but καιρός can certainly mean a decisive *period* (cf. esp. Col. 4, 5; Rom. 13, 11; also Rom. 12, 11; in D*G. Ambrst.)

[4] The verb is used in Acts 5, 6 of 'wrapping up' a corpse.

[5] Calvin (*Commentary on I Corinthians*, p. 159) says Paul 'bases his argument on the shortness of human life' but Robertson-Plummer *Commentary*, p. 155) rightly comment 'This makes good sense, but probably not the right sense.' That God should contract the time prior to the Parousia gives us no grounds for delimiting it, but simply urges us to patience and urgency in discipleship.

suggests a process already begun. τὸ σχῆμα, used in the New Testament twice only,[1] probably means the outward customs and ordinances of human life, the permanency of which is called in question; the Christian must stand over against them with a certain detachment.[2]

Such detachment is, surely, a proper expression of Christian discipleship. Héring[3] writes, 'mais ce qu'il y a de curieux, c'est que les recommandations de 30 et 31 ont une portée beaucoup plus grande, indépendante de la date de la parousie.' Paul can encourage watchfulness,[4] believing that the Parousia is near without necessarily believing that it would certainly come within a definite period of time.

I Corinthians 15

Does this chapter contain evidence that Paul believed that the Parousia must come within a few years? Lietzmann maintains that those who denied the resurrection (cf. v. 12) 'müssten denn ihre Ewigkeitshoffnung, allein auf das Erleben der Parusie eingestellt haben, was nicht unmöglich ist (vgl. I Thess. 4, 13f.)'.[5] If he were right, it is significant that Paul does *not* answer simply that this is also *his* hope! However, Lietzmann's conclusion does not necessarily follow, for there have been Christians in every generation who have substituted for the belief in the resurrection some other doctrine, often the idea of the immortality of the soul.[6] Certainly

---

[1] Here and in Phil. 2, 8; where it is clear that the meaning is 'the outward appearance.' But in view of the doubts concerning authorship of Phil. 2, 5-11 (cf. Lohmeyer, *Philipper*, p. 90; contrast Martin, *An Early Christian Confession*, pp. 8ff.), the passage cannot help very much in understanding I. Cor. 7.

[2] Cf. Rich, *Die Bedeutung*, p. 21. Calvin, *I Corinthians*, p. 160, paraphrases 'there is nothing stable or solid, for it is only a facade, or outward appearance.' Cf. Rom. 12, 2.

[3] *I Corinthiens*, p. 58. Contrast, Robertson-Plummer, *I Corinthians* p. 152, who write 'We cannot assume that his opinion would have been the same in a more peaceful period, and *after experience had proved that the Advent might be long delayed.*'

[4] It is because the End can come at any moment (cf. also I Cor. 10, 11) that Paul exhorts to 'care-lessness'; cf. exactly parallel Lk. 21, 34 (cf. 'the cares of this life'). The parallel is specially interesting since Luke is said to be concerned with an indefinite interim!

[5] *Korinther*, p. 79.

[6] For a full discussion of the views of those referred to in I Cor. 15, 12; cf. Weiss, *I Korinther*, pp. 343ff.

Paul does not address himself to such a hope, but directly to the denial of the resurrection (15, 13f.) and then to the problems arising (15, 22ff.). It seems most probable,[1] that the deniers of the Resurrection were Christians who being open to Hellenistic influences found in the idea of resurrection *per se* a source of difficulty'.[2]

The problem under discussion is certainly not the Parousia delay; the denial (v. 12) does not arise through any disillusionment —for Paul answers not that the Parousia will come (after all!), but that Christ is risen and therefore Christians too will be raised.[3]

Only two passages might possibly be taken as indicating a delimited expection in this chapter. The first is v. 23 'then they that are Christ's, at his παρουσία'. But, though this points to the next phase of salvation history (Christ the ἀπαρχὴ being a past phase, cf. v. 20), the moment of its coming is entirely undefined. ἔπειτα certainly links the two events [4] but no chronological delimitation is ventured.[5]

The other passage is vv. 51-52. Here the first person plural is taken by many [6] as meaning that Paul includes himself amongst those who will not die. This is extremely unlikely. To press the form of the expression so, would mean that in I Cor. 6, 14 Paul expected certainly to die.[7] In fact Paul probably means Christians generally-as, we suggest, he means in I Thess. 4, 15; 17.[8] Paul does

---

[1] With Davies, *Rabbinic Judaism*, p. 303; Robertson-Plummer *I Corinthians*, p. 346.

[2] Davies, *Rabbinic Judaism*, p. 303. Hence, perhaps, the argument includes the section vv. 35ff.

[3] Nor is the problem that Christians were not expected to die. I Cor. 15, 6 mentions τινὲς ἐκοιμήθησαν without more ado! If Michaelis (in *Wikenhauser Festschrift*, pp. 114f.) says that Menoud ignores this verse, we may note that Davies (*Rabbinic Judaism*) and Munck (*Paul*) do also.

[4] And they *are* linked, for Christ is the ἀπαρχὴ of this next phase.

[5] Already nearly 30 years had separated the two events. The discussion concerning the possibility of an interval between ἔπειτα and εἶτα (vv. 23, 34) (cf. Robinson, *Coming*, p. 31; Kennedy, *Last Things* p. 323) has no bearing on this question.

[6] Cf. Bultmann, *Theology*, I p. 103; Deissmann, *Paul*, p. 217; Robertson-, Plummer, *I Corinthians*, p. 376; Lietzmann, *Korinther*, p. 87; Anderson-Scott *Footnotes*, p. 140, etc. (Lietzmann indeed suggests that the non fulfilment of the verse accounts for the textual variants; but peculiarities of the construction here (πάντες οὐ ... ὀμεθα and πάντες δὲ ... ὀμεθα) may well be sufficient grounds for variations having arisen.)

[7] As Morris, *I Corinthians*, p. 232, notes.

[8] Cf. above pp. 109ff.; Héring, *I Corinthiens*, p. 150.

not write as one who will certainly be dead at the Parousia, but as one who awaits the Parousia as an event which might occur at any moment and therefore he reckons with the possibility of his being alive at that time; but this does not mean that he included himself amongst those who would necessarily be alive at its coming.

II Corinthians 5, 1-10

Here (and in Phil. 1, 23) we meet with the so-called developed view of Paul.[1] Davies [2] declares that 'there is nothing in the text to suggest Paul's hope of surviving to the Parousia'. Many, however, argue that Paul is, in fact, longing for the Parousia so that he will not have to undergo the state of nakedness (γυμνός) following death.[3] It seems at least possible that Paul does not mean that nakedness follows upon the death of *Christians*,[4] and that therefore he is not 'groaning' (στενάξομεν) because of the oppressive thought that death may come before the Lord returns. Nevertheless there *is* here a longing for the coming of the Parousia; στενάζειν as used by Paul [5] has a definite eschatological sense (cf Rom. 8, 22; 23). The hope remains, and remains undelimited.[6]

---

[1] Cf. Dodd, *Studies*, pp. 110f.; Cullmann, *Time*, p. 88; Robertson-Plummer, *I Corinthians*, p. 376; Anderson-Scott, *Footnotes*, p. 140; Davies, *Rabbinic Judaism*, pp. 310f.

[2] Cf. *Rabbinic Judaism*, p. 311 (following Cave, *Gospel*, p. 255); contrast, Kennedy, *Last Things*, p. 256.

[3] Cf. Lietzmann, *Korinther*, p. 117; Deissmann, *Paul*, p. 65; Kennedy, *Last Things*, p. 256; Robertson-Plummer, *I Corinthians*, p. 148; Sevenster, in *Studia Paulina*, p. 207.

[4] Calvin (*I Corinthians, ad loc*), Oepke (in *T.W.N.T.* I, p. 774) and Flückiger (*Ursprung*, p. 145, n. 86), think that Paul means that 'the wicked' are to be naked. Sevenster (in *Studia Paulina*, pp. 202ff.) disagrees on the grounds that we have no justification for thinking that Paul did not expect the wicked also to be raised. Yet the resurrection to a *naked* state could, surely, be envisaged by Paul? Robinson (*Body*, p. 29) maintains that 'to be absent from the body' means 'to be naked'; but there is no need to take the parenthesis of v. 3 and the negation in v. 4 as interpreting the phrase of v. 6, v. 8 and v. 9. If Paul is thinking in vv. 3f., of the putting off of the old man (cf. Col. 3, 9f., Rom. 6, 6) the longing for the 'new man' and the dread of not attaining (cf. I Cor. 9, 27), then the readiness to die or live (vv. 6ff.) is readily understandable. To be sure, Sevenster (in *Studia Paulina*, pp. 206f.) has shown that the comparison in Phil. 1, 23 is not the same as the one made in II Cor. 5, 3; at the same time, the willingness to die (Phil. 1, 23) is more easily understood if Paul is thinking of the wicked as those who, not being 'in Christ', must be 'naked'.

[5] Contrast the N.T. usage elsewhere, Jam. 5, 9; Heb. 13, 17; Mk. 7, 34.

[6] It is, anyway, extremely improbable that Paul should have so suddenly changed his views. Davies, *Rabbinic Judaism*, p. 311; Cave, *Gospel*, p. 254;

Romans 13.

This chapter is interpreted, on the one hand, as giving a re-appraisal of Paul's earlier 'world-denial' [1] and, on the other hand, as evidence that Paul still believed that the Parousia would come within a very few years.[2]

The first estimate, besides wrongly attributing to Paul in his earlier letters a simple 'world denial' [3] surely exaggerates in seeing in Rom. 13, 1-7 a simple 'world-affirmation'. Dodd thinks that here Paul grounds civil government in 'the natural moral order of the universe, but lying outside the order of grace revealed in Christ'.[4] There are, however, good reasons for understanding Paul's injunction πᾶσα ψυχὴ ἐξουσίαις ὑπερεχούσαις ὑποτασέσθω Christologically.[5] Christians are required 'to submit themselves' because the

---

Denney, *II Corinthians*, p. 175, think that II Cor. 1; 8-9 reflects the event which led to such a change. But dangers had faced Paul often enough before.

[1] Cf. Dodd, *Studies*, pp. 108ff.; *Romans*, pp. 209f.; Dodd connects his view of Rom. 13 with chapters 9-11 of which he says, 'the forecast of history in ch. 11 is hardly framed for a period of a few months' (*Romans*, p. 209). But in reply we must mention these considerations: —

a. Paul attaches to the present and future *no different* significance here than that found elsewhere. The present as the period in which the Gospel is preached is an idea found in I Cor. 9; 12, 23, II Cor. 6, 1f., 10, 15 (and cf. the interpretation of κατέχον (ων) in II Thess. 2, 6-7 above, pp. 112f.). The ultimate inclusion of the Jews, though not worked out elsewhere, is implied in the argument of the 'universalism' of I Cor. 15, 22; II Cor. 5, 14; Rom. 5, 12f.

b. The perspective of the chapters does not rule out the *possibility* of a speedy End. Already the 'grafting in of the Gentiles' can be spoken of in the past tense (cf. 11, 17 ἐνεκεντρίσθης) just as the breaking off of 'some of the branches' is past (v. 17). And although Paul hopes, by provoking his fellows to jealousy on account of the Gentiles' faith, to gain the conversion of some of them (cf. Deut. 32, 21), he does not say that Israel as a whole will have to be converted before the End comes (which might indeed suggest a *Fernerwartung*), but connects their ingrafting with the End itself (cf. 11, 26). Everything depends, therefore, on how long the 'times of the Gentiles' (cf. τὸ πλήρωμα τῶν ἐθνῶν) may be—but, significantly, Paul does not venture an opinion on this.

[2] Cf. Barrett, *Romans*, ad loc; Gore, *Romans*, II, p. 134; Sanday-Headlam, *Romans*, p. 380; Leenhardt, *Romans*, p. 339; (with reservations) Bultmann, *Theology*, I, pp. 103, 347.

[3] Cf. above on I Cor. 7, pp. 114f.

[4] *Romans*, p. 204.

[5] Even if ἐξουσίαι is not taken as a reference to the demonic powers subjected to Christ through his Cross and Resurrection (this Christological interpretation has been advocated most recently by Barth, *Shorter Commentary*, p. 158; Cullmann, *Time*, pp. 191ff.; cf. Brunner, *Romans*, pp. 108f., contrast Michel, *Römer*, p. 281; von Campenhausen, 'Zur Auslegung von

civil power is an instrument of Christ's kingly rule and because, in so far as its existence is for the good of one's neighbour, one's service of it is a part of the debt of love owed to the neighbour in whom Christ himself is mysteriously present'.[1] If this interpretation is correct, Paul is not voicing a simple world-affirmation but asserting the Lordship of Christ in the political sphere of human life, a Lordship implicit already in his earliest letters.[2]

The second estimate, that Paul 'still' thinks in Romans (especially 13, 11-12) that the Parousia will come within a few years,[3] attributes to him a delimitation of the present period which, in fact, he refuses to make.[4] Paul requires that his readers 'should know the time'— something which unbelief cannot do (cf. Mtt. 16, 2-3); this knowledge gives to Christian ethics [5] urgency and seriousness.[6] ἡ ἡμέρα

Röm. 13'. in Festschrift für A. Bertholet, pp. 97ff.; Leenhardt, Romans, p. 328 note), the Christological interpretation of the passage can stand (cf. Cranfield, 'Some observations on Romans 13; 1-7' in N.T.S. VI, pp. 241ff. contrast Barrett, Romans, p. 249.) Cranfield mentions in support of this the implicit Christological understanding in the credal formula κύριος Ἰησοῦς, the use made of Ps. 110, and such a passage as Mtt. 28, 18, and the explicit understanding in Rev. 1, 5; 17, 14; 19, 16 (in N.T.S. VI, p. 242). Barth (Shorter Commentary, p. 158) declares, 'Not a word suggests that Paul in these verses suddenly ceases to exhort "by the mercies of God" (12, 1), that he no longer appeals to Christians as such and therefore to their obedience to Jesus Christ.'

[1] Cranfield, in N.T.S. VI, p. 244.

[2] Cf. κύριος Ἰησοῦς in I Thess. 1, 1; 3. 2, 15; 19. 3, 11; 13, 4, 2. 5, 9; 23; 28 II Thess. 1, 1; 2; 7; 8; 12. 2, 1; 8; 14; 16. 3, 6; 12; 18.

[3] Strangely, Dodd accepts this, and has to speak of Paul 'reverting' to his 'old view' in the midst of his 'developed view'; cf. Studies, pp. 108f.; Romans, p. 109.

[4] Lietzmann Römer, p. 113, rightly only comments 'Die Nähe der Parusie als Motiv der Lebenserneuerung'; Sanday-Headlam, Romans, p. 378 say, 'The language is that befitting those who expect the actual coming of Christ almost immediately, but it will fit the circumstances of any Christian for whom death brings the day'; cf. also Leenhardt, Romans, p. 339.

[5] All the injunctions preceding (beginning with 12, 1-2) and those which follow (14, 1ff.) are comprehended (cf. Blass-Debrunner, Grammar, p. 480; Michel, Römer, p. 281.)

[6] If the difference between καιρός and χρόνος has sometimes been read into passages where it need not be present, Barr's criticisms, despite the service they have done, are surely too severe (as too his attack on modern lexicographical methodology; cf. Biblical Words for Time, and, The Semantics of Biblical Language). At any rate, it is clear that καιρός in Rom. 13, 11 must have the sense of divinely given opportunity, a period of special significance in the salvation history, as vv. 12f., show (cf. Leenhardt, Romans, p. 339, who compares the νῦν of 13, 11b with the eschatological νῦν in 3, 26. 5, 9; 11. 7, 6. 8, 1; 18; 22. 11, 5; 30; 31. 16, 26). But Rom. 13, 11 is a passage Barr does not discuss in Biblical Words for Time.

ἤγγικεν [1] means that the present period is a 'dawn'; the dawn, however, is not delimited—only the present is characterised *as* dawn throughout its duration.[2]

In the parenthesis of v. 11b, Paul claims νῦν γὰρ ἐγγύτερον ἡμῶν ἡ σωτηρία ἢ ὅτε ἐπιστεύσαμεν. Barrett [3] understands here, 'the lapse of time between the conversion of Paul and of his readers and the moment of writing is a significant proportion of the total interval between the resurrection of Jesus and his parousia at the last day.' But Paul could have said simply 'for you have only a few years left', had he meant this. Surely he means only that every day brings the End one day nearer. He has not ventured to suggest what proportion of the total this past period represents.[4] Each moment is a significant moment not because necessarily few moments remain, but because the entire present period is a 'dawn' and the day *could* come at any moment.

Romans 15, 19; 23

On the expression πεπληρωκέναι τὸ εὐαγγέλιον (v. 19) Barrett comments, 'he does not mean that he (or any-one else) has preached the gospel to every person . . . but that it has been covered in a representative way. The Gospel has been heard; more could not be expected before the Parousia . ' .[5] But whilst it is certainly true that Paul understands preaching (and the response of faith) directly related to the purpose for which the present time prior to the Parousia has been given (and therefore understands preaching as an

---

[1] The parallel with ἤγγικεν ἡ βασιλεία τοῦ θεοῦ is obviously important. The metaphor used by Paul can only be understood Christologically.

[2] Cf. Nygren, *Romans*, p. 436; Michel, *Römer*, p. 291; Brunner, *Romans*, p. 113. The dawn had already lasted some 25 years when Paul wrote (Dodd dates the letter in A.D. 59; Sanday and Headlam in 58.)

[3] *Romans*, ad loc. More hesitantly Leenhardt, *Romans*, p. 339 (but to say, as Leenhardt does 'he (Paul) is not interested in the chronological aspect of the event itself . . .' surely goes too far in minimising Paul's hope that the Parousia *might* come shortly.)

[4] Cf. Nygren, *Romans*, p. 436, 'When the Christian sees how time runs on, he ought thereby to be made mindful that "it is full time . . . to awake from sleep . . .".'
Paul certainly *is* referring to the period between acceptance of the gospel and the time of writing the epistle; cf. Bultmann, in *T.W.N.T.* VI, p. 215; Pallis, *Romans*, ad loc, connects with baptism (cf. Acts 19, 2); similarly Michel, *Römer*, p. 293; Brunner, *Romans*, p. 113.

[5] *Romans*, p. 211; similarly, Munck, *Paul*, pp. 47ff.; Schoeps, *Paul*, p. 101. (following Overbeck, *Christentum und Kultur*, pp. 57, 62).

eschatological activity),[1] is there really any evidence here that Paul believed the gospel could only be preached in a representative way?, that 'more could not be expected before the Parousia'?

In answering these questions in the negative, we must notice that Paul himself—before even accomplishing a complete tour of 'representative' preaching [2]—visited some of his communities more than once,[3] and stayed in some longer than one would expect if he had really believed that the Parousia's arrival was dependent upon the completion of his representative preaching.[4] Moreover, Paul's general rule (v. 20) indicates that he himself did not concern himself in detail with the administration of the communities he had founded,[5] nor did he work in places where the church had already been founded by others, but considered himself a pioneer missionary.[6]

Further, although we take πεπληρωκέναι as meaning that throughout the regions ἀπὸ ῾Ιερουσαλημ καὶ κύκλῳ μέχρι τοῦ ᾽Ιλλυρικοῦ Paul had fulfilled his task of a pioneer preaching of the gospel [7] the fact is mentioned here, and re-iterated in v. 23 *not* in the context of expounding the fulfilment of the divine pattern of salvation-history, but in the course of explaining why Paul, as a pioneer missionary, intends to visit Rome.[8] To be sure, there *is* a connection between fulfilment of the Gospel (πεπληρωκέναι τὸ εὐαγγέλιον) (and cf Col. 1, 25; II Tim. 4, 17), and the command to preach to all nations (Mk. 13, 10; Mtt. 24, 14), the former being necessitated by the latter. But the world of that time was extensive,[9] Paul's work that of a pioneer, and there is not evidence to show that Paul thought the completion of his preaching in certain parts was the same thing as the completion of all the preaching those parts would hear.[10]

---

[1] Cf. Cullmann, *Time*, pp. 157ff.; Michel, *Römer*, p. 330, Hunter, *Interpreting Paul's Gospel*, pp. 130f.

[2] Paul had, obviously, not yet been to Spain; Egypt, too, had apparently not been visited.

[3] E.g. Corinth.

[4] 18 months at Corinth, for instance (Acts 18, 11) and 2 years at Ephesus (Acts 19, 10).

[5] Cf. Dibelius, *Paul*, p. 68.

[6] Cf. II Cor. 4, 1ff., 5, 20; etc.

[7] Hence the expression νυνὶ δὲ μηκέτι τόπον ἔχων in v. 23. Pallis, *Romans*, p. 157, describes μηκέτι τόπον ἔχων wrongly as an 'irresponsible exaggeration'.

[8] The explanation is as elaborate and careful as it is, simply because it is a departure from custom.

[9] Contrast, Barrett, *Romans*, p. 277.

[10] Rom. 11, 25 speaks of τὸ πλήρωμα τῶν ἐθνῶν εἰσέλθη; similarly Lk. 21, 24. Both expressions are passive, suggesting that the fulness of the Gentiles is

Philippians, 3, 20; 4, 5

Not a few critics [1] think that Paul expressed in Philippians his 'developed' view of the future—namely, that he must die before the Parousia which (it is said) is now fading from his mind.

We admit that martyrdom certainly presents itself in this letter as a real possibility (cf. 1, 20; 2, 17). But this, surely, is to the forefront because of the nature of Paul's circumstances. Paul was in prison [2] and judgement in his case was awaited imminently (cf. 2, 23). In any case, the possibility of dying before the Parousia is not new (cf I Thess. 5, 10; II Cor. 5, 9).[3] There is no 'weariness of life' [4] here, and Paul is by no means blind to the advantage of living (ἀναγκαιότερον); indeed, his choice falls on this side (cf 1, 25). Further, Paul apparently hopes still to be released (1, 25; 2, 24) so that he can hardly be said to have viewed his death prior to the Parousia as certain.

Paul eagerly awaits the Parousia (cf. 3, 20),[5] but when he writes ὁ Κύριος ἐγγύς we cannot say that he believed the Parousia would necessarily come within a few years. Apart from the possibility that ἐγγύς[6] here has a spatial rather than a temporal significance,[7] the nearness, if temporal, is not delimited.

---

not accomplished without God's determining will. Contrast Munck, *Paul*, pp. 48f.

[1] Cf. esp. Dodd, *Studies*, pp. 108ff.; Michel, in *Z.s.T.* 1932, pp. 645ff. Sanday-Headlam, *Romans*, pp. 38f., etc.

[2] This is true whatever theory concerning the origin of the captivity epistles one takes (cf. Caesarea—Lohmeyer, *Philipper*, p. 3; or Ephesus—Michaelis, esp. *Einleitung*, ad loc; Duncan, *St. Paul's Ephesian Ministry*, and in *E.T.* LXVII, 1956, pp. 163ff.; (for other authorities); or, the traditional view, Rome—Barth, *Philippians*). Manson's suggestion ('St. Paul in Ephesus. The Date of the Epistle to the Ephesians,', in *B.J.R.L.* XXIII, 1939, pp. 182ff.) that Paul wrote from Ephesus but not in prison, rather with reference to his experiences with Gallio at Corinth (cf. Acts 18, 1ff.) makes inadequate sense of Phil. 1, 7; 13; 16. 2, 23, and has not been accepted.

[3] Cf. above, p. 119f.

[4] Cf. Heinzelmann, *Philipper*, p. 92; Thurneysen, *Philipper*, p. 423.

[5] Cf. ἀπεκδεχόμεθα which denotes 'earnest awaiting'; Rom. 8, 9; 23, I Cor. 1, 7; Gal. 5, 5; (cf. Heb. 9, 28); it is always used by Paul with reference to the End (cf. Lohmeyer, *Philipper*, *ad loc*; similarly, Vincent, *Philippians*, p. 119; Grundmann, in *T.W.N.T.* II, p. 55).

[6] ἐγγύς even in a temporal sense remains flexible. In some cases it refers to an event known to be due in a few days (Mtt. 26, 18), in others it is used of a more general nearness (Mtt. 24, 32).

[7] Dodd, *Studies*, p. 110; and Michaelis, *Philipper*, p. 67, understand the nearness as that of the fellowship of the faithful with the Lord (cf. Ps. 114, 18; 118, 151 LXX.) In support of this it is to be noted that the context in

There appears, therefore, to be no sufficient ground for thinking that Paul believed that the Parousia must come within a fixed, short number of years. The question remains whether the church has left us evidence elsewhere of such a delimited expectation, and so we address our original question next to the tradition which has been embodied in the Synoptics. Clearly the texts we shall have to examine are Mk. 9, 1 par., Mk. 13, 30 par., Mk. 14, 25 par., Mk. 14, 62 par., and Mtt. 10, 23.

Mark 9, 1

Many modern scholars [1] find in this verse indirect evidence of a delimited near-expectation in the early church. It speaks, they say, of a short delay and is addressed as a comfort and reassurance to those whose hope was beginning to waver.[2]

This interpretation, in that it sees a definitely Christological reference in Mk. 9, 1 par., is certainly preferable to those evasive views examined earlier in chapter 7.[3] Yet it is unsatisfactory, chiefly because it fails to take seriously its context.[4] In the tradition followed by all three Synoptists Mk. 9, 1 is connected on the one hand to the coming of the Son of Man in glory (Mk. 8, 38),[5] and on the

---

Phil. 4, 6 is that of prayer, as it is in the two cases cited from the Psalms. (Lohmeyer, *Philipper*, p. 169, links the nearness with that of the martyr who approaches his Lord through death; Bonnard, *Philippiens*, p. 75, mentions this interpretation but inclines against it.). Against this view Kümmel, *Promise*, p. 20, says that the eschatological tone cannot be so lightly set aside. The two ideas are, however, not incompatible. If the readiness of the Lord to hear the prayers of the faithful *were* in mind in Phil. 4, 5, it would be founded upon the eschatological nearness (near, though undelimited) which Kümmel (*Promise*, p. 20; cf. Bonnard, *Philippiens*, p. 75) takes to be primary.

[1] Cf. Bultmann, *Geschichte*, p. 128; Bornkamm, in *In Memoriam*, pp. 116 f.; Fuchs, in *V.F.* 1947-9, p. 76; Marxsen, *Markus, ad loc*; Grässer *Problem*, pp. 130f.; Conzelmann, *Mitte*, p. 88.

[2] Its *Sitz im Leben*, it is said, was the initial crisis facing the community through the non-arrival of the expected Parousia, and (it is further suggested) the saying is less general than Mk. 13, 30 and therefore reflects a situation where both disappointment at delay and hope in an imminent coming were both present.

The problem of authenticity does not here concern us; but cf. below, chapter 10, pp. 177ff.

[3] Cf. above, pp. 92ff.

[4] Besides the authorities cited above, p. 103, cf. Blunt, *Mark*, pp. 204f.; Gould, *Mark*, p. 159 (who connects with 8, 38 but not with 9, 2ff.); Klostermann, *Markus*, p. 96; Robinson, *Coming*, p. 54; Taylor, *Mark*, pp. 384f.

[5] The connection is, of course, indisputable in Mtt. 16, 28 which 'has undoubtedly taken it as a reference to the parousia' (Boobyer, *Transfiguration*, p. 60).

other hand to the Transfiguration (Mk. 9, 2ff.). Kümmel [1] and
Taylor [2] and others [3] think that the introductory formula καὶ
ἔλεγεν αὐτοῖς shows the saying to be a detached one. Nevertheless,
the link in the tradition appears firm enough and it must be given
due attention. Robinson [4] thinks the connection with 8, 38 artificial
since 8, 38 was 'added in the course of transmission.' But his arguments [5] are insufficient, and the connection to 8, 38 may well be
taken as authentic.[6] The link with 9, 2ff. is also firm. The temporal
statement (καὶ μετὰ ἡμέρας ἓξ) is unique [7] and Klostermann is no
doubt correct in thinking it refers back to Peter's confession
(8, 27f.) [8]—only he wrongly maintains that therefore Mk. 9, 1 was an
intrusion.[9]

---

[1] *Promise*, p. 25.

[2] *Mark*, p. 386.

[3] Blunt, *Mark*, pp. 204f.; Lohmeyer, *Markus*, p. 171; Hauck, *Markus*,
p. 105; Cranfield, *Mark*, p. 285.

[4] *Coming*, p. 54; similarly Taylor, *Mark*, ad loc.

[5] Robinson's two chief objections are a) that the usage 'of the Father'
τοῦ Πατρὸς here is 'unparalleled either in Jewish usage or in that of primitive
Christianity, for it equates God with 'the Father of the Son of Man', and b)
that the idea of the Son of Man as the coming judge conflicts with the earlier
tradition (represented, according to Robinson, by Mk. 8, 38; Mtt. 10, 32;
Lk. 12, 8; Mtt. 7, 22f; Lk. 13, 26f.) which represents God himself as the judge
(cf. *Coming*, p. 55). But the absence of the idea in the early church of 'Father
of the Son of Man' is accounted for by the non-usage of the term 'Son of
Man' (concerning τοῦ Πατρὸς in 8, 38 cf. most recently Van Iersel, *Der Sohn*,
pp. 103, 114f.). Concerning Robinson's second objection we cite Kümmel
(*Promise*, p. 45), '. . . the meaning (of Mk. 8, 38) is clear: whoever declares
himself for or against Jesus by open support or denial will meet with a
corresponding fate when the Son of Man appears in glory . . .' There is no
conflict here.

[6] Cf. Boobyer, *Transfiguration*, pp. 58f.; Lohmeyer, *Markus*, pp. 172f.,
Gould, *Mark*, p. 159; Robinson, *Problem*, p. 60. To be sure καὶ ἔλεγεν αὐτοῖς
reads like an editorial introduction, but this does not mean that Mark (or
his source) made a break in thought, nor that they misrepresented the
historical sequence.

[7] Cf. Hort, *Mark*, pp. 123f.; Taylor, *Mark*, p. 388; Ramsey, *Glory*, p. 113.
Lohmeyer, *Markus*, p. 173 (following Bacon, 'After six days' in *H.T.R.* 1915,
pp. 94ff.) thinks of it as a sacred-history sign (cf. Ex. 24, 15f.), but cf. Taylor,
Mark, p. 388 and Blunt, *Mark*, p. 205. Carrington, *Mark*, p. 190 (with
Riesenfeld) takes the reference as a calendrical one, and Branscomb, *Mark*,
p. 163, suggests 'perhaps in the original form of the story the voice to Jesus
and his disciples was 6 days after they went up the mount.' But both views
are rather fanciful.

[8] *Markus*, pp. 96f. cf. Taylor, *Mark*, p. 388; Cranfield, *Mark*, p. 289.

[9] The view that Mark saw the Transfiguration as a ratification of Peter's
confession is not incompatible with the view that he saw it, too, as a fulfilment in some sense of Mk. 9, 1 (cf. Boobyer, *Transfiguration*, p. 58).

If the context is taken fully into account, it suggests that the early church, so far as its views are reflected in the Synoptic tradition, did *not* regard this saying as a community-formulation sustaining it in its crisis, but as a promise fulfilled in some sense in the Transfiguration. This shows the unsatisfactory attempts to circumvent the apparent meaning of γεύσωνται θανάτου or ὧδε [1] to be entirely misplaced. This interpretation of Mk. 9, 1 is supported by tradition and by some modern scholars [2] and is not affected by the frequently raised objection [3] that τινες meant a lapse of some considerable time was anticipated prior to the fulfilment of Mk. 9, 1.[4]

In understanding Mk. 9, 1 in this way, the early church can hardly be said to have made poor sense either of Mk. 9, 1 or of the Transfiguration narrative. To be sure, not only because of the connection of Mk. 9, 1 with Mk. 8, 38, but also because the phrase

---

[1] Michaelis, *Verheissung*, p. 39 mentions (only to discard) the interpretation of γεύσωνται θανάτου here metaphorically (cf. Jn. 8, 52; 11, 26; Heb. 2, 9). In Jn. 8, 58 the argument hinges on the fact that the Jewish opponents understand γεύσωνται θανάτου as physical death; it is because 'Abraham is dead, and the prophets', yet Jesus says 'if a man keep my word he shall never taste of death' that the Jews retort 'now we know that thou hast a devil'. In Jn. 11, 26 Jesus may well be referring to spiritual death, but significantly, here he does *not* use the expression γεύσωνται θανάτου. Heb. 2, 9 is ambiguous. Behm (in *T.W.N.T.* I, p. 676) comments, 'Die Formel γεύσωνται θανάτου Mk. 9, 1 par, Jn. 8, 52 (vgl. das Logion P. Oxy 654; 5) Heb. 2, 9 . . . drückt wie ἰδεῖν oder θεωρεῖν θάνατον (Heb. 11, 5; Lk. 2, 26; Jn. 8, 51) mit sinnlicher Kraft die harte, schmerzvolle Wirklichkeit des Sterbens aus, die der Mensch erfahrt, die auch Jesus erlitten hat (vgl. Heb. 2, 9).'

Michaelis, *Verheissung*, p. 34, suggests taking ὧδε in a non-spatial sense as 'thus' and τῶν ἐστηκότων in the sense of 'those who stand as distinct from those who fall', and suggests that the saying meant 'some, at the End, will be so abiding (in faith) that they will be saved'. But probably ὧδε has a spatial force here (cf. μετ' ἐμοῦ in D 565), and, although ἵστημι is used in the N.T. of 'standing firm' (Mtt. 12, 25. 12, 26; Lk. 21, 36) the large majority of occurrences have the meaning 'being present'. There is nothing to suggest the minority usage is intended in Mk. 9, 1. Kümmel, *Promise*, p. 28, n. 33, rightly describes the suggestion as 'untenable'; cf. Cranfield, *Mark*. p. 286.

[2] Taylor, *Mark*, p. 385, mentions Chrysostom, Theophylact, Euthymius and Theodotus. Cf. also Boobyer, *Transfiguration*, pp. 27f; Barth, *C.D.* III/2, p. 499,; Cranfield, *Mark*, p. 288.

[3] Cf. Hort, *Mark*, p. 123; Gould, *Mark*, p. 159; Murray, *Future*, p. 185; Michaelis, *Verheissung*, p. 35; Kümmel, *Promise*, p. 27.; Lagrange, *Marc*, p. 227; Bornkamm, in *In Memoriam*, p. 118; Cullmann, *Early Church*, p. 152.

[4] It is not said in Mk. 9, 1 that death would exclude certain ones from seeing the awaited event (Schlatter, *Markus, ad loc*, suggests it was a question of election). The basis of selection is left entirely neutral (cf. Cranfield, *Mark*, p. 288; M. Barth, *Augenzeuge*, pp. 87ff).

ἕως ἂν ἴδωσιν τὴν βασιλείαν τοῦ θεοῦ suggests the Parousia. The Transfiguration story itself is full of overtones suggesting the Parousia; μετεμορφώθη,[1] the cloud [2] and the voice [3] all hint at the Parousia.[4] The manifestation of Christ in power in the Transfiguration scene was only temporary; but it was a *real* manifestation and therefore, in some sense, a real anticipation of the Parousia. Characteristic of the final End event is its manifest quality and its Christocentricity;[5] the Transfiguration exhibits both qualities. The central figure is without question Jesus himself, and the emphasis throughout is upon the visible nature of the occurrence.[6] The mention of Moses and Elijah can be accounted for on this view, though their presence has often proved difficult.[7] They are not merely 'predecessors and precursors of the Messiah',[8] but representatives of the Sovereignty of God as it *was* expressed in the old covenant, assembled with him in whom, in the new covenant, the Kingdom is present.[9]

The parallels, Mtt. 16, 28 and Lk. 9, 27, arouse some discussion. Matthew identifies τὴν βασιλείαν τοῦ θεοῦ ἐληλυθυῖαν explicitly with

---

[1] Omitted by Luke. Cf. Rom. 12, 2; II Cor. 3, 18. Here emphasis lies upon the *visible nature* of the transformation.

[2] The νεφέλη is reminiscent of the O.T. image of God's self-revelation and self-veiling (cf. Ex. 13, 21. 16, 10. 19, 9 etc). It is also a significant link with 8, 38; cf. Mk. 13, 26. 14, 62; (cf. further Oepke, in *T.W.N.T.* IV, pp. 910ff.).

[3] Boobyer, *Transfiguration*, p. 64f., tentatively suggests a link with the expected φωνή at the Parousia (cf. I Thess. 4, 16) though this is unlikely on account of the words spoken here (Mk. 9, 7) compared with the speaker in I Thess. 4, 16. However, the link with Mk. 8, 38 is again important. Not only does the confirmation of Sonship reflect 8, 38, but the command ἀκούετε αὐτοῦ appears to confirm the challenge of 8, 38.

[4] Boobyer, *Transfiguration*, pp. 64ff., finds other links, but in some cases rather tenuous ones. Nevertheless his conclusion seems to be justified, 'For Mark, then, it seems, the transfiguration prophesies the parousia in the sense that it is a portrayal of what Christ will be at that day, and is in some degree a miniature picture of the whole second advent scene.' (p. 87). Similarly, Ramsey, *Glory*, p. 118; Cranfield, *Mark*, pp. 286f.

[5] Cf. above, chapter 7, pp. 104ff.

[6] Cf. μετεμορφώθη ἔμπροσθεν αὐτῶν v. 2; ὤφθη αὐτοῖς v. 4; and εἶδον vv. 8, 9.

[7] For those who take the Transfiguration narrative as a resurrection story, it is of foremost difficulty. But even Boobyer, it seems, does not explain their presence very satisfactorily (*Transfiguration*, pp. 67ff.) True, Mtt. 8, 11, Lk. 13, 28f, suggest the presence of the Patriarchs and Prophets in the Kingdom; but why Moses and Elijah in particular?

[8] Ramsey, *Glory*, p. 114; following Jeremias, in *T.W.N.T.* II, pp. 930f.

[9] He who came 'not to destroy the law and the prophets, but to fulfil', Mtt. 5, 17.

Jesus, and it has been customary to view this as an explicit reference to the Parousia.[1] Such a view is difficult, however, unless the promise contained in Mtt. 16, 28 is regarded as in some sense fulfilled in the Transfiguration, for on the traditional dating of this gospel [2] eye-witnesses would by then have been few and the text should have been growing increasingly embarrassing.[3] Recently some scholars [4] have suggested that Matthew regarded the saying as fulfilled in the Resurrection and in this has imposed his own particular theology upon Mk. 9, 1; this theology, it is said, held that, 'Die gegenwärtige Kirche ist . . . . die βασιλεία des Menschensohnes, aber nicht identisch mit der Schar derer die in die Gottesherschafft eingehen'; [5] and this Kingdom of the Son of Man was inaugurated in the Resurrection and Ascension.[6] But this interpretation we find unacceptable,[7] because (a) the expression 'in his Kingdom' (ἐν τῇ βασιλείᾳ αὐτοῦ) is probably an explication of Mark's meaning, for Mark certainly links the thought of the Kingdom of God directly with Jesus himself (cf Mk. 3, 21ff.), and speaks of sending angels to gather *his* (the Son of Man's) elect (Mk. 13, 27); and because (b) it is doubtful if Matthew distinguishes between the Kingdom of God and the Kingdom of the Son in the way Bornkamm suggests, for in Mtt. 12, 28, for example, it is the 'Kingdom of God' which is mentioned;[8] and because (c) the reference in Mtt. 16, 28 is still to

---

[1] Cf. Glasson, *Advent*, p. 72 (who says Mtt. has introduced the Parousia into a saying where it was absent in Mk.; similarly Robinson, *Coming*, p. 53); Fison, *Hope*, p. 189; Kümmel, *Promise*, p. 27; Schniewind, *Matthäus*, p. 193; Filson, *Matthew*, p. 190; Allen, *Matthew*, p. 183; M'Neile, *Matthew* p. 248.

[2] Kilpatrick, *Origins*, pp. 127ff., dates the gospel between 90 and 100 A.D. Bacon, *Studies*, pp. 63ff., similarly. M'Neile, *Matthew*, p. xxiv, suggests not earlier than 80 and not later than 100 A.D. (contrast Allen, *Matthew*, pp. lxxxivf., who dates the gospel between 65 and 75 A.D.).

[3] Cf. Michaelis, *Matthäus, ad loc.*

[4] Cf. esp. Bornkamm's contributions, 'Enderwartung und Kirche im Matthäusevangelium', in *T.L.* LXXIX, 1954, pp. 34ff.; in *Dodd Festschrift*, pp. 222ff.; in *Überlieferung und Auslegung* (with G. Barth and H. J. Held), pp. 11f.; cf. also G. Barth, in *Überlieferung und Auslegung* pp. 54ff.; Stonehouse, *Matthew and Mark*, p. 240.

[5] Bornkamm, in *Überlieferung und Auslegung*, p. 40.

[6] Cf. Bornkamm, in *Überlieferung und Auslegung*, pp. 20f.

[7] Regarding the questionable methodology involved in redactional criticism, cf. above, pp. 70f.

[8] G. Barth, in *Überlieferung und Auslegung*, p. 125, admits, 'Zu einer terminologischen Unterscheidung zwischen der gegenwärtigen Königsherrschaft Jesu Christi und der zukünftigen βασιλεία τῶν οὐρανῶν hat es Matthäus jedoch nicht gebracht.'

the Parousia, and it is the Transfiguration which, in the first place
provides a proleptic manifestation of that event. It is, however, to
be noted that even if it were clear that Matthew had consciously
imposed his own theology upon Mk. 9, 1, it would not follow that he
had done so *because Mk. 9, 1 was, for him, problematical.* There is
no compulsion to see here evidence of a crisis provoked by the
Parousia delay, nor evidence that Mk. 9, 1 is being understood in a
way different from Mark's own interpretation.

Lk. 9, 27 is also understood by a number of recent scholars [1] as
evidence that Mk. 9, 1 was causing acute embarrassment in the early
church. Conzelmann thinks Mk. 9, 1 an initial explanation of the
Parousia delay which, by Luke's time was no longer any help; 'man
brauchte eine neue Lösung.' [2] But against this line of interpretation
we must note first that the context remains just as pronounced here
as in Mark and Matthew [3] and therefore the link with the coming
of the Son of Man in the glory of the Father, and the link with the
Transfiguration, is still suggested. Secondly, we may ask, if Mk. 9, 1
was really the problem Conzelmann and others suggest it was,
why has Luke not dealt more radically with it? Conzelmann [4] argues,
'Das Ende ist ja noch länger ausgeblieben; man brauchte eine
neue Lösung. Soll diese dauerhaft sein, so darf sie nicht wieder
der Bedrohung durch weitere Verzögerung ausgesetzt sein. Sie
muss also auf Angabe eines bestimmten Termins überhaupt ver-
zichten. Sie muss aber diesen Verzicht begründen können', But
Luke's easiest solution, surely, would have been to have omitted
Mk. 9, 1 altogether.[5] It is still preferable to understand Lk. 9, 27

---

[1] Cf. esp. Conzelmann, *Mitte*, pp. 95f.; Grässer, *Problem*, pp. 178ff.; Bornkamm, in *In Memoriam*, pp. 116ff.

[2] *Mitte*, p. 95. One notes how hypothetical the argument is, for Mk. 9, 1
is being understood as definitely a community-formulation, 'in der Zeit
entstanden, als man noch auf das Eintreten der Parusie in der ersten Generation, nämlich am Ende derselben, hoffen konnte' (*Mitte*, p. 95, n. 1,). If
Mk. 9, 1 is *not* so interpreted, then the Lukan variant would take on a quite
different significance.

[3] Lk. has ὡσεὶ ἡμέρα ὀκτώ but Klostermann's comment (*Lukas*, p. 107;
Matthäus, p. 142) 'sachlich mit Mc.Mtt. übereinstimmend', is probably right
(cf. Plummer, *Luke*, p. 280). Mtt. and Lk. omit Mk's καὶ ἔλεγεν αὐτοῖς and
so make the link with the preceding section even more definite.

[4] *Mitte*, p. 95.

[5] Lk. has omitted elsewhere often enough! Conzelmann himself has
collected a number of sayings (cf. *Mitte*, pp. 92ff.; also Grässer, *Problem*,
pp. 178ff.) which, he maintains, emphasise the Parousia delay, so that it
would, on his own thesis, have been enough, surely, for Lk to have omitted
Mk. 9, 1.

as a reference to the Parousia in some sense, because Luke still speaks of '*seeing* the Kingdom of God.' In 9, 26 he speaks of Jesus' glory, and in 9, 32 it is this glory which the disciples see (εἶδαν) on the mount of Transfiguration. Conzelmann [1] interprets εἶδαν thus: 'Der Ausdruck "das Reich Sehen" besagt, dass das Reich zwar *nicht sichtbar*, aber *sehbar* geworden ist. Was heisst das nun? Die Antwort liegt im heilsgeschichtlichen Verständnis des Lebens Jesu als der ausgegrenzten Darstellung des Heils innerhalb des Ganges der Heilsgeschichte. An ihm ist zu sehen, was das Reich ist. Es war in der Person Jesu anschaulich und wird am Ende der Zeiten wieder erscheinen . . .' But, whilst it is true that Luke speaks of seeing in connection with the salvation-historical significance of Jesus during his earthly ministry,[2] in 13, 28 (17, 22) and 21, 27, where 'seeing' is connected explicitly with 'the Kingdom of God' or 'the Son of Man in glory', it is clearly the future, final manifestation to which Luke here refers. Besides, we must note, as we did concerning Matthew, that even if Luke *has* consciously imposed a new significance upon Mk. 9, 1, it does not follow that he has done so because Mk. 9, 1 was an embarrassing problem for him or for those for whom Luke's gospel was written.

We therefore maintain that evidence of a delimited expectation in the early church is not forthcoming in Mk. 9, 1 or its parallels.

Mark 13, 30 par.

Is this saying evidence of a delimited Parousia expectation? [3] Two problems must be discussed in order to obtain an answer. The first is the meaning of ἡ γενεὰ αὕτη. Schniewind [4] and others [5] interpret the phrase of the Jewish nation, understood especially as the 'faithless nation'.[6] Others [7] understand it as mankind in

---

[1] *Mitte*, p. 96.

[2] Cf. esp. 2, 30 and 10, 35. 13, 15 could be included if it were not so ambiguous; however, 19, 38 suggests that it is right to see in 13, 35 a reference to the 'Palm Sunday' story. 17, 22 would be applicable on Conzelmann's understanding of it (*Mitte*, p. 96, n. 3) but if we take vv. 26ff. as interpreting v. 22 rather than v. 25, then the verse tells rather against Conzelmann.

[3] Regarding authenticity, cf. below, chapter 10, pp. 179ff.

[4] *Markus*, pp. 175f.

[5] Cf. Lohmeyer, *Markus*, pp. 281f.; Meinertz, *Theologie*, I, p. 61; Flückiger, *Ursprung*, pp. 116f. (Murray, *Future*, p. 260, cites other, older authorities.)

[6] Schniewind thinks then that Mtt. 10, 23 is support, for he takes this to mean that unbelieving Jews will persist until the End; and Rom. 9-11 is, he thinks, a Pauline version or parallel.

[7] Jerome saw it as a possible view; Bede too. Lowrie, *Mark*, p. 477 acknow-

general, whilst yet others [1] understand 'the faithful' and so 'the church'. Murray's arguments [2] against all such interpretations need no repetition, and his conclusion, that ἡ γενεὰ αὕτη means Jesus' contemporaries [3] is shared by many.[4]

The second problem is the meaning of ταῦτα πάντα. This *could* be taken to refer to the entire discourse, vv. 5-27. Many understand it so.[5] But against it is the fact that ταῦτα (πάντα) in v. 30 must 'have a similar reference, at any rate as understood by the Evangelist' [6] as the ταῦτα in v. 29; in v. 29 it is clear that the reference is only to the events *preceding* the End itself.[7] Beasley-Murray [8] objects that the addition of πάντα in v. 30 rules out any limitation of the reference to exclude vv. 24-27. However, if the reference of ταῦτα in v. 29 *is* taken as being the events preceding the End only, the πάντα of v. 30 can be understood as emphasising that *all* the 'signs' of the End (vv. 5-23) are to come upon the contemporary generation.[9] Kümmel [10] thinks it wrong to tie the exegesis down to its immediate context, which, he says, 'overlooks the original independence of the verse'. Nevertheless this context must be taken serious-

---

ledges that γενεά can mean contemporaries but adds, 'But it may equally well be translated by "age" which one can stretch much further, even infinitely far: and it seems to me more honest to give the Lord the benefit of the doubt.'

[1] Theophylact, Origen, Chrysostom, Victor of Antioch; and cf. Swete, *Mark*, p. 296; Michaelis, *Verheissung*, p. 31 (citing Luther as support). But Michaelis is reported as retracting (cf. Murray, *Mk.* 13, p. 100).

[2] *Mk.* 13, pp. 99f.

[3] Cf. esp. the other instances of the phrase ἡ γενεὰ αὕτη; Mk. 8, 38, Mtt. 11, 16. 12, 41, 42; 45. 23, 36; Lk. 11, 50. 17, 25. Cf. Buchsel, in *T.W.N.T.* I, pp. 661f.

[4] Cf. Cullmann, *Early Church*, pp. 150f.; Walter, *Kommen*, p. 81; Kümmel, *Promise*, p. 61; Klostermann, *Markus*, p. 154; Branscomb, *Mark*, p. 239; Menzies, *Earliest Gospel*, p. 241; Gould, *Mark*, p. 253, Lagrange, *Marc*, p. 348.

[5] Cf. Beasley-Murray, *Mk.* 13, pp. 100f.; Allen, *Mark, ad loc*; Kümmel, *Promise*, p. 60; Gould, *Mark*, p. 253; Lohmeyer, *Markus*, p. 282; Taylor *Mark*, p. 521; Ridderbos, *De Komst*, pp. 422f.; Cullmann, *Early Church*, pp. 150f.

[6] Barth, *C.D.* III/2, p. 500.

[7] Cf. Calvin, *Harmony*, III, pp. 151f.; Cranfield, *Mark*, p. 409; Schmid, *Markus, ad loc*; Michaelis, *Verheissung*, pp. 30f. Robinson, *Coming*, p. 86, too, but only by counting vv. 24-27 as spurious.

[8] *Mk.* 13, pp. 100f., with Lohmeyer and Allen.

[9] That the evangelist viewed πάντα in such a way is perhaps supported by the variations, cf. further below, p. 136.

[10] *Promise*, p. 60.

ly.[1] Kümmel further suggests that 'it would be a remarkable statement that definite events previous to the end will be limited to the period of this γενεά, without making a pronouncement about the actual moment of the end which alone is of importance'.[2] However, it is not here suggested that Mk. 13, 30 refers to specific events [3] but rather to the entire complex of events which may be termed 'signs of the end' and which are to be experienced, though not necessarily exhausted by,[4] the contemporary generation. In further answer to Kümmel's criticism, we suggest that an answer concerning the 'when' of the Parousia's coming is *not* lacking from the discourse but has an independent answer (vv. 32ff.), just as vv. 24-27 are distinct from vv. 5-23.

In support of this understanding of Mk. 13, 30 we discuss here briefly, the structure of Mk. 13.[5] Many scholars maintain that the discourse is at variance with itself, either because v. 32 is, they argue, irreconcilable with v. 30,[6] or because the idea of a sequence of events prior to the Parousia is thought incompatible with its sudden arrival.[7]

It is true that a series of time references runs through the discourse,[8] but it is doubtful indeed if these 'editorial touches trans-

---

[1] We discuss below the pattern of the whole discourse; cf. p. 134.

[2] *Promise*, p. 60.

[3] As Taylor, *Mark*, p. 521, says was originally the case. Feuillet, (in *R.B.* LVI, 1949, pp. 84ff., etc.), Jones, (in *Scripture*, IV, 1951, pp. 264f.), Lagrange, (*Marc*, p. 348) and others, interpret Mk. 13, 30 of the Fall of Jerusalem. But cf. above, chapter 7, p. 104. Lightfoot, (*Gospel Message*, p. 54), M. Barth (*Augenzeuge*, pp. 125ff.) (and cf. K. Barth, *C.D.* III/2, p. 501) think that Mk. 13, 30 should be referred to the Resurrection, at least as an initial fulfilment. But whilst this may have been present in the Evangelist's mind (we note that there is here no mention of 'seeing' but of events 'coming to pass'), it is better to regard the reference of 13, 30 as the entire section, vv. 5-23.

[4] Therefore Beasley-Murray, *Mk.* 13, p. 101, is wrong in saying, 'if the signs are to happen within the generation, the End is also expected to fall within the same period.'

[5] The theory of a little apocalypse underlying Mark is of no account at this point; but cf. regarding this, and the question of authenticity, below, chapter 10, pp. 179ff.

[6] Cf. Branscomb, *Mark*, p. 231; Blunt, *Mark*, p. 242.

[7] Robinson, *Coming*, p. 127; Kümmel, *Promise*, p. 97; Taylor, *Mark*, pp. 523f.

[8] Cf. οὔπω τὸ τέλος v. 7. ἀρχὴ ὠδίνων ταῦτα v. 8: εἰς πάντα τὰ ἔθνη πρῶτον δεῖ v. 10: καὶ ὅταν ἄγωσιν v. 11 ὁ δὲ ὑπομείνας εἰς τέλος v. 13: ὅταν ... τότε ... v. 14. εἰ μὴ ἐκολόβωσεν κύριος τὰς ἡμέρας v. 20: ἐν ἐκείναις ταῖς ἡμέραις μετὰ τὴν θλῖψιν v. 24: καὶ τότε ὄψονται v. 26: καὶ τότε ἀποστελεῖ v. 27: cf. also v. 30, v. 32, vv. 35f.

form the marks of time into a carefully graduated programme'.[1]
We certainly miss here the exact and somewhat esoteric temporal
references common in apocalyptic,[2] and the idea of a sudden coming
of the Parousia is compatible with preceding signs. Of course there
is no going back on Jesus' refusal elsewhere to give 'signs'.[3] But
this, the refusal to make faith easy, and so to annihilate the essential nature and possibility of faith, is not to be confused with the
admonition to recognise the true significance of events.

That v. 32 is reconcilable with v. 30 is, we suggest, apparent
through an analysis of the chapter and its structure. The pattern
of the discourse is as follows:

vv.   1- 4 Introduction. The question raised in v. 4 [4] leading to a
discourse on the End and its date, and the Signs of the
End and their dates.

vv.   5-23 The Signs of the End 'enframed at either end by warnings
against the seduction of false messiahs and prophets
with their fictitious claim ἐγώ εἰμι (vv. 5-6 and 21-23)'.[5]

vv.   24-27 The End itself.

vv.   28-31 Regarding the time of the Signs of the End, and their
significance for perceiving the time of the End itself.

vv.   32-37 Regarding the time of the End event.[6]

This pattern [7] exhibits the relationship of v. 30 to v. 32. Both the
signs and the End itself are given a time reference. But whereas

---

[1] Robinson, *Coming*, p. 127. Against him, cf. Beasley-Murray, *Future*,
pp. 214f.; Michaelis, *Verheissung*, pp. 21f.; Busch, *Zum Verständnis*; Cranfield, 'St .Mark xiii', in *S.J.T.* VI, pp. 189ff., 287ff., VII, pp. 284ff.

[2] Cf. e.g. Rev. 12, 14. 13, 5. Manson, in *Eschatology*, pp. 15f.

[3] Cf. Lk. 17, 20; Mk. 8, 12; Jn. 4, 48; etc.

[4] Posed by the prediction of the Temple's destruction (v. 2) and because
of the eschatological significance of this (cf. Schrenk, in *T.W.N.T.* III,
pp. 238ff.)

[5] Barth, *C.D.* III/2, p. 500.

[6] Including a threefold admonition to 'watch' (vv. 33, 35, 37) which
appropriately concludes the discourse.

[7] Lightfoot, *Gospel Message*, p. 49, and Lohmeyer, *Markus*, p. 267, wrongly
divide thus: vv. 5-13 the beginning of the consummation. vv. 14-27 the
consummation itself. vv. 28-37 warnings regarding the consummation.
Albertz, *Botschaft*, I/1, pp. 180f., more correctly argues that 'Nach einer
kurzen Einleitung 13; 3-4 werden die beiden Fragen behandelt: *Was* kommt
13; 5-27 und; *Wann* kommt's 13; 28-37?' He does not, however cross refer
the two sections in the second group to the two sections in the first, as we
suggest is correct. He simply divides each group into seven, '. . . in Anlehnung
an den apokalyptischen Gebrauch der Siebenzahl . . .

the signs will occur within the immediate future (though not necessarily exhausted by that immediate future), the End itself is not so delimited. In both cases a parable is attached to enforce the significance of this time reference. The events of vv. 5-23 are 'signs', as the fig-tree is a sign, that 'he is nigh, even at the doors'. In the case of the End itself, the short parable of the returning lord is equally appropriate: he *will* return, but since his servants do not know when, they must constantly be on watch.

Thus it is reasonable to interpret Mk. 13, 30 as not providing a delimited expectation of the Parousia. The question remains whether by their alterations, Matthew and Luke provide evidence that Mk. 13. 30 *was* understood as signifying a delimited hope which, for the later Evangelists, was problematical.

We turn first to Mtt. 24, 34. G. Barth [1] maintains, 'Bei Mtt. tritt die Naherwartung zurück, die Paränese tritt in den Vordergrund.' If he is right, it would be very surprising indeed for Matthew to include v. 34 in the discourse, if this *were* understood, either by him or by the early church as a whole, as expressing a delimited Parousia expectation. It would be insufficient to contend that Matthew, by the addition of parables emphasising delay [2] has counterbalanced the effect of v. 34 (as Bornkamm holds),[3] since if Mk. 13, 30 really meant what Bornkamm suggests it did, it would have required much more radical treatment than mere counterbalancing.

Next, Lk. 21, 32. Conzelmann [4] thinks Mk. 13, 30 expressed a delimited expectation which Luke found problematical and removed by means of two expedients. The first is the new meaning (according to Conzelmann)[5] which Luke gave to γενεά, namely 'humanity in general'; but, in fact, an examination of Luke's use of this word tells against Conzelmann's thesis.[6] The second is the omission of

---

[1] *Überlieferung und Auslegung*, p. 51.
[2] A questionable interpretation of Mtt. 25; but cf. below, pp. 202ff.
[3] In *In Memoriam*, pp. 116f.
[4] *Mitte*, pp. 107ff.
[5] *Mitte*, p. 122.
[6] Mk. 8, 12; par Mtt. 16, 4 (cf. 12, 39); Lk. 11, 29. It is not Lk. but Mtt. who alters Mk's explicit ἡ γενεὰ αὕτη to simple γενεά. Lk. 11, 31; 32 show no difference from Mtt. 12, 41, 42, and the omission of Mtt.'s final phrase (14, 25) is insignificant.

Mk. 8, 38 uses the phrase, but Lk. *and* Mtt. omit, so no conclusion can be drawn for a specific Lukan usage.

Mk. 9, 19 is paralleled exactly, Mtt. 17, 17; Lk. 9, 41.

ταῦτα which Conzelmann argues allows πάντα to relate ". . . nicht auf die berichteten Einzelheiten, sondern auf das Ganze des gött- lichen Planes'.[1] However, in its context Lk. 21, 23, if an expression for the entire sweep of salvation-history, would appear to embrace the events of vv. 27-28, and so to delimit *the End also* to the con- temporary generation! (since we cannot accept Conzelmann's interpretation of γενεά here). In fact, the omission of ταῦτα is probably to be understood as a stylistic alteration [2] signifying no alteration of Mark's meaning, namely that the *signs* of the End will come upon that generation.

There is, therefore, no reason to see a Parousia-delay crisis loo- ming behind Mk. 13,30 or its parallels.

Mark 14,25 par.

Two questions concern us here. The first is, to what future event does the saying refer? Many [3] think there is no reference to the Parousia at all. Others [4] hold that the Parousia is only indirectly in mind, the primary reference being to the Resurrection; (meals prior to the Ascension [5] are regarded as an initial fulfilment.) We suggest that the primary reference is, in fact, the Parousia. The expression τῆς ἡμέρας ἐκείνης is most naturally understood of the final Day of the Lord [6] and since 'that day' is hardly essential to the

---

Mk. 13, 30 (the case in question) is also exactly paralleled.

Lk. 11, 50-51 shows some variation from Mtt. 23, 35-36, but the use of γενεά remains exactly similar. The same is true of Lk. 7, 31 Mtt. 11, 16.

Lk. 16, 8 does not refer to the contemporary generation, but neither does it refer to 'humanity in general'.

Lk. 17, 25, against Conzelmann, means the contemporaries under whom the Son of Man suffered.

Lk. 1, 48; 50 would support Conzelmann, except that the problem of compilation (cf. e.g. Creed, *Luke, ad loc*) makes this indecisive for specific Lukan usage.

[1] *Mitte*, p. 122.

[2] Mk. 13, 29 has ταῦτα followed in v. 30 by ταῦτα πάντα. Mtt. has changed this rather unbalanced form by using πάντα ταῦτα both times (Mtt. 24, 33-34). Lk. on the other hand has also smoothed the style but by a different ex- pedient; he has shortened Mk. using Mk's ταῦτα in 21, 31 and his πάντα in 21, 32, thereby retaining the overall sense of ταῦτα πάντα.

[3] Cf. Glasson, *Advent*, p. 114; Dodd, *Parables*, p. 56; Robinson, *Coming*, pp. 42, 149.

[4] Cf. Barth, *C.D.* III/2, p. 502; Cranfield, *Mark*, p. 428; M. Barth, *Abend- mahl*, pp. 43f.

[5] Cf. Lk. 24, 31-35, Jn. 21, 5; 12; 15, Act. 1, 4. 10, 41.

[6] Cf. ביום ההוא e.g. Is. 2, 11; Jer. 4, 9; Amos 2, 16; etc. or the plural בימים ההם e.g. Jer. 31, 29; 33, 15; Joel 3, 1; etc. Contrast Robinson, *Coming*,

contrast being drawn, should be taken in this way. Further, the word καινὸν should be taken as expressing otherness[1] and πίνω καινὸν ἐν τῇ βασιλείᾳ τοῦ θεοῦ suggests the expected Messianic banquet.[2] Perhaps a *secondary* reference might be the Resurrection and the post-resurrection meals.[3]

The second question is, whether there is any temporal delimitation? Schweitzer [4] understood it as delimiting the expectation of the Parousia, and M. Barth [5] though referring the saying to the Resurrection, also thinks it carries a temporal delimitation. Kümmel [6] seems to think a certain interval is presupposed, neither very long nor very short. But whilst the verse clearly foresees a period of separation from the disciples, 'über die Dauer dieser Trennung wird freilich nichts ausgesagt. Dass sie sehr kurz sein soll ergibt sich aus unserem Text nicht.' [7] Jeremias [8] has conclusively

---

p. 42, n. 1 (but in 2, 20 with which Robinson compares this expression, 'that day' is essential to the point).

[1] Cf. Swete, *Mark, ad loc*; Cadoux, *Theology*, p. 47; Michaelis, *Verheissung*, p. 28, Jeremias, *Eucharistic Words*, p. 172. Black, *Aramaic Approach*, pp. 71f., suggests 'until I am renewed in the Kingdom of God' as the meaning of the Aramaic. Our argument is not affected.

[2] Cf. Mtt. 22, 1-14. 26, 29; Lk. 14, 15. 22, 30; Rev. 19, 9. Dalman, *Words*, pp. 110ff.; Lohmeyer, *Markus*, p. 304; S.-B. *Kommentar*, IV, pp. 1154ff. For this imagery in the Qumran sect cf. Cullmann, in *J.B.L.* LXXIV, 1955, p. 215.

[3] Though Calvin's suggestion may still be the clue regarding these post-resurrection meals; cf. *Harmony*, III, p. 211.

The church's celebration of the last supper may similarly be understood (as indeed it was from early days—cf. Dix, *Shape of the Liturgy*, pp. 259ff.) as, in a sense, a fulfilment of this verse: a fulfilment which points to further and final fulfilment. But the reference to a repeated 'last supper' is hardly primary (contrast Carrington, *Mark*, p. 317).

[4] Cf. *Mystery*, p. 89; similarly Menzies, *Earliest Gospel*, pp. 224f.; Grässer, *Problem*, pp. 53f.

[5] *Abendmahl*, p. 43.

[6] *Promise*, p. 77. Actually, Kümmel appears to have three views concerning this verse. On p. 32 he says 'it is equally clear that Jesus foresees between his imminent death and this eschatological "coming" a certain interval of time about the length of which nothing is said in this word.' On p. 31, '. . . it follows that Jesus expects the coming of the Kingdom of God to be in the near future, and that he feels it to be so near that he can impress its proximity on his disciples by limiting his abstinence to the dawning of the Kingdom of God.' And on p. 77, 'the prediction . . . has meaning in fact only if the Kingdom of God is not expected in the most immediate future and if the disciples are to come together for meals for some time without their departed Lord. So the expectation of a *considerable interval* . . . is evident. (My italics).

[7] Bosch, *Heidenmission*, p. 180; cf. Lohmeyer, *Markus*, p. 305.

[8] *Eucharistic Words*, pp. 165ff. cf. Leaney, *Luke*, p. 267; Kümmel, *Promise*, p. 31; Cranfield, *Mark*, p. 428; Barth, *C.D.* III/2, p. 603.

shown that the verse is a vow of abstinence; the most natural understanding of this vow is that Jesus, recognising that 'his hour' (Jn. 13, 1) was imminent and that death was at hand, dedicated himself to this vocation.[1] Death was so near that he could make this his last meal. There is, however, no indication at all when the next, the καινός meal would take place. It is simply said that the time had arrived for ordinary human sustenance to be no longer appropriate or necessary.

This brings us to the parallels. Mtt. 26, 29 is essentially the same.[2] The addition of μεθ' ὑμῶν makes explicit what is already implicit in Mark; and the substitution of ἀπ' ἄρτι for Mark's οὐκέτι is best understood as a stylistic alteration.[3] Luke too, in 22, 18,[4] substitutes for reasons of style ἀπὸ τοῦ νῦν for Mark's οὐκέτι. Still the meaning is that from the time of that meal onwards, that which sustains human life would have no place or necessity in Jesus' life.[5] Conzelmann [6] thinks that Luke has toned down the idea of the nearness of the Parousia, particularly in his expression ἕως οὗ ἡ βασιλεία τοῦ θεοῦ ἔλθῃ. But the allusion would still appear to be to the Parousia and an awaited Messianic meal.[7] It is apparent that for all three Evangelists the vow cannot have meant a Parousia Nächsterwartung,[8] and we find no good reason for supposing this saying held any delimited expectation for them at all.

---

[1] Cf. Jeremias, *Eucharistic Words*, p. 171, 'Jesus . . . prepares himself with a resolute will to drink the bitter cup which the Father offers Him.'

[2] Not insignificantly, the volume *Überlieferung und Auslegung* nowhere discusses this verse.

[3] Cf. Lagrange, *Matthieu*, p. 498; Mtt. uses ἀπ' ἄρτι 7 times, Mk. and Lk. not at all. Luke uses ἀπὸ τοῦ νῦν 5 times, Mtt. and Mk. not at all.

[4] Most agree that Mk. follows a primary tradition over against Lk. cf. Jeremias, *Eucharistic Words*, pp. 87ff., 118ff. for the evidence.

[5] It is doubtful whether the post-resurrection meals are intended to be understood as necessary to Jesus' life; cf. above p. 137.

[6] *Mitte*, p. 106.

[7] Plummer, *Luke*, p. 495, thinks the allusion cannot be to such a messianic meal; he thinks it impossible because 'if αὐτὸ means the paschal lamb, in what sense could Jesus partake of that in the future?' He himself, however, in referring to the fulfilment of the saying in terms of the Christian Eucharist, obviously extends the meaning. Cf. Manson, *Luke*, p. 239; Jeremias, *Eucharistic Words*, pp. 116, 172.

[8] Else why have they included the saying? Similarly a *Nächsterwartung* is excluded from Mk. 14, 28 par., simply by the fact that the Evangelists record it. This reference, in any case, is perhaps best regarded as a prediction of the Resurrection, or of the gentile mission (cf. Schweitzer, *Mystery*, p. 144; Lohmeyer, *Markus*, p. 312, who interpret as *Nächsterwartung*).

Mark 14, 62 *par.*

Once more we pose the question, Does this verse speak of a delimited Parousia expectation? A number of critics find, in fact, no reference here to the Parousia [1] but this view seems unlikely to be correct.[2] Some argue [3] that Luke and Matthew speak only of an immediate exaltation (and that Mark omitted the phrase ἀπ' ἄρτι (ἀπὸ τοῦ νῦν) to conform with Mk. 13, 26 and the idea of the Son of Man being seen at the End. But the Matthean and Lukan variations are readily understandable [4] and there is not sufficient reason for taking the Markan version here as secondary.[5]

Robinson [6] maintains that ἐκ δεξιῶν καθημένων τῆς δυνάμεως and ἐρχόμενον μετὰ τῶν νεφελῶν τοῦ οὐρανοῦ are parallel expressions, one static and the other dynamic, for the same conviction, namely vindication. The allusion to Ps. 110, 1 certainly suggests coronation (and so, vindication); but the imagery of the Psalm is also strongly reminiscent of the awaited final Messianic reign, open and manifest and universal.[7] Similarly Dan. 7, 13 is not exhausted by the idea of vindication but points to the End manifestation of God's rule. Glasson [8] argues that Dan. 7, 13 does not suggest a *descent*; however, the whole scene of Dan. 7 is enacted *on earth* so that although the

---

Taylor, *Mark*, p. 549, Cranfield, *Mark*, p. 429 and Lagrange, *Marc*, p. 384, take it as a reference to the Resurrection appearances (which fits well with the context, and means taking προάξω in a temporal rather than spatial sense, which is permissible (cf. Mk. 6, 45); Hoskyns and Davey, *John*, pp. 425f., and Evans, in *J.T.S.* V, 1954, pp. 3ff., take προάξω in a spatial sense and think in terms of the Gentile mission in which Jesus leads the disciples. (Surprisingly Bosch, *Heidenmission*, makes no mention of Mk. 14, 28. 16, 7; Mtt. 26, 32. 28, 7.)

[1] Cf. Feuillet, in *R.B.* LVI, 1949, pp. 72ff.; Guy, *Last Things*, pp. 76ff.; Walter, *Kommen*, p. 90; Taylor, *Mark*, pp. 568f.; Glasson, *Advent*, pp. 63ff.; Robinson, *Coming*, pp. 43f.; Dodd, *Parables*, pp. 51f.; Lagrange *Matthieu*, p. 508; *Marc*. p. 402 (following Loisy, *Synoptiques*, II, p. 606); Gould, *Mark*, p. 279.

[2] If only because of the general objection raised in chapter 7 above; cf. esp. pp. 103ff.

[3] Cf. Glasson, *Advent*, pp. 63f.; Robinson, *Coming*, pp. 43.

[4] Cf. below, pp. 143f.

[5] Cf. Streeter, *Four Gospels*, pp. 321f.; Lightfoot, *History and Interpretation*, pp. 180f.; Montefiore, *Synoptic Gospels*, II, p. 337; Kümmel, *Promise*, p. 50, n. 102.

[6] Cf. *Coming*, p. 45.

[7] Cf. Grundmann, in *T.W.N.T.* p. 38; Kissane, *Psalms*, II, p. 194.

[8] *Advent*, p. 64; similarly Robinson, *Coming*, p. 45; Taylor, *Mark*, p. 569.

Son of Man comes to the Ancient of Days, this is not to be interpreted as an ascent to heaven, but as a coming *on earth*.[1]

Those who find here no reference to the Parousia argue that ὄψεσθε refers to a spiritual experience and must not be taken literally.[2] Glasson[3] says we should compare with Jn. 8, 28 and Heb. 2, 9 but these are *not* able to support his argument[4] and Kümmel[5] rightly concludes 'to transfer ὄψεσθε to a spiritual experience is as arbitrary as to contest that Dan. 7, 13 points to an eschatological cosmic event'. We therefore accept that this passage refers to the Parousia.[6]

The next problem of interpretation is, whether or not the prediction here is delimited. Otto,[7] for example, thinks there is an *immediate* expectation, but the fact that Mark has recorded the saying suggests that he did not understand it in this way.[8] Others think there is a delimitation, though allowing for a short interval,[9] and some conclude that there is here no distinction in perspective

---

[1] Ps. 110 also is clearly set upon the earth. Cf. Beasley-Murray, *Future*, p. 259 (following Dalman, *Words*, p. 241, n. 2, and Rowley, *Relevance*, p. 30, n. 1.).

[2] Lagrange, *Marc*, p. 403 writes, 'Le terme "vous verrez" ne signifie pas toujours "vous verrez de vos yeux" (cf. Dt. 28, 10; Ps. 48, 11; Ps. 88, 49).'

[3] *Advent*, p. 65.

[4] Heb. 2, 9 uses, in fact, βλέπειν and certainly refers to an experience of *faith* (contrast the unbelieving Sanhedrin), for the letter is written by a believer to believers (cf. 2, 1. 13, 7 etc.). That which is already true of Christ (i.e. his sovereignty) is 'seen' (2, 9) by an exercise of that faith referred to in 11, 1 as πραγμάτων ἔλεγχος οὐ βλεπομένων. It is not a question here of *un*belief witnessing the unmistakable manifestation of Christ's rule.

Jn. 8, 28 speaks not of 'seeing' but of 'knowing' (γνώσεσθε). It is not enough to say that this is the equivalent in John's language of what Mark, in 14, 62, means, for this is begging the question. Again it is possible that believers are in mind (cf. Barrett, *John, ad loc*), and not unbelievers as in Mk. 14, 62.

Of course, if the records gave us an account of a confession from the high priest similar perhaps to that of the centurion (Mk. 15, 39-40) then there might arise the question whether the evangelist understood Mk. 14, 62 in this sense; but there is no such record (Indeed Mtt. 27, 62ff., Acts 4, 1f. 5, 33f., suggest continued opposition). cf. further Michaelis, in *T.W.N.T.* V pp. 315ff. [5] *Promise*, p. 50, n. 102.

[6] Cf. Cranfield, *Mark*, p. 444; Rawlinson, *Mark*, p. 222; Lohmeyer, *Markus*, p. 329; Sjöberg, *Verborgene Menschensohn*, p. 102; M'Neile, *Matthew*, p. 402; Schniewind, *Matthäus*, p. 265.

[7] *Kingdom of God*, pp. 227f.

[8] Grässer, *Problem*, pp. 30f., thinks that *because the saying presupposes a delay*, it is a community-saying!

[9] Cf. Cullmann, *Early Church*, p. 152; Allen, *Matthew*, p. 284; Jeremias, in *T.B.* XX, 1941, pp. 219f.; Conzelmann, *Mitte*, p. 77, n. 2.

between the expectation of the Resurrection and of the Parousia.[1] It is, however, doubtful if a reference to the Resurrection is in mind here (expect perhaps as the presupposition of exaltation and the Parousia), for in what sense, we might ask, would the judges addressed *see* the Resurrection, or resurrection appearances? It is also unlikely that the Evangelists understood that the event foretold would necessarily occur within a short time. This contention is, we suggest, supported by the following considerations:

First, Mk. 14, 62 is addressed to the high priest personally. But this does not necessarily mean that the high priest was expected to live until the Parousia occurred; it is rather the assurance that he who now rejects the Messiah will one day see him in unmistakable clarity when he comes as Judge.[2] It is the high priest, and Sanhedrin, who, as representatives of God's people, *should* recognise their Messiah: it is they who, having rejected him, must see their rejection confounded when the truth concerning Jesus' person and work is openly manifested at the Parousia.[3]

Secondly, the addition in Matthew (26, 64) of ἀπ' ἄρτι supports our interpretation. Some, indeed, interpret ἀπ' ἄρτι as 'soon',[4] but the phrase is probably intended to emphasise the contrast between what *from that time* (ἀπ' ἄρτι) ceases—namely Jesus' lowly status—and that which will be seen at his Parousia *whenever that occurs*. Thus the temporal aspect of ἀπ' ἄρτι refers to the past-present side of the contrast rather than to the future side.[5] This is certainly the case with Mtt. 23, 39 and 26, 29 where it is the *cessation* of the past-present mode of Jesus' ministry which ἀπ'

---

[1] Cf. Schniewind, *Matthäus*, p. 265; Lohmeyer, *Matthäus*, p. 329; M'Neile, *Matthew*, p. 402.

[2] This interpretation is to be found in Calvin, *Harmony*, III, p. 257; Montefiore, *Synoptic Gospels*, II, p. 337; Cranfield, *Mark*, pp. 444f. (following J. P. Bercovitz, 'The Parables of the Messiah', an unpublished Edinburgh University doctoral thesis.) Kümmel, *Promise*, p. 67, concludes, 'Mk. 14, 62 gives no indication at all of the time when the Son of Man will be seen, and makes no mention whatever of the resurrection.'

[3] Cf. Barth, *C.D.* III/2, pp. 503f.

[4] Cf. Allen, *Matthew*, p. 284; Lohmeyer, *Matthäus*, p. 369.

[5] Montefiore suggests, 'From henceforth you have nothing more to expect than that you will see . . .' *Synoptic Gospels*, II, p. 337. Debrunner's suggestion (*Conjectanea Neotestamentica* XI, 1947-8; cf. Blass-Debrunner, *Grammar*, p. 8 para 12, 3) that we should read ἀπαρτί, is accepted by Michaelis ('Exegetisches zur Himmelfahrtspredigt', in *K.r.S.* CVIII, 1952, pp. 115f.), mentioned by Cranfield, (*Mark*, p. 445), and rejected by Kümmel (*Promise*, p. 51, n. 102) on the grounds that Lk. shows a similar need for alteration by his ἀπὸ τοῦ νῦν which parallels Mtt's ἀπ' ἄρτι. We might add that the saying

ἄρτι emphasises, leaving open the moment when the new future mode shall begin.[1]

Thirdly, Lk. 22, 69 is understandable on our interpretation of Mk. 14, 62. Luke has several alterations which many think [2] to be due to the problematical nature of Mk. 14, 62 for Luke and his contemporaries. Actually, Matthew's acceptance of the saying should suggest that this is an unlikely conclusion, but Luke himself gives us a clue as to the reason for the alterations. By his omission of ὄψεσθε and the phrase ἐρχόμενων μετὰ τῶν νεφελῶν τοῦ οὐρανοῦ he has focussed attention upon the period of exaltation.[3] This then forms an appropriate background against which he sets his Acts narrative of the work of the disciples during that period of exaltation. More explicitly than Mark or Matthew [4] he speaks of this exaltation, thus giving a double focus to the church's life: the exaltation— the ground and possibility of the church's activity and the object of its faith: the Parousia (cf. Acts 1, 6-11) [5] which is the end of that possibility and the constant object of the church's hope.[6]

Again, therefore, we find no incontravertible evidence of a delimited expectation, only the open possibility that now that the

---

in Mtt. 26, 64, opening as it does with πλὴν λέγω ὑμῖν would probably have been emphasis enough without the Evangelist adding another emphatic term ἀπαρτί. The suggestion is perhaps not very likely.

[1] Thus Mtt. recognises that Mk. 14, 62, like Mk, 14, 25, is a contrast between a hidden ministry which is now brought to a close and the future open manifestation which can come at any moment after.

[2] Cf. Cadbury, *Luke-Acts*, p. 295; Montefiore, *Synoptic Gospels*, II p. 615; Grässer, *Problem*, pp. 30f.; Conzelmann, *Mitte*, p. 77, n. 2, etc.

[3] Lk.'s phrase ἀπὸ τοῦ νῦν is, as Mtt's ἀπ' ἄρτι, an emphasis upon the contrast between what is from that time onwards to cease, and what is at an unspecified future moment to take its place.

[4] Cullmann, *Early Church*, p. 152 (cf. also *Peter*, p. 201) claims that even in Mk. 14, 62 'Jesus distinguishes between the moment when the Son of Man will sit at the right hand of God and the moment when he will return.' Robinson, *Coming*, p. 51, claims that Jesus does 'nothing of the sort.' Since both clauses are subordinated to the promise 'ye shall see' (ὄψεσθε), it is probable that the saying refers to the scene at the moment of the Parousia, when Jesus is to be seen both in the supreme position of authority (cf. Grundmann, in *T.W.N.T.* II, p. 38) and also 'coming'. This, of course, is different from the point brought out by Fison (*Hope*, pp. 192f.) and Cranfield, (*Mark*, p. 444), that the *order* of the saying is significant.

[5] Cf. below, pp. 146ff.

[6] Leaney (*Luke*, p. 276) says that for Luke the event referred to is hidden from unbelieving eyes. But for Luke the Parousia remains an open manifestation, certainly *not* hidden (cf. Acts 1, 6f.), and that to which he refers in 22, 69 is hidden precisely because it is *not* the Parousia (cf. Sjöberg, *Verborgene Menschensohn*, p. 235).

lowly ministry has ceased, the final manifestation can come at any moment.

Matthew 10, 23

Schweitzer [1] demanded, rightly, that this saying should be interpreted with reference to its context; he, however, wrongly understood this context.[2] There can be no doubt that the chapter is a composite compilation,[3] as an analysis shows. Matthews opens this, his second discourse, with the calling and authorising of the Twelve—apparently a detached saying in the tradition;[4] this gives the discourse its theme. Matthew then records instructions relating to the disciples' commission (vv. 5ff.) reminiscent of Mk. 6, 7-13, Lk. 9, 1-6, 10. Matthew expressly limits this mission by vv. 5-6 to 'the lost sheep of the house of Israel', and we are most probably to understand this with reference to the short preaching tour of the Twelve during Jesus' own ministry.[5] With Mtt. 10; 16 we enter upon a new section, drawn from Mk. 13,[6] which closes with v. 23.

---

[1] *Quest*, pp. 357ff.; cf. also Burkitt, *Beginnings*, p. 138; Werner, *Formation*, pp. 71ff.   [2] Cf. chapter 3 above, p. 38.

[3] Cf. Schniewind, *Matthäus*, pp. 124f.; Allen, in *Oxford Studies*, pp. 235f.; Streeter, *Four Gospels*, pp. 263ff.; Kilpatrick, *Origins*, p. 35; M'Neile, *Matthew*, pp. 133f.; Kümmel, *Promise*, p. 63; Glasson, *Advent*, pp. 103f.; Robinson, *Coming*, pp. 76f.; Flückiger, *Ursprung*, p. 26; Lagrange, *Matthieu*, pp. 204f., Grässer, *Problem*, p. 18; Bornkamm, in *Überlieferung und Auslegung*, p. 15; G. Barth, in *Überlieferung und Auslegung*, pp. 93f. Lohmeyer, *Matthäus*, unfortunately fails here.

The compositeness of the discourse is borne out by an analysis of the other Matthean discourses (chs 5-7, 13, 18 and 23-25); all, including ch. 10, close with the sentence καὶ ἐγένετο ὅτι ἐτέλεσεν ὁ Ἰησοῦς. There appears to be a conscious pattern in this chapter:—

vv. 5-15 'mission to Jews'. ending ἀμὴν λέγω ὑμῖν v. 15.

vv. 16-23 'mission to all', ending ἀμὴν γὰρ λέγω ὑμῖν v. 23.

vv. 24-42 'various sayings', ending ἀμὴν λέγω ὑμῖν v. 42.

[4] Mk. 3, 13-19 places it between an account of preaching and healing in Galilee (3, 7ff.) and the dispute with the scribes (3, 20f.). Lk. 6, 12-16 follows the dispute with Pharisees (6, 1ff.) and the healing of the man with the withered hand (6, 6f.), and is the immediate prelude to the Sermon on the Plain (6, 17ff.).

[5] Cf. Calvin, *Harmony*, I, *ad loc*. Mk. and Lk. do not state that the tour (Mk. 6, 7ff., Lk. 9, 1ff.) was confined to Israelite territory, but there is nothing to suggest the contrary (Lk's πανταχοῦ in 9, 6 presumably means 'everywhere they went', rather than 'they went everywhere'.) Lk's mission of the Seventy may be intended to suggest a gentile mission contrasted with the mission of the Twelve (understand) to Jews.

[6] The differences are very minor and understandable; contrast the divergencies between Lk. 21 and Mk. 13. Cf. Lagrange, *Matthieu*, p. 204. M'Neile, *Matthew*, p. 133.

The theme here is 'witness under persecution' and v. 18 suggests that the horizon apparent in Mtt. 28, 19 is present here also. The Evangelist speaks here not of a specific missionary enterprise, but of mission as such, of mission in general.[1] The final section of the discourse (vv. 24-42) drawn from diverse sources, continues the same theme.

If then we are to understand the chapter as composite, v. 23 must, in the first instance, be interpreted by reference to its context in vv. 16-22 and the wide missionary activity envisaged there. Two possible interpretations then present themselves. Either v. 23 means 'you will not have exhausted every refuge offered by Israel's cities before the Son of Man is come'; or it means, 'you will not have completed the work of mission amongst Israel's recalcitrant peoples, until the Son of Man is come'. The former,[2] it is said, is supported by the addition in D θ f 1, f 13 al, of καν εκ ταυτης διωκωσιν υμας φευγετε εις την αλλην. But this is not strong support[3] and Montefiore rightly comments 'v. 23 seems to mean . . . not "you will not exhaust the cities in your flight from one to the other, before the Son of Man comes", which would be a very odd remark.'[4] The second alternative gives to τελέσητε its natural meaning of 'bringing to an end' (cf. Lk. 12, 50), rather than the unnatural meaning 'come to an end'.[5] It is, surely, not necessary to separate (as many do)[6] v. 23a from v. 23b. Bosch[7] holds that '23a redet von der Flucht der Jünger, während 23b von der Ausführung einer Aufgabe in den Städten Israels—also gerade *nicht* von einer Flucht!—redet'. But v. 23a is given missionary significance (as part of the missionary strategy) not only by its conjunction with v. 23b but by its setting in this missionary discourse, vv. 16-23.

---

[1] G. Barth in *Überlieferung und Auslegung*, p. 94 says, 'die Aussendungsrede spricht nun von Aussendung der Jünger überhaupt . . .'

[2] Cf. Glasson, *Advent*, p. 103; Klostermann, *Matthäus*, p. 89.

[3] The idea of flight is only reinforced; nothing is added as to its purpose.

[4] *Synoptic Gospels*, II, pp. 149f. cf. Robinson, *Matthew*, p. 92; Michaelis, *Matthäus*, II, p. 94.

[5] Cf. Kümmel, *Promise*, p. 62; Beasley-Murray, *Future*, p. 198.

[6] Cf. Kümmel, *Promise*, pp. 62f.; Montefiore, *Synoptic Gospels*, p. 150; Bosch, *Heidenmission*, p. 156; G. Barth, in *Überlieferung und Auslegung*, p. 94, n. 1; Grässer, *Problem*, pp. 137f. Contrast, Bammel, in *S.T.* XV, 1962, pp. 8of.; Beasley-Murray, *Future*, p. 198, 'The two halves of the saying are sometimes regarded as independent, but if so they are cunningly put together. They form a coherent whole as they stand.'

[7] *Heidenmission*, p. 156.

Verse 23 is therefore at once a *discouragement* of hasty martyrdom, and of easy optimism; and at the same time an *encouragement* in suggesting that the anticipated failure of the Jewish mission is part of the entire salvation-history and is not something for which the disciples are made to feel responsible—they themselves will not succeed in winning the Jews to allegiance of the gospel.[1]

The reference to the 'coming of the Son of Man' has been variously interpreted as the fall of Jerusalem,[2] as the Resurrection [3] or as Pentecost.[4] But, as M'Neile points out, 'the meaning of "the coming of the Son of Man" is too distinctive in the gospels to allow us to suppose' that these interpretations are valid.[5] Kümmel, agreeing with this, concludes, 'Then the meaning of the saying appears clearly to be: the parousia of the Son of Man will arrive before the disciples have finished proclaiming the Kingdom of God in Israel. Thereby the coming of the Kingdom of God is transferred here also to the lifetime of Jesus' disciples . . .'.[6] However, the delimitation referred to in Kümmel's second sentence does not at all follow of necessity from his first observation; we suggest that such a delimitation is *not* involved here. V. 23b is neutral in respect of the duration of the work involved,[7] simply affirming that it will not be completed before the parousia; and if v. 23a is understood in connection with v. 23b and the entire mission charge, this too is undelimited.

This interpretation is able to make sense of the juxtaposition of 10, 5 to 10, 18. It might perhaps be said that Matthew has simply not realised their incongruity—but, in view of the skill with which the discourse appears to be compiled, this seems unlikely. Schniewind [8] and others [9] are probably right in suggesting that the discourse is so arranged as to display the pattern 'to the Jew first,

---

[1] Cf. Cullmann, in *E.M.*, 1941, pp. 98ff.

[2] E.g. Lagrange, *Matthieu*, p. 205; Schmaus, *Dogmatik*, p. 34. Robinson, *Coming*, pp. 76ff.

[3] E.g. Barth, *C,D.* III/2, pp. 499f.; Stonehouse, *Matthew and Mark*, p. 240.

[4] E.g. Calvin, *Harmony*, I p. 458; Fison, *Hope*, p. 194.

[5] *Matthew*, p. 142. and cf. above, chapter 7, pp. 102f.

[6] *Promise*, p. 63.

[7] Cf. Bosch *Heidenmission*, p. 157, 'Über die Zeitdauer bis zur Parusie ist damit noch nichts gesagt, weil kein Anlass besteht, die zweite Person (im Verbum τελέσητε) zu pressen, also darunter die Zwölf zu verstehen . . .'

[8] *Matthäus*, pp. 130f.

[9] Cf. Flückiger, *Ursprung*, pp. 126f.; Michaelis, *Matthäus, ad loc.*; Beasley-Murray, *Future*, p. 198; Robinson, *Matthew*, pp. 87f.; G. Barth, in *Überlieferung und Auslegung*, p. 94; Schlatter, *Matthäus*, ad loc.

and also to the Greek' (Rom 1, 16; 2, 10; cf. 9-11). Thus the discourse is not only a series of instructions but offers also an overall plan of mission; vv. 5-15 'to the Jew first', vv. 16-23 'and also to the Greek',[1] v. 23 actually having relevance for both sections. We conclude [2] that there is *no* necessarily delimited expectation here.

With Mtt. 10, 23 we complete this review of the Synoptic evidence and it is now time to address our original question (is there any certain evidence of a delimited Parousia hope in the thought of the early church?) to the remainder of the New Testament material; to Acts, Hebrews, the Catholic Epistles, John and Revelation.

Acts 1, 6-11

Haenchen [3] and others [4] maintain that Acts 1, 6-11 gives us the contemporary situation against which Luke's own theological standpoint was directed. So, it is said, he here depicts the early church's delimited expectation and goes on to oppose it with the 'compensatory factors'—the Spirit and the Mission, hallmarks of the 'epoch of the Church.'

On the other hand it is entirely possible to interpret Acts 1, 6 as a question of the disciples prior to the Ascension and the coming of the Spirit—as it purports to be! Narrow nationalism [5] is answered by the prophecy of world mission (v. 8) and the enquiry about the

---

[1] πορεύεσθε δὲ μᾶλλον to be sure means 'go rather', not 'go first' (though the superlative μάλιστα can certainly mean 'first, first and foremost'), and perhaps the saying referred originally to the short preaching tour of the Twelve.

[2] Against Streeter, *Four Gospels*, p. 255; Cullmann, *Early Church*, p. 152; Kümmel, *Promise*, p. 63, etc.

[3] *Apostelgeschichte*, pp. 114ff., 120ff.

[4] Grässer, *Problem*, pp. 205ff.; Conzelmann, *Mitte*, p. 127.

[5] Jackson and Lake, *Beginnings* IV, p. 8 (cf. I, pp. 317ff.) argue that the nationalism and reluctance to undertake the Gentile mission (cf. Acts 5, 16) prove that Jesus did not command such a mission (cf. Mtt. 28, 19; Mk. 13, 10; Mk. 16, 15). Flückiger, *Ursprung*, pp. 213ff., contends that a special revelation of the risen Lord was needed to rouse the disciples from their nationalistic hope, and again a special revelation was needed to turn them to the heathen. Bruce, *Acts, ad loc*, thinks 'this interest in the hope of an earthly and national kingdom (cf. Mk. 10, 35ff.) gave place after Pentecost to the proclamation of the spiritual kingdom of God . . .' Bosch, *Heidenmission*, p. 187 argues (surely correctly), 'dass es in den Auseinandersetzungen der Apostelzeit gar nicht um das grundsätzliche *Recht* der Heidenmission ging, sondern vielmehr um die *Bedingungen*, unter denen die Mission erfolgen darf, um den Verkehr zwischen Juden und Heiden, um die theologischen Auseinandersetzungen zwischen Gesetz und Evangelium . . .'

date of the end is forbidden (v. 7); question and answer are both understandable in the context given them here, and though they serve as a foil to the pattern traced out in the subsequent chapters, this does not mean that the context is necessarily fictitious.

Haenchen [1] argues that in v. 7 'die Erwartung des nahen Welt-endes verneint wird', but, in fact, the date of the end is not spoken of either as near or as far off; curiosity concerning the date is simply rejected and forbidden.[2]

The rebuke by the 'men in white' (v. 11) is interpreted by Haenchen in similar manner: 'Das βλέπειν εἰς τὸν οὐρανόν wird . . . verboten . . . weil es die Naherwartung des Endes ausdrückt, die Lukas nicht nennt, sondern nur mit dieser Haltung beschreibt,'[3] But it is very strange that Luke—if he understood the rebuke in this way and himself was opposing such a Naherwartung—should have added v. 11b. On Haenchen's interpretation of v. 11a, the verse should read, 'Why stand ye gazing? This same Jesus will *not* come for a long time . . .' whereas the disciples are actually en-couraged by these words to await the Parousia. The disciples' attitude, gazing into heaven, can be understood as a wistful longing for Jesus' presence, and perhaps as a forlornness at his departure; only in this light can v. 11b become intelligible and appropriate.[4]

Luke traces, in the chapters following, the development of the gospel's progression.[5] Grässer [6] maintains that thereby the Parousia

---

[1] *Apostelgeschichte*, p. 114.

[2] Cf., of course, Mk. 13, 32. Stauffer, in *Background of the N.T.*, pp. 285f., regards this as evidence that the early church had an intense *Naherwartung* and that Jesus had not. This, however, overlooks the fact that it is the dis-ciples prior to Pentecost who are depicted here, and that their immediate hope is represented as bound up with their nationalism of that time.

[3] *Apostelgeschichte*, pp. 120f. Calvin, *Harmony*, I, pp. 43ff., thinks that one of the reasons for the rebuke was that 'they hoped he would return again straightway, that they might enjoy the sight of him again . . .' 'before such time as they begin to work they will have their wages.'

[4] Renan was, then, perhaps not so far wrong as Haenchen suggests (*Apostelgeschichte*, p. 120, n. 4) in understanding the angels' words as com-fort; cf. Jacquier, *Actes*, p. 21.

[5] Cf. Dibelius, *Studies*, pp. 192ff.; Foakes-Jackson, *Acts*, p. 3; Haenchen, *Apostelgeschichte*, p. 92; O'Neill, *Acts*, p. 174.

[6] *Problem*, p. 208. Cf. Haenchen, *Apostelgeschichte*, p. 90.; Conzelmann, *Mitte*, passim.; Jackson-Lake, *Beginnings*, IV, p. 8. Cadbury, in *Background of the N.T.* p. 319, whilst recognising a lack of emphasis in Luke-Acts on vivid, urgent expectation, thinks this is due 'not so much to changing pers-pectives of a delayed Parousia, as to practical considerations of the Christian teachers . . .'

is pushed into the background. Yet the promise of the Parousia standing here at the outset of the church's life and work serves rather as a constant reminder that the history being narrated is to come to an end, that the opportunity for mission is temporary, and therefore that the missionary task of the church is urgent, forbidding idle wistfulness and lethargic sorrow.[1]

Hebrews 1, 10, 25. 10, 37

The writer certainly appears to treat the Parousia as *near*.[2] Thus in 1, 2 the period of the old covenant is contrasted with ἐπ' ἐσχάτου τῶν ἡμερῶν τούτων;[3] 10, 25 suggests that the approaching of 'the Day' must be a motive of Christian obedience,[4] and 10, 36f. exhorts to patience (ὑπομονῆς),[5] adding a reference to Is. 26, 20 and Hab. 2, 3-4, as encouragement and assurance.[6]

Our thesis is certainly *not* that the New Testament does not regard the Parousia as near, but that this nearness is not delimited. In none of these passages cited is there such a delimited hope. It is because God's final word to man spoken in Jesus Christ *has come* (1, 1-2) that the present is characterised as 'last days',[7] and that

---

[1] Cf. further, below chapter 12.

[2] Some, e.g. Wickham (*Hebrews, ad loc*, 10, 25), Westcott (*Hebrews*, p. 239), think that the writer has the fall of Jerusalem in mind. Robinson (*Coming*, p. 27) thinks the letter leaves no room for a Parousia; he argues that 6, 1 does not include the Parousia under the τὸν τῆς ἀρχῆς . . .λόγον. But the Parousia is *not* an object of faith so much as of hope and the omission is understandable (ὁ ἐρχόμενος in 10, 37 also tells against Robinson if this is to be interpreted as a Messianic title; cf. Strobel, *Untersuchungen*, p. 81). Barrett, in *Background of the N.T.* pp. 363ff., argues for a Parousia expectation in Hebrews; cf. also Spicq, *Hébreux, ad loc* 10, 37; Héring, *Hébreux*, pp. 20f.; Windisch, *Hebräerbrief*, in Excursus to 9, 28, pp. 86f.

[3] Cf. Manson, *Hebrews*, pp. 88f.; Westcott, *Hebrews, ad loc*. Michel, *Hebräerbrief*, p. 35 writes, 'Das Besondere des Urchristentums liegt in der Gewissheit, das das Weltende eingesetzt hat; dieseTage sind die letzten Tage.'

[4] Cf. Manson, *Hebrews*, p. 89. Of 2, 1 he writes, 'The writer brings in the eschatological note which . . . rings through and through his practical warnings to his readers' (*op cit* pp. 47ff.)

[5] Cf. also παρρησίαν v. 35. Strobel, *Untersuchungen*, p. 81.

[6] On this passage cf. esp. Strobel, *Untersuchungen*, pp. 79ff. 11, 40 might also be mentioned (cf. Windisch, *Hebräer*, p. 87) as evaluating highly the place of the writer and his contemporaries in the salvation-history plan. 12, 26, too, if the reference to Hag. 2, 6 were completed! (Cf. Michel, *Hebräer*, p. 241; Strobel, *Untersuchungen*, p. 84.)

[7] Cf. further chapter 9 below.

the present demands a complex of faith (involving obedience and repentance) and hope.[1]

The present is evaluated as a period wherein Christ reigns,[2] and wherein Christians obey him, living in faith in what is unseen (cf. 11, 1f.) and in hope of what will be revealed (namely Jesus Christ, cf. 12, 2; 13, 8 etc.); hope that this may occur soon, and assurance that it will come at the appointed time (οὐ χρονίσει); it is not far distant (μικρὸν ὅσον ὅσον).[3] But μικρὸν ὅσον ὅσον is a relative expression and does not delimit the present period, only defining it as 'short'.[4]

James 5, 7-9

5, 7 probably begins a concluding section of the Epistle applicable to all the preceding teaching,[5] thus depicting the Parousia of Christ [6] as the motive for ethical obedience and persistent discipleship. Three particular expressions require comment. The first is ἕως τῆς παρουσίας τοῦ κυρίου. The conjunction ἕως is certainly temporal, but the phrase does not define the present period prior to the Parousia as long or short, only characterising it as a time during which patience is necessary, in contrast to a time to come—at an unspecified date.[7]

The second expression is in v. 8, ὅτι ἡ παρουσία τοῦ κυρίου ἤγγικεν.

---

[1] In this respect cf. Michel, *Hebräer*, p. 233, 'eschatologische Erwartung ist nur dann echt, wenn sie mit der Nähe des Endes rechnet'. Strobel, *Untersuchungen*, p. 304, 'Glauben—das bedeutet in konkreten *Naherwartung* leben.' We shall hope to show that the N.T. relates hope and faith inextricably and knows of a tension between 'already accomplished' and 'not yet revealed'; but that a *Nächsterwartung*, or delimited *Naherwartung* is not inherent in faith and that *faith* can reckon with a period prior to the Parousia at the same time as *hope* regards it as near.

[2] Cf. Heb. 2, 5ff. Whether this is regarded as contrasting Christ's reign with mans' not reigning, or Christ's present unseen reign with his future manifest rule, is here of no import; clearly he is king.

[3] On ὅσον ὅσον cf. Blass-Debrunner, *Grammar*, para 304, pp. 159f.

[4] What this means is, of course, our question in the next chapter.

[5] οὖν is emphatic if only because it is the sole occurrence here in the whole Epistle.

[6] It is not impossible that τοῦ κυρίου here refers to God (cf. Bousset, *Kyrios Christos*, p. 273 n. 4; Windisch, *Katholische Briefe*, p. 3, cf. 3, 9; 5, 4. But there is no compulsion to take it in this way (cf. Dibelius, *Jakobus*, p. 224; Ropes, *James*, p. 297; Mayor, *James*, p. 157.

[7] Calvin, *Catholic Epistles*, pp. 347f., comments, 'The confusion of things which is now seen in the world will not be perpetual, because the Lord at his coming will reduce things to order . . .'

In 4, 8 ἐγγίσει is used of the relationship of the believer to God and vice versa [1] and the idea is that of accessibility: God is 'ready' for relationship with the humble (v. 6 f.). 5, 8 might perhaps be intended to be understood in a similar way. Or ἤγγικεν may be meant in its temporal sense, in which case the writer is affirming that the Parousia *is* (temporally) near, but at the same time there is no delimitation of its coming.[2]

The third expression is ὁ κριτὴς πρὸ τῶν θυρῶν ἕστηκεν v. 9.[3] Closer parallels than Bar. 48, 39 and Is. 26, 20 are Is. 3, 13 where God is depicted as standing to judge,[4] indicating his *readiness*; and Rev. 3, 20 which depicts a present situation of undefined duration. The most significant parallels are Mk. 13, 29; Mtt. 24, 33 par (cf. Acts 5, 9) where nearness is the theme.[5] This nearness, however, even if understood temporally [6] is quite undelimited, not ruling out the possibility that the Parousia might remain 'near' without coming for some time.[7]

In 4, 13-17 we find confirmation of this interpretation. James,

---

[1] In the LXX 'Oft geht das Wort auf das Verhältnis von Gott und den Frommen' (Preisker, in *T.W.N.T.* II, p. 330. cf. Ps. 33, 19; 118, 151; 144, 18).

[2] Knowling, *James*, p. 130, wants to interpret in terms of the fall of Jerusalem, and therefore gives a very early date for the letter (cf. pp. xxxivff.) which most commentators reject.

[3] Whether the Judge is Christ or God is again open to question, cf. 5, 7. Cf. Dibelius, *Jakobus, ad loc.*

[4] In Is. 3, 13 the action of the verse is probably still future (cf. v. 14. 'The Lord will enter into judgement'), but the 'standing' נצב and 'arising' עמד indicate that he is now ready to perform his judgements.

[5] Jeremias (in *T.W.N.T.* III, p. 174) writes, 'vor der Tür stehen, dh. im Begriff stehen einzutreten, ist Ausdruck für grösste Nähe.'

[6] It is perhaps plausible to suggest that a spatial reference is here intended. Jeremias (in *T.W.N.T.* III, pp. 174f.), arguing for a temporal connotation, says, 'Die Verwendung des räumlichen Bildes als Zeitangabe ist hellenistisch' (authorities op. cit. p. 174, n. 8). The hellenistic origin of the usage here, he thinks, is supported by the plural αἱ Θυραι for the singular (a classical usage). However αἱ Θυραι is not necessarily a hellenistic usage; the plural occurs both with דלת and with פתח frequently in the O.T. (cf. Jud. 3, 23; 16, 2; Neh. 3, 3; 7, 3) presumably because 'doors were often made with two leaves' (Warren, in *H.D.B.* II, p. 434). In a metaphorical sense, the plural usage is almost invariable; 'the doors of heaven', Ps. 78, 23; cf. Job. 38, 8; 41, 14; etc. It is interesting that the phrase occurs in the N.T. in the plural (excepting where the meaning is obviously influenced by architectural detail, cf. Jn. 20, 26; Acts 5, 19, 5, 23; 16, 26; 27; 21, 30) in just those places where Jewish influence is said to be most present. So perhaps Jeremias' argument is not altogether convincing.

[7] 5, 3 does not denote a delimited expectation either; ἐν ἐσχάταις ἡμέραις is doubtless an expression for the Judgement time.

fulminating against those who take sovereign control of their lives, does not argue 'you say "to-day or to-morrow . . .", but you forget that the Parousia is to come within a year or two'! The uncertainty of 'to-morrow' he connects first with the transitoriness of human life (v. 14),[1] and then with the sovereignty of God (v. 15).

I Peter 4, 7

ἤγγικεν here means that the End is near, but not in a delimited sense; it might come at any moment (thought it might also dealy!) and this 'readiness' to occur is made the basis for an exhortation to soundness of mind and sobriety.[2] Many interpret it as delimiting the present,[3] but without sufficient ground. In favour of our interpretation we may compare I Peter 4, 5, τῷ ἑτοίμως ἔχοντι κρῖναι; ἑτοίμως is used not infrequently to denote the readiness of the End to break in to the present order.[4] Further, in 1, 5 it is said that salvation is ἑτοίμην ἀποκαλυφθῆναι ἐν καιρῷ ἐσχάτῳ.

The Epistle recognises an essential unity between the Parousia on the one hand and the death, resurrection and ascension of Christ on the other (cf. 1, 3f., 1, 14, 1, 19f.) Christ is already exalted as Lord (1, 21; 3, 22) and nothing remains but that he should be 'revealed' (1, 8; 1, 13) or 'manifested' (5, 4). In the meantime, though this revelation is ready and near, and with it judgement and salvation, men are given occasion to repent and believe (1, 7; 13; 22 etc.).[5]

II Peter 3

It is often said that II Peter 3 reflects a crisis provoked by the

---

[1] Recognising that those addressed may die within a year or two, and before the Parousia occurs.

[2] Similarly in James 5, 8 nearness is the ground for exhortation to patience; cf. Selwyn, *I Peter*, p. 216; Windisch, *Katholische Briefe, ad loc*; Beare, *I Peter*, p. 158.

[3] Calvin, *Catholic Epistles*, p. 127, suggested besides the nearness of Christ's return, the nearness of each individual's death; but this seems unlikely as it is not suggested by the context, and νήφω is regularly used in the N.T. (cf. I Thess. 5, 6; 5, 8; II Tim. 4, 5; I Pet. 1, 13; 5, 8 — the only occurrences besides here) of an attitude appropriate to the nearness of the *End*.

[4] Cf. Mtt. 22, 4; 8. 24, 44 par., 25, 10; etc.

[5] This is why the writer can speak (in 1, 20) of the incarnation of Christ as occurring 'at the end of time'. 'That was the climax, the final chapter. All subsequent history is but epilogue, a period in which men have opportunity to come to terms with the meaning of their lives, as it has been revealed in history . . .' Cranfield, *I & II Peter*, p. 112.

'unexpected' Parousia delay.[1] This view, however, receives serious set-back when the chapter is compared with earlier eschatological material, especially II Thess. 2, and Mk. 13. Such comparison suggests that the writer reiterates substantially the same tradition as is already found in the Synoptics and in Paul.[2]

Käsemann[3] argues that the eschatology of II Peter 3 is de-Christologised,[4] de-ethicised[5] and de-centralised;[6] but comparison with the earlier material again shows that the Christology is

---

[1] Cf. the Commentaries of Knopf, Hauck, Wand and Windisch, *ad. loc.*; and Käsemann, 'Eine Apologie der urchristlichen Eschatologie', in *Z.T.K.* XLIX, 1952, pp. 272ff., etc.

[2] Mk. 13	II Thess. 2	II Pet. 3
1. Warning to take heed, vv. 5-6, 21-23.	Warning to take heed, vv. 2-3.	Warning to take heed, vv. 1-3.
2. Signs of the end, vv. 7-9, 11-13, 14-20.	Signs of the end. vv. 3-4.	Signs of the end. vv. 2-3.
3. Proclamation of gospel, v. 10.	Proclamation of gospel,? vv. 6-7.	Proclamation of gospel, v. 9.
4. Final End, vv. 26-27.	Final End, v. 8.	Final End, vv. 9-10.
5. Imminence of End, vv. 28-31.	Imminence of End, v. 7.	Imminence of End, vv. 8-9.
6. Ignorance of date, v. 32.	Ignorance of date (presupposed by vv. 2-3.)	Ignorance of date, v. 8.
7. Exhortation to watch, vv. 33-37.	Exhortation to stand fast, vv. 13ff.	Exhortation to watch, vv. 10-16.

[3] In *Z.T.K.*, XLIX, 1952, pp. 272ff.

[4] The chapter, he argues, 'has a Christological flavour, in that it is Christ who destroys at the judgement; but otherwise the eschatology is thoroughly anthropological.'

[5] No longer, he says, is it the new resurrection life which is the spur to Christian obedience, but rather the impersonal expectation of reward and punishment to be meted out at the last day.

[6] Eschatology, he argues, has been made a 'last chapter' of dogmatics, in a manner consistently copied since but actually foreign to the apostolic understanding of eschatology.

parallel,[1] the ethics similarly orientated,[2] and the place and status of eschatology the same.[3]

Many critics maintain that a crisis (caused by the Parousia dealy) is reflected in the (so-called) new arguments adduced by the writer to 'emphasise the certainty of the end and to account in some measure for the delay'. These arguments are as follows:

1. The witness of the Flood to the coming world destruction,[4] vv. 5-7. This, however, is already paralleled to some extent by Lk. 17, 26 (Mtt. 24, 37); to be sure the emphasis in Luke (and Matthew) is upon *suddenness*, but the parallelism of imagery remains. If there *is* an element of newness in the argument, it can be accounted for by the mockers' objections which are being met: they apparently argued from the non-arrival of the Parousia (v. 4) to a denial of salvation-history as such.[5] It is particularly appropriate in reply to point to a momentous *past* activity of God in the salvation-history which is also a prototype of the momentous act still awaited.

2. The idea of a final world conflagration.[6] But the prototype of the Flood and the judgement of Sodom and Gomorrah by fire probably gave rise to this imagery. Already fire and judgement are conjoined in the Old Testament,[7] and II Peter 3, 7. 3, 12-13 connect the End with judgement. Lk. 17 connects the destruction of Sodom and Gomorrah with the Flood narrative as parallel

---

[1] The climax of Mk. 13 comes in vv. 26-27 (apart from 'for my sake' in vv. 9 and 13, the only mention of Christ), and II Thess. 2 speaks of 'the Lord Jesus' (v. 8) only in connection with this central phase of the salvation-plan.

[2] Mk. 13, 13 suggests the ultimate goal of Christian faith as an incentive for obedience; similarly 13, 33-37. In II Thess. 2, the eschatological motive of ethics is not isolated out but is none the less present, cf. vv. 13-15 (cf. similar motivation, Rom. 13, 8-14, Phil. 4, 4-7, I Thess. 5, Heb. 10, 24f., Jam. 5, 7-11, I Pet. 4, 7-11).

[3] In the sense that primitive Christianity regarded the hope of the Parousia as something to be 'read off' from the past acts of the salvation-history acknowledged in faith, then hope and its content *is* derivative—and, in a sense, a 'final chapter'; but this is as true of Mk. 13 and II Thess. 2 as of II Pet. 3.

[4] Cf. Michel, 'Grundzüge urchristlicher Eschatologie', in *Z.s.T.* 1932, pp. 66off.

[5] Cf. v. 4, 'All things continue as they were from the beginning of creation.'

[6] Cf. Knopf, *Petri und Judae, ad loc.*; For the idea of a conflagration outside the N.T., cf. Zeph. 1, 18; 3, 8; Sib. Orac. IV/172f., V/155f., Ps. Sol. 15, 6; II Esdras 13, 10. Qumran Thanksgiving Ps. 3, 19f.

[7] Cf. e.g. Gen. 19, 24; Ex. 9, 24; 24, 17; Lev. 10, 2. etc.

examples of God's consuming wrath.[1] Also in II Thess. 2, 8 (1, 7) fire and the End judgement are brought together.

3. The impossibility of knowing the date of the End.[2] But this (v. 8) is precisely the assertion of Mk. 13, 32 (cf. Mtt. 24, 36; Acts 1, 7). It is also presupposed in II Thess. 2, 2-3. The balance of imminence and ignorance found in Mk. 13[3] and II Thess. 2[4] is maintained by the writer here also. Significantly the reminiscence of Ps. 90, 4 is given an unique expansion which 'rules out the possibility of taking the meaning to be merely that God's time is measured on a bigger scale than man's.'[5] The expansion shows that the writer is concerned to maintain the open possibility of the End coming at any moment; only man is ignorant of the date.[6] This possibility (emphasised too by the 'sign' of the scoffers' presence),[7] leads to an exhortation to watchfulness in face of the suddenness of the End, (v. 10).[8]

4. God's patience in allowing time for repentance.[9] This, v. 9, is but another way of describing the present time as an opportunity for the preaching of the gospel, for which we may compare Mk. 13, 10 (and II Thess. 2; 6-7 if the interpretation adopted above be accepted).[10]

5. Repentance and the coming of the End (v. 12).[11] Knopf[12]

---

[1] So cf. Lk. 17, 29 (II Pet. 2, 6). Fire, as a medium of destruction at the end would be readily suggested rather than water (cf. Gen. 9, 8ff. 15).

[2] Käsemann (in Z.T.K. XLIX, 1952, pp. 272ff.) regards it as a speculative argument. Knopf (Petri und Judae, ad loc) as 'ein neuer Gedanke'; Moffatt (General Epistles, ad loc.) calls it 'a new application'; Hauck (Kirchenbriefe, ad loc), a tacit abandonment of Mtt. 24, 34.

[3] Cf. above, p. 133.

[4] The μυστήριον τῆς ἀνομίας is 'already at work' pointing to the End; but there is no attempt to determine the date; cf. above, pp. 111ff.

[5] Cranfield, I & II Peter, p. 189; cf. Wand, General Epistles, ad loc.; James, II Peter, ad loc.

[6] Ps. 90, 4 would suffice as it stands if the writer were intent only on refuting the suggestion that the Lord delays beyond the appointed time. 'In God's sight—and after all they live in His sight—not only is nearness distance, but distance nearness' (Barth C.D. III/2, p. 510).

[7] Cf. v. 3 ἐπ' ἐσχάτων τῶν ἡμερῶν. Cf. Jn. 2, 18; II Tim. 3, 1; Jude 18.

[8] Hence the 'thief' imagery, Mtt. 24, 43; Lk. 12, 39; Rev. 3, 3; 6, 15.

[9] Cf. Michel, in Z.s.T. 1932, pp. 66off.

[10] The theme of repentance (cf. Ezek. 18, 23; 33, 11; I Tim. 2, 4; Rom. 11, 23; I Clem. 8, 5; etc.) is coupled with that of an imminent End in Lk. 13, 6-9. On the 'grace-character' of the present cf. Flückiger, Ursprung, pp. 121ff., and below, chapter 12.

[11] Cf. Knopf, Petri und Judae, pp. 320ff.

[12] Petri und Judae, p. 320.

writes 'Merkwürdig und sehr beachtenswert ist die in σπεύδοντας liegende Anschauung: σπεύδειν kann unmöglich heissen: entgegen-eilen und auch nicht: sehnsüchtig erwarten, sondern σπεύδειν trans. heisst: etwas beschleunigen: schaffen, dass es schneller kommt.' Mauer,[1] however, disputes this, claiming that the intrans. sense of σπεύδειν is preferable here. Even if the trans. sense is taken [2] there is not necessarily a *direct* correlation of repentance with the End, as though the former effected the latter, but rather the obverse side of v. 9 is made explicit; in this sense Acts 3, 20 can be seen as a clear parallel. In neither case, therefore, is v. 12 entirely novel.

6. The appeal to Paul, vv. 15-16. The essence of the appeal is to support for the teaching given, from outside of the writer's own personal authority. In Mk. 13, 31 a similar appeal to veracity is made [3] and again in II Thess. 2, 15. Käsemann argues [4] that 'faith' is in II Peter 3 made 'acceptance of the Apostolic testimony'— but this is nothing new! [5]

These are the so-called new arguments. A number of scholars further maintain that the number of ideas brought together here reflects the writer's embarrassment at the situation and the views of the mockers (showing what a great problem the community was facing). But vv. 17-18 exhort the community *not* to succumb to the false views of the mockers, implying that it has not yet done so, and it is probable that the writer has brought the full truth to the remembrance [6] of the community from pastoral concern lest it should fall. It is by no means necessarily embarrassment which leads the pastor to relate the whole case against some evil, but a recognition of the real danger which that evil presents to the faithful.

But further than this, the comparison with earlier tradition shows that the writer has not 'sought out' all the possible arguments against the mockers, but has faithfully reproduced the total

---

[1] in *T.W.N.T.* VI, p. 726; cf. p. 727 n. 7; similarly Cranfield, *I & II Peter*, p. 191.

[2] With e.g. Wand, *General Epistles, ad loc*; Moffatt, *General Epistles, ad loc.*

[3] In this case, of course, the appeal does not pass to another speaker, yet corroboration is made in the strongest terms.

[4] In *Z.T.K.* XLIX, 1952, pp. 272ff.

[5] Cf. Paul's insistence that he himself 'received' his gospel and that it was this 'tradition' that he preached to others (I Cor. 15, 1; 3. Gal. 1, 9; Phil. 4, 9; II Thess. 3, 6; etc).

[6] Remembrance is emphasised throughout the epistle; cf. 1, 12; 1, 13; 1, 15; 3, 1; 3, 8.

pattern and particular truths [1] of the primitive tradition. In particular, he has retained the complex pattern of ignorance as to date, imminence of the End, and the grace character of the present.

To be sure, the scoffers present a menace.[2] But it is one amongst a number of diverse difficulties and dangers which faced the primitive communities.[3] Hauck [4] will see here evidence of the supposed crisis through which the church passed—'Nur unter Schmerzen lernte die Kirche, wie unser Brief zeigt, dass die ursprüngliche Wiederkunftserwartung, welche das Ende ganz nahe glaubte (Mtt. 24, 34; Mk. 9, 1; cf. I Thess. 4, 15 'wir'), nicht zu halten sei. Nur ungern gab man dieser doch notwendigen Einsicht Raum.' We suggest that the whole of our review so far of the New Testament evidence tells against this understanding both of the earliest Christian hope and of the situation addressed in II Peter 3.[5]

I John 2, 18; etc.

Are we to understand ἐσχάτη ὥρα ἐστίν as evidence, at last, of a delimited expectation? [6] Or is the meaning here akin to that suggested for I Peter 1, 20; 4, 7; Jam. 5, 8 etc.? A review of the letter [7] reveals that the writer's chief concern is with the nature of the present period prior to the Parousia,[8] rather than with its duration.

---

[1] Naturally, with some variation of order and some alteration of expression.

[2] Cf. also I Clem. 23, 3f., II Clem. 11, 2 (Sanh 97 re Ps. 89, 50).

[3] Cf. Reicke, *Diakonie, Festfreude und Zelos*, pp. 233ff., who traces the connection between the various false views and practices in the early communities; a connection between eschatological impatience, materialism, libertinism, revelry and eucharistic unseemliness and anti-social zealotism.

[4] *Kirchenbriefe, ad loc.*

[5] Cf. Cranfield, *I & II Peter*, p. 188, 'It is significant that the author writes not as someone wrestling with his own doubts and perplexity and endeavouring to find a way through them, but as someone who recognises a bogus problem for what it is. It is significant too that the fact that the first generation of Christians has passed away does not lead him to re-formulate it in different terms. On the contrary, he re-iterates, unembarrassed, the primitive message.'

[6] Brooke, *Johannine Epistles*, p. 51, for example, thinks the writer expected the End definitely within 'the remaining years of his own lifetime . . .'

[7] 1; 5-10 present fellowship. 2; 1-6 present knowledge of this fellowship. 2; 7-11 present possibilities of 'light and dark'. 2; 12-17 nature of truth in the present. 3; 1-12 ambiguous nature of the Christian life. 3; 13-24 present persecution. 4; 1-6 proving the spirits. 4; 7-21 complex character of obedience 5; 1-12 present possession of eternal life. 5; 13-21 ambiguous nature of the present.

[8] Bultmann (in 'Die kirchliche Redaktion des ersten Johannes Briefes', in *In Memoriam*, pp. 189ff.) wants to count the references to the Parousia

It seems, therefore, most probable that the expression ἐσχάτη ὥρα (without the article) [1] is intended to reinforce this interest in the general character of the present. Even if we understand ἐσχάτη ὥρα as *'the* last hour' [2] it is arbitrary to suppose that the writer has divided the present into a series of hours and means *'the last period* of the interval between the first and second comings of the Christ'.[3]

The presence of antichrists [4] is taken by the writer as a sign that the present *is* ἐσχάτη ὥρα; already light shines in the darkness (2, 7-11), darkness παράγεται, antichrist is in the world ἤδη (4, 3). The present contains the open possibility that the Parousia can occur at any moment.[5]

John 21, 20-23

Many [6] think that the explanation of v. 23 is an early christian apologetic accounting for the Parousia delay. Against this we must notice that the context reaches back to v. 15 where Jesus is represented as commissioning Peter and predicting his death. In contrast to this the saying in v. 22 is solicited and is not directed to the

---

in this letter (2, 28; 3, 2; 4, 17) as redactional interpolations into the basic eschatology of the Johannine writings which is 'vergeschichtlicht'. Cf. against this, Nauck, *Die Tradition* pp. 121ff., 'der Verfasser des I Joh. ebenso wie seine Tradition neben der gegenwärtigen Heilsgewissheit die Hoffnung auf eine zukünftige Vollendung festhält.' (p. 130).

[1] Gore, *Johannine Epistles*, p. 124 thinks 'the omission can hardly be unintentional.' Westcott, *Johannine Epistles*, p. 55, says the anarthrous phrase 'seems to mark the general character of the period and not its specific relation to "the end".' But Blass-Debrunner, *Grammar* (p. 134 para 256; p. 143 para 276) noting the omission of the article with ordinals and with predicate nouns, say 'I Jn. 2, 18 is understandable.' (p. 134); and Moule, *Idiom*, p. 111, warns against building too much upon the omission of the article (though, unfortunately he does not discuss I Jn. 2; 18, 28).

[2] With RV, RSV, Moffatt, NEB.

[3] Brooke, *Johannine Epistles*, p. 51; Cf. Dodd. *Johannine Epistles*, pp. 48ff. This seems to be on *a priori* grounds an unlikely interpretation: would the writer suppose that, some 65 years having already elapsed, another 65 years could not possibly occur because of the presence of 'antichrist's' in the world? Whilst their presence is a sign of the end, the writer would, surely, not be unmindful of their presence in the preceding 65 years.

[4] The extent to which the writer has 'demythologized' the apocalyptic image of the antichrist is of little consequence here; but it is doubtful whether Dodd (*Fourth Gospel*, p. 50) is justified in saying that here 'the conflict between Christ and Antichrist is fought out upon the field of the mind.'

[5] Cf. too, ἐάν in 2, 28; 3, 2.

[6] Cf. Grässer, *Problem*, p. 135; Barrett, *John*, p. 488; Bultmann, *Johannes*, p. 544; Carpenter, *Johannine Writings*, p. 249; Strachan, *Fourth Gospel*, p. 338.

disciple in question but to Peter: we are, therefore, *not* to see two parallel predictions but a continuous dialogue with Peter. It is doubtless Peter's curiosity that prompts his question,[1] and the answer given is not a straightforward one.[2] It consists of a) a reminder of Peter's proper concern,[3] and b) a hypothesis concerning the beloved disciple. This *is* a hypothesis (as the form ἐὰν ... θέλω suggests),[4] positing a fate as different from that predicted for Peter as may be—μένειν ἕως ἔρχομαι.[5]

The explanation, v. 23, confirms that this *was* but a hypothesis and there is no necessity to suppose 'that the original meaning of the saying ... was that which it was popularly supposed to have',[6] nor is there justification for linking the false understanding of v. 22 with Mk. 9, 1.[7] The repudiation is straightforward and dispassionate,[8] suggesting no underlying crisis. The passage is evidence that there existed some in the church at that time who held to a false hope, but there is no suggestion that every member of the community or the responsible leaders of the church [9] were misled.

---

[1] Cf. Temple, *Readings*, pp. 409; Hoskyns-Davey, *John*, p. 668; Lagrange, *Jean*, p. 533; Calvin, *John*, II. p. 296. But some find here the problem whether martyrdom or life is better; cf. Schlatter, *Johannes*, p. 373; partially, Strachan, *Fourth Gospel*, p. 338.

[2] Temple, *Readings*, p. 410 sees the real point, 'The Lord does not answer speculative questions or satisfy curiosity.'

[3] σύ is emphatic; cf. e.g. Bernard, *John*, p. 711.

[4] Bernard, *John*, p. 711 maintains that the emphasis is on ἐὰν θέλω; contrast Bultmann, *Johannes*, p. 554; Barrett, *John*, p. 488.

[5] This 'abiding' should be referred to the Parousia. It is true that μενειν is regularly used in the 4th Gospel (and the Johannine Epistles) in a spiritual sense (cf. Hauck, in *T.W.N.T.* IV, pp. 578ff.) (hence Westcott, *John, ad loc*; Strachan, *Fourth Gospel*, p. 250; Hoskyns-Davey, *John*, p. 668, interpret μενειν in this way here); but Christ's coming is decisive for the meaning here (and it is thus understood by Carpenter, *Johannine Writings*, p. 249; Lightfoot, *John*, p. 343; Bernard, *John*, p. 711; Barrett, *John*, p. 488). Bernard *John*, p. 711, rightly says of the coming, 'to apply it to the coming of Christ at a disciple's death is a desperate expedient of exegesis.'

[6] Barrett, *John*, p. 488.

[7] As Bultmann, *Johannes*, p. 555; Bauer, *Johannes*, p. 239; Barrett, *John*, p. 488; contrast Michaelis, *Verheissung*, pp. 48f. The promise in Mk. 9, 1 is clearly to 'some' (τινες), and there is no evidence that this was ever narrowed down to a single individual; hence Barrett, *John*, p. 488, admits, 'this expectation, however, was possibly local; there seems to be no evidence for it except in John.' Cf. Streeter, *Four Gospels*, pp. 476f.

[8] Temple, *Readings*, p. 410, can comment, '*Incidentally* the recalling of this episode makes it possible to explain and dissipate the rumour ...'

[9] ἐξέρχομαι ... εἰς should probably be understood (with RV) as 'went forth amongst', suggesting simply that the idea went around.

Revelation 1, 1; etc.

Our original question is addressed, finally, to the expressions ἃ δεῖ γενέσθαι ἐν τάχει (1, 1), ἔρχομαι ταχύ (3, 11. 22, 7; 12; 20) and ὁ καιρὸς γὰρ ἐγγύς ἐστιν (22, 10). At the outset we must notice that the present period is evaluated highly as a time of watching [1] and repentance [2]—and, perhaps, of the proclamation of the gospel; [3] so that the place of the present is not underestimated. More important, we must notice that throughout the book there is a note of delay [4] which militates against the interpretation of the above expressions as delimiting the End. Whilst we suggest that there is here no delimited hope, there *is* the conviction that the End is 'near'.[5] What this nearness means, or meant for the early church, is now our problem.

---

[1] 3, 3 is particularly important (cf. Mtt. 24, 43 par Lk. 12, 39f., and I Thess. 5, 4). The thought that Jesus will come at an hour unknown is still present (it is not meant that if the church at Sardis watches, then Jesus will come at a moment anticipated!, but rather that he will then not come with the disastrous consequences of a thief in an unprepared household.)

[2] Cf. 2, 5; 2, 10; 2, 16; 2, 21; 3, 3; 3, 11; 3, 18.

[3] Many (e.g. Schmidt, *Aus der Johannes Apokalypse*, p. 18; Lohmeyer, *Offenbarung*, p. 57; Kiddle, *Revelation*, p. 110; Charles, *Revelation*, p. 161.) think that all four horsemen in Rev. 6, 1ff., are to be understood as representing plagues. But recently Cullmann (*Time*, pp. 16off) has presented a strong case for understanding the rider of the white horse as personifying the preaching of the gospel. We mention in support of this view the following evidence:

a. White, in 1, 14; 2, 17; 3, 4; 3, 5; 3, 18; 4, 4; 6, 11; 7, 9; 7, 13; 14, 14; 19, 11; 19, 14; and 20, 11 (i.e. every reference in Revelation besides 6, 2) is, in this book, a heavenly attribute.

b. νικω predominantly has the sense of overcoming by non violent means (cf. 2, 7; 2, 17; 2, 26; 3, 5; 3, 12; 3, 21; 21, 7; contrast 11, 7; 12, 11; 13, 7; 17, 14), and essentially *divine* action is denoted. (Of course the plagues are not regarded as outside of divine control).

c. If the conquering of the first horseman is a plague, it must be that of war—which the second also brings (though there *is* some duplication amongst the other plagues).

d. The parallelism between this horesman and that of 19, 11f. is very striking; sovereignty and warfare concern both. The horseman of 6, 1f. has a bow; in 19, 11f. he has a sharp sword (perhaps 'bow' is mentioned in 6, 2 to differentiate it from the great sword of the second rider, 6, 4). Rev. 1, 16; Eph. 6, 17; Heb. 4, 12 present the idea of the Word of God as a powerful weapon.

e. If thus interpreted, the four 'signs' parallel Mk. 13 par. and II Thess. 2., II Peter, 3, which include amongst the signs of the End, preaching of the gospel.

[4] Cf. 6, 1. 6, 10. 7, 3. 9, 5; 10. 10, 11. 11, 3. 12, 6; 14. 13, 5.

[5] Kiddle, *Revelation*, p. xxxi., rightly notes that the sequence of events in Revelation connected by 'then'. 'after this', 'does not indicate strict sequence.' cf. further, Rissi, *Zeit und Geschichte in der Offenbarung Johannes*.

CHAPTER NINE

THE EARLY CHURCH'S NEAR EXPECTATION
OF THE PAROUSIA

That the early church certainly thought of the Parousia as (in some sense) near has become evident in our examination of those passages in which a delimited expectation is often understood—wrongly, in our opinion—to be present. The perspective of I Thess. 4, 13f. (cf. I Cor. 15, 51) is that of watchful expectancy, not of certainty that the Parousia will not occur for centuries or millennia.[1] II Thess. 2, 7 speaks of τὸ μυστήριον τῆς ἀνομίας already at work (ἤδη ἐνεργεῖται), stamping the present with the character of the End.[2] The apparent stability and permanency of the world and its institutions are called in question (cf. I Cor. 7, 31). Paul can speak of an 'earnest expectation' (ἀποκαραδοκία) (Phil. 1, 20, Rom. 8, 19),[3] and of 'groaning' (στενάζω) (II Cor. 5, 2, Rom. 8, 23), showing the intensity and earnestness of hope. Expressions such as ἐν ταῖς ἐσχάταις ἡμέραις,[4] ἐπ' ἐσχάτου τῶν ἡμερῶν τούτων,[5] ἐπ' ἐσχάτου τοῦ χρόνου,[6] and ἐσχάτη ὥρα [7] designate the present in its unique relationship to the End. Paul characterises the present as a dawn (Rom. 13, 11f.) and Christians as those 'on whom the end of the ages has come' (I Cor. 10, 11); he maintains that ὁ κύριος ἐγγύς (Phil. 4, 5). The present generation must experience all the signs (political, cosmic and personal) of the End (cf. Mk. 13, 28ff. par.), signifying

---

[1] Cullmann, *Early Church*, p. 152, says 'no one reckoned on the period between the ascension and the return of the Master lasting for centuries.' Certainly they did not write from the perspective that the period prior to the End would *definitely* be very long.

[2] Cf. Frame, *Thessalonians*, p. 264; Bornkamm, in *T.W.N.T.* IV, p. 830. Cf. I Jn. 4, 4.

[3] Delling, in *T.W.N.T.* I, p. 392, makes no allusion to the Christological basis of this earnest hope. But Phil. 1, 20f. has in mind the perfection of salvation in Christ, and Rom. 8, 18ff. has the 'revealing of the sons of God' (8, 17) as the object of creation's ἀποκαραδοκία.

[4] Cf. Acts 2, 17, II Tim. 3, 1.

[5] Cf. Heb. 1, 2, II Pet. 3, 3.

[6] Cf. Jude 18, I Pet. 1, 20.

[7] Cf. I Jn. 2, 18.

that the Parousia of Jesus is not far distant. The End comes 'quickly' (ταχύ) (Rev. 22, 7; 12; 20, cf. Heb. 10, 37).

Significantly, this belief that the Parousia is not far off appears to persist even in those parts of the New Testament where it is often said that near-expectation is missing. Here we mention first, the Epistle to the Ephesians. Many conclude that here all hope of a speedy End has been subsumed under the concepts of catholicity and of the 'summing up of all things in Christ' (cf. 1, 10; 1, 23; 4, 14f.)[1] But the expression in 5, 16 ἐξαγοραζόμενοι τὸν καιρόν suggests that the hope of a speedy End is not entirely lacking; the verb ἐξαγοράζομαι seems to imply urgency,[2] and this because αἱ ἡμέραι πονηραί εἰσιν and because the present God-given opportunity for repentance and faith is not unlimited but has its determined measure.

Secondly, we draw attention to Jn. 14, 19; 16, 16f., where, we suggest, it is correct to understand a near-expectation of the Parousia in the expression μικρὸν . . . μικρόν. Clearly John's peculiar methodology must be borne in mind[3] and this, surely, allows us to draw out of the theme of 'departure—return' in chapters 13—17 not solely the thought of Jesus' departure in death and his return at the Resurrection,[4] nor solely the thought of his departure in the Ascension and 'coming' in the Spirit,[5] but also the thought of his departure and absence in this interim and his return at the Parousia; the Evangelist is likely to have had in mind the situation of the disciples in the last hours before the Passion, *and* the situation of his *readers*.[6] In this case, μικρόν has relevance for the expectation

---

[1] Cf. Hort, *Prolegomena*, p. 142; Abbott, *Ephesians*, p. xx; Westcott, *Ephesians*, p. xxxv; Allan, *Ephesians*, p. 40; Goodspeed, *Ephesians*, p. 65 Mitton, *Ephesians*, pp. 238f.; Nineham, in *Studies in Ephesians*, pp. 33f.

[2] In Dan. 2, 8 the phrase is used *in malam partem*. Buchsel, in *T.W.N.T.* I, p. 128, comments, 'es bedeutet, entsprechend dem Sinn des ἐκ in vielen Kompositis, auch ein *intensives Kaufen*, ein Kaufen, das die vorhandenen Möglichkeiten ausschöpft. So Kol. 4, 5, Eph. 5, 16 τὸν καιρὸν ἐξαγοραζόμενοι. Καιρός steht hier für das, was die Zeit an Möglichkeiten enthält. Das soll unter Aufwand von "Kosten", von Anstrengungen, "restlos ausgenützt", angeignet werden.' Cf. further Abbott, *Ephesians*, pp. 195f.

[3] Cf. Barrett, *John*, p. 409, 'Most of this language is marked by a studied ambiguity . . .'

[4] As in Murray, *Jesus according to St. John*, pp. 280f; Strachan, *Fourth Gospel*, p. 296; Bernard, *John*, pp. 512f.; Tasker, *John*, pp. 182ff.

[5] As in Calvin, *John*, II, pp. 147f.; Bauer, *Johannes*, p. 199; Temple, *Readings*, pp. 293ff.; Holwerda, *Spirit*, esp. pp. 65ff.

[6] Cf. Barrett, *John*, p. 409.

of the Parousia, and the idea of the speedy coming of the End is not entirely lacking.

Thirdly, in Luke's gospel, where the emphasis is so frequently said to rest on the present duration as an indefinitely long period,[1] two passages deserve special notice. The first is Lk. 13; 6-9. Lk. 3, 9 (Mtt. 3, 10) has already declared that judgement is not far distant, ἤδη ... ἡ ἀξίνη πρὸς τὴν ῥίζαν, and in 13, 6ff. the opportunity for repentance is shown to be strictly limited and short.[2] The extra year's grace is wrested from the owner of the vineyard [3] and there is yet time for repentance; [4] but the present time is the final opportunity and has therefore a crucial, urgent character. It is not yet too late to repent; but the time is limited . . .[5]

The other passage is Lk. 18, 1-8. As it stands now, this parable speaks not simply of prayer in general (cf. v. 1) but of the prayerful longing of the faithful for the Parousia (cf. v8b); if this is the meaning imposed by Luke [6] it is especially significant that he has emphasised ἐν τάχει.[7] Although the possibility of delay is envisaged [8] this idea is held in tension by the ἐν τάχει.[9] As in the case of the parable Lk. 13; 6-9, there is a tension of delay and nearness; though the End delays, it is near, and though near there is yet time to repent. There is little warrant for understanding ἐν τάχει as 'suddenly' or 'unexpected';[10] in keeping with its general New

---

[1] Cf. Conzelmann, *Mitte*, p. 129; Cadbury, *Luke-Acts*, p. 292; Grässer, *Problem*, pp. 178.; Creed, *Luke*, p. lxxii.

[2] Leaney, *Luke*, p. 207, comments, 'Only a short time for the inhabitants to change their ways.'; cf. also Creed, *Luke*, p. 181.

[3] Cadbury, *Luke-Acts*, p. 296 is surely wrong in holding that the chief point of the parable is the vinedresser's delay. It is not without significance that Conzelmann makes only fleeting reference to the parable; *Mitte*, p. 55, n. 2 ('Jesus dürfe nach 13, 18f. die Frist nicht eigenmächtig abkürzen').

[4] Cf. Jeremias, *Parables*, p. 157.

[5] If this is Luke's alternative for Mk. 11; 12-14, Mtt. 21; 18-22 (cf. Creed, *Luke*, p. 181), it is particularly important to notice that he has recorded a parable more definitely emphasising urgency.

[6] As many think; cf. Klostermann, *Lukas*, p. 177 (who mentions Jülicher and J. Weiss); Jeremias, *Parables*, pp. 115f.; Bultmann, *Geschichte*, p. 108.

[7] By placing ἐν τάχει at the end of the sentence Lk. has given it special emphasis (cf. Plummer, *Luke*, p. 415; Cranfield, 'The Parable of the Unjust Judge', in S.J.T. xvi, 1963, pp. 297 ff.)

[8] But Cadbury, *Luke-Acts*, p. 296, goes too far; cf. also Geldenhuys, *Luke* p. 448 (following Zahn), 'According to the context the teaching here is that the final events will be very long in coming . . .'

[9] To say that the parable cannot speak of a near End because it envisages delay (*cf. authorities in n. 1 above*) is to exhibit an unjustified monism.

[10] Zahn, *Lukas, ad loc*; Jeremias, *Parables*, p. 116; Geldenhuys, *Luke*,

Testament usage [1] it means 'without undue delay'. Some [2] understand v. 8b as toning down the eager hope of the faithful contained in v. 8a; but 8b does not so much tone down 8a as explicate its serious demand— '. . . the saints must remember (this is the point of v. 8b) that the Parousia, when it comes, will mean judgement for them as well as for their persecutors. Will they themselves be found faithful, when the Lord comes.'[3]

Besides these two important passages, we might mention Lk. 13, 22ff., where the theme is, 'strive to enter . . . before it is too late', and Lk. 12; 57-59, where the emphasis is upon hasty repentance. It appears that Luke is not unsympathetic to the hope of a speedy End nor unaware of the tension between this hope and the need to take full advantage of the present opportunity for obedience.

The writer of the Pastorals, too, has laid great weight on the significance of the present, and the care with which he seeks to regulate the life and worship of the community suggests that he did not believe the End must certainly come within a few years.[4] Nevertheless, certain expressions appear to hint, at least, at the idea of the Parousia's nearness. I Tim. 4, 1, ἐν ὑστέροις καιροῖς is the first, where the exact phrase may have been chosen from stylistic grounds,[5] but it is difficult to dismiss from it the sense inherent in ἔσχαται ἡμέραι.[6] Even if ὕστεροι καιροί means simply a time later than that at which the warning purports to have been penned,[7] it is

---

p. 448; Grässer, *Problem*, p. 38, n 3, take it in this way. But Arndt and Gingrich, *Lexicon*, p. 814, do not mention this as a possibility (similarly Liddell and Scott). Jeremias, *Parables*, p. 116 offers as support the LXX of Dt. 11, 17; Jos. 8, 18f and Ps. 2, 12 but Cranfield, 'The Parable of the Unjust Judge' has shown that these references tell rather against the translation of ἐν τάχει as 'suddenly'.

[1] Cf. Acts 12, 7; 22, 18; 25, 4; Rom. 16, 20; I Tim. 3, 14; Rev. 1, 1 etc.

[2] Klostermann *Lukas*, p. 179, quotes Wellhausen that 8b 'erscheint als redaktionelles Nachtrag: hier wird ein Dämpfer aufgesetzt (cf. Mal 3, 2): sie sollen nicht so eifrig nach seinem Tage rufen'. cf. also Conzelmann, *Mitte*, p. 103; Grässer, *Problem*, p. 38.

[3] Cranfield, 'The Parable of the Unjust Judge' in S. J.T. xvi, 1963, pp. 297ff.

[4] Cf. the emphasis on the writer's own ministry of the gospel in the present period (I Tim. 1, 12; 2, 7; II Tim. 1,3; 1, 11; 2, 1f., 4, 7; 4, 17); on sound doctrine (I Tim. 1, 5f., 1, 18ff., 2, 5f., 3, 15; 4, 1f.)and on moral uprightness (I Tim. 6, 3f., 6, 11f., II Tim. 1, 6f., 2, 14).

[5] Cf. Dibelius, *Pastoralbriefe*, p. 40, 'Die Wahl der Ausdruck ὕστεροι καιροί (nicht ἔσχαται ἡμέραι) ist vielleicht durch den künstlich-futurischen Charakter der Stil . . . bedingt'. (Those who favour Pauline authorship would take another view here.)

[6] Cf. Spicq, *Pastorales*, p. 136.

[7] As Dibelius, *Pastoralbriefe*, p. 40; Parry, *Pastoral Epistles*, p. 24; Easton, *Pastoral Epistles*, pp. 138f., maintain.

pregnant with overtones of the Parousia.[1] Next, I Tim. 6, 14 ἦν καιροῖς ἰδίοις δείξει. Here there seems to be no need to discern polemic against Parousia-delay grumbling!,[2] nor should we conclude that the Parousia is thought of as far distant:[3] the End *is* to appear at its own (divinely) appointed time, and the stress lies in the assurance and urgency contained in that thought. Another expression is ἐν ἐσχάταις ἡμέραις in II Tim. 3, 1. Falconer comments, '. . . though the men are present, the end is not thought to be so near as in Paul's epistles.'[4] But Spicq's comment,[5] 'ἐν ἐσχάταις ἡμέραις désignet la période qui précède immédiatement la parousie . . . Mais rien n'est dit de la durée de ces derniers temps . . .' is, surely, right. The character of the present is referred to as an interim bounded by the Parousia which can occur at any moment.[6] In II Tim. 4, 1 we meet the expression τοῦ μέλλοντος κρίνειν. RV, RSV, Moffatt and NEB all translate, 'who shall judge', but it might perhaps be that we should understand a sense of nearness here, and 'that his appearing to judge is not far off.'[7]

So we have some grounds for saying that the sense of nearness persists. Since this, as we have argued, appears to be an undelimited nearness, no belief being held that the End *must* come within a specified period, it is now necessary to define it more narrowly, and this we do in the first place by drawing attention to its origins. Our examination of Old Testament and inter-testamental expectation[8] emphasised how Israel's hope that God would intervene decisively in history was *based consistently upon the fact of his past and present activity in the salvation-history. The same is true also of the early church* as we find its hope conveyed in the New Testa-

---

[1] Cf. II Thess. 2, 3f., which, perhaps, the writer had in mind?

[2] As e.g., Falconer, *Pastoral Epistles*, p. 157, holds.

[3] As e.g., Guthrie, *Pastoral Epistles*, p. 116, suggests.

[4] *Pastoral Epistles*, p. 89.

[5] *Pastorales*, p. 366; contrast Guthrie, *Pastoral Epistles*, p. 156.

[6] Because it is the character of the present which is referred to, perhaps, the article is omitted (cf. Spicq, *Pastorales*, p. 366; Lock, *Pastoral Epistles*, *ad loc*), though Parry (*Pastoral Epistles*, p. 62) takes the omission as grounds for translating 'times of extremity', in a general sense.

[7] Falconer, *Pastoral Epistles*, p. 94. Arndt-Gingrich, *Lexicon*, pp. 501f., noting the frequent occurrence (84x) of μέλλω with present infinitive in the N.T., say that this can mean 'on the point of . . .', but place II Tim. 4, 1 under the second meaning, the weakened sense used as a periphrasis for the future. Blass-Debrunner, *Grammar*, p. 181 para 356, 'Μέλλειν with the infinitive expresses imminence.'

[8] Cf. above, chapter 2.

ment. Two features, in particular, in the salvation-history events created and sustained the early church's intense Parousia hope.

1. The first is their conviction that in Jesus Christ ἤγγικεν ἡ βασιλεία τοῦ θεοῦ (Mk. 1, 15 par.). This particular reference, since it appears to be a summary of Mark's (or of his source),[1] clearly reflects the early church's understanding of Jesus' message (however much this may have coincided with Jesus' own understanding of it.).[2] ἤγγικεν here most probably means 'has come (near)'. The LXX usage [3] may be inconclusive,[4] but the parallelism here with πεπλήρωται must, surely, be decisive,[5] for there can be no doubt as to the meaning of this word.[6]

At the same time, the flexibility of the word ἤγγικεν (reflected in the LXX usage, and manifest in the temporal and spatial possibilities it contains) [7] helps to suggest that the 'coming' of the Kingdom of God was not understood in a straightforward, but in a complex manner,[8] and this is, surely, because the expression ἡ βασιλεία τοῦ θεοῦ held for the early church a special significance (over against its meaning in Judaism). It is not that the early church saw in the proclamation simply a call to repent in order to

---

[1] Most agree that Mk. 1, 15 is an editorial compilation; cf. Rawlinson, *Mark*, p. 13; Sharman, *Son of Man*, pp. 99f.; Lohmeyer, *Markus, ad loc*; Lagrange, *Marc*, p. 18; Percy, *Botschaft*, p. 20; Branscomb, *Mark*, p. 25; Klostermann, *Markus*, p.14. etc.

[2] Cf. Percy, *Botschaft*, p. 21; Rawlinson, *Mark*, p. 251.

[3] Cf. Dodd, *Parables*, p. 44 (and in *E.T.* XLVII, pp. 936f., 138ff.) Kümmel, *Promise*, pp. 21ff.; Campbell, in *E.T.* XLVIII, pp. 91f.; Clark, in *J.B.L.* LIX, 1940, pp. 367f.; Black, in *E.T.* LXIII, 1952, pp. 298f. Dodd argues that 'ἤγγικεν could be used to translate Hebrew and Aramaic verbs meaning "arrive" without being untrue to their meaning', and Black (following M. Paul Joüon, in *Recherches de Science Religieuse*, Tome XVII (1927), p. 538) concludes that 'the parallel at Mk. 1, 15 πεπλήρωται like the parallel at Lam. 4, 19 (18) may be taken to support the translation of ἤγγικεν = qᵉrabhath by "the Kingdom of God has come".' But contrast Kümmel, Campbell and Clark.

[4] Because although the majority usage might tell against Dodd's view, Kümmel (*Promise*, p. 24) acknowledges that 'the translators of the Septuagint occasionally stretch the meaning of ἤγγικεν to the marginal case of "approaching to".'

[5] Cf. Lohmeyer, *Markus, ad loc*; Flückiger, *Ursprung*, pp. 96ff.; Black, in *E.T.* LXIII, 1952, pp. 298f.

[6] Cf. Delling, in *T.W.N.T.* VI, p. 289f.; also III, p. 463 n. 37, '. . .Mk. 1, 15: von dem καιρός schlechthin, der, von Gottes Volk auf Grund der Verheissung erwartet, mit dem Auftreten Jesu gekommen ist.'

[7] Preisker, in *T.W.N.T.* II, pp. 330f., and Fuller, *Mission and Message*, pp. 20f., give details.

[8] Kümmel, *Promise*, p. 23, n. 13 complains that no explanation is given

attain salvation,[1] nor simply the challenge to decide for God, against all the attraction of the world,[2] not yet simply the promise that the End was soon to arrive,[3] but rather that it saw in this proclamation a *Christological affirmation*: 'The Kingdom has come close to men in the person of Jesus and in his person it actually confronts them.'[4] Jesus' healings and exorcisms are a pointer to this fact (cf. Mtt. 12, 28; Lk. 11, 20).[5] (Significantly φθάνειν [6] whose precise meaning is disputed [7] is probably a further indication that the Kingdom's presence though real, is complex).[8] Jesus' preaching is essentially a self-offering (cf. Lk. 4, 16ff., Jn. 4, 26f., etc.), his teaching concerns final judgement and final forgiveness (Mk. 2, 9f.)

Since this theme has been elaborated more than once [9] we do no more here than draw attention to the fact that the basic affirmation that the Kingdom of God has come (near) in the person of Jesus Christ, runs throughout the New Testament. The pre-New Testament hope in the coming of the Kingdom of God looked for three major events: the judgement upon sinners, the blessing of the faithful, and the overthrow of all rebellious powers (and so, essentially, the renewal of the world). Each aspect is seen in the New Testament as fulfilled—in Christ.

In Christ, the final judgement is enacted. That is certainly the conviction of those elements in the New Testament witness which point to the vicarious judgement of sin in and through the

---

why ἤγγικεν should have been used in the tradition, if it was meant to mean 'has come'. It may perhaps be that ἤγγικεν was thought specially suitable in view of its flexibility to denote the real, though Christological and proleptic, presence of the Kingdom of God.

[1] As Case, *A New Biography*, pp. 244f., maintains.

[2] Cf. Bultmann, *Theology*, p. 21 holds this.

[3] As Schweitzer, *Mystery*, pp. 69f., holds.

[4] Cranfield, *Mark*, p. 68.

[5] Cf. also Mk. 3, 27; 7, 37; 5, 19; Is. 35, 5-6, 61, 1. Hence the Fourth Gospel designates them as σημεῖα (cf. 20, 30).

[6] The word nowhere else appears in the gospels. But cf. Phil. 3, 16, Rom. 9, 31, II Cor. 10, 14, I Thess. 2, 16 and 4, 15.

[7] Kümmel, *Promise*, p. 106, finds the old meaning 'to anticipate' only in I Thess. 4, 15 and concludes that the meaning 'has arrived' is therefore conclusive for Mtt. 12, 28 par. Morgenthaler, *Kommendes Reich*, pp. 36f., however, suggests that an examination of its usage shows it to have a proleptic character.

[8] Cf. Cullmann, *Time*, p. 71; Michaelis, *Matthäus*, *ad loc* Mtt. 12, 28; Flückiger, *Ursprung*, p. 95.

[9] Cf. esp. Cullmann, *Time*, pp. 121-174; Filson, *New Testament*; Barth, *C.D.* III/2, pp. 437ff.; Stauffer, *Theology*, pp. 51ff., etc.

death of Jesus (cf. Mk. 10, 45, Rom. 6, 10; 8, 1; II Cor. 5, 14 etc.).[1]
This judgement, though focussed in the Cross, in fact embraces the
entire incarnation (cf. Mk. 10, 45, Jn. 13, 4-11, Phil. 2, 6ff.) Though,
to be sure, 'All that Jesus does and all that he teaches is directed
towards man, who is "lost", not in order to judge him or to lecture
him, but in order to save him, to bring him back to God . . .',[2] yet
judgement of man's sin *is* brought to a head and, in its finality
enacted in the Cross (cf. esp. Gal. 3, 10).[3]

In no greater detail we call attention, secondly, to the belief
reflected in the New Testament that in Christ the final blessing
of the just has been accomplished. It had been expected that the
faithful would receive at the Messiah's hand, reward for their
uprightness.[4] This hope was indeed not unfulfilled, but the 'faithful'
have been narrowed down to the one man Jesus Christ.[5] This is
most clearly expressed in the numerous passages which speak
of Christ's exaltation (cf. Acts 5, 31; Rom. 3, 24; 5, 1; 4, 25; Eph. 1,
3 etc.)[6] which is regarded not as something which has occurred to
him *only*, but to him as representative.[7]

Finally, in Christ—so the New Testament witness maintains—the
final subjugation of rebellious powers has occurred. Already in
his ministry (through exorcisms and miracles particularly) Jesus
exercised God's sovereignty against disorder and disease.[8] But the
subjugation is especially bound up with the crucifixion and resurrection (cf. Acts 2, 36; Eph. 1, 20-23; Phil. 2, 9). Even death
itself has been 'abolished' (καταργήσαντος) (II Tim. 1, 10), so that
it can be said, 'whosoever believes on me shall never die.' (Jn. 11,

---

[1] Cf. Richardson, *Theology*, pp. 215f.; Calvin, *Institutes* II, 16/5 and thereto
cf. van Buren, *Christ in our Place*, pp. 40ff.

[2] Brunner, *Dogmatics*, II, p. 281.

[3] Cf. Luther's exposition, in *Galations*, Clarke ed., pp. 279ff.

[4] Cf. above, chapter 2, esp. pp. 14f.

[5] Cf. Manson, *Teaching*, pp. 171ff.; Cullmann, *Time*, pp. 115f.

[6] Calvin rightly warns against artificially separating the Cross from the
Resurrection and Ascension (cf. van Buren, *Chist in our Place*, pp. 81ff.);
yet the Resurrection and Ascension have special place in the point we wish
to make here.

[7] Cf. esp. Eph. 1, 3ff., 2, 6-7, II Cor. 1, 10; I Cor. 15, 20f.; Phil. 3, 20;
Col. 3, 3f., I Pet. 1, 3f., etc.
Calvin (*Institutes* II, 16/16) writes, 'For since he entered there in our
flesh and, as it were, in our name, it follows, as the apostle says, that in a
certain manner we sit together with him now in heaven (Eph. 2, 5), since
we do not hope for heaven with a bare hope, but possess it in our Head.'
Cf. also van Buren, *Christ in our Place*, pp. 86ff., Barth, *C.D.* IV/2, pp. 3ff.

[8] Cf. Jn. 20, 30; Lk. 10, 18; Mk. 3, 27. Manson, *Jesus*, pp. 33ff.

26). Hence the great stress in the New Testament upon Ps. 110 [1] and Christ's exaltation to the position of authority at God's right hand: 'His resurrection is the victory of the new creation over the old'.[2]

So the final events of the End are, in a real sense, already accomplished—in Christ. This is the first factor upon which the New Testament insistence upon the nearness of the End is based. It is a specific understanding of the past phases of salvation-history as these have been brought to a head in Christ.

2. The second factor on which the near hope is based is the presence of the Spirit in the life of the early church, and its meaning for the church. Throughout the New Testament, the Spirit is regarded as having a twofold focus, both vital for the Parousia hope.

The first focus is the historical life and work of Jesus Christ. The Spirit is regarded as in some way contemporising this historical person and work: [3] 'The Spirit's office is confined to revealing and communicating Christ to the believer'.[4] To be sure Matthew and Mark, whether in accord with the actual historical situation,[5] or perhaps because of some express purpose [6] 'contain astoundingly few statements about the Spirit'; [7] for Luke, 'the chief thing for which the Spirit is responsible is the preaching of the disciples . . .',[8] preaching being the proclamation of Christ's person and work, the contemporising of the Word.

Paul regards the presence of the Spirit as mediating the presence

---

[1] Cf. Rom. 8, 34; I Cor. 15, 25; Col. 3, 1; Eph. 1, 20; Heb. 1, 3; 8, 1; 10,13; I Pet. 3, 22; Acts 2, 34; 5, 31; 7, 55; Rev. 3, 21; Mtt. 22, 44; 26, 64; Mk. 12, 36; 14, 62; 16, 19; Lk. 20, 42; 22, 69. Cf. Cullmann, 'The Kingship of Christ and the Church in the N.T.', in *Early Church*, pp. 105ff.; Caird, *Principalities and Powers*, pp. 8off.; Leivestad, *Christ the Conqueror, passim*.

[2] Visser 't Hooft, *Renewal*, p. 33. Barth, *Humanity of God*, p. 47, writes, 'He is in his person the covenant in its fulness, the Kingdom of heaven which is at hand, in which God speaks and man hears, God gives and man receives, God commands and man obeys, God's glory shines in the heights and thence into the depths, and peace on earth comes to pass among men in whom he is well pleased.'

[3] Cf. Dillistone, *The Holy Spirit in the Life of To-day*, pp. 27f.; Barth, *C.D.* I/1, pp. 515ff.; Hamilton, *Holy Spirit*, pp. 3ff.

[4] Hamilton, *Holy Spirit*, p. 12.

[5] Cf. Barrett, *H.S.G.T.*, pp. 140ff.; Schweizer, *Spirit* (ET of the article in *T.W.N.T.* VI, pp. 330ff.)

[6] It could, perhaps, be argued that there had been a conscious attempt to focus attention solely on the person of Christ and that therefore teaching concerning the Spirit was kept to a minimum?

[7] Schweizer, *Spirit*, p. 35, and cf. pp. 25-36.

[8] Schweizer, *Spirit*, p. 43.

of the ascended Christ (cf. Rom. 8, 9-10, I Cor. 3, 7; II Cor. 3, 11),
so that the events accomplished in the death and resurrection of
Christ are communicated to the believer: 'The Spirit is the Spirit
of Christ because his office is to communicate the benefits of Christ's
work.'[1] The judgement, the new life, the 'new creation' effected in
Christ's person and work, the imperative and the indicative of the
Cross and Resurrection, are echoed by the Spirit in the believer.[2]

The same can be said of the Spirit in John. The Fourth Evangelist
'proclaims, more clearly even than Paul, the present actuality
of the salvation which is one day to be consummated'[3] and,
concentrating more consciously on the interval between Jesus'
ascension and the Parousia than the Synoptists, 'interprets its real
significance. This interval is eschatologically a continuation of
the present kingdom manifested in the earthly ministry of Jesus'.[4]
It is, indeed, so intimately bound up with that historical ministry
that that ministry is contemporised in the interval through the
Spirit who is 'the eschatological continuum in which the work of
Christ, initiated in his ministry and awaiting its termination at
his return, is wrought out.'[5] The Paraclete sayings (cf. Jn. 14, 16;
14, 26; 15, 26; 16, 7; 16, 13f.) emphasise most particularly this
relationship between Christ's historical life and work, and the
Spirit present with the believer.[6]

The other focus which the Spirit has is the second coming of
Christ and the presence of the Kingdom in its consummate form.
The first focus is a backward reference, the second looks forward.
This forward look arises from the conviction that the presence of the
Spirit is a sign of the End and an assurance that the present is
already somehow an anticipation of the Last Age.[7] Whether the
Baptist spoke of a bestowal of the Spirit or not,[8] it is evident

---

[1] Hamilton, *Holy Spirit*, p. 15.

[2] Schweizer, *Spirit*, pp. 73f.

[3] Cf. Schweizer, *Spirit*, p. 88; Barrett, *John*, pp. 57ff.

[4] Holwerda, *Spirit*, p. 85; and cf. chapters 1-3.

[5] Cf. Barrett, *John*, pp. 74ff.; Holwerda, *Spirit*, pp. 25ff.; Schweizer, *Spirit*, pp. 92f.; Barrett, 'The Holy Spirit in the Fourth Gospel,' in *J.T.S.* (NS) I, 1950, pp. 1ff.

[6] Cf. Barrett, *John*, pp. 75ff.; Schweizer, *Spirit*, pp. 95ff.

[7] For the expectation that the last times would witness an outpouring of the spirit cf. Joel 2, 28f.; Is. 44, 3, Ezek. 36, 26f.; 37, 14; 39, 29, Test. Lev. 18, 11. Cf. Schweizer, *Spirit*, pp. 12f.; Taylor, *Mark*, p. 157; Cranfield, *Mark*, p. 50; Lampe, *Seal*, pp. 27ff.

[8] Cf. Eisler, *Messiah Jesus and John the Baptist*, pp. 275ff.; Barrett, *H.S.G.T.*, pp. 126f.; Taylor, *Mark*, p. 157. Contrast Cranfield *Mark*, p. 50.

that the Synoptic tradition (cf. Mk. 1, 8; Lk. 3, 16; Mtt. 3, 11; cf. Jn. 1, 33) saw his witness to Jesus as a testimony to his eschatological significance: 'while John administers the eschatological sacrament of baptism, the coming one will actually bestow the eschatological gift of the Spirit.'[1] This is as clear in the Fourth Gospel[2] as in Paul,[3] but is perhaps most explicit in the terms used by Paul with reference to the Spirit—ἀρραβών (II Cor. 1, 22; 5, 5; Eph. 1, 14) and ἀπαρχή (Rom. 8, 23): 'Der Geist, den Gott ihnen gegeben hat, ist den Christen Gewähr für künftigen vollen Heilsbesitz.'[4]

This understanding of the person and work of Jesus Christ, and this understanding of the presence and work of the Holy Spirit, are the basis of the early church's insistence upon the nearness of the Parousia. It is a matter of the (now frequently stated)[5] tension between 'already' and 'not yet'. Not between certain End events which have been accomplished and certain others which have not yet been fulfilled,[6] but between the End events fulfilled in a mystery already (fulfilled, that is, in the hidden ministry of Christ), and the manifestation of their fulfilment in openness which has not yet occurred and which therefore involves acute tension in the present.

We may enlarge upon this briefly. Clearly the ambiguity concerning the Sovereignty of God, to which the End events were expected to put an end, continued in the Ministry of Jesus: the presence of the Kingdom of God in his person and work was a

---

[1] Cranfield, *Mark*, p. 49.

[2] Cf. Holwerda, *Spirit*, pp. 65ff.; Barrett, in *J.T.S.* (NS) I, 1950, pp. 1ff., *John*, pp. 74ff.

[3] Cf. Hamilton, *Holy Spirit*, pp. 17ff.

[4] Behm, in *T.W.N.T.* I, p. 474; cf. Barrett, *H.S.G.T.* p. 153; Hamilton, *Holy Spirit*, pp. 20f.; Schweizer, *Spirit*, pp. 64f.; Cullmann, *Time*, p. 155; Sanday and Headlam, *Romans*, p. 209; cf. also Gal. 6, 8; Rom. 14, 17; I Cor. 4, 20.

[5] Cf. Ridderbos, *De Komst*, pp. 68f.; Cullmann, *Time*, pp. 86f.; *Early Church*, pp. 153f.; Jeremias, in *T.B.* XX, 1941, pp. 22f.; Filson, *New Testament*, pp. 65ff.; Cranfield, *Mark*, p. 408; Morgenthaler, *Kommendes Reich*, p. 73; Flückiger, *Ursprung*, pp. 208f.

[6] Hence, perhaps, we might suggest that Cullmann's 'D-Day' analogy is not altogether satisfactory, for it suggests that though the victory of Cross and Resurrection was decisive, it was only partial; clearly Cullmann himself does not want to assert such a partial victory (cf. *Early Church*, p. 111, where he contends that even in Heb. 10, 15; I Cor. 15, 25, we have to do with a contrast between a present subjection and a future annihilation, rather than a present partial subjection contrasted with a future complete one).

mystery (cf. Mk. 4, 11),[1] and was anything but the obvious, irrefutable, unambiguous display of sovereignty awaited. Though God was really revealing himself in his Word [2] he revealed himself and his rule in the 'Son of Man' who 'must first serve as the servant of the Eternal and suffer and die as a ransom for all'.[3] The final judgement occurred in the obedience of this Son of Man, an obedience 'even unto the death of Cross' (Phil. 2, 8). The final blessing occurred in a form equally hidden and equally Christocentric; participation in the exaltation by the believer is certainly not apparent (cf. e.g. I Jn. 3, 2; Col. 3, 4). The final subjugation of the ἐξουσίαι has occurred in total obscurity, indeed in the apparent triumph of rebellious powers over Christ.[4] Preiss rightly asserts, 'the primitive church saw itself constrained by its Lord to tear in two the traditional eschatology; on the one hand stands what has already been realised by the life, death and resurrection of Jesus, and on the other, what will only come through the Parousia'.[5]

Further, the present time is by no means that era of bliss, of unambiguous rule, of the triumph of right and the punishment of wrong which was awaited. Only through the exercise of faith can the present be regarded as the time of the End; the present Lordship of Christ is acknowledged only more or less, only here and there, only in faith.[6] By the presence of the Spirit the believer is involved in an acute tension between 'now' and 'then'. It is in this understanding of past and present centred on Christ and mediated to us through the Spirit, that the early church has found itself compelled to live in imminent expectation of the End.[7] One is perhaps tempted at this point to suggest that a concept of revelation demands that

---

[1] Cf. Cranfield, *Mark*, p. 153, 'The Incarnate Word is not obvious. Only faith could recognise the Son of God in the lowly figure of Jesus of Nazareth...'

[2] Cf. Baillie, *The Idea of Revelation in Recent Thought*, pp. 76ff.

[3] Preiss, *Life in Christ*, p. 68.

[4] I Cor. 2, 8f. suggests that not even the ἄρχοντες were aware of the significance of the Crucifixion. Cf. Cullmann, *Early Church*, pp. 111f. Stauffer, *Theology*, p. 125.

[5] *Life in Christ*, p. 49.

[6] Hence the church is that sphere within the Regnum Christi in which His Lordship is more or less openly acknowledged, in contrast to other spheres where it is none the less real, but unconfessed. Cf. Cullmann, *Early Church*, pp. 105f.

[7] How inadequate by comparison the explanation that the imminent hope was essentially a mistake but served a good purpose in that it encouraged moral earnestness and allowed elasticity and mobility! cf. Sanday and Headlam, *Romans*, pp. 379f.

the open manifestation inherent in the final events should occur imminently (i.e. by definition it is an urgent necessity).[1] And, to be sure, the present ambiguity and the hidden character of the revelation in Jesus Christ, cry out for the display of that revelation in unambiguous manner.[2] But Barth [3] has warned against finding a basis for the Parousia hope in a deduction from some general insight, or from an analysis of a concept. The New Testament hope rests not on an analysis nor upon a general insight, but upon the event and acknowledgement of revelation. The early church looked for the return of their Lord not simply because the ambiguity of the past and present cried out for it, but because Christ'showed himself to them as the One he once was, as the One who was with them and indeed in them, but also as the One who stood before them as eternally future'.[4]

The nearness of the end is bound up with the person of Jesus Christ, in whom the events of the end, including their open, unambiguous manifestation, coinhere. In him, death, resurrection, ascension and Parousia belong together. They do not belong together as a general principle [5] but as a matter of theological, or more exactly of Christological fact.[6]

The Christological unity of the End events is thus the mainspring of the End's nearness. This has two important corollaries. The first is that this Christological unity and this imminence are factors difficult to express; the situation is complex, the older eschatological pattern shattered,[7] and the nearness of the End, whilst not without chronological connotation [2] is nevertheless

---

[1] Revelation, of course, involves not only confrontation with an object but an adequate perception of that object; cf. Torrance, in *Essays in Christology*, pp.13ff.

[2] Hence the emphasis within the N.T. is upon the Parousia as the open manifestation of that which has occurred in Christ, in principle and in hiddenness; cf. above chapter 7, pp. 103ff. Richardson, *Theology*, pp. 53f.; this was already perceived by F. D. Maurice, in *The Kingdom of Christ*, (SCM ed.) II, pp. 283f.

[3] *C.D.* IV/I, pp. 322ff.

[4] Barth, *C.D.* IV/I, pp. 326f.

[5] 'We must be careful not to formulate the answer in a way which would give to this final coming and consummation any other necessity than that of the free grace of God'. Barth, *C.D.* IV/I p. 324.

[6] Cf. Cranfield, *Mark*, p. 408; in *Essays in Christology*, pp. 89ff.; Barth, *C.D.* III/2, pp. 490f.; Camfield, 'Man in his time,' in *S.J.T.* III, 1950, pp. 127ff.

[7] Cf. Preiss, *Life in Christ*, p. 49; Cullmann, *Time*, pp. 81ff.

[8] Cf. Preiss, *Life in Christ*, p. 59; Barth, *C.D.* III/2, pp. 490f.

independent of temporal delimitation. It can, therefore, be expressed only obliquely. This accounts for the variety of the New Testament expressions for this nearness [1] and for the use of terms which are either ambiguous or flexible.[2] It accounts, too, for the otherwise irreconcilable juxtaposition of exhortations to watch expectantly beside warnings to patient endurance in face of the possibility of a delay.[3]

The second corollary of this Christological imminence is that when and where the significance of the person and work of Jesus Christ is inadequately grasped, or the presence and purpose of the Holy Spirit is imperfectly perceived and understood, then and there the imminence of the End will either evaporate,[4] or will be expressed in a faulty manner—sometimes in the form of a temporally delimited expectation.[5]

Already within the New Testament there are signs of eschatological misunderstandings which the New Testament writers have to oppose.[6] In the Thessalonian community there were those who sought to anticipate the End (cf II Thess. 2, 2) and inclined to moral laxity, social irresponsibility and political anarchy.[7] Paul counters this by a repetition of the significance of Christ's work and of the present period of salvation-history. The materialistic eschatology reflected in the Corinthians' excesses in the eucharist (cf I Cor. 11, 17ff.) is attacked by Paul with an insistence upon a Christological-

---

[1] Cf. the imagery of 'standing at the door' (Mk. 13, 29 par., Jam. 5, 9; cf. Rev. 4, 1), 'later times' (I Tim. 4, 1), 'the last days' (II Tim. 3, 1; Jam. 5, 3), 'a last hour' (I Jn. 2, 18; 28), 'the last times' (Jude 18); the imagery of day and night (Rom. 13, 11f., Heb. 10, 25), the expression 'the Kingdom of God is at hand' ((Mk. 1, 15 par. etc., cf. Phil. 4, 5; I Pet. 4, 7) and the expressions of haste (Heb. 10, 37f., II Pet. 3, 9; Rev. 22, 7)).

[2] Cf. ἐγγύς, ἐγγίζειν (Mk. 1, 15; Mtt. 3, 2; 4, 17; 10, 7; Rom. 13, 12; I Pet. 4, 7; etc.), and ἔφθασεν (Mtt. 12, 28; Lk. 11, 20).

[3] Cf. e.g. Mk. 13, 28-30 with Mk. 13, 32-37: Mtt. 25, 5 with Mtt. 25, 13: II Pet. 3, 8 with II Pet. 3, 9.

[4] Into a gentle hope or a pious optimism; whereas 'das gesamte Neue Testament die Nähe des Endes verkundet und in dieser Spannung lebt: Das Reich Gottes ist nahe herbeigekommen...' (Albertz, Botschaft, II/1, pp. 206.) Cf. 'The second coming was one of the primary motives for the Christian life', Barclay, Mind, p. 218.

[5] Cf. Cullmann, in K.r.S. XI, 1942, pp. 178.

[6] Cf. the detailed discussion in Reicke, Diakonie, Festfreude und Zelos, Pt. 3, pp. 233ff.

[7] Cf. II Thess. 3, 6f, 11, rebuking disorderliness; II Thess. 3, 12 and I Thess. 4, 10-12 encouraging quietness and responsible work; II Thess. 3, 11 rebuking 'busybodies'.

eschatological scheme whereby the eucharist is both and ἀνάμνησις (I Cor. 11, 24; 25) and an anticipation of the Parousia (ἄχρι οὗ ἔλθῃ 11, 26).[1] In II Peter, the eschatological scepticism or impatience is met with a reaffirmation of the reality of salvation-history, of the work of Christ, and of the purpose of the present interim (cf esp. II Pet. 1, 16-21, 3, 14-18). When these factors are perceived it can and must still be maintained that 'the Lord is not slack concerning his promise'.[2]

Other, less obvious, instances of eschatological misunderstanding can be found within the New Testament,[3] generally reflecting Judaistic or heathen pressures towards a materialising of eschatology and an anticipation of the End through inadequate appreciation of the purpose of the present opportunity.

In post-New Testament times (up to, and including, the present) such errors continue, often involving a temporal delimitation of the end.[4] But the New Testament writers maintain a thoroughly Christological eschatology and therefore consistently oppose such misunderstandings. It only remains now to pose the question whether this Christological eschatology was maintained by the New Testament writers on their own initiative, or whether they have followed (in principle at least) Jesus' own understanding and teaching.

---

[1] Jeremias' thesis that ἀνάμνησις here means 'God will remember me' (*Eucharistic Words*, pp. 162ff.) even if correct (but cf. Jones, in *J.T.S.* VI, 1955, pp. 183ff.), does not rule out the fact that the Eucharistic rite was a 'proclamation of the Lord's death'; cf. Héring, *I Corinthiens*, p. 103; Plummer, *Luke*, p. 246, Reicke, *Diakonie, Festfreude und Zelos*, pp. 257ff. If the Last Supper has, at least, Passover associations (cf. Jones, in *J.T.S.* VI, 1955, pp. 188f.) it is noteworthy that 'the Passover at the time of Jesus looked both backwards and forwards. God's people remember at the feast the merciful immunity afforded the houses sprinkled with the blood of the Paschal lambs and their deliverance from servitude in Egypt' (Jeremias, *Eucharistic Words*, p. 137; cf. Preiss, *Life in Christ*, p. 90). The forward reference is focussed in the expression ἄχρι οὗ ἔλθῃ (cf. Jeremias, *Eucharistic Words*, pp. 115f., 136f.).

[2] Cf. οὐ βραδύνει; Blass-Debrunner, *Grammar*, para. 180, 5.

[3] Cf. Mtt. 24, 31-51 (Lk. 12, 35-46) perhaps reflects an actual situation of revelry and violence connected with a materialistic eschatology; cf. zealostistic impatience in James (1, 3f., 1, 12; 3, 17f; 5, 7f.) connected with misunderstanding as to the significance of the present (4, 13ff.). Cf. Reicke, *Diakonie, Festfreude und Zelos*, pp. 233ff.

[4] Cf. the examples mentioned in chapter 12, below, pp. 215ff.

CHAPTER TEN

DID JESUS DELIMIT HIS EXPECTATION OF THE PAROUSIA?

In this chapter we pose the third of our questions (cf. p. 107). We seek an answer by enquiring into the authenticity of those sayings which are often taken as expressing a delimited hope (Mk. 9, 1. 13, 30; etc.); if they seem to be authentic, then we enquire further into their possible original meaning.

Mark 9, 1

Although the authenticity of this verse has been recently very much under fire, many modern scholars accept it as a saying of Jesus [1] and indeed there seems insufficient reason for regarding it as anything but authentic.

Many [2] argue that this is a word of comfort composed in a time when belief in the near approach of the End was beginning to wane,

---

[1] Cf. Taylor, *Mark*, p. 386; Rawlinson, *Mark*, p. 116; Kümmel, *Promise*, p. 27; Schniewind, *Markus*, p. 212; Schlatter, *Markus, ad loc*; Lohmeyer *Markus*, pp. 217f.; Flückiger, *Ursprung*, p. 117; Morgenthaler, *Kommendes Reich*, p. 53; Cullmann, *Early Church*, p. 150; Cranfield, *Mark*, pp. 285f.; Michaelis, *Verheissung*, pp. 34f.; and in *Wikenhauser Festschrift*, pp. 111f.; Robinson, *Coming*, p. 89; Lagrange, *Marc*, p. 226; Bosch, *Heidenmission*, p. 144; Streeter, in *Oxford Studies*, pp. 429f.; Guy, *Last Things*, pp. 80f.; Ridderbos, *De komst*, pp. 427f.; Manson, *Jesus*, p. 70; Dodd, *Parables*, pp. 53f.; Beasley-Murray, *Mark* 13, p. 108; and *Future*, pp. 183f.; Swete, *Mark*, p. 175; Duncan, *Son of Man*, p. 182; Glasson, *Advent*, p. 112; Walter, *Kommen*, p. 96; Nicklin, *Gleanings*, p. 346; Manson, *Teaching* p. 278; Hunter, *Mark*, p. 91; Johnson, *Mark*, p. 153 (possibly).

[2] Cf. Bultmann, *Geschichte*, p. 128; Bornkamm, in *In Memoriam*, pp. 116f.; Grässer, *Problem*, pp. 131ff.; Marxsen, *Markus, ad loc*; Percy, *Botschaft*, p. 177 (tentatively); Fuchs, in *V.F.* 1947-8, pp. 76f.; Conzelmann, *Mitte*, pp. 95f.; Branscomb, *Mark*, p. 159; Menzies, *Earliest Gospel*, p. 173; (Kümmel, *Promise*, p. 27, n. 28, adds K. Kundsin *Das Urchristentum*, 1929, p. 15; Guignebert, *Jesus*, pp. 333f., is not certain; Loisy, *Marc, ad loc*, and Hauck, *Markus*, p. 106 think the saying originally forecast that all would live to the Parousia and that Mk.9, 1 has been modified because some disciples had already died. Percy, *Botschaft*, p. 177 n. 2, rightly comments, 'eine solche bewusste Änderung einer so deutlichen Aussage mutet aber an sich weniger wahrscheinlich an.'

for it speaks of a *delay* of the Parousia, whereas 'Jesus, who expected it to come if not before his death at least very shortly after, could scarcely have deferred the Coming, as he does here, to a time when most of his disciples would have died, as was evidently the case when this was written'.[1] However, most who arrive at such a conclusion are working with a radical redactional-critical methodology [2] which in this case assumes that no delay prior to the Parousia was anticipated by Jesus or the earliest disciples, whereas this is precisely the point in question, not to be assumed. They also maintain that the saying speaks definitely of a delay, which is questionable.[3]

If this were a community saying, it is difficult to imagine how exactly it originated: [4] although Matthew and Luke alter Mark here,[5] we have no evidence that the early church (or Mark himself) felt free to create sayings prefaced with the solemn asseveration αμην λέγω ὑμῖν.[6]

On the other hand, it is sometimes argued in favour of authenticity, 'the fact that this prediction was not realised must have caused such serious difficulties that they would hardly have been created.' [7] This, however, is no answer to the criticism just mention-

---

[1] Menzies, *Earliest Gospel*, p. 173.

[2] Cf. above chapter 5, pp. 68f.; cf. Cullmann, in *T.L.* I, 1958.

[3] Cf. above, chapter 8, pp. 125f.

[4] Michaelis, in *Wikenhauser Festschrift*, p. 116, poses the question. Bornkamm, in *In Memoriam*, pp. 118f., says I Thess. 4, 15 shows how such prophecies were put into the mouth of the Lord. But, in fact, Paul uses this device ('for this I say by the word of the Lord') to differentiate what is really of the Lord—whether by tradition or by direct inspiration—from his own advice; cf. also I Cor. 7, 6; 12; 25; 40.

[5] Cf. above, chapter 8, pp. 128ff. Sjöberg, *verborgene Menschensohn*, p. 239.

[6] Cf. above chapter 7, esp. p. 98; it is important that without exception αμην λέγω ὑμῖν is found throughout the N.T. only as introducing a word of Jesus and was apparently not current in the early church, not even in its prophetic pronouncements (cf. e.g. I Cor. 15, 51; I Thess. 5, 1f., II Pet. 3, 3; etc.) Certainly Matthew appears to favour the phrase as an introductory formula (31x; cf. Lk. 6x, Mk. 13x, Jn. (doubled) 25x), but this may be due to more careful preservation (rather than invention) prompted by his Jewish-liturgical interests (cf. M'Neil, *Matthew*, p. xviii; Kilpatrick, *Origins*, p. 77). The omission of αμην in Mtt. 12, 31; 26, 29; where the Markan parallels have it suggests, surely, that Matthew was not casually adding the clause wherever he fancied. Luke's infrequent usage could well be due to his concern to remove Jewish formulae; cf. Dalman, *Words*, p. 227.

[7] Kümmel, *Promise*, p. 27; cf. Bosch, *Heidenmission*, p. 144; Schniewind, *Markus*, pp. 121f.

ed for, as Bornkamm [1] and others [2] reply, the saying would prove difficult only for the *later* generation. Besides, the argument is founded upon the view that the verse was necessarily an embarrassment, whereas evidence of this is lacking.[3]

The most that we are justified in saying is that there are no compelling reasons against authenticity. But this does not mean that the verse is evidence that Jesus held to a delimited Parousia hope. In the first place, the context given in the Synoptics may well be the original one, Jesus himself referring to the Transfiguration (as we suggested the context indicates).[4] On the other hand, if the context is secondary the expression γεύσωνται θανάτου may have had a metaphorical meaning (ruled out as it stands only by the context).[5] There is insufficient reason for agreeing with Taylor [6] that this reflects Jesus' *early* view of an imminent Parousia, or for agreeing with Schwietzer's view.[7] We can only say that the pericope appears to be authentic, and does not necessarily delimit the date of the End.

Mark 13, 28f., 30. *par*

The authenticity of vv. 28f., 30 par. cannot be discussed without a comment on the authenticity of the discourse as a whole. The history of the Little Apocalypse theory [8] has been exhaustively recounted by Beasley-Murray.[9] Many regard such a theory as laudable,[10] whilst others, though not accepting necessarily the idea

---

[1] In *In Memoriam*, pp. 116f.

[2] Grässer, *Problem*, p. 133; Conzelmann, *Mitte*, p. 95, n. 1.

[3] Michaelis, *Verheissung*, p. 35, argues that the application by the early Fathers to the Transfiguration was an embarrassment solution (cf. Ramsey, *Glory*, p. 132; Klostermann, *Markus*, p. 85); but, as suggested above (chapter 8, pp. 125ff.) the context supports such an interpretation.

[4] Cf. above, chapter 8 pp. 125ff.

[5] The phrase could be used metaphorically; cf. *S.-B. Kommentar* I, p. 751 and above, chapter 8, p. 127.

[6] *Mark*, p. 386; cf. Guy, *Last Things*, p. 80.

[7] *Quest*, pp. 357ff.; Cf. Barrett, *H.S.G.T.*, pp. 156f.

[8] Put forward by T. Colani, *Jesus-Christ et les croyances messianiques de son temps*, 1864; and W. Weiffenbach, *Der Wiederkunftsgedanke Jesu*, 1873.

[9] *Future*, chapters 1 and 2.

[10] Cf. Moffatt, *Introduction*, p. 209, who counts it a 'sententia recepta of synoptic criticism'; Streeter, in *Oxford Studies*, pp. 179ff. Bultmann, *Geschichte*, pp. 129f.; Hauck, *Markus*, p. 153; Klostermann, *Markus*, pp. 131f.; Hölscher, in *T.B.* XII, 1933, pp. 193ff.; Grant, *Earliest Gospel*, p. 62; Redlich, *Mark*, pp. 29f.; Glasson, *Advent*, p. 76; Dibelius, *Fresh Approach*, pp. 119ff.;

12

of a Little Apocalypse, regard the chapter with varying degrees of scepticism.[1] The main arguments against authenticity are as follows:

i. That the discourse is out of character with Jesus' teaching elsewhere.[2] But the contents of the chapter can, in fact, be paralleled considerably.[3] Further, the discourse *form* is not necessarily a sign that the *contents* are unauthentic.[4]

ii. That it is internally inconsistent, v. 32 and the emphasis on a sudden End being (it is said) out of keeping with the idea of preceding 'signs'.[5] But signs encouraging watchfulness and expectancy are capable of being held in tension with the idea of suddenness.[6]

iii. That the apparent privacy of the teaching is a mark of secondariness.[7] Against this, however, we must notice how suitable private instruction is in the case of material of an apocalyptic character (if not an 'apocalypse'):[8] other sayings appear to have been spoken in private,[9] and in this particular case one might well expect some caution and privacy—'Apart from other considerations, it would have been indiscreet for Jesus and his followers to discuss in the open the anticipated ruin of the temple, involving as it did that of the city and nation also'.[10]

Rawlinson, *Mark*, pp. 180f.; Branscomb, *Mark*, p. 231; Goodspeed, *Life*, pp. 186f.; Bacon, *Mark*, pp. 121f. Hunter, *Mark*, ad loc.

[1] Cf. Grässer, *Problem*, pp. 152f.; Robinson, *Coming*, pp. 119f,; Lowrie, *Mark*, pp. 469f.; Major, in *Mission and Message*, pp. 159f.; Guy, *Last Things*, p. 58f.; Kümmel, *Promise*, p. 98; Lohmeyer, *Markus*, p. 285; Montefiore, *Synoptic Gospels*, I, pp. 296f.; Fison, *Hope*, p. 126; Taylor, *Mark*, pp. 636f.; Menzies, *Earliest Gospel*, p. 233; Blunt, *Mark*, p. 242; Manson, *Teaching*, p. 261; Dodd, *Parables*, p. 52; Duncan, *Son of Man*, p. 179; Johnson, *Mark*, p. 219.

[2] Cf. Manson, *Teaching*, p. 262; G. Barth, in *Überlieferung und Auslegung*, pp. 56.; Kümmel, *Promise*, pp. 102ff.

[3] Cf. Beasley-Murray, *Mark* 13, p. 9; and cf. Lightfoot, *Gospel Message*, p. 54, who traces parallelism between ch. 13 and chs. 14-15 (similarly M. Barth, *Augenzeuge*, pp. 125ff.); Busch, *Zum Verständnis, passim*; Michaelis, *Verheissung*, pp. 22f.; Bosch, *Heidenmission*, p. 151 Cranfield, *Mark*, p. 389.

[4] Cf. Mk. 4, for example. Cf. Beasley-Murray, *Future*, p. 205 (contrast Glasson, *Advent*, p. 78).

[5] Cf. Taylor, *Mark*, p. 523; Guy, *Last Things*, pp. 59f.; Branscomb, *Mark*, pp. 231f.; Kümmel, *Promise*, pp. 102f.; Robinson, *Coming*, p. 127.

[6] Cf. above, pp. 133f.

[7] Cf. Hölscher, in *T.B.* XII, 1933, pp. 193f.; Dibelius, *Fresh, Approach*, pp. 119f.; Major, *Reminiscences*, p. 43; Dodd, *Apostolic Preaching*, p. 61.

[8] Cf. esp. Rowley, *Relevance*, pp. 109f.

[9] Cf. Daube, 'Public Pronouncement and Private Explanation in the Gospels', in *E.T.* LVII, 1946, pp. 175ff.; Beasley-Murray, *Future*, p. 205; Turner, in *New Commentary*, ad loc; and cf. Mk. 4, 10; 7, 17; 9, 28; and 10, 10.

[10] Beasley-Murray, *Mark* 13, p. 25; cf. also *Future*, pp. 205ff.

iv. That Mk. 13, 14 (Mtt. 24, 15) reveals secondariness.[1] But this verse, if not authentic to Jesus,[2] is intelligible as a Markan editorial device,[3] or dark hint,[4] without supposing that Mark is referring to a written source.

v. That the discourse fits better the early church situation;[5] but only on *a priori* views of cleavage between Jesus and the early church's understanding [6] could this be an argument against authenticity.[7]

There therefore seems good reason for the judgement, 'that 13; 5-37 does give us substantially our Lord's teaching',[8] to which a number of scholars incline.[9] If we are not able to treat the chapter as an authentic discourse,[10] we certainly are justified in weighing

---

[1] Cf. Kümmel, *Promise*, p. 103; Major, *Reminiscences*, p. 43; Klostermann, *Markus*, p. 151; Glasson, *Advent*, pp. 78f.; Grässer, *Problem*, pp. 161f.

[2] J. Schmid, *Mark, ad loc.*; and Cranfield, *Mark*, p. 403, regard this as a possibility.

[3] Cf. Cranfield, *Mark*, p. 403; Lagrange, *Marc*, p. 341; Beasley-Murray, *Mark* 13, p. 57; Ridderbos, *De Komst*, p. 403.

[4] Cf. Turner, in *New Commentary, ad loc*; Taylor, *Mark*, p. 512; Schniewind, *Markus*, p. 163; Beasley-Murray, *Mark* 13, p. 57.

[5] Cf. e.g. Menzies, *Earliest Gospel* (aimed at soothing excitement) Streeter, in *Oxford Studies*, p. 180 (when delay was a problem, to encourage); Glasson, *Advent*, pp. 186f., (the early church building up its Parousia hope) (similarly Robinson, *Coming*, pp. 120f.; Dodd, *Parables* pp. 52f.); Taylor, *Mark*, pp. 640.; Grässer, *Problem*, pp. 152f. Bultmann, *Geschichte*, p. 129; Klostermann, *Markus*, pp. 131f.; Fison, *Hope*, p. 126 (shows signs of re-interpretation of the primitive hope); etc.

[6] Cf. above chapter 3, p. 40; chapter 4, p. 56 and chapter 5, pp. 70f.

[7] Grässer, *Problem*, p. 153, n. 2, charges Beasley-Murray's 'uncritical' evaluation with not even asking if a pericope can be better explained as an early church composition. In his Commentary, *Mark* 13 p. 8, n. 1, Beasley-Murray seems to have noted the charge and answers, 'I cannot pretend to be writing this book apart from faith, nor do I expect any to read it but men of faith . . .' The task of the exegete is obviously under discussion, and a radical difference must exist between those who understand exegesis as attempting to make sense of the N.T. witness, and those who regard it as constructing early church history and thought.

[8] Cranfield, *Mark*, p. 390.

[9] Cf. Beasley-Murray, *Future*, pp. 172ff.; *Mark* 13, pp. 17f.; Michel, in *Z.s.T.*, 1932, pp. 625ff.; Schniewind, *Markus*, pp. 132ff.; Burkitt, *Beginnings*, pp. 63f.; K & S Lake, *Introduction*, p. 32; Cranfield, in *S.J.T.* VI, 1953, pp. 189ff.; Allen, *Mark*, pp. 163f.; Turner, in *New Commentary ad loc*; Stonehouse, *Matthew and Mark*, pp. 113f.; Lightfoot, *Locality and Doctrine*, p. 48; *Gospel Message*, p. 54; Lagrange, *Marc*, pp. 334f.

[10] As Schlatter, *Markus, ad loc.*; Rowley, *Relevance*, pp. 109f.; Busch, *Zum Verständnis*, pp. 44f. (a farewell discourse); see Beasley-Murray, *Future*, pp. 205ff., and *Mark* 13, pp. 10f. (and the important note 1, p. 11.)

each pericope on its own merits,[1] allowing at least the possibility of authenticity.

Verses 28f. (which even Grässer [2] thinks could be authentic) can be understood as an exhortation to see in the calamities mentioned (vv. 5-23) an indication that the End (vv. 25-27) is near.[3] Or, discounting the context, vv. 28f. may have referred to some other crisis whose imminence could be indicated by certain signs. Feuillet [4] suggests that the parable pointed to the new world which would follow Jerusalem's destruction: but this seems unlikely, for as Kümmel [5] contends, 'the subject of ἐγγύς ἐστιν becomes completely nebulous' on this interpretation. Dodd [6] refers it to the present situation and its significance. It is true (as Dodd maintains) that ταῦτα γινόμενα, since it must refer to vv. 5-23 and not to vv. 24-27,[7] is slightly awkward, but this does not necessarily 'suggest that a parable is used by the compiler for a purpose for which it was not originally intended'[8] compilation itself being a sufficient explanation of the awkwardness.[9]

ἐστιν ἐπὶ θύραις, as Beasley-Murray notes[10] 'accords better with a personal subject',[11] and the context given to the parable in Mark 13 seems more likely than alternatives suggested. In *no case* is it possible to find here evidence of a delimited Parousia expectation.[12]

The same can be said of Mk. 13, 30 par. If v. 30 is an isolated

---

[1] With Kümmel, *Promise*, p. 98; Schniewind, *Markus*, p. 132; Beasley-Murray, *Future*, pp. 205f.; Cranfield, *Mark*, p. 390; Lohmeyer, *Markus*, p. 267; Marxsen, *Markus*, p. 101; Bosch, *Heidenmission*, p. 152.

[2] *Problem*, p. 152.

[3] Cf. Cranfield, *Mark*, p. 408; Bosch, *Heidenmission*, pp. 139, 152.

[4] In *R.B.* LVI, 1949, pp. 82f.; cf. Sharman, *Son of Man*, pp. 98f.; Jones, in *Scripture*, IV, 1949-51, pp. 222ff.

[5] *Promise*, p. 21, n. 5.

[6] *Parables*, p. 137 n. 1 (in agreement with his treatment of the parables in general; cf. above, chapter 4, pp. 64f. appended note); cf. Jeremias, *Parables*, p. 96; Robinson, *Coming*, p. 71; Taylor, *Mark*, p. 520; B.T.D. Smith, *Parables*, pp. 90f. (other authorities cited by Beasley-Murray, *Mark* 13, p. 95): Hunter, *Mark*, p. 125 suggests the interval between death and resurrection.

[7] Cf. above, chapter 8, pp. 132f.

[8] Taylor, *Mark*, p. 520.

[9] Beasley-Murray, *Future*, p. 211 (similarly Cranfield, *Mark*, pp. 407f.) contends that the structure of the discourse exlains the apparent awkwardness.

[10] *Mark* 13, p. 97.

[11] Cf. Jam. 5, 8; Rev. 3, 20 and the general O.T. usage.

[12] Cf. the discussion above chapter 8, pp. 132ff.

unit [1] then there is no necessity to take ταῦτα πάντα as a reference to the End coming within the generation [2]. Grässer [3] objects on the grounds that the End is the important theme, but of course, taken out of context v. 30 is removed from such criticism. Depending on the original context, it might refer to the destruction of Jerusalem and the events leading to it,[4] or to the preceding events only,[5] or perhaps to something entirely different!

If the context is retained [6] it is hardly a 'word of comfort composed in days of disappointment',[7] for we have no evidence that the early church was prepared to compose such a saying,[8] and besides, the context demands that ταῦτα refers to *signs*.[9] It appears that Jesus may well have predicted here that the contemporary generation must experience all the preliminary signs and therefore could expect the End at any moment. But this does not mean that he held to a delimited expectation, only rather that he had that undelimited near-expectation which we have seen to have characterised the early church.[10]

Mark 14, 25 par.

Concerning the exegesis of this verse, nothing need here be added to the discussion above.[11] The only question here is whether we have to do with a genuine word of Jesus or not.

---

[1] Cf. Bultmann, *Geschichte*, p. 130; Grässer, *Problem*, pp. 128f.; Kümmel, *Promise*, p. 60; Branscomb, *Mark*, p. 239; Manson, *Sayings*, p. 333; Robinson, *Coming*, p. 86.

[2] So Michaelis, *Verheissung*, pp. 30f.; This is the effect given by Robinson *Coming*, p. 86 (cf. Glasson, *Advent*, p. 79) in dismissing Mk. 13, 24-27 as unauthentic.

[3] *Problem*, pp. 128f.; cf. Kümmel, *Promise*, p. 60.

[4] Cf. Feuillet, in *R.B.* LVI, 1949, pp. 82f.; Taylor, *Mark*, p. 521; Flückiger, *Ursprung*, p. 116; Lagrange, *Marc*, p. 348; Jones, in *Scripture*, IV, 1949-51, pp. 222ff.

[5] Cf. Sharman, *Son of Man*, pp. 98.

[6] The context is objected to by Rawlinson, *Mark*, p. 192; Taylor, *Mark*, p. 523; Manson, *Teaching*, p. 262; on the grounds that it is said to be difficult to reconcile Mk. 13, 30 with Mk. 13, 32. But cf. above, chapter 8, pp. 133ff.

[7] Cf. Grässer, *Problem*, p. 128; Bultmann, *Geschichte*, p. 130; Branscomb, *Mark*, p. 239.

[8] Cf. above, p. 180.

[9] Cf. above, chapter 8, pp. 132ff.

[10] Cf. above, chapter 8, p. 160. So Stonehouse, *Matthew and Mark*, p. 113; Cranfield, *Mark*, p. 409; Barth, *C.D.* III/2, pp. 601f.; Contrast, Beasley-Murray, *Mark* 13, p. 101; Kümmel, *Promise*, pp. 60f. Lohmeyer, *Markus*, *ad loc*; Manson, *Jesus*, pp. 65f; Marxsen, *Markus*, pp. 132f.; Hadorn, *Zukunft und Hoffnung*, p. 95; Cullmann, *Early Church*, pp. 150f.

[11] Cf. above, chapter 8, pp. 136ff.

Bultmann [1] has suggested that vv. 22-25 are added by Mark to an older tradition and that these verses are 'nicht in erster Linie aus dem Glauben, sondern aus dem Kult . . . erwachsen', through hellenistic cultic practice.[2] The question as to which version is to be preferred cannot be discussed here,[3] but v. 25 (Mtt. 26, 29; Lk. 22, 18) remains substantially unaffected. In view of the imagery of a feast as type of the joys of the righteous in the Old Testament and post-Old Testament literature,[4] and the strong Semitic flavour of v. 25,[5] it is most unlikely that the saying stems from a non-Palestinian source, and it can certainly be authentic.[6] There seems to be no adequate reason why the interpretation suggested above (chapter 8, pp. 137f.), containing an *un*delimited Parousia hope, should not go back to Jesus himself.

Mark 14, 62 par.

Not a few critics regard the whole scene of the Sanhedrin trial as fictitious.[7] Two main reasons are given:

The first is that no sympathetic eye-witnesses would have been present.[8] Yet 'this fact does not necessarily discredit the account, since knowledge of what happened, even if we allow for the absence of a biographical interest, must have been available'.[9] Further, the

---

[1] *Geschichte*, pp. 285f., 301, 333.

[2] He continues, 'Vielmehr hat V. 22-25, die Kultlegende aus hellenistischen Kreisen der paulinischen Sphäre, offenbar ein Stück verdrängt, das als organische Fortsetzung von V. 12-16 das Paschamahl schilderte.' (*Geschichte*, pp. 285f.)

[3] Cf. esp. Jeremias, *Eucharistic Words*, pp. 72ff.; Kümmel, *Promise*, pp. 30ff.; Manson, *Jesus*, pp. 134ff.; Bosch, *Heidenmission*, p. 175. (who cites further authorities, notes 1 and 2).

[4] Cf. Dalman, *Words*, pp. 110f.; S.-B. *Kommentar*, IV, pp. 1144ff.; Volz, *Jüdische Eschatologie*, pp. 331f.; Taylor, *Mark*, p. 547.

[5] Cf. Jeremias, *Eucharistic Words*, pp. 125f.; Taylor, *Mark*, p. 547.

[6] Cf. Taylor, *Mark*, p. 547; Lagrange, *Marc*, p. 381; Cranfield, *Mark*, pp. 427f.; Jeremias, *Eucharistic Words*, p. 71, pp. 118f.; Percy, *Botschaft*, p. 175; Bosch, *Heidenmission*, pp. 175f.; Rawlinson, *Mark*, pp. 204f.; Kümmel, *Promise*, p. 82; Robinson, *Coming*, p. 92, n. 2.

[7] Cf. esp. Winter, *On the Trial of Jesus*; Blinzler, *The Trial of Jesus*, throughout this section. For the view cited, cf. Taylor, *Mark*, authorities cited p. 644 n. 1; Bultmann, *Geschichte*, pp. 290f.; Grässer, *Problem*, pp. 172f.; Dibelius, *Tradition*, p. 213.

[8] Cf. esp. Dibelius, *Tradition*, p. 213; Bultmann, *Geschichte*, p. 291; Grässer, *Problem*, p. 172; Tödt, *Menschensohn*, p. 33.

[9] Taylor, *Mark*, p. 563; cf. also Cranfield, *Mark*, p. 439; Kümmel, *Promise*, p. 50.

lack of biographical detail suggests faithfulness of compilation.[1] It is, surely, entirely credible that a member of the Sanhedrin later recounted the facts; either a sympathiser (if πάντα in v. 64 is not pressed),[2] or a later convert.[3]

The second objection is that Mark places the scene at night[4] though such was, apparently, forbidden.[5] However, we cannot say with certainty that the rules embodied in Tractate Sanhedrin (c 200 A.D.) applied at the time of Christ.[6] Further, it may well be that Mark is describing an informal, preliminary sitting of the Sanhedrin,[7] rather than merely duplicating a second form of the same narrative.[8] It is inherently probable that hasty counsel should have been taken in such a situation, immediately prior to the feast, with the Sanhedrin anxious to avoid a disturbance.[9] Perhaps John's expression in Jn. 18, 13 'to Annas πρῶτον' supports this.[10] Grässer[11] objects to this because a definite judgement is given. But of course, the point of the enquiry would be to come to a definite decision, and Taylor[12] rightly notes that they only concluded (v. 64) that he 'was worthy of death' (ἔνοχον εἶναι θανάτου), which is a decisive basis for action without necessarily being a legal sentence.

In any case, illegal trials have been known before and since, and it is possible that even if the regulations (Sanhedrin iv-vii) were in force, the account is still essentially accurate.[13] The same may be said concerning all the apparent irregularities.[14] The desire

---

[1] Taylor, *Mark*, p. 563, speaks of 'artless details . . . characteristic of an eye-witness'; but artless details would, surely, also occur in free composition.

[2] With Lagrange, *Marc*, p. 398; Cranfield, *Mark*, p. 439.

[3] Cf. Taylor, *Mark*, p. 565; Kümmel, *Promise*, p. 50; Cranfield, *Mark*, p. 439.

[4] Cf. v. 53. Mtt. 26, 57; contrast Lk. 22, 54; 66. Bultmann, *Geschichte* p. 291; Grässer, *Problem*, pp. 172f.

[5] Cf. San. iv-vii. Danby, *Mishnah*, pp. 386f.; S.B. *Kommentar*, I, pp. 1020f.; Montefiore, *Synoptic Gospels*, I, p. 352; Barrett, *Background*, pp. 179ff.

[6] Cf. Rawlinson, *Mark*, pp. 217f., following Danby, in *J.T.S.* XXI, pp. 51f.; Taylor, *Mark*, p. 645.

[7] Cf. Cranfield, *Mark*, p. 440; Kümmel, *Promise*, p. 50.

[8] As Bacon, *Mark*, p. 200; Taylor, *Mark*, p. 646 suggest; contrast e.g. Williams, in *Oxford Studies*, pp. 406ff.

[9] Cf. Mk. 11, 18; 1, 12; 14, 2; Lk. 22, 6; Jn. 11, 47ff.

[10] Cf. Taylor, *Mark*, p. 646; Barrett, *John, ad loc*, takes the expression simply as an indication of Annas' lasting influence.

[11] *Problem*, pp. 172f.

[12] *Mark*, p. 645.

[13] Cf. Montefiore, *Synoptic Gospels*, I, p. 351.

[14] See Rawlinson, *Mark*, pp. 218f.; Taylor, *Mark*, p. 645

to remove Jesus and yet avoid a disturbance could provide adequate motive. Therefore we conclude that there is not sufficient ground for rejecting the trial scene outright.[1]

There are three other main attacks upon the authenticity of Mk. 14, 62 par in particular. First: Grässer [2] regards the verse as suspect because, he maintains, it presupposes a delay of the Parousia which contrasts (he says) with Jesus' view. He suggests it was composed in its present form by first-generation Christians when the delay was a problem and yet hope in an imminent coming had not been given up. This *a priori* criterion is, surely, unsatisfactory; [3] in any case we have found [4] no temporal delimitation here, only the conviction that Jesus is *no longer* to appear in the lowly role of the Servant, but is next to come in glory. On Grässer's premiss, might one not expect that the early church would have created something *more* encouraging and definite? But the matter of a delay, contained in 14, 62, can hardly be made the criterion of authenticity or unauthenticity, since it is the matter of an interval which is under discussion.

The second objection is that the idea of Christ's exaltation is early church theology [5] and this verse is said to be a reading back of such a theology into historical events. To be sure, one central feature of the earliest confessional statements *is* Christ's present Lordship,[6] but this conviction is never expressed in terms of the 'Son of Man'. The only occurrence of ὁ υἱὸς τοῦ ἀνθρώπου in the determinate form outside the gospels, Acts 7, 56, speaks of exaltation; but the image is that of standing (ἑστῶτα) and is probably prompted rather by the idea of welcoming the martyr than by the theme of Lordship.[7] The indeterminate occurrences do not support Grässer's view: Heb. 2, 6 (quoting Ps. 8, 4f.) refers to man in general: [8] Rev. 1, 13 purports to describe a vision and is an unique picture: Rev. 14, 14 depicts the exalted Lord *at the opening of the*

---

[1] Cf. Héring, *La Royaume*, pp. 111f.; 120; Taylor, *Mark*, pp. 563f.; Cranfield, *Mark*, pp. 439f.; Dodd, *Parables*, p. 91, n. 1.

[2] *Problem*, pp. 175f.

[3] Cf. above, chapter 5, pp. 70f.

[4] Cf. above, chapter 8, p. 138.

[5] Cf. Grässer, *Problem*, pp. 174f.

[6] Cf. Cullmann, *Confessions*, pp. 58f.; Cranfield, in *Essays in Christology*, pp. 83f.; Cullmann, *Christology*, pp. 195ff.

[7] Cf. Williams, *Acts*, p. 112.

[8] Cf. Arndt-Gingrich, *Lexicon*, p. 843.

Parousia scene. Hence Lohmeyer [1] rightly says that there is 'no later analogy' [2] and that this supports the authenticity of Mk. 14, 62.

The final argument against authenticity is that the early church is said to reflect its own Christology here. Tödt [3] maintains, '. . . die *Formulierung* des Menschensohnspruches in Mk. 14, 62 der nach-österlichen Gemeinde zuzuschreiben ist, die mit Hilfe der Schrift das Verhör Jesu vor dem Synedrion schilderte und dabei ein besonderes Interesse an dem Verhältnis der christologischen Würde-prädikate zueinander hatte'. Tödt maintains that Jesus is represent-ed as openly declaring his authority and status. [4] However, it is significant that an air of ambiguity remains even here: this is particularly the case in Mtt. 26, 64, σὺ εἶπας and Lk. 22, 70 ὑμεῖς λέγετε (cf. Lk. 22, 67f.) which, while assenting [5] nevertheless suggest vagueness. [6] It is possible, too, that we should read συ ειπας ὀτι (with θ f 13 pc) in Mk. 14, 62. [7] In any case the immediate insistence upon the term 'Son of Man', although the expression ὁ υἱὸς τοῦ Εὐλογητοῦ was mentioned (v. 61) suggests that despite the clear affirmation ('Εγώ εἰμι) there is still veiledness. [8] Tödt also holds [9] that authentic 'Son of Man' sayings are not composed of Old Testament quotations in the manner of Mk. 14, 62, par. He con-trasts Lk. 12, 8f., Mtt. 24, 27; 37, 39 (authentic) with Mk. 14, 62; 8, 38; 13, 26f. This criterion of evaluation is, however, open to question. First, the early church's relative non-usage of the term Son of Man tells against the argument, particularly since in vv. 60-62 the term 'Son of Man' (with apparently conscious intention) is introduced over against the phrase ὁ υἱὸς τοῦ Εὐλογητοῦ. [10] Secondly, if Mk. 2, 28 par., for example, is a comment of the evangelist or his

---

[1] *Markus*, pp. 330f.; followed by Manson, *Jesus*, p. 115; Kümmel, *Promise*, p. 50.

[2] Percy, *Botschaft*, p. 226, n. 2 disputes, but on inadequate ground.

[3] *Menschensohn*, p. 34; cf. also Branscomb, *Mark*, p. 280.

[4] *Menschensohn*, p. 34.

[5] Cf. Blass-Debrunner, *Grammar*, p. 260.

[6] Cf. Sjöberg, *verborgene Menschensohn*, p. 102; Swete, *Mark*, ad loc.

[7] So Taylor, *Mark*, p. 568; cf. Wilson, in Peake's *Commentary* (new edition), pp. 816f.; Cranfield, *Mark*, p. 444 (possible).

[8] Cf. Sjöberg, *verborgene Menschensohn*, pp. 102, 129; contrast Jeremias, *Eucharistic Words*, p. 78; Lagrange, *Marc*, p. 462; Goodspeed *Problems*, pp. 64f.

[9] *Menschensohn*, p. 33.

[10] Robinson, *Coming*, p. 57, n. 2, rightly comments, 'If something like Mk. 14, 62 is not authentic, then it is hard to see how it entered the tradition . . .'

source, as seems likely,[1] we have a clear case of an early christian 'Son of Man' saying *not* composed of Old Testament quotes (cf also Mtt. 12, 32). On the other hand, there is much to be said in favour of the authenticity of sayings which *are* a pastiche of quotations or allusions (cf e.g. Mk. 4, 32-Dan. 4, 12; 21, Ezek. 17, 23; 31, 6), and this applies to Son of Man sayings too, for the grounds on which the authenticity of Mk. 8, 38 par. (cf. I Enoch 61, 8; 10. 62, 2)[2] and Mk. 13, 26 (cf. Is. 13, 10; Zech. 12, 10f., Dan. 7, 13f.)[3] is challenged are inadequate. It is important to notice that of all the Son of Man sayings in the gospels it is precisely those which speak of his future glory which contain Old Testament (or Pseudepigrapha)

---

[1] Cf. Rawlinson, *Mark*, p. 34; Taylor, *Mark*, p. 220; Cranfield, *Mark*, p. 118.

[2] Many—cf. esp. Glasson, *Advent*, pp. 74f.; Sharman, *Son of Man*, p. 12; Taylor, *Mark*, p. 384; Robinson, *Coming*, pp. 54f.—think the Q saying (Mtt. 10, 32 = Lk. 12, 8) original and this to be a later interpretation. Robinson's arguments are a) that God is represented as Father of the Son of Man, so that Son of Man and Son of God are identified in an unparalleled manner: but cf. Iersel, *Der Sohn*, p. 115, n.1 and b) that the Q saying speaks of Son of Man as Advocate, whereas here—in accordance with early church theology—he is represented as judge. But cf. I Jn. 2, 1; Heb. 7, 25 etc., which suggest that the early church still held to the idea of Jesus as advocate. Moreover, as Kümmel, *Promise*, p. 45, and Schniewind, *Markus*, *ad loc* (cf. also *Nachgelassene Reden*, p. 11) note, the Q saying in dissolving the ambiguity of the Son of Man has the marks of secondariness over against Mk. 8, 38.

[3] Glasson, *Advent*, p. 185f.; and 'Mark 13 and the Greek O.T.' in *E.T.* LXIX, 1957-8, pp. 213ff.; Robinson, *Coming*, p. 57, contend that the vv. 25-27 are unauthentic because two of the quotations apparently depend on the LXX rendering for their significance (there can be no difficulty in occurrence of LXX language *as such*, which can be explained as assimilation). Thus:—

Mk. 13, 25 from Is. 34, 4. Hebrew reads וְנָגֹלּוּ כַסֵּפֶר הַשָּׁמַיִם 'the heavens shall be rolled together as a scroll'. Whereas LXX reads καὶ πάντα τὰ ἄστερα πεσεῖται 'and all the stars *shall fall*'. Mark clearly is assimilated to the LXX version: but the point is not changed—it remains that of the dissolution of the cosmic structure! Mk. 13, 27 alluding to Zech. 2, 6: Hebrew reads 'For I have spread you abroad as the four winds of the heaven. Flee from the land of the north . . .' LXX renders 'From the four winds of heaven will I gather your'. But (in answer to Glasson) the context of Zech. 2, 6 is clearly one of gathering—Glasson (*Advent*, p. 187) seems to think the Hebrew speaks of an injuction to scatter, whereas it speaks of gathering the scattered. Further, 'he shall gather together his elect from the four winds', is reminiscent not only of Zech. 2, 6 but also of Deut. 30, 3f., Jer. 32, 37; Ezek. 34, 13 and 36, 24—all of which speak of gathering scattered people; it may well be *this* general picture which Mk. 13, 27 depicts, coupled with the phrase 'the four winds' from Zech 2—a convenient short phrase for the longer passages in the other references listed.

references.[1] But it is precisely in this sphere that we would expect such references or allusions. Where the present situation of the Son of Man is spoken of, there is no necessity to call in traditional imagery: but how else ought one to speak of heaven, of glory, of the End, but in traditional imagery?[2]

We conclude that there is no sufficient reason for counting Mk. 14, 62 par. unauthentic. Although on the interpretation offered above,[3] the argument from non-fulfilment[4] is ruled out, there is much to suggest authenticity; as a community saying it is not definite enough to be a word of comfort to waning hope, nor violent enough to be a word of vengeance on the persecutors of the Lord. Hence we take this verse as evidence of Jesus' own Parousia hope, but if the interpretation suggested above[5] is valid, there is once again no question of a delimited expectation, only the conviction that the lowliness of the Son of Man's present situation is no longer relevant: he is next to be seen (at whatever date) in his true glory.

Matthew 10, 23

The authenticity of this verse, much disputed,[6] is challenged on the following grounds:

a. It is said to be irreconcilable with Mk. 13, 10 (cf. Mtt. 24, 14. 10, 18. 29, 19) and the view that Jesus envisaged a future Gentile mission.[7] Actually, just for this reason Kümmel accepts its authenti-

---

[1] Although O.T. allusions or quotations *can* be used in Son of Man sayings referring to his present situation (cf. Lk. 1, 10; Mtt. 18, 11 in some Manuscripts, Ezek. 34, 16) and with reference to his coming Passion (cf. Jn. 3, 13; 14; Numb. 21, 8; 9., Mk. 10, 45.? Is. 53) and the Parousia of the Son of Man can be spoken of (just *mentioned*) without reference to O.T. (or Pseudepigrapha) passages (cf. Mtt. 10, 23; 16, 28; 24-27; Lk. 17, 24), all the passages where the Parousia of the Son of Man is spoken of in any detail include O.T. (or Pseudepigrapha) references or allusions (cf. Mtt. 16, 27 = Mk. 8, 38 = Lk. 9, 26; cf. Lk. 12, 8; 10.—I Enoch 61, 8; 10. 62, 2. Mtt. 13, 41f.—Zeph. 1, 3; Dan. 12, 3. Mtt. 19, 28—Dan. 7, 9, 10. Mtt. 24, 29f., cf. Lk. 21, 27f., Mk. 13, 26f.—Is. 13, 10; Zech. 12, 10f., Dan 7, 13f., etc. Mtt. 25, 31—Zech. 14, 5. Mtt. 26, 64 = Mk. 14, 62 = Lk. 22, 69—Ps. 110, 1; Dan. 7, 13? Jn. 1, 51—Gen. 28, 12. Rev. 14, 14—Dan. 7, 13.

[2] Cf. Cranfield, *Mark*, p. 406 (following Schlatter, *Matthäus*, p. 710).

[3] Cf. above chapter 8, pp. 140f.

[4] Cf. Manson, *Jesus*, p. 115; Otto, *Kingdom of God*, p. 277; Kümmel, *Promise*, p. 50.

[5] Cf. above, chapter 8, pp. 140f.

[6] Taylor, *Names*, p. 29, n. 1 says, 'probably the saying has suffered in critical estimation from the use made of it by Schweitzer . . .'

[7] Cf. e.g. Manson, *Teaching*, p. 221.

city,[1] though we suggest that this rather too readily dismisses Mk. 13, 10 par.[2] and the Gentile mission as a factor in Jesus' future outlook.[3] Nevertheless, there is not necessarily a conflict between Mk. 13, 10 par. and Mtt. 10, 23. *Even in its present* context, the formal difficulty (v. 23 and v. 5 against v. 18) is capable of being reconciled;[4] taken out of context the formal difficulty need not even exist.

b. It is said that the verse fits the early church situation better.[5] But the formal difficulty in vv. 5, 18 and 23 supports authenticity, and Taylor more cautiously comments, 'it may well have been *re-interpreted* by Matthew in the light of the controversy regarding the Gentile Mission; but it is difficult to think that it was *invented* for this purpose.'[6]

c. It is said that the verse was invented as a word of comfort in the Parousia-delay 'crisis'.[7] However, in its present context the saying looks more like an admonition not to be slack in missionary zeal nor to sell one's life cheaply in view of the need for mission.[8] Surely free composition could conceive a less negative and less ambiguous 'comfort' than this?

d. It is said that since the verse delimits the End, it (with Mk. 9, 1. 13, 30 par.) is unauthentic, being contrary to Jesus' view.[9]

---

[1] *Promise*, p. 85. Bultmann, *Theology*, I, p. 55, says this saying stems from the Jerusalem church justifying its restriction of its missionary work to Jews only.

[2] Cf. below, chapter 11, pp. 204ff.

[3] Cf. Schlatter, *Matthäus, ad loc*; Flückiger, *Ursprung*, pp. 25f.; Beasley-Murray, *Future*, pp. 198f.; Jeremias, *Promise*, pp. 40ff.; Bosch, *Heidenmission*, pp. 132ff.

[4] See above, chapter 8, pp. 143ff.

[5] Cf. Manson, *Teaching*, p. 221; Cadoux, *Historic Mission*, pp. 292f. Sharman, *Son of Man*, p. 29; Glasson, *Advent*, p. 104; Duncan, *Son of Man* pp. 181f. (reflects the eager expectation of the Jewish-Christian church); Bultmann, *Theology* I, p. 42; Robinson, *Coming*, p. 80 (possibly); Kilpatrick, *Origins*, p. 122; Bammel, in *S.T.* XV, 1962, pp. 91f.

[6] *Names*, p. 29. Robinson, *Coming*, p. 76 suggests (tentatively) that v. 23a embodies the 'oracle' referred to in Eusebius (Hist. III 5, 3) meaning 'if they persecute you in this city (i.e. Jerusalem) flee to the other (by pre-arrangement, Pella), but it seems rather unlikely that an administrative detail should be turned into a solemn directive of this nature.

[7] Grässer, *Problem*, pp. 18f., 137ff.

[8] Cf. esp. Michaelis, *Matthäus*, II, p. 93f.; Schniewind, *Matthäus ad loc*; Robinson, *Matthew*, p. 92; Calvin, *Harmony*, I, pp. 456f.

[9] I.e. a complete reversal of the position held by Schweitzer, *Quest*, pp. 357ff. (cf. also Burkitt, *Beginnings*, p. 138; Klostermann, *Matthäus*, p. 89.) So cf. e.g. Heard, *Introduction*, pp. 245f.; Streeter, *Four Gospels*, pp. 520f.

But at least in its present context we doubt whether it delimits the End in the way suggested [1] (and this should not, in any case, be used as the criterion of authenticity[2]).

Some think that the non-fulfilment of this saying guarantees its authenticity; [3] but this argument rests on an understanding of the saying which we do not accept.[4] Nevertheless, not a few scholars accept its authenticity.[5] In its favour we repeat the point emphasised concerning Mk. 14, 62; [6] the early non-usage of the term 'Son of Man', and the entire lack of evidence that the early community invented sayings prefaced with the solemn introduction αμην λέγω ὑμῖν.

If the saying *is* judged authentic, the question has to be asked, does it reflect a delimited hope in Jesus' outlook? In one sense, the interpretation suggested above *is* delimited—but the delimitation is conceptual, not chronological: i.e. 'you will not finish this work until. . . .' rather than 'on or before the year "X" the Son of Man will come.' And it is not impossible that the original meaning has been retained by Matthew, even though he has imparted a new context to it. If the context is dismissed altogether, we cannot say with any certainty to what the saying referred. It is possible that the Resurrection was in mind,[7] and it is possibly significant that the verse does no say 'Ye shall *see* . . .'[8]. On the other hand, as Robinson says, there is no 'suggestion that 10, 23 is to be referred to a different and earlier moment, say, than 16, 27'.[9] Though Barth thinks that the verse referred to the Resurrection *as a pro-*

(the heightening of Apocalyptic); Taylor *Names*, p. 29 rightly points out that compared with 13, 41; 19, 28; 24, 30 and 25, 31; Mtt. 10, 23 is marked by simplicity and sobriety.

[1] Cf. above chapter 8, pp. 143ff.

[2] Beasley-Murray, *Future*, p. 185, p. 198; Kümmel, *Promise*, p. 64; Cullmann, *Early Church*, p. 151, accept the delimitation which they find in the saying, yet still accept its authenticity. It is simply inadequate to reconstruct Jesus' teaching by such radical surgical procedure.

[3] E.g. Schniewind, *Matthäus, ad loc*; Jeremias, *Promise*, p. 20.

[4] Cf. above, chapter 8, pp. 144ff.

[5] Cf. esp. Beasley-Murray, *Future*, p. 185; *Mark* 13, pp. 108f.; Manson, *Jesus*, pp.. 64ff.; Taylor, *Names*, p. 29; Montefiore, *Synoptic Gospels*, I, p. 150; Jeremias, *Promise*, p. 20; Bosch, *Heidenmission*, pp. 156f.; Kümmel, *Promise*, pp. 60ff.; Cullmann, *Early Church*, p. 150.

[6] Cf. above, p. 186f.

[7] Cf. Stonehouse, *Mathew and Mark*, p. 239; Barth, *C.D.* III/2, pp. 499f.

[8] Cf. above, chapter 7, pp. 105ff.

[9] *Coming*, p. 49, n. 1. cf. also Kümmel, *Promise*, p. 67.

lepsis of the Parousia, in the absence of any guidance to make this clear (contrast the case of Mk. 9, 1 where the context directs us) it cannot be at all certain that the Resurrection is intended. Besides the flight or mission thoughout Israel would neither be feasible in the short interval before the Resurrection—so obviously so, as to rule the saying in this case rather pointless. Some [1] suggest that the saying referred in the first place to the fall of Jerusalem. But other references to the coming of the Son of Man do not support this interpretation [2] and the Christocentricity of the expression should be preserved.[3] Many whish to separate v. 23a from v. 23b,[4] but whilst this must remain a possibility, Beasley-Murray is perhaps more probably right in maintaining that the two parts 'form a coherent whole as they stand'.[5] If G. Barth is right that 'der ursprüngliche Sinn ist ungewiss',[6] the most we may say is that the verse does not force us to conclude that Jesus held to a delimited Parousia hope.

The discussion of this chapter has necessarily been rather negative and tentative. It appears that the Parousia in Jesus' outlook was *in some sense* near, but that evidence is lacking that he held to a delimited hope. In the following chapter, still somewhat tentatively, though, we hope, less negatively, we shall enquire into the nature of this nearness in the mind of Jesus himself.

---

[1] Cf. Guy, *Last Things*, pp. 77f.; Addis, in *Oxford Studies*, p. 385; Lagrange, *Matthieu*, pp. 204f. (following Schanz, he also suggests 'La venue du Fils de l'homme commence à la résurrection et se termine avec la Parusie'); Robinson, *Coming*, pp. 91f.

[2] Cf. esp. Mtt. 16, 28; 13, 41; 24, 30; 25, 31.

[3] Cf. above, chapter 7, pp. 104ff.

[4] Cf. Bosch, *Heidenmission*, pp. 156f.; Streeter, *Four Gospels*, Montefiore, *Synoptic Gospels, ad loc*; G. Barth, in *Überlieferung und Auslegung*, p. 94, n. 1; Manson, *Teaching*, pp. 221f. cf. above, p. 140.

[5] *Future*, p. 198; cf. also Bammel, in *S.T.* XV, 1962, pp. 80f.

[6] In *Überlieferung und Auslegung*, p. 94, n. 1.

CHAPTER ELEVEN

JESUS' NEAR EXPECTATION OF THE PAROUSIA

In this chapter we raise the fourth and final question proposed above, namely in what sense exactly (if undelimited) did Jesus think of the End as imminent?

The discussion in chapter 10 resulted in the negative conclusion that we have no evidence that Jesus definitely delimited his expectation. This conclusion is confirmed in a positive way by Mk. 13, 32 par. Mtt. 24, 36 where Jesus' knowledge concerning the End excludes knowledge of its date. Of course in order for this verse to be acceptable here as evidence, its authenticity must be upheld. Bultmann [1] regards it as a creation of the Jewish-Christian apocalyptist: others [2] suggest it is a community saying, prompted by the Parousia-delay 'crisis'. However, against all objections to authenticity, we must regard it as doubtful that a saying, so embarrassing from early days [3] would have been invented.[4] Schniewind [5] rightly notes that the present interim period could be given an interpretation in the entire salvation-history scheme in terms much less embarrassing (as, for instance, in II Peter 3) without recourse to such a 'solution' as this. Some [6] argue that the expression 'the Son

---

[1] *Geschichte*, p. 130; cf. Klostermann, *Markus*, p. 138.

[2] Cf. Grässer, *Problem*, p. 82; Conzelmann, *Mitte*, p. 179, n. 1.

[3] The verse certainly occasioned early embarrassment to be sure; and this may well account for its omission by Luke and the modified form of the saying in Acts 1, 7. Yet—and this is particularly true in relation to the Arian controversy later—difficulty arose not so much through any 'non-fulfilment' as through the proposition itself that Jesus could admit to ignorance: it is certainly such an embarrassment which Acts 1, 7 avoids.

[4] Cf. e.g. Schmiedel, in *E.B.* II, col. 1881; Lagrange, *Marc*, p. 350 Taylor, *Mark*, p. 522; Lohmeyer, *Markus*, p. 283; Glasson, *Advent*, p. 97; Cullmann, *Christology*, pp. 286f.; Duncan, *Son of Man*, p. 106; Beasley-Murray, *Mark 13*, p. 109; Branscomb, *Mark*, p. 239; Cranfield, *Mark*, pp. 410f.; Kümmel, *Promise*, p. 42; Robinson, *Coming*, p. 87; Michaelis, *Verheissung*, p. 46; Schniewind, *Markus, ad loc.*; Fison, *Hope*, p. 127; Bosch, *Heidenmission*, p. 146.

[5] *Markus, ad loc.*

[6] Cf. Bultmann, *Geschichte*, p. 130; Bousset, *Kyrios Christos*, p. 52; Dalman, *Words*, p. 194; Kümmel, *Promise*, p. 42; Grässer, *Problem*, pp. 77f.; Klostermann, *Markus*, p. 138.

. . . the Father' is characteristic of the early church's vocabulary, not of Jesus'. But in answer we make the following three points: (a) the formulation of the saying could be attributed to the early church without the content of the verse being necessarily unauthentic;[1] (b) though a disputed text can hardly be used to confirm the authenticity of another disputed saying, yet Mtt. 11, 27 should not be altogether ruled out of court here. It is not impossible that Jesus spoke of 'the Son' and of 'the Father', however rarely or ambiguously:[2] (c) Iersel[3] notes what is too often overlooked, that the formulation here in terms of 'Son. . . Father' actually exposes and heightens the embarrassing character of the saying, for it is precisely as Son (to whom the Father delivers up all things, Mtt. 11, 27; Lk. 10, 22) that Jesus' ignorance is problematical. The gospels are not hesitant about Jesus' ignorance of certain things,[4] but the omission of this passage by Luke (with the significantly re-phrased expression in Acts 1, 7, whether a parallel version of the same saying, or an authentic second pronouncement) and the omission in some later manuscripts of Matthew[5] suggest that this particular *expression* of ignorance *was* an embarrassment.[6] It seems, therefore, quite probable that not only the concept but also the actual formulation of this saying is authentic.[7]

The verse should not be interpreted as meaning ignorance of the precise moment only (which interpretation has already been

---

[1] So cf. Kümmel, *Promise*, p. 42.

[2] Cf. Richardson, *Theology*, p. 151; Cranfield, *Mark*, p. 411; Schniewind *Markus, ad loc.*; Lohmeyer, *Markus, ad loc.*; Robinson, *Problem*, p. 81, n. 1; Beasley-Murray, *Mark* 13, pp. 105f.; Allen, in *Oxford Studies*, p. 312; Cullmann, *Christology*, pp. 286f.

[3] *Der Sohn*, pp. 117ff.

[4] Cf. e.g. Mk. 5, 9; 5, 31-32; 6, 38; 8, 5; 8, 27f., 10, 37.

[5] οὐδὲ ὁ υἱός omitted from Mtt. 24, 36 by ℵ ca W. fl. 565. 700. Sy⁸, pesh. etc. cf. also the omission in Mk. 13, 32 by Codex Montanensis and one Vulgate MS (cf. Taylor, *Mark*, *ad loc.*); cf. Gore, *Dissertations*, pp. 111f.

[6] Thus Iersel, *Der Sohn*, pp. 117f.; cf. M'Neile, *Matthew*, p. 356. Even to-day, the expression in this explicit form causes difficulty: Dom Graham, for instance (in *Christ of Catholicism*, p. 195) writes, 'He could refrain from satisfying the undue curiosity of the disciples on a matter which they had no right to enquire (Acts 1, 7) . . . As touching a point which the Father had not charged him to reveal, he could even profess his ignorance (Mk. 13, 32) . . . But deep within his mind there was no absence of knowledge, whether of the past, present or future . . .'

[7] Iersel, *Der Sohn*, p. 119 (following Taylor, Schniewind, etc.) is surely right, 'Die Annahme der Authentizität dieses Logions stellt den Exegeten und Historiker eigentlich vor geringere Probleme als die Leugnen derselben.'

challenged); [1] even if, as many hold,[2] the context is secondary this contention stands. Further, it is entirely speculative whether this saying corresponds (as some argue) [3] to a 'high point' in Jesus' development: as Branscomb comments, 'No such dependence can be put on the chronological arrangement of the Gospels as to warrant a reconstruction of the story on the basis of the present order of Jesus' sayings' [4] and any other arrangement would require some *a priori* view of Jesus' development upon which the arrangement could proceed!

Another evasion of the verse's apparent meaning is to suppose that the Parousia is only a secondary reference and that the saying on Jesus' lips referred to some other event.[5] However, as many object,[6] the expression τῆς ἡμέρας ἐκείνης most naturally refers to the *End*.

Thus we find in Mk. 13, 32 par. confirmation of the conclusion that Jesus at no time delimited the coming of the Parousia. At the same time, the sense of 'nearness' *is* present in Jesus' expectation —particularly, as we have seen, in Mk. 14, 25 (with its emphasis on a near cessation of Jesus' lowly ministry) and Mk. 13, 30 (with the certainty that every sign of the End being 'at the door' would

---

[1] Cf. above, chapter 7, pp. 99f. Amongst those who hold that the confession is of a particular day only, we mention particularly, Branscomb, *Mark*, p. 239; Schlatter, *Markus, ad loc.*; Beasley-Murray, *Future*, pp. 189f.; *Mark* 13, pp. 105f.; Guy, *Last Things*, p. 57; Nicklin, *Gleanings*, p. 347; Guignebert, *Jesus*, p. 346; K. & S Lake, *Introduction* p. 32. Contrast particularly, Cranfield, *Mark*, pp. 410f.; Lagrange *Marc*, p. 349; Schniewind, *Markus, ad loc.*; Taylor, *Mark, ad loc.*; Lohmeyer, *Markus, ad loc.*; Kümmel, *Promise*, p. 42. (M'Neile, *Matthew*, p. 355, is surely wrong in suggesting that the verse means 'God alone possesses knowledge *concerning* the day and hour, i.e. what it will be like—the terror and glory of it, all that it will mean to the bad and the good.' Jesus has just given considerable account of its significance and character. On the other hand, as Klostermann (*Markus*, p. 138) points out, some comment on the *date* of the End is typical conclusion for such a discourse as has preceded.

[2] Cf. e.g. Iersel, *Der Sohn*, p. 121; Taylor, *Mark*, p. 522; Glasson, *Advent*, p. 97; Menzies, *Earliest Gospel*, p. 242.

[3] Cf. Goguel, *Life*, pp. 570f.

[4] *Mark*, p. 239.

[5] Cf. Glasson, *Advent*, p. 97 (who claims that 'that day' in Lk. 17, 31 refers to the fall of Jerusalem; but we doubt this, for in v. 30 'the day when the Son of Man is revealed' suggests much rather the Parousia); Feuillet, in *R.B.* LVI, 1949, p. 87; Bowman, *Intention*, p. 61.

[6] Iersel, *Der Sohn*, p. 121; Lagrange, *Marc*, p. 350; Taylor, *Mark*, p. 522; Kümmel, *Promise*, p. 42; Michaelis, *Verheissung*, pp. 45f.; Grässer, *Problem*, pp. 77f.; Beasley-Murray, *Future*, p. 189.

come upon that contemporary generation). This nearness is to be
expounded, we suggest, by an examination of the tension inherent
in Jesus' self-consciousness. (Some, recognising a tension between
Jesus' near expectation and the confession of Mk. 13, 32 interpret
this as a tension within Jesus' self-consciousness, but somewhat
inadequately expound this tension. Beasley-Murray, for example,
suggests that Jesus held two complementary attitudes: 'one derived
from his consciousness of willing to do his Father's will and which
would see no obstacle compelling a postponement of the End to distant times; the other bore the stamp of his filial obedience and readily subordinated itself to the sovereign will of the father, leaving
to him the decision of times'.[1] Kümmel, on the other hand, rather
lamely concludes, 'it must be frankly confessed that we do not know
how to strike a balance between these two series of assertions'.[2])
To be sure, the degree of our knowledge of Jesus' self-consciousness
and the precise lines to be drawn in some areas are matters of much
debate. Yet for our purpose it will be sufficient to draw attention
to two features of Jesus' self-understanding about which there
should now be little doubt.

The first feature in Jesus' self-understanding to which we
draw attention is the eschatological significance which he attached
to his own person and work. Mtt. 12, 28 is important here.[3] The
presence of the Kingdom could be recognised in Jesus' person and
work where men had eyes to see.[4] Lk. 17, 21 is also relevant.
Much discussion continues over this saying, but it seems best [5]
to regard the proximity of the Kingdom spoken of as that same proximity due to the presence of Jesus Christ. ἐντὸς ὑμῶν can, it is
true, mean 'within you', in the sense of 'within your soul, or personality': P. M. S. Allen, indeed, noting [6] that Liddell and Scott

---

[1] *Mark* 13, p. 109; following Schlatter, *Matthäus*, p. 714.

[2] *Promise*, p. 151.

[3] See above, p. 167: for a discussion of the verse, cf. esp. Kümmel, *Promise*,
pp. 106f.; Dodd, *Parables*, p. 43; Otto, *Kingdom of God*, p. 103; Manson, in
Eschatology, p. 10; Michaelis, *Matthäus, ad loc*; Schniewind, *Matthäus, ad
loc*; Flückiger, *Ursprung*, p. 95; Morgenthaler, *Kommendes Reich*, pp. 36f.;
Bultmann, *Theology*, I, p. 41.

[4] To be sure, such a presence was a μυστήριον (cf. Mk. 4, 11) and most
could not discern it; but there were those who had eyes to see and ears to
hear the indications of its presence.

[5] We cannot dogmatise. Beasley-Murray, *Future*, p. 173, rightly says, it is
so ambiguous, 'there is no room for dogmatism' in its interpretation.

[6] In *E.T.* XLIX, 1938, pp. 276f.; and *E.T.* L, 1939, pp. 233f.

give no examples of ἐντός meaning 'among' thinks that such a translation would be a 'violation of the known usage of the word εντός'. A. Sledd [1] on the other hand, maintains that the examples which Allen offers prove only that ἐντός means 'within a certain group' or in a certain locality, not necessarily within a single individual. C. H. Roberts [2] cites papyri evidence in favour of the translation 'within', but Kümmel [3] successfully contests this evidence.

The chief reasons against understanding ἐντὸς ὑμῶν in an 'interiorised' sense in Lk. 17, 21 are fairly conclusive; they are, (a) that such an idea would not accord with the general treatment of the Kingdom of God theme in the New Testament as a whole, which regards the Kingdom as an external event.[4] Dodd's demythologized Kingdom-concept is clearly apparent when he writes (of this verse), 'although revealed in history, it essentially belongs to the spiritual order where categories of space and time are inapplicable'.[5] As Flückiger [6] holds, such an 'inward' view would be unique in the New Testament. (b) that the essential contrast being made in Lk. 17, 21 is not between an external view of the Kingdom of God and an internal one, but between the Pharisaic contention that the date of the End can be determined μετὰ παρατηρήσεως and Jesus' affirmation that it is rather ἐντὸς ὑμῶν. The translation 'the Kingdom of God is amongst you' has greater relevance as a reply here than an interpretation of the Kingdom's nature in psychological terms. (c) that 'within you' would, clearly, be strange as addressed to unbelieving Pharisees. If—as Kümmel holds [7]—this is a detached saying the setting might be Lukan; but the difficulty would remain, for Luke could be expected to spot the inappropriateness of ἐντὸς ὑμῶν with the Pharisees as object (if he had meant an 'interior' interpretation). Otto [8] wants to understand ἐντὸς ὑμῶν impersonally and so eliminate the difficulty, but there is no evidence to support

---

[1] In *E.T.* L, 1939, pp. 235f.

[2] In *H.T.R.* XLI, 1948, pp. 1ff.

[3] *Promise*, p. 35, n. 54 (following H. Riesenfeld and A. Wikgren, in *Nuntius Sodalicii Neotestamentici Upsaliensis* II, 1949, pp. 11f. and IV, 1950, pp. 27f.) cf. also Griffiths, in *E.T.* LXIII, 1951-2, pp. 30f.

[4] Cf. Conzelmann, *Mitte*, p. 106; Beasley-Murray, *Future*, p. 175; Morgenthaler, *Kommendes Reich*, pp. 56f.

[5] *Parables*, p. 84, n. 1.

[6] *Ursprung*, p. 102; similarly, Morgenthaler, *Kommendes Reich*, p. 56.

[7] *Promise*, p. 34.

[8] *Kingdom of God*, p. 135.

such a view. Therefore in the present context and in view of the general idea of the Kingdom of God in the Gospels, it seems most likely that the Evangelist meant 'among you' and that he has faithfully recorded Jesus' meaning. In his own person and work, the Kingdom was present amongst men.

Mk. 1, 15,[1] though probably a summary of the evangelist or his source, is not improbably a true picture of Jesus' own message and again the proximity of the Kingdom in the ministry of Jesus himself is central. This aspect of Jesus' self-understanding [2] involves the conviction that where God is, there is eschatological glory; i.e. the revelation of God's presence cannot altogether be hidden, but insistently breaks forth.[3] Hence on those occasions where Jesus' divinity is particularly affirmed,[4] there the revelational character of the End glory is to the fore.

Without labouring the point, we may say with some confidence that Jesus regarded his own person and work in eschatological terms. This eschatological self-understanding is, however, not to be assessed in isolation, for there is a duality in Jesus' self-understanding. If his eschatological self-consciousness is assessed alone, we are left with a picture of Jesus such as Schweitzer portrayed, where there is little account of a grace-motif and where we are left wondering how Jesus' life, death and resurrection could have had any crucial role to play in salvation-history.[5] Beside the eschatological motif there runs throughout the gospel records a *grace* character which is most dominant where expression is given to Jesus' self-consciousness.

In this connection we notice the explicit references to his mission (Mk. 10, 45; 2, 17; 1, 38,[6] Jn. 13, 1ff.), in all of which the grace

---

[1] Cf. above, chapter 6, p. 90.

[2] Cf. further Jeremias, *Parables*, pp. 96f., concerning Jesus' self-understanding in eschatological categories.

[3] Cf. Kittel and von Rad, in *T.W.N.T.* II, pp. 236ff.

[4] Cf. esp. his baptism, Mk. 1, 9-11 par.; the Transfiguration, Mk. 9, 2-8 par.; the exorcisms, Mk. 1, 23f., etc.

[5] The lack of this grace motif in Consistent Eschatology (noted especially by Flückiger, *Ursprung*, pp. 121-151) has already been criticised (above, chapter 3, p. 45); it accounts in part for the fact that in assessing the ultimate meaning of Jesus' life Schweitzer had to adopt an exemplary interpretation coupled with the philosophy of reverence for life.

[6] The reference *may* be to Jesus' departure from Capernaum; but—and Luke's expression (Lk. 4, 43 ὅτι ἐπὶ τοῦτο ἀπεστάλην) supports this—it *may* be a reference to his entire ministry and his 'coming from God'; cf. Cranfield, *Mark*, pp. 89f.

motif is central. The same motif characterises and underlies the
healing miracles where any desire to parade spectacular powers
or to win popular acclaim is wholly put aside, and yet *compassion*
enjoins healing action.[1] Healing is concerned especially with
restoration to wholeness and soundness [2] and it is not accidental
that in Mk. 2, 2-12 the eschatological blessings of forgiveness and
healing are so intimately interwoven.[3] It is in this connection that
Jesus' work and words are subsumed under the term 'gospel'
εὐαγγέλιον; not only because they share the nature of good news,
but also because they form the content of the good news of salvation.[4]

It is because of this grace character that the End events as
they occurred in the life, death and resurrection of Jesus Christ,
were *veiled*. Men were thereby given time and occasion to respond
with freedom and integrity to the demand to repent and believe.
The eschatological motif strives to *reveal*, since the End (by definition) is the open manifestation of God's divine rule, unambiguous
and irrefutable. But the grace motif strives to *veil*, so that men
should not be overcome in their situation by the glory and power
of God's rule, but should have time and opportunity to make up
their minds in responsibility and freedom to the demand which God,
in his sovereign rule, makes upon them. There is here no contradiction; but there is a real tension.[5]

To be sure, just as the eschatological element in Jesus' understanding of his person and work taken *alone* provides us with a
distorted view of his self-understanding, so the grace motif taken
alone gives an inadequate, demythologized picture. It is when
these two elements are taken together and allowed to inform each

---

[1] Cf. Strachan, *Fourth Gospel*, pp. 2ff.; Richardson. *Miracles*, pp. 29f.
σπλαγχνίζομαι found 12x in the Synoptics is written of Jesus in 8 cases, and
(except in Mk. 9, 22 where it is besought of Jesus) it is elsewhere illustrative
of his attitude (Mtt. 18, 27; Lk. 10, 33; 15, 20).

[2] Cf. Mk. 5, 23 ἵνα σωθῇ καὶ ζήσῃ; Cairns, *The Faith that Rebels*, pp. 48ff.

[3] As. e.g. Richardson, *Miracles*, pp. 66f., following Creed, *Luke*, p. 78,
argues, there is no reason why the debate (vv. 5-10) should not have an
authentic basis in the ministry of Jesus.

[4] Cf. Friedrich, in *T.W.N.T.* II, pp. 705ff. ('Jesus ist der Freudenbote der
erwarteten Endzeit', p. 715).

[5] Seen in the light of this fundamentally Christological tension the ex-
planations of duality in Jesus' thought in terms either of pastoral expediency
or of epistemological necessity appear totally inadequate; cf. above, chapter 7, pp. 100ff.

other that we perceive how the grace element in Jesus' ministry formed the raison d'être of the veiledness of his eschatological person and work. For it is only as the End confronts man in an oblique, tangential manner, that man has even the possibility of a personal, free response to that End, its judgement and its command. Borchert expresses it in this way, 'Our liberty is a slight thing which can only be preserved in the twilight. If God were to reveal the Son clearly and indisputably to the world by external means, the liberty, development, and faith of mankind would be shattered in pieces'.[1]

It is now our intention to allow this two-fold character in Jesus' self-consciousness to illuminate a reconstruction of his outlook upon the future, and so perceive the sense in which he regarded the End as 'Near'. This we do, not because there can be any *a priori* basis for believing that Jesus' view of the future must have been characterised by the same motifs as characterised his self-consciousness, but rather because the evidence of the gospel witness suggests that the same duality of motifs *does* in fact hold sway in both areas.

First, the eschatological motif. This, if assessed alone [2] leads to a future expectation characteristic of frenzied apocalyptists which in no way does justice to the sense of unhurried order and certainty in Jesus' ministry and outlook.[3] But neither may it legitimately be denied nor re-interpreted in such a drastic manner as to dissolve its original character.[4] Under this heading we consider the conviction that the End is near. In its future reference this nearness is not unconnected to a chronological proximity (hence it is not enough to understand it as 'eternity always menacing time',[5] for there is a real compression of the present chronological period in the interests of the inbreak of the End in its fully manifest form).[6] It is again a question of the nearness of glory, of open manifestation of divinity,[7] which breaks through even in Jesus'

---

[1] *Original Jesus*, p. 398; cf. also Torrance, 'A Study in N.T. communication', in *S.J.T.* III, 1950, pp. 298ff.

[2] As in Consistent Eschatology.

[3] Cf. e.g. Mtt. 26, 18; Mk. 1, 15; Jn. 7, 6; 7, 8; Mtt. 18, 7; Mk. 13, 7 and the frequent occurrence of δεῖ (cf. Grundmann, in *T.W.N.T.* II, pp. 21ff.).

[4] Cf. above, chapters 4 and 5.

[5] Cf. Barth's criticism of this, *C.D.* III/2, pp. 490ff.

[6] Cf. Mk. 13, 20 par. 'except the Lord had shortened the days . . .'

[7] Cf. the future reference of Mk. 4, 21 (whether we understand by ὁ λύχνος Jesus' word or Jesus himself—Schniewind, *Markus, ad loc*, thinks this latter meaning 'liegt . . . nicht unbedingt nahe', but cf. Cranfield, in

lowly ministry and which must ever be regarded as near at hand since its advent in that hidden, veiled ministry. The open, universal and unambiguous manifestation of the End can be postponed,[1] yet because it belongs to the End to be open and unambiguous, its manifestation must be near throughout all postponements.[2]

It is from this conviction that Jesus insists upon watching and expectant waiting. The parables of 'crisis' have been subjected by many [3] to a critical re-interpretation and it has been claimed that they referred originally not to the Parousia but to that crisis in which Jesus' contemporaries were placed on account of his presence among them. We have seen, however, that there is no necessary ground for thinking that they could not, originally, have had the Parousia as their subject. Indeed, properly understood, the crisis in which his contemporaries were placed by Jesus' presence amongst them was (and still is!) the crisis of the nearness of the End, involving the Parousia as the crisis itself.[4]

The same must be said of the collection of Parousia parables in Mtt. 24-25. Grässer [5] calls Mtt. 24, 45-51 a product of the early community contending with the unexpected Parousia delay! Dodd [6] maintains that originally the master's departure and return had no stress but were merely framework; the parable 'pilloried the religious leaders of the Jews as God's unfaithful servants . . . it had sharp point directed to the actual situation.' Both, however, seem to

---

Interpretation, IX, 1955, pp. 150-155 and *Mark*, p. 164) there is an ultimate purpose of unveiling, of revelation.

[1] There is a real Parousia delay. But if this is thought of as an unexpected event, then the grace-character of Jesus' ministry is underestimated (there is a failure to see that the presence of the Holy Spirit amongst men, making faith and repentance possible, is of a piece with Jesus' own ministry); conversely, if this is regarded as a 'natural' phenomenon, and not the express gift of God's compassion (cf. II Peter 3, 9), then the urgency of the present time and the transitoriness of present institutions (particularly 'the church') will be overlooked. Hence, as Barth, *C.D.* III/2, pp. 509f., says Consistent Eschatology fails to reckon adequately with the Holy Spirit, and Realised Eschatology fails to reckon with the church's transitoriness.

[2] Cf. Cranfield, *Mark*, p. 408.

[3] Cf. above, chapter 4, esp. pp. 64f.

[4] The veiled Eschaton *must* threaten to become unveiled because the Eschaton *is* the universal, unambiguous manifestation of God's sovereignty. The antagonism of Realised Eschatology towards eschatology (and cf. Bultmann and others against traditional eschatology), sheds light on the need felt to re-interpret the crisis, but it does not excuse or justify that re-interpretation.

[5] *Problem*, p. 90; cf. Bultmann, *Geschichte*, p. 125.

[6] *Parables*, pp. 158ff.; Klostermann, *Matthäus, ad loc.*

underestimate the relevance of the parable with the Parousia as subject, to the contemporary situation in Jesus' ministry; it is spoken of those who held *no* 'near-expectation',[1] that is, those who failed to see that the universal manifestation of Jesus in glory could not be far off. The certainty and nearness of the End's coming (i.e. the eschatological motif) did not inform their use of the present period of opportunity (i.e. the grace-motif). This understanding of the parable does not necessitate finding another *Sitz im Leben* than that given it by the evangelist.

Of Mtt. 25, 1-13 Glasson says, it 'probably referred to the situation in Israel when Jesus came ... to a time of crisis and opportunity in Israel's life, a day of visitation for which the majority were not ready ... the reference is not to some future consummation but to the attitude of the Jewish leaders who treated lightly the great invitation.'[2] Objections to authenticity also arise, on account (a) of the presence of allegory;[3] but this can no longer be regarded as sufficient grounds [4] and Meinertz [5] is justified in regarding it as a parable with allegorical aspects which can well be authentic. (b) the presence of apparent confusion of thought: Kümmel for instance, thinks v. 13 probably has been added by the evangelist, since it 'wrongly emphasises watchfulness instead of preparedness.'[6] However, the interchange of these two related themes may be no accident, nor unoriginal—indeed it is difficult to imagine how watchfulness can rule out preparedness, or vice versa.[7] (c) Jeremias holds that the metaphor of the bridegroom as used of Messiah is 'wholly foreign to the O.T.' [8] and that the idea comes into the church's thought first with Paul. However, as Meinertz again points out [9] the relation of JHWH to Israel is often depicted

---

[1] Cf. Michaelis, *Verheissung*, p. 92; Flückiger, *Ursprung*, p. 119.

[2] *Advent*, p. 93; following Dodd, *Parables*, pp. 172f.

[3] Cf. Bultmann, *Geschichte*, p. 125; Bornkamm, in *In Memoriam*, p. 119; Grässer, *Problem*, pp. 119ff.; Klostermann, *Matthäus, ad loc.*; cf. Jeremias, *Parables*, p. 41.   [4] Cf. the modifications to Jülicher's thesis, above p. 54.

[5] In 'Die Tragweite des Gleichnisses von den zehn Jungfrauen' in *Synoptischen Studien für A. Wikenhauser*, pp. 94f.

[6] Cf. *Promise*, p. 57; similarly Jeremias, *Parables*, p. 41; Grässer, *Problem*, p. 86; Klostermann, *Matthäus, ad loc.*

[7] Cf. Schniewind, *Matthäus*, p. 250; Meinertz, in *Synoptischen Studien für A. Wikenhauser*, pp. 94f.

[8] *Parables*, pp. 41f.; also in *T.W.N.T.* IV, pp. 1095f.

[9] In *Synoptischen Studien für A. Wikenhauser*, pp. 95f.; cf. also Kümmel, *Promise*, p. 57, n. 123; Cranfield, *Mark*, pp. 109f.; Michaelis, *Verheissung*, pp. 10f.

as that of bridegroom to bride,[1] and there is no reason why this metaphor could not be authentic to Jesus.

Grässer [2] and Bornkamm [3] contend that the delay (cf. χρονίζοντος) is emphasised—thus fitting in well, they say, with the situation of the early church faced with the Parousia delay and consequent 'crisis'. To be sure, the delay *is* emphasised,[4] but in this sense: that the five foolish virgins wrongly reckoned on a delay and did not take sufficiently seriously the nearness of the bridegroom! Of course, it was their original lack of oil which caused them to be absent when he arrived, but the crux of the parable lies in the fact that they were caught unprepared, they were hoping for time which was not allowed them, and the bridegroom arrived whilst they were still making preparations.[5] Again, the parable is seen to have adequate relevance to Jesus' contemporaries of whom it was required that they should recognise the urgency of the situation and the need to be prepared for the bridegroom's revelation and to be awaiting him.

Mtt. 25, 14-30 is again interpreted by Dodd [6] as referring originally to the crisis brought about by Jesus' ministry, and he thinks that the Parousia reference is secondary, the departure and return of the master only framework. Grässer [7] rightly maintains that the parable's true reference *is* the Parousia (though he exaggerates, in keeping with his thesis, the element of delay). The crisis of Jesus' presence in lowliness involves the idea of the Parousia as that for which men must now prepare.

The need for awaiting, as an imminent possibility, the coming of Jesus Christ in glory is coupled with the urgent summons to preach the gospel. This brings us to the second element in Jesus' future expectation (corresponding to the other element in his self-consciousness) namely the grace-motif. For it is this grace motif

---

[1] Cf. Ezek. 16, 7ff., Hos. 1-3, Is. 65, 5; Ps. 45, 3.

[2] *Problem*, p. 126.

[3] In *In Memoriam*, pp. 119f.

[4] Contrast Michaelis, in *Synoptischen Studien für A. Wikenhauser*, pp. 117f.; Strobel, *Untersuchungen*, pp. 233f.

[5] It is the fact that the five foolish were not watching at the crucial moment (the point of v. 13) which is the climax of the parable and its purpose; their lack of oil—and failure to reckon with a long interval—is only the framework to show how easily they were led into a position of unpreparedness.

[6] *Parables*, pp. 146ff.; cf. also Robinson, *Coming*, pp. 65f.

[7] *Problem*, pp. 114f.

which underlies the Parousia delay and stands in tension with the eschatological impulse towards open manifestation of the End. We repeat, the grace element must not be omitted from our reconstruction of Jesus' outlook upon the future any more than it *alone* can be taken as the whole key to his expectation.

Under this head, the exceptation of a future community in which Jesus' own mission might be continued, would need to be considered: the choosing of the Twelve, their training and their commissioning, etc. But some attention has already been devoted to this question [1] and this must suffice for our purposes. The major question which must occupy us here is whether or not Jesus anticipated a future gentile mission: whether the grace element in his self-consciousness informed his future hope in this way. Before discussing Mk. 13, 10 and 14, 7-9, there are two objections to the idea of a gentile mission in the mind of Jesus which we must mention.

The first is that Jesus limited himself to Israel during his own ministry and apparently directed the disciples to similar limitation during his presence with them.[2] However, this limitation *can* be understood in part as a matter of order ('to the Jew first',[3]) and in part as a matter of principle, the universality of his demand upon Israel revealing his basic attitude: Israel is God's vehicle for the inclusion of the Gentiles.[4] So that, in both respects a wider mission, far from being excluded, appears rather to be presupposed. Further, the instances where Jesus, during his ministry, met with Gentiles,[5] suggest that notwithstanding his self-limitation he was not unmindful of the place of the Gentiles in the entire salvation-history plan.[6]

---

[1] Cf. above, chapter 7, pp. 96ff.

[2] Cf. Mtt. 10, 6; 15, 24. Bosch, *Heidenmission*, p. 93, following his treatment of Jesus' self-limitation to Israel writes, 'Auf Grund des vorangehenden Kapitels könnte man versucht sein, Harnacks Urteil eine Heidenmission habe überhaupt nicht im Horizonte Jesu gelegen, beizupflichten. Die Tatsache der universalen Mission der Jünger nach Jesu Tod wäre dann *bestenfalls* daraus zu erklären, dass in seiner Botschaft etwas "Allgemeinmenschliches", "Universales", "Supranationales" oder "Innerliches" steckte, das die Jünger zu einer solchen weltweiten Tätigkeit anspornte. Und *schlimmstenfalls* würde man die nachösterliche Heidenmission daraus erklären müssen, dass die Jünger ihrem Meister ungehorsam waren oder ihn verhängnisvoll missverstanden haben'.

[3] Cf. Bosch, *Heidenmission*, pp. 110f.; cf. above, pp. 145f.

[4] Cf. Is. 42, 6; 49, 6; etc. Rowley, *Missionary Message*, pp. 39f.

[5] Cf. esp. Mtt. 8, 5-13 par.; Mtt. 15, 21-28 (Mk. 7, 24-30) (Lk. 7, 1-10, cf. Jn. 4, 46-53); Mk. 5, 1-20 par.

[6] Cf. Bosch, *Heidenmission*, p. 115; Jeremias, *Promise*, pp. 46f.

The second matter is that many think the early church would not have been reluctant to undertake the Gentile Mission if Jesus had told them to embark upon it.[1] However, this is again perhaps to be seen partly as a matter of order—to the Jew first [2]—and in part as a matter of disobedience and natural reluctance to embark upon a course of action of such magnitude and consequence. Besides, there were (according to Acts 7) some who wished to engage in a Gentile mission; and apparently there were some who quite spontaneously did so.[3] Further, to some extent, the early discussion regarding the Gentile mission centred not upon whether or not the Gentiles should be evangelised, but whether or not they should become Jews *also*.[4] In any case, an appeal to the disciples' behaviour is a dubious methodological principle; it is, for example, wrong to conclude that Jesus never spoke of his death and resurrection, simply because these events apparently took the disciples by surprise.

Apart from these objections which, we suggest, are based on rather inadequate grounds, Mk. 13, 10 and 14, 7-9 cannot be evaded. Jeremias [5] who thinks that Jesus' work held significance and promise for the nations, but that this involved not a mission to the Gentiles but their ingathering at the End, claims that neither passage gainsays his thesis. Concerning Mk. 14, 7-9 par. he argues that the preaching referred to is angelic proclamation (cf. Rev. 14, 6f.) and that the original meaning (which has been re-interpreted by Mark and Matthew) ran thus—'Amen, I say unto you, when the triumphal news is proclaimed (by God's angel), to all the world, then will her act be remembered (before God), so that he may be gracious to her (at the last judgement)'.[6] Three objections to this interpretation, however, must be raised:

i. Jeremias' interpretation of εἰς μνημόσυνον has been strongly criticised by D. R. Jones: [7] even without entirely opposing Jeremias' understanding, it would surely be necessary, with Richardson to remember that εἰς μνημόσυνον 'may contain not merely one

---

[1] Cf. e.g. Cadoux, *Historic Mission*, p. 142.
[2] Hence the early practice of preaching in synagogues was not merely expediency, but conformity to this pattern.
[3] Even during Jesus' ministry, cf. Mk. 1, 28; 1, 45; 5, 20, etc.
[4] Cf. Jeremias, *Promise*, p. 25; and above p. 146 n.5.
[5] *Promise, passim.*
[6] *Promise*, p. 22; cf. also in *Z.N.W.* XLIV, 1952-3, pp. 103f.; *Eucharistic Words*, pp. 163f.; similarly Lohmeyer, *Markus, ad loc.*
[7] In *J.T.S.* VI, 1955, pp. 183ff.

meaning but several, and several reminiscences and overtones of different biblical themes and passages.' [1] Hence Beasley-Murray rightly contends that 'each case must be taken on its merits'.[2] To restrict εἰς μνημόσυνον here necessarily to a remembrance before God seems hardly justified: indeed 'in the absence of any indication here that the reference is to God's remembering the woman, it seems clear that the ordinary meaning should be preferred.'[3]

ii. Although τὸ εὐαγγέλιον may reflect early christian vocabulary [4] this does not necessarily cast doubts upon the authenticity of the passage as a whole [5] which is, in fact, well attested by the introductory formula αμην δὲ λέγω ὑμῖν and by the absence of the woman's name.[6] The prevailing Markan usage is entirely against Jeremias' interpretation. It may well be too, that Rev. 14, 6 should be understood in terms of angelic powers behind the christian mission, rather than as a single event to occur at the End (Rev. 1-14, 14 is, after all, concerned with the events of the *interim*, and 14, 6ff. appear to have in mind a prolonged activity—cf. v. 12.)

iii. Jeremias takes ὅπου ἐὰν in a temporal sense and as a single moment, 'when'—(as he says in Mk. 14, 14). But ὅπου ἐὰν whether temporal or local is indefinite (in Mk. 14, 14 too), and bearing in mind the clause 'ye have the poor always with you . . .' (Mk. 14, 7) an activity of some duration and amidst the ordinary circumstances of life appears to be envisaged.

Kilpatrick [7] thinks there is nothing to show that the object of preaching here (or in Mk. 13, 10) is any other than the Jewish population of Palestine and the Dispersion. On the other hand, there is nothing to suggest that it *is* so restricted, and the phrase εἰς ὅλον τὸν κόσμον definitely inclines to the opposite meaning.[8] Jeremias himself understands this as 'the entire world'.[9]

---

[1] *Theology*, p. 368, n. 1.

[2] *Mark* 13, p. 40.

[3] Cf. Cranfield, *Mark*, p. 418.

[4] Cf. Rawlinson, *Mark*, p. 198; Bultmann, *Geschichte*, pp. 37f.; Taylor, *Mark*, p. 529; Klostermann, *Markus*, p. 158; Lagrange, *Marc*, p. 370.

[5] Contrast Bultmann, *Geschichte*, pp. 37f.; Loisy, *Synoptiques*, II, p. 497; Klostermann, *Markus*, p. 158.

[6] Cf. Lagrange, *Marc*, p. 370; Rawlinson, *Mark*, p. 198; Taylor, *Mark*, p. 529.

[7] In *Studies in the Gospels*, pp. 145ff.

[8] Cf. Cranfield, *Mark*, p. 399.

[9] τὸν κόσμον in Mk. 8, 36 (the only other occurrence not counting Mk. 6, 15 in Mark) obviously means the entire world, as does the prevailing N.T. usage.

The other passage, Mk. 13, 10 par. is equally disputed. Many scholars [1] regard it as unauthentic, partly because its vocabulary seems to be distinctly Markan,[2] partly because v. 11 follows on naturally upon v. 9 [3] so that v. 10 seems to be an interruption, and partly because v. 10 is prosaic whereas vv. 9 and 11 are poetic.[4] However, it is quite possible that the verse expresses in the vocabulary of the church a thought which may well be authentic to Jesus [5] and the arrangement can be accounted for in terms of compilation.[6] Many scholars, therefore, regard the verse as most probably genuine.[7]

Jeremias [8] interprets the saying on similar lines to his understanding of Mk. 14, 9, and Kilpatrick [9] follows this interpretation. However, the same objections apply. Witness and suffering are both addressed to the disciples as *their* lot during the interim (there is no hint of an angelic activity!). Of course, it is true, as Bosch writes, 'Das Leiden ist eigentlich des Jüngers Teil und Beitrag; die Mission dagegen ist nicht seine Sache sondern Sache Gottes . . .'[10] But—as Bosch goes on to point out—neither is concerned with a passive expectation but with an active participation during the interim. The coming in of the heathen is effected through missionary preaching by the disciples.

Thus, preaching 'to the Gentiles' is placed side by side with the other 'signs' of the End as an activity which characterises the interim, and gives it the character of 'grace-time'. Yet, here especially, we perceive that duality of motifs characteristic of Jesus' outlook; for just as mission stamps the interim with the character of grace, so this mission, being a necessary[11] preliminary

---

[1] Cf. Lohmeyer, *Markus*, p. 272; Blunt, *Mark*, p. 239; Kümmel, *Promise*, pp. 84f.; Grässer, *Problem*, pp. 5f., 159ff.; Klostermann, *Markus, ad loc.*

[2] Cf. Taylor, *Mark*, p. 507 for the evidence.

[3] Cf. Burney, *Poetry*, pp. 118f.; Lohmeyer, *Markus ad loc.*

[4] But cf. Burney, *Poetry*, pp. 118f., followed by Beasley-Murray, *Future*, pp. 198f.

[5] Cf. Taylor, *Mark*, p. 508.

[6] Cf. Cranfield, *Mark*, p. 399.

[7] Cf. Meinertz, *Theologie*, I, p. 64; Schniewind, *Markus, ad loc*; Bosch, *Heidenmission*, pp. 149ff.; Cranfield, *Mark*, p. 399; Cullmann, *Time*, p. 149; Michaelis, *Verheissung*, pp. 19f.; Beasley-Murray, *Future*, pp. 194ff.

[8] *Promise*, p. 22.

[9] In *Studies in the Gospels*, pp. 145ff.

[10] *Heidenmission*, p. 167.

[11] πρῶτον δεῖ, i.e. a divine necessity. *Studies in the Gospels* pp. 149f. punct-uates in a way which separates this πρῶτον δεῖ (with εἰς πάντα τὰ ἔθνη) from

of the End continually points forward to the End. It is itself only made possible by the grace-motif allowing the End to be withheld, and it is a sign, a testimony that the End is near. The view that missionary preaching is in any way a substitute or compensation for the early expectation of the Parousia [1] is therefore wholly false. The missionary command and its fulfilment form an integral part of Jesus' outlook upon the future and shed light on the manner in which he conceived the Parousia to be imminent. Only the motif of grace withholds that which properly belongs to the complex of eschatological events which ended with the Ascension and Exaltation.

So we find, in Jesus' understanding of the future, the twin themes, eschatology and grace. On the one hand the sure and certain hope that the End, being the revelation of his person and work, the end of all ambiguity and contradiction, must be near; the presence of the Eschaton guarantees the nearness of the manifestation proper to the Eschaton. On the other hand, the conviction that God will allow men 'time for amendment of Life and the grace and comfort of his Holy Spirit': [2] time, that is, in which to enter *freely* into the significance of Christ's work, to exercise faith, and hope and love.

κηρυχθῆναι: but (cf. Cranfield, *Mark*, p. 398) this leaves κηρυχθῆναι τὸ εὐαγγέλιον rather pointless.

[1] Cf. Conzelmann, *Mitte*, p. 116; Grässer, *Problem*, pp. 199f.

[2] 1928 B.C.P., alternative form of absolution.

CHAPTER TWELVE

THE SIGNIFICANCE OF THE NEW TESTAMENT IMMINENT EXPECTATION FOR THE LIFE OF THE CHURCH TO-DAY

Jesus' own understanding of the future has been elucidated by an examination of the duality of motifs present in his self-concious-ness, a duality which informed also his expectation for the future. The hope of the early church, on the other hand, has been recon-structed by an examination of its assessment of the past (princi-pally its assessment of the person and work of Jesus Christ as the fulfilment of salvation-history), and of the present (principally the working of the Holy Spirit amongst them, interpreted as a foretaste of the End). Despite the differences of approach, the content and significance of the future outlook is, in both cases, entirely similar: for both are founded upon the conviction that the End has—*in a hidden manner*—come; that its coming in manifest form cannot therefore be far off, though for the moment it is held back in the interests of grace, allowing an opportunity to be given to men to repent and believe.

There is, therefore, no question of abandoning an *outmoded* hope; no necessity to re-interpret (or demythologize) an expression of the early church's expectation which is now no longer tenable. Much rather, because the essence of the New Testament hope is Christological, it is possible for our hope to be similarly orientated and our assessment of the purposes of the present time similarly informed by that hope. If Jesus, or the early church, had orientated their hope about some delimited expectation, then we would indeed be forced to revise their hope, to orientate ours differently from theirs, to re-interpret and refashion their hope in order to make it meaningful and relevant to-day. But such, as we have tried to maintain, was *not* the case: Jesus and the early church as a whole, based their future expectation upon the conviction that the End was in Jesus Christ (though hidden), and that therefore the End in its manifest, unambiguous, universal form could not be far off: but they persistently refused to allow the sense of nearness to be turned into a belief that the End would definitely come within a certain number of years. They steadfasty rejected such a delimitation because beside the eschatological motif in the salvation-history they reckoned with the grace motif and realised that the time for repentance and faith could not be limited by men and that the provision of God's mercy could not be measured nor forecast.

In this chapter we propose to allow the undelimited but imminent Parousia hope to illuminate the character of the present and its significance in the total salvation-history pattern. We suggest that four major characteristics of the present, understood as grace-time, should be considered: they are:

1. The present period must be regarded as a time given in order to facilitate *repentance and faith*. The grace motif of Jesus' life, death and resurrection is entirely 'of a piece' with the provision of the present time before the final, universal, open display of the End. The vicarious nature of Christ's work is not considered in the New Testament as absolving men from aligning themselves to that work through repentance and faith. The demand for such alignment is inherently bound up in the vicarious work itself, and so the provision of an opportunity wherein such repentance and faith can be effected is as much a part of the 'gospel'—of grace—as the events of the life, death and resurrection of Jesus Christ are 'gospel'. The entire dependence of men for salvation upon the grace of God is not divorced from the response of faith and repentance required of man,[1] and it is the grace motif which is responsible for providing an opportunity and a time for this.[2] However, the provision of this opportunity is not altogether 'natural', self-evident or obvious, but actually stands in tension with the eschatological impulse towards the glorious revelation proper to the End events. This tension, which—if we may speak in this way—is a divine tension based upon God's purpose both to reveal his rule and also to give men time to respond to it freely in faith, gives rise to a human tension of a similar nature. The Christian is, on the one hand, thankful for the opportunity to repent and is not over anxious that the occasion should be cut short prematurely (cf. e.g. Lk. 13, 8) yet, on the other hand, being himself caught up in the ambiguity

---

[1] Cf. questions 56, 86 and 87 of the Heidelberg Catechism.

[2] Cf. Eph. 2, 8. The entire matter, even faith itself, is subsumed under the concept of grace.

of the present, being involved in suffering and endurance [1] the Christian hopes and prays for the End to come speedily (cf. I Cor. 16, 22; Rev. 22, 20). Hence the provision of time (cf. Mk. 13, 10) to repent and believe stands side by side with the shortening of the time (Mk. 13, 20) for the sake of the elect. The New Testament is clear that the present ('now' [2]) is *the* opportunity which men have to repent and believe,[3] and that the End delays only for this purpose—and not indefinitely. It is man's final chance. It is man's final *chance*, because the End *is* held back, God *is* patient and wills to give men time for repentance and faith and obedience: it is man's *final* chance, for the End delays not naturally, not indefinitely, not unintelligibly, but solely because it is held back by God's mercy, all the while remaining near, ready to arrive, belonging to the complex of events broken off at the Ascension, belonging as the *revelation* of that which has already occurred in Christ in lowliness and hiddenness.

2. Because the present grace-time spells the opportunity for men to repent and believe, the present is also to be seen as the *era of the church*, of those called to repentance and faith and obedience who hear the call and, more or less, here and there, attempt to understand and respond to it. We have already suggested [4] reasons for thinking that in all probability Jesus envisaged that 'his mission and message should be enshrined and mediated in a community living under his allegiance'.[5] This community has a two-fold purpose. In the first place it is the community in which Jesus Christ is recognised and openly acknowledged.[6] In the second place, it is the community through which Jesus Christ is proclaimed to 'those outside', and so through which his gracious ministry is continued. Thus the church is the eschatological community partaking in the blessings of the End through its relationship with Christ. It is also the community specially established to further the purpose of grace by participating in furthering the occasion of repentance and faith through constant witness. Both aspects are present in

---

[1] Cf. Mk. 13, 9; Rev. 5, 1of., etc.
[2] Cf. Stählin, in *T.W.N.T.* IV, pp. 110ff.
[3] Cf. Mk. 1, 15; Acts 3, 20; Lk. 13, 6-9 (cf. Michaelis, *Gleichnisse*, p. 98, who thinks this parable referred *originally* not simply to Jews but to all men).
[4] Above, chapter 7, pp. 95ff.
[5] Turner, *Jesus, Master and Lord*, p. 262.
[6] Cf. Cullmann, *Early Church*, pp. 105ff., *Time*, pp. 185f.

embryo in the choosing of the Twelve (Mk. 3, 13f., par.) 'that they might be with him' (sharing in the eschatological nature of his person and work, anticipating the End through union with him), and 'that he might send them forth' (participating in his ministry by preaching and calling forth repentance and faith). In both respects, the church's character and purpose are parallel to her Lord's who himself was 'sent' by God.[1]

3. Following from this, the present grace-time can be designated the time of the *Christian mission*. 'The time of Jesus' life on earth and of his presence in the Spirit is the time of grace, for it is the time of the proclamation of the Word'.[2] The mission of the church is already prefigured in the short preaching tour which the Twelve undertook during the earthly ministry of Jesus (Mk. 6, 7ff. par., cf. also Lk. 10, 1ff.) and is continued in his absence—though in this mission his hidden presence is assured.[3] The mission is paramount in the church's life; persecution must not hinder the progress of mission—indeed, it is anticipated that the mission will be costly[4]. The mission is especially to the fore in the Epistles [5] and it is evident that Paul himself was entirely dedicated to the service and progress of the gospel.[6] The variety of the gifts which Christians possess he subsumes under the overall purpose of edifying—particularly edifying the unbeliever (cf. I Cor. 14, 23ff.).

Of course, according to the New Testament, witness is not exhausted by the idea of preaching. Nor is repentance and faith simply regarded as confession of faith if this is understood as an intellectual conviction orally expressed. The witness which the

---

[1] This idea, not prominent in the Synoptics (cf. Mk. 1, 38; 12, 6) is emphasised by the Fourth Gospel—cf. Jn. 3, 17; 24. 5, 36; 38. 6, 29; 57. 7, 29. 8, 22. 10, 36. 11, 42. 17, 3; 8; 18; 21; 23; 25 ἀποστέλλω: and 4, 34. 5, 23f; 30; 37. 6, 38f; 44. 7, 16; 17; 28; 33. 8, 16; 18; 26; 29. 9, 4. 12, 44f.; 49. 13, 20. 14, 24. 15, 21. 16, 5. πέμπω cf. Rengstorf, in *T.W.N.T.* I, pp. 397ff.; Barrett, *John*, pp. 403f.

[2] Holwerda, *Spirit*, p. 84.

[3] Cf. Mtt. 28, 20. Jn. 15, 26-27 (Mk. 16, 20).

[4] The interim period is characterised by distress and persecution under which witness is to be carried out. This includes domestic distress (cf. Lk. 14, 26. Mk. 13, 12), cosmic distress (cf. Mk. 13, 8), and political distress (cf. Mk. 13, 8 par.). In point of fact, the Christian mission has apparently progressed mainly under the utmost persecution (cf. e.g. K. S. Latourette, *The Unquenchable Light*).

[5] Cf. Rom. 11, 25. 15, 19ff. I Cor. 1, 18ff. 9, 13; 23. II Cor. 3, 6. 4, 3f. 5, 18f. 6, 2-3. 9, 13. 10, 16. Gal. 1, 6ff. Phil. 1, 12ff. etc.

[6] Cf. esp. I Cor. 9, 23 and 9, 13.

New Testament demands in the present includes the whole field of Christian ethics: 'Not one of us is only a Christian; we are all also a bit of the world. And so we are necessarily also concerned with worldly attitudes, with translations of our responsibility into this realm. For the Confession of Faith claims to be fulfilled in its application to the life we all live, to the problems of our actual existence in the theoretical and practical questions of our everyday life . . .'.[1] Mk. 14, 7ff. speaks of a ministry to the poor which obviously includes the alleviation of need such as the price of the ointment would have furthered.[2] In the authority which Jesus gives his disciples (Mk. 6, 7ff.) to 'cast out unclean spirits' it is made apparent that the physical needs of men (in all their variety) must also be the concern of those who preach 'that men should repent'. As Mtt. 25, 31-46 makes evident, such ministration to those in need is regarded as ministry to Christ himself (even where it is not recognised by the doer as such [3]). A definite ministry to society at large seems to be envisaged in the expression (Mtt. 5, 13 par.) 'ye are the salt of the earth': perhaps Mk. 9, 50 is a fundamentally different saying from Mtt. 5, 13: but its meaning is very similar if the clue to its interpretation is the salting of sacrifices: [4] whilst Mark sees the effect of 'salting' in individualistic terms, Matthew thinks of the entire Christian community as the necessary salt apart from which the entire world is unacceptable to God (cf. Mtt. 5, 14).

This entire ministry to the world is a part of the church's witness to the world, being a confession of its allegiance to Jesus Christ. The tension between eschatology and grace, between already accomplished and not yet revealed, between longing for the End and thankfulness for its delay, is nowhere more apparent than in this sphere of Christian faith and witness. For ethics, Christian

---

[1] Barth, *Dogmatics in Outline*, p. 32.

[2] One wonders whether in the phrase εὖ ποιῆσαι in Mk. 14, 7 there might be an allusion to preaching the gospel to the poor? Cf. Is. 61, 1-2 (Lk. 4, 18 par. 7, 22 par.). Whereas v. 5 uses the verb δοθῆναι, v. 7 does not speak of *giving*, but of *doing good*.

[3] Some wish to understand 'brethren' as only needy *Christians*, but this seems unlikely; 'for, while all the individuals denoted by "all the nations" (whichever sense we give it) would be sure to have had some opportunity to succour a fellow man in need, it is obvious that they certainly could not all be assumed to have had a chance to succour a needy Christian', Cranfield, 'Diakonia', in *L.Q.H.R.* CLXXXVI, 1961, p. 276.

[4] Though, perhaps, the reference is to the ordinary domestic use of salt.

ethics, are at the same time an aspect of faith, an aspect of the purpose for which this grace-time is given us, and also an aspect of the End, a participation already in the blessing of the End. Christian ethics are at once a testimony to the world of the world's failure and condemnation and at the same time an assertion that God has reconciled the world to himself and that men can enter into the service of God. Christian ethics, made possible by the delay of the End (and so by grace) spring from participation in the End, from thankfulness to God for his work in Jesus Christ [1] (and so are eschatological). The constant tension in Christian ethics, between a tendency towards world affirmation (the desire to anti-cipate the time when the adversary the devil no longer goes about as a roaring lion!), and the tendency towards world denial (the desire to opt out of the struggle against evil by not coming into contact with it!) testifies to the twofold character of the present as an eschatological period (the world *is* reconciled—Col. 1, 20. II Cor. 5, 19, etc.) and as a grace-time prior to the End manifestation (the world still awaits its 'deliverance'—Rom. 8, 18f.). The same twofold character of the present time is also emphasized by the fact that Christian ethics are imposed as a free response. They are demanded as part of the response of faith, to be undertaken responsibly and urgently, and with utter obedience: and yet they spring from thankfulness, and are entered into with joy and confidence. In this sphere of Christian ethics, the eschatological situation of the present grace-time can be discerned in all its complexity; our understanding of the situation brought about by the advent of the End in Christ, its advent in hiddenness and the holding back of its advent in openness, makes sense of Christian ethics and of the tension within

---

[1] So the Heidelberg Catechism's third section (in which good works are discussed) is entitled 'of Thankfulness'. Calvin, in grounding ethics at least partially on a general law of God rather than upon a specifically Christol-ogical foundation, emphasises this character of ethics less, but cf. Book III of the Institutes. The responsive character of ethics is brought out by Luther (cf. e.g. his comments on Gal. 4, 8ff.) The Westminster Confession is similarly orientated (cf. Ch. XVI 'Of good works'). And the Scottish Confession of 1560 asserts, 'So that the cause of gude warkis, we confess to be not our free wil, bot the Spirit of the Lord Jesus, who dwelling in our hearts be trewe faith, bringis furth sik warkis as God has prepared for us to walke in . . . and thir thingis they do, not be their awin power, bot be the power of the Lord Jesus, without whom they were able to do nothing' (taken from Barth, *Knowledge of God and Service of God*, Gifford Lectures for 1937-8, pp. 113f. Barth's text is based on Sir John Skene's *Acts of the Parlia-ment of Scotland*, 1424-1579.).

faith and obedience and releases the disciple for obedience both with joyfulness and with serious urgency. *Now* is the time for Christian ethics; yet not with anxiety and distress as though all depended on our own good works, but from thankfulness and joy because the world *is* reconciled: yet not without seriousness and urgency as though we had all the time in the world, but with the utmost urgency since this opportunity to express our faith and make our witness to the world is dependent entirely on grace and on the withholding of the End.

4. The present grace-period is the *era of the Holy Spirit.* In one sense the Spirit stamps the present as the eschatological time of the End. He is the real presence of Christ with his church.[1] In Acts 2, 16f. Peter asserts that Pentecost has fulfilled the prophecy of Joel 2, 28-32, thus characterising the present as 'the last days'.[2] The same concept is contained in the choice of the two terms used to define the Spirit's presence ἀπαρχή und ἀρραβών.[3] Both testify to the real anticipation of the End, and also encourage a straining forward to the final manifestation of the End in its unambiguous form.[4]

In another sense the Spirit stamps the present as the grace period in which men are given occasion to repent and believe. For it is the Spirit who sustains the mission of the church—indeed He inaugurated it.[5] The Spirit mediates the presence of Christ to the believing community speaking to the community of Christ.[6] He

---

[1] Cf. esp. Mtt. 28, 20. Jn. 14, 17-18.

[2] Clearly that did not mean that he thought that the End had occurred in its final, open form. Joel 2, 31 speaks of that which will occur 'before the great and terrible day of the Lord come'.

[3] Cf. the discussion above, chapter 9, pp. 169ff.

[4] Cf. e.g. Rom. 8, 23 where the ἀπαρχή of the Spirit is spoken of in connection with the Christian 'groaning', waiting for the adoption, the redemption of our body: or II Cor. 1, 22, which speaks of the ἀρραβών of the Spirit in connection with being sealed (σφραγισάμενος) by God—clearly a reference to the yet future redemption which the Christian awaits (cf. v. 10).

[5] To be sure the mission *is* commanded by Christ (cf. our discussion above, chapter 11, pp. 205ff) and *is* at least prefigured in the preaching tour of the Twelve. But it is the Spirit who actually sets the mission in motion. Of Jn. 16, 7 Barrett writes, 'The thought is identical with that of 7, 39; the coming of the Spirit waits upon the glorifying of Jesus. The Spirit is the agent of the creation of the Church and the salvation of the world; in this sense the coming of the Spirit depends upon the completion of the work of Christ' (*John, ad loc*).

[6] Cf. Jn. 14, 26. 15, 26-27. 16, 13ff. I Cor. 12, 3. Eph. 2, 18. etc.

also mediates Christ through the community to those outside.[1]
He not only guides the witnessing but leads the geographical progress
of the gospel.[2] As Barth writes, '. . . there is a dominion of the Holy
Spirit. It corresponds to the dominion of Christ, between his
resurrection and return. Christ's resurrection, in a sense, might
have been the end. Does it not declare the end of this world and
the beginning of the Kingdom of God? But God did not will it so.
He inserted between the resurrection and the Kingdom of God,
the Dominion of Christ, the Dominion of the Holy Spirit. We may
still repent, we may still live on, at once facing toward resurrection
and return, during these final times which make God's mercy and
his patience manifest to us'.[3]

Thus the present time is a time of grace, made possible by
the patience (μακροθυμεῖ)[4] of God in withholding the End: it is a
time for repentance and faith, the time of the Church and of the
church's mission: the time of the Holy Spirit. And whilst these
features testify to the grace-character of the present, they also
testify to its eschatological nature, being signs that the present *is*
grace-time, *is* 'the last days', and that the End *is* at hand. The grace-
time, though not temporally delimited, is not unending: the End
waits to break in.

Two important corollaries follow from this understanding of
the character of the present and the nearness of the End. Though
the present is not unending, it is not within *our* knowledge nor
is it our prerogative to delimit the present time and specify how
much time yet remains. Throughout the Christian era there have
been those who have thought to reconstruct from the contemporary
political, cosmic or domestic situation, a programme whereby the
further duration of the interim could be estimated if not exactly
defined. This occurs particularly (and understandably easily!)
where a sense of the urgency of the church's missionary task is
perceived. It would serve no purpose here to describe exhaustively
the number of occasions on which this has happened; but it may
illustrate how easily men have fallen into the error if we select
instances through the history of the church.[5]

---

[1] Cf. Mk. 13, 11 par. Jn. 15, 26-27. 16, 7f. Acts 5, 32.

[2] Cf. Acts 13, 2. 16, 6f. 21, 11. (also 10, 44f. 11, 18).

[3] Barth, *The Faith of the Church*, pp. 111f.

[4] Cf. II Pet. 3, 9; 15. Interestingly the B.F.B.S. New Testament has a
marginal reference from Lk. 13, 8 to II Pet. 3, 9; 15.

[5] For another historical survey cf. Glasson, *Appearing*, pp. 43ff.

Already in II Thessalonians 2 we meet with some who, because of misunderstanding of Paul's preaching, sought to anticipate the End, and because of their belief in its proximity (if not its actual presence) apparently ceased working altogether (cf. 3, 10f.).

Montanism is an example. The Montanists maintained that 'as the dispensation of the Father had given place to the dispensation of the Son when Christ came to earth, so now the dispensation of the Son had given place to the dispensation of the Spirit'.[1] The coming of the Spirit marked for Montanus the immediate heralding of the Parousia and the establishment of the New Jerusalem in Phrygia itself. An ethic of world-denial and an enthusiastic anti-cipation of the imminent end followed. As Greenslade remarks, its 'enthusiasm was not purely and specifically Christian; it smacked of the fanaticism of those Asiatic cults of which Montanus had once been a priest, a fanaticism which the English bishops of the eigh-teenth century found in Methodist enthusiasm'.[2] Undoubtedly Montanus failed to see that the 'sign' of the Spirit stamped the present not only as an eschatological time *but also* as grace time.[3]

An example from the time of the Reformation is Luther himself. Not untypical of this Reformer, his desire to translate his under-standing of eschatology into the terms of ordinary practical involvement in life resulted in some inconsistencies. Partly the man's unsettled personality was responsible for this, but partly too was his mixed background with his strict scholastic intellectual training rubbing shoulders with his fascination for the popular apocalyptic writings of his generation. On the one hand, this background led him away from attempting to translate eschatology in chronological terms for scholastic theology was not inclined to consider categories of space and time as having real bearing in the rule of God; but on the other hand, this background led him almost involuntarily towards relating time to the Kingdom of God in a false, delimited manner. For the most part realisation that the inbreak of God's final and unambiguous rule could not be far off expressed itself in a proper sense of urgency and his resolve, in 1530, to publish his translation of the Book of Daniel without

---

[1] F. F. Bruce, *The Growing Day*, p. 87.

[2] *Schism in the Early Church*, p. 109.

[3] Cf. Cullmann, 'Early Christianity and Civilisation', originally in *Verbum Caro* V (Nos. 17-20), 1951; now in English in *Early Church*, pp. 207ff.

further ado reveals only a due sense of the open possibility that the End could come at any moment, a realisation that God would not indefinitely delay his final coming.[1] Consistently with this, Luther was scornful of attempts to date the End,[2] an activity in which not a few of his contemporaries engaged. At the same time, he himself was guilty on occasions of trying to do the self-same thing. As Torrance says, his 'fervid eschatological expectation kept up its force until Luther's death, but it became more and more calculating'.[3] In a revised edition in 1545 of his book Suppatatio annorum mundi, first issued in 1541, he determined that there were strictly speaking just 500 years remaining before the End, but since God had promised to 'shorten the days' the Parousia could occur at any moment; there might be only 100 years left. This is just the sort of delimitation which a sense of urgency can easily prompt, but which, as even Luther at his wisest knew, should be guarded against and avoided.

In the early part of the nineteenth century, millenarianism, with a strong belief that Christ's Advent was about to dawn, spread in Evangelical circles, chiefly owing to the books by Hatley Frere [4] and Lewis Way.[5] Both maintained 'that the view which had prevailed since the time of Augustine, that the Second Coming of Christ would be at the end of the world, was contrary to Scripture, and that the earlier view of the second and third centuries was the true one, that Christ would return and reign on earth for a thousand years . . .' [6] The result was a growth in the expectation that Christ was about to return, and whilst some found in this a motive for increased activity, others were 'afloat on prophesying, and the immediate work of the Lord is disregarded for the uncertain future'.[7]

An example from the present day may serve to complete the sketch. It is chiefly amongst the smaller sects that Christ's return is calculated, and a notable case is Seventh-Day Adventism. Right

---

[1] Torrance, *Kingdom and Church*, p. 19.

[2] 'In 1533, Luther had to deal severely with Michel Stifel for calculating that the world would end at 8o. a.m. on 19th October 1533'; Torrance, *Kingdom and Church*, p. 20.

[3] *Kingdom and Church*, p. 21.

[4] *A combined view of the prophecies of Daniel, Esdras and St. John*, 1815.

[5] *Thoughts on the Scriptural Expectations of the Christian Church*, 1823.

[6] G. R. Balleine, *A History of the Evangelical Party*, p. 137.

[7] Quoted by Balleine, *A History of the Evangelical Party*, p. 137 from E. Bickersteth's *Memoir*, Vol. II, p. 43.

at its inception, the founder William Miller 'as a result of his original studies in the Scriptures . . . became convinced that the end of the world would come on 10th December, 1843. His enthusiasm was such that he gathered tens of thousands of followers who watched in vain for the expected Advent of Christ. Nothing daunted he essayed another prophecy, and, blaming an error in mathematics for the fiasco, advanced the date by a year'.[1]

It is an easy and subtle step from the assertion that Christ's return is 'near' to declaring that it will come at a definite date. Yet it is instructive to notice how—at least in the examples we have cited—non-New Testament factors have helped to achieve what we maintain is essentially a non-New Testament standpoint. Thus, in the case of Montanism, Phrygia (and Asia Minor as a whole) was noted for its enthusiastic cults. In Luther's case, as has been pointed out, the influence of popular apocalypticism was strong upon him. The 19th century example was strongly influenced (as one of the titles of the important publications makes clear) by the apocalypticism of Daniel and Esdras. Seventh-Day Adventism derives much of its encouragement from the fact that the 'institutional' churches do not (generally speaking) hold, or manifest an awareness of, the idea of the nearness of the End in any sense, and its own calculating tendency is, in part, a revolt against indifference.

However, the transition, though subtle and easy, is fundamental. 'Die Zeichen der Zeit, auf die zu achten Jesus uns ausdrücklich auffordert, zeigen unmissverständlich an, dass "das Feld weiss geworden ist zur Ernte", dass das "Ende dieser Weltzeit" bevorsteht. . . .' and yet, 'Es ist selbstverständlich völlig wertlos und verkehrt, darüber zu streiten, *wie* "nahe" Jesu Wiederkunft ist . . .'.[2] Recognition of the character of the present time should make us aware of the nearness of the End, held back in the interests of grace, but should not lead us to suppose that we can, or ought to delimit the date of the End.

That is the first corollary which follows from what we have said about the nearness of the End. The other is this: that the

---

[1] J. O. Sanders and J. Stafford Wright, in a pamphlet, *Some Modern Religions*, p. 16.

[2] Hermann Leitz, *Die christliche Hoffnung und die letzten Dinge*, pp. 94 and 149.

church is required to recognise that its task in this present interim period must be pursued with intense urgency, 'whilst it is yet to-day'.[1] Though we cannot say that the End will certainly come tomorrow, or next year, its *nearness* should drive the church to serious, responsible and urgent obedience to its tasks. The provision of a grace-time is not to be taken for granted as self-evident or 'natural'. Self-evident and natural it certainly is *not*, for Jesus' 'life, death, resurrection and *Parousia* belong together as parts of an indivisible whole, as moments in the great and all-decisive movement of God to man now breaking into the world'.[2] The present opportunity for repentance and faith and obedience is the time of God's patience; this merciful provision must not be allowed to blind us to the urgent necessity imposed upon us but should rather undergird that sense of urgency. Nevertheless, this sense of urgency must not become an anxious matter, as though the End's coming were dependent not on God's mercy but on our faithfulness in performing our task. To be sure, the church must witness with zeal! 'Within the time of God's patience, she announces the grace and judgement accomplished in Jesus Christ, which on his return will be revealed in glory and in public.' [3] But the coming of the End is not withheld on account of the church's zeal or lack of it, but on account of the patience of God.[4]

We suggest that where the person and work of Jesus Christ is evaluated in terms of eschatology *and* grace, there too the present time will be recognised both as eschatological and the provision of grace. The End will be regarded indeed as near, as ready to break in at any moment, as held back only by the merciful patience of God who wills that men should repent whilst there is time: but the End's coming will not be delimited, either by our calculations or by our imagining that its coming is determined by our success in witnessing. It is for God only to decide (Mk. 13, 32).[5]

---

[1] Cf. Barth, *C.D.* III/2, pp. 468ff.
[2] Camfield, 'Man in his Time', in *S.J.T.* III, 1950, p. 133; cf. Cranfield, in *Essays in Christology*, pp. 89ff.
[3] Barth, *The Faith of the Church*, p. 118.
[4] Cf. Cullmann, 'Eschatologie und Mission', in *E.M.* 1941, pp. 98ff.
[5] See further, Preiss, *Life in Christ*, p. 71.

PERIODICALS CITED, WITH ABBREVIATIONS USED

A.T.R.	Anglican Theological Review
B.J.R.L.	Bulletin of the John Ryland's Library
	Ecumenical Review
E.M.	Evangelisches Missionsmagazin
E.T.	Expository Times
Ev.T.	Evangelische Theologie
H.J.	Hibbert Journal
H.T.R.	Harvard Theological Review
	Interpretation
J.B.L.	Journal of Biblical Literature
J.R.	Journal of Religion
J.T.S.	Journal of Theological Studies
J.E.H.	Journal of Ecclesiastical History
K.r.S.	Kirchenblatt für die reformierte Schweiz
L.Q.H.R.	London Quarterly and Holborn Review
N.R.T.	Nouvelle Revue de Theologie
N.T.	Novum Testamentum
N.T.S.	New Testament Studies
R.B.	Revue Biblique
R.H.P.R.	Revue d'Histoire et de Philosophie religieuses
R.S.R.	Recherches de Science Religieuse
	Scripture
S.J.T.	Scottish Journal of Theology
S.T.	Studia Theologica
S.T.U.	Schweizerische theologische Umschau
T.B.	Theologische Blätter
	Theology
T.L.	Theologische Literaturzeitung
T.Q.	Theologische Quartalschrift
T.R.	Theologische Rundschau
T.T.	Theology To-day
T.Z.	Theologische Zeitschrift
U.S.Q.R.	Union Seminary Quarterly Review
	Verbum Caro
V.F.	Verkundigung und Forschung
V.s.P.	Verhandlungen des schweizerischen Pfarrvereins
Z.A.W.	Zeitschrift für die alttestamentliche Wissenschaft
Z.N.W.	Zeitschrift für die neutestamentliche Wissenschaft
Z.s.T.	Zeitschrift für systematische Theologie
Z.T.K.	Zeitschrift für Theologie und Kirche
	Zwischen den Zeiten

BIBLIOGRAPHY OF AUTHORITIES CITED
OR CONSULTED

Abbreviations, where used, are given first

Abbott, *Ephesians*: T. K. Abbott, *The Epistles to the Ephesians and to the Colossians*, Edinburgh, 1897.

Ackermann, *Jesus*: H. Ackermann, *Jesus. Seine Botschaft und deren Aufnahme im Abendland*, Göttingen, 1952.

Addis, W. E. 'The Criticism of the Hexateuch compared with that of the Synoptic Gospels', in *Oxford Studies*, ed. W. Sanday, pp. 367ff.

Albertz: *Botschaft*: M. Albertz, *Die Botschaft des Neuen Testaments*. I (1-2), II (1-2), Zürich, 1947f.

Albright, W. F. *From Stone Age to Christianity*, Baltimore, 1940.

Allen, *Ephesians*: J. A. Allen, *The Epistle to the Ephesians*, London, 1959.

Allegro, *Scrolls*: J. M. Allegro, *The Dead Sea Scrolls*, Harmondsworth, 1956. 'Further Messianic references in Qumran Literature', in *J.B.L.* LXXV, 1956, pp. 182ff.

Allen, E. L. 'A Theology of Involvement', in *T.T.* XI, 1954, pp. 179ff.

Allen, P. M. S. 'Luke 17; 21. The Kingdom of God is within you', in *E.T.* XLIX, 1937, pp. 276f.

Allen, *Mark*: W. C. Allen, *The Gospel according to St. Mark*, London, 1915.

——, *Matthew*: *The Gospel according to St. Matthew*, Edinburgh, 1907.

——, 'The Book of Sayings used by the Editor of the First Gospel', in *Oxford Studies*, ed. W. Sanday, pp. 235ff.

——, 'The Aramaic Background of the Gospels', in *Oxford Studies*, ed. W. Sanday, pp. 287ff.

Allmen, *Vocabulary*: J. J. Allmen, ed. *Vocabulary of the Bible*, London, 1958.

Althaus, *Letzten Dinge*: P. Althaus, *Die Letzten Dinge*, Gütersloh, 1949 (5th ed.).

Anderson, *Introduction*: G. W. Anderson, *A Critical Introduction to the Old Testament*, London, 1959.

——, 'Hebrew Religion', in *The Old Testament and Modern Study* ed. H. H. Rowley, pp. 283ff.

Anderson, H. 'The Historical Jesus and the Origins of Christianity', in *S.J.T.* XIII, 1960, pp. 113ff.

Anderson-Scott, *Footnotes*: C. A. Anderson-Scott, *Footnotes to St. Paul*, Cambridge, 1935.

Argyle, A. W. 'Does "Realised Eschatology" make sense?', in *H.J.* LI, 1952-3, pp. 385f.

Arndt-Gingrich, *Lexicon*: Arndt, W. F. and Gingrich, F. W., *A Greek-English Lexicon of the N.T. and other early Christian Literature*. Cambridge, 1957.

Bacher, W. art. 'Synagogue', in *H.D.B.* IV, pp. 640f.

Bacon, *Mark*: B. W. Bacon, *The Gospel of Mark, its Composition and Date*, New Haven, 1925.

——, *Studies*: *Studies in Matthew*, New York, 1930.

——, 'After six days', in *H.T.R.* 1915, pp. 94ff.

Bailey, J. W. 'The Temporary Messianic Reign in the Literature of Early Judaism', in *J.B.L.* LII, 1934, pp. 170ff.

Baillie, J. *The Idea of Revelation in Recent Thought*, London, 1956.
Baldensperger, *Selbstbewusstsein Jesu*: W. Baldensperger, *Das Selbstbewusstsein Jesu im Lichte der messianischen Hoffnung seiner Zeit*, Strassburg, 1888.
Balleine, G. R. *A History of the Evangelical Party*, London, 1911.
Bammel, E. 'Matthäus 10, 23' in *S.T.* XV, 1962, pp. 79ff.
Barclay, *Mind*: W. Barclay, *The Mind of Jesus*, London, 1957.
Barr, A. 'Hope in the New Testament', in *S.J.T.* III, 1950, pp. 68ff.
——, 'Bultmann's Estimate of Jesus', in *S.J.T.* VII, 1954, pp. 337ff.
——, 'More Quests of the Historical Jesus', in *S.J.T.* XIII, 1960, pp. 394f.
Barr, J. *Biblical Words for Time*, London, 1962.
——, *The Semantics of Biblical Language*, London, 1961.
Barrett, *H.S.G.T.*: C. K. Barrett, *The Holy Spirit and the Gospel Tradition*, London, 1947.
——, *John*: *The Gospel according to St. John*, London, 1955.
——, *Romans*: *A Commentary on the Epistle to the Romans*, London, 1957.
——, *Luke the Historian*: *Luke the Historian in Recent Research*, London, 1961.
——, *The New Testament Background*: *Selected Documents*, London, 1956.
——, *Yesterday, To-day and Forever*; *the New Testament Problem*, Durham, 1959.
——, 'Paul and the Pillar Apostles', in *Studia Paulina*, pp. 1ff.
——, 'The Background of Mk. 10, 45', in *N.T. Essays*, ed. A.J.B. Higgins, pp. 2ff.
——, 'The Holy Spirit in the Fourth Gospel', in *J.T.S.* I, 1950, pp. 1ff.
——, 'The Place of Eschatology in the Fourth Gospel', in *E.T.* LIX, 1947, pp. 302ff.
——, 'New Testament Eschatology', in *S.J.T.* VI, 1953, pp. 136ff., and 225ff.
——, 'Myth and the New Testament; the Greek word "mythos" ', in *E.T.* LXVIII, 1956, pp. 345ff.
Barth, G. 'Das Gesetzverständnis des Evangelisten Matthäus', in *Überlieferung und Auslegung*', by G. Barth, G. Bornkamm and H. J. Held., pp. 54ff.
Barth, K. *Church Dogmatics*, Edinburgh, 1936f.
——, *Ein Versuch*: *Rudolf Bultmann; ein Versuch ihn zu verstehen*, Zürich, 1952. (E.T. in *Kerygma and Myth*, II, ed. H. W. Bartsch).
——, *Shorter Commentary*: *A Shorter Commentary on Romans*, London, 1959.
——, *Church and State*, London, 1939.
——, *Knowledge of God and Service of God*, London, 1938.
——, *The Epistle to the Romans*, Oxford, 1933.
——, *The Humanity of God*, London, 1961.
——, *The Faith of the Church*, London, 1960.
Barth, *Augenzeuge*: M. Barth, *Der Augenzeuge. Eine Untersuchung über die Wahrnehmung des Menschensohnes durch die Apostel*. Zürich, 1946.
——, *Abendmahl*: *Das Abendmahl. Passamahl, Bundesmahl und Messiasmahl*. Zürich, 1945.
Bartsch, H. W. ed. *Kerygma and Myth*, i-ii. London, 1954, 1962.
Bauer, *Johannes*: W. Bauer, *Das Johannesevangelium*. Tübingen, 1933.
Baumgartner, W. 'The Wisdom Literature', in *The Old Testament and Modern Study*, ed. H. H. Rowley, pp. 200ff.
Beardsley, W. A. 'Was Jesus more Optimistic than Paul?' in *J.B.L.* XXIV, 1956, pp. 264ff.

Beare, *I Peter*: F. W. Beare, *The First Epistle of Peter*, Oxford, 1947.
Beasley-Murray, *Future*: G. R. Beasley-Murray, *Jesus and the Future*, London, 1954.
——, *Mark* 13: *A Commentary on Mark* 13, London, 1957.
——, 'A Century of Eschatological Discussion', in *E.T.* LXVI, 1953, pp. 312ff.
Bell, G. K. A. and Deissmann, A. ed. *Mysterium Christi*, London, 1930.
Benecke, P. V. M. art. 'Claudius', in *H.D.B.* I, pp. 446f.
Bennett, J. C. 'A Theological Conception of Goals for Economic Life', in *Goals of Economic Life*, ed. A. Dudley-Ward.
Bentzen, A. *King and Messiah*, London, 1955.
——, *Daniel*, Tübingen, 1937.
Bercowitz, J. P. The Parables of the Messiah. Unpublished Edinburgh doctoral thesis.
Bernard, *John*: J. H. Bernard, *The Gospel according to St. John*, Edinburgh, 1928.
Bethune-Baker, *Introduction*: J. F. Bethune-Baker, *An Introduction to the early history of Christian Doctrine*, London, 1903.
Bevan, E. R. *Jerusalem under the High Priests*, London, 1904.
——, *Later Greek Religions*, London, 1927.
——, *Christianity*, Oxford, 1933.
Bieneck, *Sohn Gottes*: J. Bieneck, *Sohn Gottes als Christusbezeichnung der Synoptiker*, Zürich, 1951.
Bigg, C. *The Epistles of St. Peter and St. Jude*, Edinburgh, 1901.
Black, M. *An Aramaic Approach to the Gospels and Acts*, Oxford, 1946.
——, 'The Son of Man in the Teaching of Jesus', in *E.T.* LX, 1948, pp. 32ff.
——, 'The Parables as Allegory', in *B.J.R.L.* XLII, 1960, pp. 273ff.
——, 'The Son of Man in the old Biblical Literature', in *E.T.* LX, 1948, pp. 11f.
——, 'The Fulfilment of the Kingdom of God; Luke 22; 16' in *E.T.* LVII, 1945, pp. 25f.
——, 'The Kingdom of God has come', in *E.T.* LXIII, 1951, pp. 298ff.
Black, M. and Rowley, H. H. ed. *Peake's Commentary on the Bible*. Revised and reset, London, 1962.
Blass-Debrunner, *Grammar*: F. Blass and A. Debrunner, *A Greek Grammar of the N.T. and other early Christian literature*, Cambridge, 1961.
Blinzler, J. *The Trial of Jesus*, Westminster Md., 1959.
Blunt, *Mark*: A. W. F. Blunt, *The Gospel according to St. Mark*, Oxford, 1929.
Boman, T. *Hebrew Thought compared with Greek*, London, 1960.
Bonnard, *Philippiens*: P. Bonnard, *L'Épitre de Saint Paul aux Philippiens*, Neuchâtel, 1950.
Bonsirven, *Judaïsme*: J. Bonsirven, *Le Judaïsme palestinien au temps de Jesus-Christ*, (2 volumes) Paris, 1935.
Boobyer, *Transfiguration*: G. H. Boobyer, *St. Mark and the Transfiguration Story*, Edinburgh, 1942.
——, 'The Interpretation of the Parables of Jesus', in *E.T.* LXII, 1950, pp. 131ff.
Borchert, *Original Jesus*: O. Borchert, *The Original Jesus*, London, 1933.
Bornkamm, *Jesus*: G. Bornkamm, *Jesus of Nazareth*, London, 1960.
——, 'Die Verzögerung der Parusie', in *In Memoriam E. Lohmeyer*, ed. W. Schmauch, pp. 116ff.
——, 'Enderwartung und Kirche im Matthäusevangelium', in *T.L.Z.* LXXIX, 1954, pp. 341ff.

Bornkamm, with G. Barth and H. J. Held, *Überlieferung und Auslegung im Matthäusevangelium*, Neukirchen, 1961 (2nd ed.).
——, 'Enderwartung und Kirche im Matthäusevangelium', in *The N.T. Background*, ed. W. D. Davies and D. Daube, pp. 222ff.
Bosch, *Heidenmission*: D. Bosch, *Die Heidenmission in der Zukunftschau Jesu*, Zürich, 1959.
Bousset, W. *Kyrios Christos*, Göttingen, 1921 (2nd ed.).
——, *Die Religion des Judentums in späthellenistischen Zeitalter*, 3rd ed. H. Gressmann, Tübingen, 1926.
Bowman, *Intention*: J. W. Bowman, *The Intention of Jesus*, London, 1945.
——, 'From Schweitzer to Bultmann', in *T.T.* XI, 1954, pp. 16off.
——, 'The Background of the term "Son of Man" ', in *E.T.* LIX, 1948, pp. 288ff.
Box, *Ezra*: G. H. Box, *The Ezra Apocalypse*, London, 1912.
——, *Judaism in the Greek Period*, Oxford, 1932.
Brandon, *Fall of Jerusalem*: S. G. F. Brandon, *The Fall of Jerusalem and the Christian Church*, London, 1951.
——, 'Myth and the Gospel', in *H.J.* LI, 1952-3, pp. 121ff.
Branscomb, *Mark*: B. H. Branscomb, *The Gospel of Mark*, London, 1937.
Bright, J. *A History of Israel*, London, 1960.
Brockington, *Apocrypha*: L. H. Brockington, *A Critical Introduction to the Apocrypha*, London, 1961.
Brooke, *Johannine Epistles*: A. E. Brooke, *The Johannine Epistles*, Edinburgh, 1912.
Brown, W. Adams. art. 'Parousia', in *H.D.B.* III, pp. 674ff.
Browne, L. E. *Early Judaism*, Cambridge, 1920.
Bruce, *Acts*: F. F. Bruce, *Commentary on the Book of the Acts*, London, 1954.
——, *Biblical Exegesis*: *Biblical Exegesis in the Qumran Texts*, London, 1960.
——, *Second Thoughts on the Dead Sea Scrolls*, Grand Rapids, 1956.
——, *The Growing Day*, London, 1951.
——, *The Teacher of Righteousness in the Qumran Texts*, London, 1956.
——, 'Eschatology', in *L.Q.H.R.* 1958, pp. 99f.
Brunner, *Das Ewige*: E. Brunner, *Das Ewige als Zukunft und Gegenwart*, Zürich, 1953. (E.T. *Eternal Hope*, London, 1954).
——, *Romans*: *The Letter to the Romans*, London, 1959.
——, *Dogmatics*: *Dogmatics I. The Christian Doctrine of God*, London, 1949.
Bultmann, *Geschichte*: R. Bultmann, *Die Geschichte der synoptischen Tradition*, Göttingen, 1931 (2nd ed.).
——, *Jesus*: *Jesus and the Word*, London, 1935.
——, *Primitive Christianity*: *Primitive Christianity in its Contemporary Setting*, London, 1956.
——, *Theology*: *Theology of the New Testament*, London, 1952, 1955. (2 vols).
——, *Johannes*: *Das Evangelium des Johannes*, Göttingen, 1950 (11th ed.).
——, *Essays Philosophical and Theological*, London, 1955.
——, *History and Eschatology*, Edinburgh, 1957.
——, 'New Testament and Mythology', in *Kerygma and Myth*, ed. H. W. Bartsch, pp. 1ff.
——, 'History and Eschatology', in *N.T.S.* 1954, pp. 5ff.
——, 'Das Befremdliches des christlichen Glaubens', in *Z.T.K.* LV, 1958, pp. 185ff.
——, 'Heilsgeschichte und Geschichte. Zu Oscar Cullmann's Christus und die Zeit', in *T.L.Z.* XI, 1948, pp. 659f.
——, 'Reich Gottes und Menschensohn', in *T.R.* 1937-9, pp. 1ff.

Bultmann, 'What is Demythologizing', in *The Listener*, 5th February, 1953.
———, 'Die kirchliche Redaktion des ersten Johannesbriefes', in *In Memoriam E. Lohmeyer*, ed. W. Schmauch, pp. 189ff.
Buren; *Christ in our Place*: P. van Buren, *Christ in our Place. The Substitutionary Character of Calvin's Doctrine of Reconciliation*. Edinburgh, 1957.
Burkitt, *Gospel History*: F. C. Burkitt, *The Gospel History and its Transmission*, Edinburgh, 1911 (3rd ed.).
———, *Beginnings*: *Christian Beginnings*, London, 1924.
———, *Jesus Christ. An Historical Outline*, London, 1932.
———, *Sources*: *Earliest Sources for the Life of Jesus*, London, 1922 (2nd ed.).
Buri, *Die Bedeutung*: F. Buri, *Die Bedeutung der neutestamentlichen Eschatologie für die neuere protestantische Theologie*, Bern, 1934.
———, 'Zur Diskussion des Problems der ausgebliebenen Parusie', in *T.Z.* 1947, pp. 426ff.
———, 'Das Problem': 'Das Problem der ausgebliebenen Parusie', in *S.T.U.* 1946, pp. 101ff.
Burney, *Poetry*: C. F. Burney, *The Poetry of our Lord*, London, 1926.
Burrows, M. *The Dead Sea Scrolls*, London, 1956.
Burton, *Galations*: E. de W. Burton, *The Epistle to the Galations*, Edinburgh, 1921.
Busch, *Zum Verständnis*: F. Busch, *Zum Verständnis der synoptischen Eschatologie*; *Markus 13 neu untersucht*, Gütersloh, 1938.
Buse, S. J. 'Spatial imagery in N.T. Teaching about the Kingdom of God', in *E.T.* LX, 1948, pp. 82f.
Butterfield, H. *Christianity and History*, London, 1949.
Cadbury, *Luke-Acts*: H. J. Cadbury, *The Making of Luke-Acts*, London, 1927.
———, 'Acts and Eschatology', in *The New Testament Background*, ed. W. D. Davies and D. Daube, pp. 300ff.
Cadoux, *Historic Mission*: C. J. Cadoux, *The Historic Mission of Jesus*, London, 1941.
Cadoux, *Theology*: A. T. Cadoux, *The Theology of Jesus*, London, 1940.
———, *Parables*: *The Parables of Jesus, their Art, and Use*, New York, 1931.
Caird, *Principalities and Powers*: G. B. Caird, *Principalities and Powers. A Study in Pauline Theology*, Oxford, 1956.
———, *The Apostolic Age*, London, 1955.
Cairns, *Gospel*: D. S. Cairns, *A Gospel without Myth? Bultmann's Challenge to the Preacher*, London, 1960.
———, *The Image of God in Man*, London, 1953.
———, *The Faith that Rebels*, London, 1928.
Calvin, *Institutes*: J. Calvin, *The Institutes of the Christian Religion*, 2 vols. London, 1961.
———, *Harmony*: *Commentary on a Harmony of the Evangelists, Matthew, Mark and Luke*, Edinburgh, 1845 (C.T.S. ed.).
———, *John*: *Commentary on the Gospel according to John*, Edinburgh, 1847 (C.T.S. ed. *John 1-10*, Edinburgh, 1959. D.W. and T.F. Torrance ed.).
———, *Acts*: *Commentary on the Acts of the Apostles*, Edinburgh, 1844 (C.T.S. ed.).
———, *Romans*: *Commentary on the Epistle of Paul the Apostle to the Romans*, Edinburgh, 1849 (C.T.S. ed.).
———, *Corinthians*: *Commentary on the Epistles of Paul the Apostle to the Corinthians*, Edinburgh, 1848 (C.T.S. ed. *First Corinthians*, Edinburgh 1960. D.W. and T.F. Torrance ed.).

Calvin, *Philippians*: *Commentary on the Epistles of Paul the Apostle to the Philippians, Colossians and Thessalonians*, Edinburgh, 1851 (C.T.S. ed.).
——, *Commentary on the Epistles to Timothy, Titus and Philemon*, Edinburgh, 1856 (C.T.S. ed.).
——, *Hebrews*: *Commentary on the Epistle to the Hebrews*, Edinburgh, 1853 (C.T.S. ed.).
——, *Catholic Epistles*: *Commentary on the Catholic Epistles*, Edinburgh, 1855 (C.T.S. ed.).
Camfield, F. W. 'Man in his Time', in *S.J.T.* III, 1950, pp. 127ff.
Campbell, J. Y. 'The Kingdom of God has Come', in *E.T.* XLVIII, 1936-7, pp. 91f.
Campenhausen, 'Zur Auslegung': H. von Campenhausen, 'Zur Auslegung von Röm 13', in *Festschrift für A. Bertholet*, pp. 97ff.
Carpenter, *Johannine Writings*: J. E. Carpenter, *The Johannine Writings*; *A Study of the Apocalypse and the Fourth Gospel*, London, 1927.
Carrington, *Mark*: P. Carrington, *According to Mark. A Running Commentary on the Oldest Gospel*, Cambridge, 1960.
Case, S. J. *Jesus*; *A New Biography*, Chicago, 1927.
Cave, *Gospel*: S. Cave, *The Gospel of St. Paul*; *a Re-interpretation in the light of the Thought of his Age and Modern Missionary Experience*, London, 1928.
Charles, *Revelation*: R. H. Charles, *The Revelation of St. John*, Edinburgh, 1920.
——, *Eschatology*: *A Critical History of the Doctrine of a Future Life in Israel, in Judaism and in Christianity, or Hebrew, Jewish and Christian Eschatology from preProphetic Times till the close of the N.T. Canon*, London, 1913 (2nd ed.).
——, *Apochrypha*: *The Apocrypha and Pseudepigrapha in English with Introductions and critical explanatory notes on the several books* (ed. R. H. Charles), Oxford, 1913 (2 vols).
——, *Daniel*: *The Book of Daniel*, Oxford, 1929.
——, *Religious Development*: *Religious Development between the Testaments*, London, 1914.
Clarke, K. W. 'Realised Eschatology', in *J.B.L.* LIX, 1940, pp. 367ff.
Clarke, W. K. Lowther, 'The Clouds of Heaven; an eschatological study', in *Theology*, XXXI, 1935, pp. 63ff. and 128ff.
Clavier, H. 'The Kingdom of God; its coming and mans' entry into it', in *E.T.* LX, 1948, pp. 24ff.
Colani, T. *Jésus Christ et les Croyances Messianiques de son Temps*, Strassburg, 1864 (2nd ed.).
Coniectanea Noetestamentica XI in honorem A. Fridrichsen, Lund, 1947.
Conzelmann, *Mitte*: H. Conzelmann, *Die Mitte der Zeit*, Tübingen, 1960 (3rd ed. E.T. *The Theology of St. Luke*, London, 1960).
——, 'Gegenwart und Zukunft in der synoptischen Tradition', in *Z.T.K.* LIV, 1957, pp. 277ff.
——, 'Die formgeschichtliche Methode', in *S.T.U.* III, 1959, pp. 54ff.
——, 'Zur Methode der Leben-Jesu-Forschung', in *Z.T.K.* LVI, 1959, pp. 54ff.
Cook, *Old Testament*: S. A. Cook, *The Old Testament*; *a Re-interpretation*, Cambridge, 1936.
Corell, A. *Consummatum Est*; *Eschatology and Church in the Gospel of St. John*, London, 1958.
Craig, C. T. 'Realised Eschatology', in *J.B.L.* LVI, 1937, pp. 17ff.

Cranfield, *Mark*: C. E. B. Cranfield, *The Gospel according to St. Mark*, Cambridge, 1959.
——, *I and II Peter*: *I and II Peter and Jude*, London, 1960.
——, *The Epistle of James*; *Four Studies*, London (undated).
——, 'The Parable of the Unjust Judge and the Eschatology of Luke-Acts', in *S.J.T.* XVI, 1963, pp. 297ff.
——, 'St. Mark 4,1-34', in *S.J.T.* IV, 1951, pp. 398ff. and V, 1952, pp. 49ff.
——, 'The Witness of the New Testament to Christ', in *Essays in Christology*, ed. T.H.L. Parker, pp. 71ff.
——, 'Mark 13', in *S.J.T.* VI, 1953, pp. 189ff. and 287ff., and VII, 1954, pp. 284ff.
——, 'Some observations on Romans 13; 1-7', in *N.T.S.* VI, pp. 241ff.
——, 'Diakonia', in *L.Q.H.R.* CLXXXVI, 1961, pp. 276ff.
Creed, *Luke*: J. M. Creed, *The Gospel according to St. Luke*, London, 1930.
——, 'The Kingdom of God has come', in *E.T.* XLIX, 1937, p. 184.

Cripps, *Amos*: R. S. Cripps, *The Book of Amos*, London, 1920.
Cross, F. L. ed. *Studies in Ephesians*, London, 1956.
      ed. *The Jung Codex*, London, 1955.
Cullmann, *Christology*: O. Cullmann, *The Christology of the N.T.* London, 1959.
——, *Time*: *Christ and Time*, London, 1951.
——, *State*: *The State in the New Testament*, London, 1957.
——, *Peter*: *Peter, Disciple, Apostle and Martyr*, London, 1953.
——, *Early Church*: *The Early Church*, London, 1956 (ed. A. J. B. Higgins).
——, *Worship*: *Early Christian Worship*, London, 1953.
——, *Confessions*: *The Earliest Christian Confessions*, London, 1949.
——, *Baptism*: *Baptism in the N.T.* London, 1950.
——, 'Das Wahre': 'Das Wahre durch die ausgebliebene Parusie gestellte neutestamentliche Problem', in *T.Z.* III, 1947, pp. 178ff.
——, 'Unzeitgemässe Bemerkungen': 'Unzeitgemässe Bemerkungen zum "historischen Jesus" der Bultmannschule', in *Der historische Jesus und der kerygmatische Christus*, ed. H. Rigstow and K. Matthiae, Berlin, 1960, pp. 266ff. (E.T. 'Out of season remarks on the "historical Jesus" of the Bultmann School', in *U.S.Q.R.* XVI, 1961, pp. 131ff).
——, 'Der johanneische Gebrauch doppeldeutiger Ausdrücke als Schlüssel zum Verständnis des vierten Evangeliums', in *T.Z.* IV, 1948, pp. 360ff.
——, 'Parusieverzögerung und Christentum — der gegenwärtige Stand der Diskussion', in *T.L.* LXXXIII, 1958, pp. 2ff.
——, 'Neutestamentliche Eschatologie und die Entstehung des Dogmas', in *K.r.S.* XI, 1942, pp. 161ff.
——, 'Eschatologie und Mission', in *E.M.* 1941, pp. 98ff.
——, 'Die Hoffnung der Kirche auf die Wiederkunft Christi', in *V.s.P.* 1942, pp. 27ff.
——, 'Le caractère eschatologique du devoir missionaire et de la conscience , apostolique de S. Paul. Étude sur le κατεχον(ων) de 2. Thess 2,6-7', in *R.H.P.R.* 1936, pp. 210ff.
——, 'The Significance of the Qumran Texts for Research into the Beginnings of Christianity', in *J.B.L.* LXXIV, 1955, pp. 215ff.
——, *Heil als Geschichte*, Tübingen, 1965.
Dahl, N. A. *Das Volk Gottes*, Oslo, 1941.
——, 'Die Theologie des N.T.', in *T.R.* XXII, 1954, pp. 21ff.
——, 'The Parables of Growth', in *S.T.* V, 1952, pp. 132ff.

Dalman, *Words*: G. Dalman, *The Words of Jesus*, Edinburgh, 1909.
——, *Jesus Jeshua*, London, 1929.
Danby, H. *The Mishnah*, Oxford, 1933.
Daube, D. 'Public Pronouncement and Private Explanation in the Gospels', in *E.T*. LVII, 1946, pp. 175ff.
Davidson, *Theology*: A. B. Davidson, *The Theology of the Old Testament*, Edinburgh, 1904.
Davidson, F. and Stibbs, A. M. ed. *The New Bible Commentary*, London, 1953.
Davies, *Rabbinic Judaism*: W. D. Davies, *Paul and Rabbinic Judaism*, London, 1948.
Davies, W. D. and Daube, D. ed. *The Background of the New Testament and its Eschatology; in honour of C. H. Dodd*, Cambridge, 1956.
Deissmann, *Paul*: A. Deissman, *Paul; a Study in Social and Religious History*, London, 1926.
——, *Light from the East*, London, 1927.
Delling, *Zeitverständnis*: G. Delling, *Das Zeitverständnis des N.T.*, Gütersloh, 1940.
Denney, *II Corinthians*: J. Denney, *The Second Epistle to the Corinthians*, London, 1910 (5th ed.).
Dibelius, *Paul*: M. Dibelius, *Paul*, London, 1953 (edited and completed W. G. Kümmel).
——, *Studies*: *Studies in the Acts of the Apostles*, London, 1956.
——, *Jakobus*: *Der Brief des Jakobus*, Göttingen, 1957 (9th ed.).
——, *Pastoralbriefe*: *Die Pastoralbriefe*, Tübingen, 1931 (2nd ed.).
——, *Thessalonicher*: *An die Thessalonicher I, II*, Tübingen, 1923 (2nd ed.).
——, *Tradition*: *From Tradition to Gospel*, London, 1934.
——, *Fresh Approach*: *A Fresh Approach to the New Testament and early Christian Literature*, London, 1936.
Dillistone, F. W. *The Holy Spirit in the Life of To-day*, London, 1946.
——, 'Time and the Church', in *S.J.T*. VI, 1953, pp. 156ff.
Dix, Dom G. *The Shape of the Liturgy*, London, 1945.
Dobschütz, E. von. *The Eschatology of the Gospels*, London, 1910.
Dodd, *Parables*: C. H. Dodd, *The Parables of the Kingdom*, 1936 (revised ed.).
——, *Apostolic Preaching*: *The Apostolic Preaching and its Developments*, London, 1936.
——, *History*: *History and the Gospel*, London, 1938.
——, *Fourth Gospel*: *The Interpretation of the Fourth Gospel*, Cambridge, 1953.
——, *Studies*: *New Testament Studies*, Manchester, 1954.
——, *Romans*: *The Epistle of Paul to the Romans*, London, 1932.
——, *Johannine Epistles*: *The Johannine Epistles*, London, 1946.
——, *Coming of Christ*: *The Coming of Christ*, Cambridge, 1952.
——, *Authority*: *The Authority of the Bible*, London, 1947.
——, *The Bible and the Greeks*, London, 1935.
——, 'The Appearance of the Risen Christ; an Essay in Form Criticism of the Gospels', in *Studies in the Gospels*, ed. D. E. Nineham, pp. 9ff.
——, 'The Kingdom of God has come', in *E.T*. XLVIII, 1936, pp. 138ff.
——, 'The Primitive Catechism and the Sayings of Jesus', in *N.T. Essays*, ed. A. J. B. Higgins.
Driver, *Daniel*: S. R. Driver, *The Book of Daniel*, Cambridge, 1900.
Du Bose, *Gospel*: W. P. Du Bose, *The Gospel in the Gospels*, London, 1906.
Duhm, B. *Der kommende Reich Gottes*, Tübingen, 1910.
Duncan, *Son of Man*: G. S. Duncan, *Jesus, Son of Man*, London, 1947.
——, *St. Paul's Ephesian Ministry: a Reconstruction*, London, 1929.

Duncan, 'Were Paul's Imprisonment Epistles written from Ephesus?' in *E.T.* LXVII, 1956, pp. 163ff.

Dupont-Sommer, A. *The Dead Sea Scrolls*, Oxford, 1952.

Easton: *Pastoral Epistles*: B. S. Easton, *The Pastoral Epistles*, London, 1948.

——, *Christ in the Gospels*, London, 1930.

Ecumenical Studies, *The Meaning of Hope in the Bible* (No. A/5) Geneva, 1952.

Edersheim, A. *The Life and Times of Jesus the Messiah* (2 vols.) London, 1883.

Edgar, S. L. 'New Testament and Rabbinic Messianic Interpretation', in *N.T.S.* V, 1958, pp. 47ff.

Edghill, *Amos*: E. A. Edghill, *Commentary on Amos*, London, 1914.

Ehrhardt, A. 'The Construction and Purpose of the Acts of the Apostles', in *S.T.* XII, 1958, pp. 45ff.

Eichrodt, *Theology*: W. Eichrodt, *Theology of the Old Testament*, I. London, 1961.

——, 'Heilserfahrung und Zeitverständnis im A.T.' in *T.Z.* XII, 1956, pp. 103ff.

Eisler, R. *The Messiah Jesus and John the Baptist*, London, 1931.

Eissfeldt, O. 'Jahve als König', in *Z.A.W.* XLVI, 1928, pp. 81ff.

Engnell, *Studies*: I. Engnell, *Studies in Divine Kingship in the Ancient Near East*, Uppsala, 1943.

Evans, O. E. 'Demythologizing', in *L.Q.H.R.* 1958, pp. 104ff.

Evans, C. F. 'I will go before you into Galilee', in *J.T.S.* V, 1954, pp. 3ff.

——, 'Kerygma', in *J.T.S.* VII, 1956, pp. 25ff.

Evanston Speaks: *Reports from the Second Assembly of the World Council of Churches, August* 15-31, 1954, London, 1954.

Falconer, *Pastoral Epistles*: Sir R. Falconer, *The Pastoral Epistles*, Oxford, 1937.

Farrer, A. *A Study in St. Mark*, London, 1951.

Feine, *Theologie*: P. Feine, *Theologie des Neuen Testaments*, Leipzig, 1910.

Ferré, N. 'Present Responsibility and Future Hope', in *T.T.* VIII, 1952, pp. 483ff.

Festschrift Rudolf Bultmann zum 65. Geburtstag überreicht, Stuttgart & Köln, 1949.

Feuillet, A. in *R.S.R.* XXXV, 1947, pp. 303ff. and XXXVI, 1948, pp. 544ff.

——, in *R.B.* LVI, 1949, pp. 61ff. and 360ff. and LVII, 1950, pp. 43ff. and 180ff.

——, and Robert, A. ed. *Introduction à la Bible*, Tournai, 1959.

Filson. *Matthew*: F. V. Filson, *Commentary on the Gospel according to St. Matthew*, New York, 1960.

——, *New Testament*: *The New Testament against its Environment*, London, 1950.

Fison, *Hope*: J. E. Fison, *The Christian Hope*, London, 1954.

Flew, *Perfection*: R. Newton Flew, *The Idea of Perfection*, Oxford, 1934.

——, *Church*: *Jesus and His Church*, London, 1943 (2nd ed.).

Flückiger, *Ursprung*: F. Flückiger, *Der Ursprung des christlichen Dogmas*, Zürich, 1955.

Foakes-Jackson, *Acts*: F. J. Foakes-Jackson, *The Acts of the Apostles*, London, 1931.

——, and K. Lake *The Beginnings of Christianity* (5 vols.) London, 1920-33.

Forsyth, P. T. *The Person and Place of Jesus Christ*, London, 1909.

Foster, J. 'Eschatology and the Hope of a New World', in *E.T.* LIV, 1942, pp. 10ff.

Frame, *Thessalonians*: J. E. Frame, *Commentary on I and II Thessalonians*, Edinburgh, 1912.

Frankfurt, H. *Kingship and the Gods*, Chicago, 1948.

Fridrichson, A. J. ed. *The Root of the Vine; Essays in Biblical Theology by A. Fridrichson and other members of Uppsala University*, London, 1953.

Fritsch, C. T. 'The Message of Apocalyptic for To-day', in *T.T.* X, 1953, pp. 357ff.

Frost, *Apocalyptic*: S. B. Frost, *Old Testament Apocalyptic, its Origin and Growth*, London, 1952.

Fuchs, E. 'Die Frage nach dem historischen Jesus', in *Z.T.K.* LIII, 1956, pp. 210ff.

——, 'Christus das Ende der Geschichte', in *Ev.T.* 1949, pp. 447ff.

——, 'W. G. Kümmel: Verheissung und Erfüllung', in *V.F.* 1947, pp. 75f.

Fuller, *Mission and Achievement*: R. H. Fuller, *The Mission and Achievement of Jesus*, London, 1954.

Gardner, P. art. 'Mysteries', in *E.R.E.* IX, pp. 81ff.

Gaster, *Scriptures*: T. H. Gaster, *The Scriptures of the Dead Sea Sect in English Translation*, London, 1957.

Geldenhuys, *Luke*: N. Geldenhuys, *Commentary on the Gospel of Luke*, London, 1950.

George, *Communion*: A. R. George, *Communion with God in the N.T.*, London, 1953.

Glasson, *Advent*: T. F. Glasson, *The Second Advent*, London 1947 (revised ed.).

——, *Appearing*: *His Appearing and His Kingdom*, London, 1952.

——, 'Mark 13 and the Greek O.T.', in *E.T.* LXIX, 1957, pp. 213ff.

——, 'The Kerygma: is our version correct? in *H.J.* LI, 1953, pp. 129ff.

Gloege, G. *Reich Gottes und Kirche*, Gütersloh, 1929.

——, *Das Reich Gottes im N.T.*, Leipzig, 1928.

Gogarten, *Demythologizing*: F. Gogarten, *Demythologizing and History*, London, 1955.

——, 'Theologie und Geschichte', in *Z.T.K.* L, 1953, pp. 339ff.

Goguel, *Life*: M. Goguel, *The Life of Jesus*, London, 1933.

——, *Birth*: *The Birth of Christianity*, London, 1953.

Goodenough, E. R. *An Introduction to Philo Judaeus*, New Haven, 1940.

——, 'John, a Primitive Gospel', in *J.B.L.* LXIV, 1945, pp. 145ff.

Goodspeed, *Introduction*: E. J. Goodspeed, *An Introduction to the N.T.* Chicago, 1937.

——, *Life*: *The Life of Jesus*, New York, 1950.

——, *Ephesians*: *The Meaning of Ephesians*, Chicago, 1933.

——, *New Solutions of N.T. Problems*, Chicago, 1927.

Gore, *Dissertations*: C. Gore, *Dissertations on Subjects connected with the Incarnation*, London, 1896.

——, *Romans*: *St. Paul's Epistle to the Romans* (2 vols.), London, 1900.

——, *Johannine Epistles*: *The Epistles of St. John*, London, 1920.

——, *Belief in Christ*, London, 1922.

——, and H. L. Goudge and A. Guillaume, *A New Commentary on Holy Scripture, including the Apocrypha*, London, 1928.

Goudge, *I Corinthians*: H. L. Goudge, *The First Epistle to the Corinthians*, London, 1911 (revised ed.).

——, 'The Parable of the Ten Virgins', in *J.T.S.* XXX, 1929, pp. 267ff.

Gould, *Mark*: E. P. Gould, *The Gospel according to St. Mark*, Edinburgh, 1896.

Grässer, *Problem*: E. Grässer, *Das Problem der Parusieverzögerung in den synoptischen Evangelien und in der Apostelgeschichte*, Berlin, 1957.

Graham, *The Christ of Catholicism*: Dom A. Graham, *The Christ of Catholicism; A Meditative Study*, London, 1947.

Grant, *Earliest Gospel*: F. C. Grant, *The Earliest Gospel*, New York, 1943.

——, *The Gospels, their Origin and their Growth*, London, 1957.

Greenslade, S. L. *Schism in the Early Church*, London, 1953.

Gressmann, H. *Der Ursprung der israelitisch-jüdischen Eschatologie*, Göttingen, 1905.

Griffiths, J. G. 'ἐντὸς ὑμῶν — Lk. 17,21', in *E.T.* LXIII, 1951, pp. 30f.

Guignebert, C. *Jesus*, London, 1935.

Guthrie, *Pastoral Epistles*: D. Guthrie, *The Pastoral Epistles*, London, 1957.

——, *The Pastoral Epistles and the Mind of Paul*, London, 1955.

Guy, *Last Things*: H. A. Guy, *The New Testament Doctrine of the Last Things*, London, 1948.

——, *Prophecy*: *New Testament Prophecy; its Origin and Significance*, London, 1947.

——, *The Life of Christ*, London, 1951.

——, *The Origin of the Gospel of Mark*, London, 1954.

——, *The Acts of the Apostles*, London, 1953.

Haak, E. 'Exegetische-dogmatische Studie zur Eschatologie I Thess. 4,13-18' in *Z.s.T.* XV, 1938, pp. 544ff.

Hadfield, P. 'Iranean Influence on Jewish and Christian Apocalyptic', in *L.Q.H.R.* 1958, pp. 216ff.

Hadorn, D. W. *Zukunft und Hoffnung*, Gütersloh, 1914.

Haenchen, *Apostelgeschichte*: E. Haenchen, *Die Apostelgeschichte*, Göttingen, 1956.

Hamilton, *Holy Spirit*: N. Q. Hamilton, *The Holy Spirit and Eschatology in Paul*, Edinburgh, 1957.

Haroutunian, J. 'The Christian Hope and the Modern World', in *T.T.* X, 1953, pp. 312ff.

Harper, W. R. *Amos and Hosea*, Edinburgh, 1905.

Harris, *Testimonies*: J. R. Harris and V. Burch, *Testimonies*, Cambridge 1916.

Harrison, *Pastoral Epistles*: P. N. Harrison, *The Problem of the Pastoral Epistles*, Oxford, 1921.

Hastings, *H.D.B.*: J. Hastings, ed. *A Dictionary of the Bible* (5 vols.) Edinburgh, 1904.

——, *E.R.E.*: *Encyclopaedia of Religion and Ethics* (13 vols.) Edinburgh, 1908-26.

——, *D.C.G.*: *A Dictionary of Christ and the Gospels* (2 vols.) Edinburgh, 1906.

Hatch and Redpath, *Concordance*: E. Hatch and H. A. Redpath, *A Concordance to the Septuagint and other Greek versions of the O.T.* (4 vols.) Oxford, 1897-1904.

Hauck, *Lukas*: F. Hauck, *Das Evangelium des Lukas*, Leipzig, 1934.

——, *Kirchenbriefe*: *Die Kirchenbriefe*, Göttingen, 1954 (7th ed.).

——, *Markus*: *Das Evangelium des Markus*, Leipzig, 1931.

Headlam, *Life and Teaching*: A. C. Headlam, *The Life and Teaching of Jesus the Christ*, London, 1923.

Heard, *Introduction*: R. Heard, *An Introduction to the N.T.*, London, 1950.

Heaton, *Daniel*: E. W. Heaton, *The Book of Daniel*, London, 1956.

Hebert, *Authority*: A. G. Hebert, *The Authority of the Old Testament*, London, 1947.

Heim, K. *Jesus the Lord*, Edinburgh, 1959.
Heimann, E. 'Comparative Economic Systems', in *Goals of Economic Life*, ed. A. Dudley Ward.
Heinzelmann, *Philipper*: G. Heinzelmann, *Der Brief an die Philipper*, Göttingen, 1959 (8th ed.).
Held, H. J. 'Matthäus als Interpret der Wundergeschichten', in *Überlieferung und Auslegung*; by, G. Barth, G. Bornkamm and H. J. Held.
Henderson, *Myth*: I. Henderson, *Myth in the New Testament*, London, 1956.
Héring, *Le Royaume*: J. Héring, *Le Royaume de Dieu et sa Venue*, Paris, 1937.
——, *II Corinthiens*: *La Seconde Épitre de Saint Paul aux Corinthiens*, Neuchâtel, 1958.
——, *Hebreux*: *L'Épitre aux Hebreux*, Neuchâtel, 1954.
——, *I Corinthiens*: *La Première Épitre de Saint Paul aux Corinthiens*, Neuchâtel, 1949.
——, 'St. Paul a-t-il ensigné deux résurrections?' in *R.H.P.R.* XII, 1932, pp. 300ff.
Higgins, A. J. B. ed. *N.T. Essays: Studies in Memory of T. W. Manson*, Manchester, 1959.
——, *The Lord's Supper in the N.T.*, London, 1952.
——, 'Son of Man Forschung since the "Teaching of Jesus" ', in *N.T. Essays*, ed. A. J. B. Higgins, pp. 119ff.
Hölscher, G. 'Der Ursprung der Apokalypse Mk. 13', in *T.B.* XII, 1933, pp. 193ff.
Holmes-Gore, V. A. 'The Ascension and the Apocalyptic Hope', in *Theology*, XXXII, 1936, pp. 356ff.
Holmstrom, F. *Das eschatologische Denken der Gegenwart*, Gütersloh, 1936.
Holwerda, *Spirit*: D. E. Holwerda, *The Holy Spirit and Eschatology in the Gospel of John*, Kampen, 1959.
Hommel, F. 'The Apocalyptic Origin of the Expression "Son of Man" ', in *E.T.* XI, 1899, pp. 341ff.
Hooft, *Renewal*: W. A. V. 't Hooft, *The Renewal of the Church*, London, 1956.
Hooke, *Kingdom of God*: S. H. Hooke, *The Kingdom of God in the Experience of Jesus*, London, 1949.
——, *The Origins of Early Semitic Ritual*, London, 1938.
——, ed. *The Labyrinth*, London, 1935.
——, ed. *Myth and Ritual*, London, 1933.
Hooker, M. D. *Jesus and the Servant*, London, 1959.
Hort, *Prolegomena*: F. J. A. Hort, *Prolegomena to St. Paul's Epistles to the Romans and the Ephesians*, London, 1895.
Hoskyns, E. C. and Davey, F. N. *The Riddle of the New Testament*, London, 1931.
——, *The Fourth Gospel* (2 vols.), London, 1940.
Hoskyns, E. C. 'Das überweltliche Reich Gottes im N.T.,', in *T.B.* VI, 1927, pp. 115ff. (with articles by K. L. Schmidt, C. H. Dodd, G. Kittel and A. E. J. Rawlinson).
Howard, *Christianity*: W. F. Howard, *Christianity according to St. John*, London, 1943.
——, *Fourth Gospel*: *The Fourth Gospel in recent Criticism and Interpretation*, London, 1931.
Hunter, *Mark*: A. M. Hunter, *The Gospel according to St. Mark*, London, 1948.
——, *Paul*: *Paul and his Predecessors*, London, 1961 (revised ed.).
——, *Parables*: *Interpreting the Parables*, London, 1960.
——, *Words and Works*: *The Words and Works of Jesus*, London, 1950.

Hunter, *Design for Life*: an exposition of the Sermon on the Mount, Mtt. 5-7, London, 1953.
——, *Interpreting the N.T. 1900-1950*, London, 1951.
——, *Interpreting Paul's Gospel*, London, 1954.
Hutton, W. R. 'The Kingdom of God has come', in *E.T.* LXIV, 1952, p. 89.
Iersel, *Der Sohn*: B. M. F. van Iersel, *Der Sohn in den synoptischen Jesusworten*, Leiden, 1961.
Iremonger, F. A. *William Temple, Archbishop of Canterbury*: His Life and Letters, London, 1948.
Jacob, *Theology*: E. Jacob, *Theology of the Old Testament*, London, 1958.
Jacquier, *Actes*: E. Jacquier, *Les Actes des Apôtres*, Paris, 1926.
James, *II Peter*: E. R. James, *The Second Epistle General of Peter and the General Epistle of Jude*, Cambridge, 1912.
——, *The Apocryphal New Testament*, Oxford, 1924.
Jeremias, *Parables*: J. Jeremias, *The Parables of Jesus*, London, 1954.
——, *Eucharistic Words*: The Eucharistic Words of Jesus, Oxford, 1955.
——, *Promise*: Jesus' Promise to the Nations, London, 1958.
——, *Unknown Sayings*: Unknown Sayings of Jesus, London, 1957.
——, *Jesus als Weltvollender*, Gütersloh, 1930.
——, 'Eine neue Schau der Zukunftsaussagen Jesu', in *T.B.* XX, 1941, pp. 216ff.
——, 'The Present Position in the Controversy concerning the Problem of the Historical Jesus', in *E.T.* LXIX, 1957, pp. 333ff.
——, *Die Briefe an Timotheus und Titus*, Göttingen, 1934.
——, 'Zum Problem der Deutung von Jes. 53 im palästinischen Judentum', in *Mélanges offerts à M. Goguel*, pp. 118ff.
——, and W. Zimmerli, *The Servant of God*, London, 1957.
Johnson, A. R. *Sacral Kingship in Ancient Israel*, Cardiff, 1955.
——, 'The Psalms', in *The O.T. and Modern Study*, ed. H. H. Rowley, pp. 181ff.
Johnson, *Mark*: E. Johnson, *The Gospel according to St. Mark*, London, 1962.
Johnson, S. E. 'Bultmann and Mythology', in *A.T.R.* XXXVII, 1954, pp. 29ff.
Johnston, *Church*: G. Johnston, *The Doctrine of the Church in the New Testament*, Cambridge, 1943.
Jones, A. 'Did Christ foretell the end of the world in Mk. 13?' in *Scripture*, 1951, pp. 264ff.
Jones, D. R. 'ἀνάμνησις in the Septuagint and the Interpretation of I Cor. 11,25', in *J.T.S.* VI, 1955, pp. 183ff.
Jones, G. V. *Christology and Myth in the N.T.*, London, 1956.
Jouen, P. 'Notes Philologiques sur les Évangiles', in *R.S.R.* XVII, 1927, pp. 538ff.
Jülicher, A. *Die Gleichnissreden Jesu*, Tübingen, 1910 (2nd ed.).
Käsemann, E. 'Das Problem des historischen Jesus', in *Z.T.K.* LI, 1954, pp. 125ff.
——, 'Eine Apologie der urchristlichen Eschatologie', in *Z.T.K.* XLIX, 1952, pp. 272ff.
Kelly, *Creeds*: J. N. D. Kelly, *Early Christian Creeds*, London, 1950.
——, *Doctrines*: Early Christian Doctrines, London, 1958.
Kennedy, *Last Things*: H. A. A. Kennedy, *St. Paul's Conception of the Last Things*, London, 1904.
——, *St. Paul and the Mystery-Religions*, London, 1913.

Kent, *Old Testament*: C. F. Kent, *The Growth and Content of the O.T.*, London, 1926.

Kiddle, *Revelation*: M. Kiddle, *The Revelation of St. John*, London, 1940.

Kilpatrick, *Origins*: G. D. Kilpatrick, *The Origins of the Gospel according to St. Matthew*, Oxford, 1946.

——, *The Trial of Jesus*, Oxford, 1953.

——, 'The Gentile Mission in Mark, and Mk. 13,9-11', in *Studies in the Gospels*, ed. D. E. Nineham, pp. 145ff.

Kiss, J. 'Zur eschatologischen Beurteilung der Theologie des Apostels Paulus', in *Z.s.T.* XV, 1938, pp. 379ff.

Kissane, *Psalms*: E. J. Kissane, *The Book of Psalms* (2 vols.), Dublin, 1953-4.

Kittel, G. ed. *Theologisches Wörterbuch zum Neuen Testament*, Stuttgart, 1933f.

Klausner, J. *Jesus of Nazareth*, London, 1925.

——, *Messianic Idea: The Messianic Idea in Israel from its beginning to the completion of the Mishnah*, London, 1956.

Klostermann, *Markus*: E. Klostermann, *Das Markusevangelium*, Tübingen, 1926 (2nd ed.).

——, *Matthäus*: *Das Matthäusevangelium*, Tübingen, 1927 (2nd ed.).

——, *Lukas*: *Das Lukasevangelium*, Tübingen, 1928 (2nd. ed.).

Knopf, *Petri und Judae*: R. Knopf, *Die Briefe Petri und Judae*, Göttingen, 1912 (7th ed.).

Knowling, *James*: R. J. Knowling, *The Epistle of James*, London, 1904.

Knox, *Acts*: J. Knox, *The Acts of the Apostles*, Cambridge, 1948.

——, *Jesus, Lord and Christ*, New York, 1958.

Köhler, *Theology*: L. Köhler, *Old Testament Theology*, London, 1957.

Körner, J. 'Endgeschichtliche Parusieerwartung und Heilsgegenwart im N.T und ihrer Bedeutung für eine christliche Theologie', in *Ev.T.* XIV, 1954, pp. 177ff.

Kraemer, H. *The Christian Message in a non-Christian World*, Edinburgh, 1938.

Kraus, H. J. *Die Königsherrschaft Gottes im A.T.*, Tübingen, 1951.

Kümmel, *Promise*: W. G. Kümmel, *Promise and Fulfilment*, London, 1957.

——, *Kirchenbegriff*: *Kirchenbegriff und Geschichtsbewusstsein in der Urgemeinde und bei Jesus*, Uppsala, 1943.

——, *Das Neue Testament. Geschichte der Erforschung seiner Probleme*, München, 1958.

——, 'Futurische und präsentische Eschatologie im ältesten Urchristentum', in *N.T.S.* V, 1958, pp. 113ff.

——, 'Die Eschatologie des Evangeliums', in *T.B.* XV, 1936, pp. 225ff.

Kuhl, C. *The Old Testament: Its Origins and Composition*, Edinburgh, 1961.

Kuhn, K. G. 'Die beiden Messias Aarons und Israels', in *N.T.S.* 1954-6, pp. 168ff.

Kundsin, K. *Das Urchristentum im Lichte der Evangelienforschung*, Giessen, 1929.

Kuss, O. 'Jesus und die Kirche im N.T.' in *T.Q.* 1954, pp. 28ff. and 150ff.

Lacey, T. A. *Authority in the Church*, Oxford, 1928.

Ladd, G. E. 'Eschatology and the Unity of the N.T. Theology', in *E.T.* LXVIII, 1956-7, pp. 268ff.

Lagrange, *Marc*: M.-J. Lagrange, *Évangile selon Saint Marc*, Paris, 1929 (4th ed.).

——, *Matthieu*: *Évangile selon Saint Matthieu*, Paris, 1923.

——, *Jean*: *Évangile selon Saint Jean*, Paris, 1948 (7th ed.).

Lake, *Introduction*: K. and S. Lake, *An Introduction to the N.T.*, London, 1938.
Lambeth Conference 1958; *the Encyclical letter, Resolution and Reports*, London, 1958.
Lampe, *Seal*: G. W. H. Lampe, *The Seal of the Spirit*, London, 1951.
Lauk, *II Thessaloniens*: W. Lauk, *II Thessaloniens, II Petrus, Judas*, Stuttgart, 1955.
Lawton, J. S. *Conflict in Christology*, London, 1947.
Leaney, *Luke*: A. R. C. Leaney, *A Commentary on the Gospel according to St. Luke*, London, 1958.
Leckie, *World to Come*: J. H. Leckie, *The World to Come and Final Destiny*, Edinburgh, 1918.
Lee, E. K. *The Religious Thought of St. John*, London, 1950.
Leenhardt, *Romans*: F. J. Leenhardt, *The Epistle to the Romans*, London, 1961.
Leitz, H. *Die christliche Hoffnung und die letzten Dinge*, Baden-Baden, 1948.
Leivestad, R. *Christ the Conqueror; Ideas of Conflict and Victory in the N.T.* London, 1954.
Levertoff, O. 'Eschatological Teaching in the Gospels', in *Theology*, XXXII, 1936, pp. 339ff.
Liddell and Scott, *Lexicon*: H. G. Liddell and R. Scott, *A Greek-English Lexicon*, Oxford, 1925.
Lietzmann, *Römer*: H. Lietzmann, *An die Römer*, Tübingen, 1933 (4th ed.).
——, *Korinther*: *An die Korinther I, II*, Tübingen, 1931 (3rd ed.).
——, 'Bemerkungen zum Prozess Jesu', in *Z.N.W.* XXX, 1931, pp. 211ff.
Lightfoot, *History and Interpretation*: R. H. Lightfoot, *History and Interpretation in the Gospels*, London, 1935.
——, *Locality and Doctrine*: *Locality and Doctrine in the Gospels*, London, 1938.
——, *Gospel Message*: *The Gospel Message of St. Mark*, Oxford, 1950.
——, *John*: *St. John's Gospel: a Commentary* (ed. C. F. Evans) Oxford, 1956.
Lindblom, J. *The Servant Songs in Deutero-Isaiah*, Lund, 1951.
Lock, *Pastoral Epistles*: W. Lock, *The Pastoral Epistles*, Edinburgh, 1924.
Lohmeyer, *Markus*: E. Lohmeyer, *Das Evangelium des Markus*, Göttingen, 1937 (ed. W. Schmauch, Göttingen, 1958).
——, *Philipper*: *Der Brief an die Philipper*, Göttingen, 1956 (11th ed.).
——, *Offenbarung*: *Die Offenbarung des Johannes*, Tübingen, 1926.
——, *Galiläa und Jerusalem*, Göttingen, 1936.
——, 'Vom Sinn der Gleichnisse Jesu', in *Z.s.T.* XV, 1938, pp. 319ff.
Lohse, E. 'Lukas als Theologe der Heilsgeschichte', in *Ev.T.* XIV, 1954, pp. 256ff.
——, 'Zur neutestamentlichen Eschatologie', in *V.F.* 1956, pp. 184ff.
Loisy, *Synoptiques*: A. Loisy, *Les Évangiles synoptiques*, (2 vols.) Paris, 1907.
——, *Marc*: *L'Évangile selon Marc*, Paris, 1912.
Lowrie, *Mark*: W. Lowrie, *Jesus according to St. Mark; An Interpretation of St. Mark's Gospel*, London, 1929.
Luther, *Galations*: M. Luther, *St. Paul's Epistle to the Galations*, London, 1953.
Major, *Reminiscences*: H. D. A. Major, *Reminiscences of Jesus by an Eye-Witness* (*St. Mark*), London, 1925.
——, and T. W. Manson, and C. J. Wright, *The Mission and the Message of Jesus*, London, 1941.
Malevez, *Christian Message*: L. Malevez, *The Christian Message and Myth; The Theology of Rudolf Bultmann*, London, 1958.

Manson, *Teaching*: T. W. Manson, *The Teaching of Jesus*, Cambridge, 1931.
——, *Sayings*: *The Sayings of Jesus*, London, 1949.
——, *Studies in the Gospels and Epistles* (ed. M. Black) Manchester, 1962.
——, *The Servant Messiah*, Cambridge, 1953.
——, 'The Son of Man in Daniel, Enoch and the Gospels', in *B.J.R.L.* XXXII, 1949, pp. 171ff.
——, 'The New Testament Basis of the Doctrine of the Church', in *J.E.H.* I, 1950, pp. 1ff.
——, 'St. Paul in Ephesus: the date of the Epistle to the Ephesians', in *B.J.R.L.* XXIII, 1939, pp. 182ff. (now in *Studies in the Gospels and Epistles*, ed. M. Black).
——, 'Realised Eschatology and the Messianic Secret', in *Studies in the Gospels*, ed. D. E. Nineham, pp. 209ff.
——, 'The Life of Jesus: Some tendencies in present day research', in *The Background of the New Testament*, ed. W. D. Davies and D. Daube, pp. 211ff.
——, ed. *A Companion to the Bible*, Edinburgh, 1939.
Manson, *Jesus*: W. Manson, *Jesus the Messiah*, London, 1943.
——, *Luke*: The Gospel according to St. Luke, London, 1930.
——, 'The Son of Man and History', in *S.J.T.* V, 1952, pp. 113ff.
——, *Hebrews*: *The Epistle to the Hebrews*, London, 1951.
——, and others, *Eschatology*, Edinburgh, 1953.
Marsh, J. *The Fulness of Time*, London, 1952.
Martin, *Philippians*: R. P. Martin, *The Epistle of St. Paul to the Philippians*, London, 1959.
——, *An Early Christian Confession*: *Phil. 2,5-11 in recent interpretation*, London, 1960.
Martin-Achard, *Israël*: R. Martin-Achard, *Israël et les nations: la perspective missionaire de l'Ancien Testament*, Neuchâtel, 1959.
Marxsen, *Markus:* W. Marxsen, *Der Evangelist Markus: Studien zur Redaktionsgeschichte des Evangeliums*, Göttingen, 1956.
Maurice, F. D. *The Kingdom of Christ* (2 vols.) London, 1958 (ed. by A. R. Vidler).
Mayor, *James*: J. B. Mayor, *The Epistle of St. James*, London, 1910.
McCown, C. C. 'In History or Beyond History', in *H.T.R.* XXXVIII, 1945, pp. 151ff.
McKinnon, J. *The Historic Jesus*, London, 1931.
MacKintosh, H. R. *The Doctrine of the Person of Jesus Christ*, Edinburgh, 1913.
M'Neile, *Matthew*: A. H. M'Neile, *The Gospel according to St. Matthew*, London, 1915.
——, *St. Paul*: *St. Paul: his life, letters and christian doctrine*, Cambridge, 1920.
MacQuarrie, J. *An Existentialist Theology. A Comparison of Heidegger and Bultmann*, London, 1955.
——, *The Scope of Demythologizing: Bultmann and his Critics*, London, 1960.
——, 'Existentialism and the Christian Vocabulary', in *L.Q.H.R.* 1961, pp. 250ff.
Meinertz, M. *Theologie des Neuen Testaments* (2 vols.), Bonn, 1950.
——, 'Die Tragweite des Gleichnisses von den zehn Jungfrauen', in *Synoptischen Studien für A. Wikenhauser*.
Mélanges offerts à M. Maurice Goguel: Aux sources de la Tradition Chrétienne, Neuchâtel, 1950.

Menzies, A. *The Earliest Gospel*, London, 1901.

Metzger, *Journeys*: H. Metzger, *St. Paul's Journeys in the Greek Orient*, London, 1955.

Michael, *Philippians*: J. H. Michael, *The Epistle of Paul to the Philippians*, London, 1928.

Michaelis, *Verheissung*: W. Michaelis, *Der Herr verzieht nicht die Verheissung: Die Aussagen Jesu über die Nähe des Jüngsten Tages*, Bern, 1942.

——, *Zur Engelchristologie*: *Zur Engelchristologie im Urchristentum*, Basel, 1942.

——, *Philipperbrief*, Leipzig, 1935.

——, *Matthäus*: *Das Evangelium nach Matthäus* (2 vols.) Zürich, 1948.

——, *Gleichnisse*: *Die Gleichnisse Jesu*, Hamburg, 1956.

——, *Einleitung*: *Einleitung in das Neue Testament*, Bern, 1954.

——, 'Zur Frage der Aeonenwende', in *T.B.V*, 1939, p. 113.

——, 'Exegetisches zur Himmelfahrtspredigt', in *K.r.S.*, 1952, pp. 115ff.

Michel, *Römer*: O. Michel, *Der Brief an die Römer*, Göttingen, 1955.

——, *Hebräer*: *Der Brief an die Hebräer*, Göttingen, 1957 (10th ed.).

——, 'Grundzüge urchristlicher Eschatologie', in *Z.s.T.* IX, 1932, pp. 645ff.

Miegge, *Gospel*: G. Miegge: *Gospel and Myth in the thought of Rudolf Bultmann*, London, 1958.

Migne, *P.G.* J. P. Migne, ed. *Patrologia, Series Graeca*.

——, *P.L.*: *Patrologia, Series Latina*.

Milligan, Thessalonians: G. Milligan, *St. Paul's Epistles to the Thessalonians*, London, 1908.

Minear, *Christian Hope*: P. S. Minear, *The Christian Hope and the Second Coming*, Westminster, Md., 1954.

——, *Images of the Church in the New Testament*, London, 1961.

——, 'The Coming of the Son of Man: an exegesis of Mtt. 25, 31-46', in *T.T.* X, 1953, pp. 489ff.

——, 'Between two worlds', in *Interpretation*, V, 1951, pp. 27ff.

——, 'The Time of Hope in the N.T.', in *S.J.T.* VI, 1953, pp. 337ff.

——, 'Time and the Kingdom', in *J.R.* XXIV, 1944, pp. 21ff.

Mitton, *Ephesians*: C. L. Mitton, *The Epistle to the Ephesians: Its Authorship, Origin and Purpose*, Oxford, 1951.

Moffatt, *General Epistles*; J. Moffatt, *The General Epistles, James, Peter and Judas*, London, 1928.

——, *Introduction*: *An Introduction to the Literature of the New Testament*, Edinburgh, 1933 (3rd ed.).

Montefiore, *Synoptic Gospels*: C. G. Montefiore, *The Synoptic Gospels* (2 vols), London, 1927 (2nd ed.).

——, *Liberal Judaism and Hellenism*, London, 1918.

Morgenthaler, R. *Kommendes Reich*, Zürich, 1952.

——, 'Formgeschichte und Gleichnissauslegung', in *T.Z.* VI, 1950, pp. 1ff.

Morris, *I Corinthians*: L. Morris, *The First Epistle of Paul to the Corinthians*, London, 1958.

——, *Thessalonians*: *The Epistles of Paul to the Thessalonians*, London, 1956.

Moule, *Idiom*: C. F. D. Moule, *An Idiom Book of N.T. Greek*, Cambridge, 1953.

——, *Colossians*: *The Epistles to the Colossians and to Philemon*, Cambridge, 1957.

——, *The Meaning of Hope*: *A Biblical exposition with concordance*, London, 1953.

Mowinkel, S. *Psalmenstudien* I-II, Amsterdam, 1961.

——, *He that Cometh*, Oxford, 1956.

Muirhead, L. A. *The Eschatology of Jesus*, London, 1904.
——, art. 'Eschatology', in *H.D.C.G.* I, pp. 525f.
Munby, D. L. *Christianity and Economic Problems*, London, 1956.
Munck, *Paul*: J. Munck, *Paul and the Salvation of Mankind*, London, 1959.
——, 'Israel and the Gentiles in the N.T.' in *J.T.S.* II, 1951, pp. 3ff.
Munz, P. *Problems of Religious Knowledge*, London, 1959.
Murray, J. M. *The Life of Jesus*, London, 1926.
Murray, *John*: J. O. F. Murray, *Jesus according to St. John*, London, 1936.
Nairne, *Epistle of Priesthood*: A. Nairne, *The Epistle of Priesthood: Studies in the Epistle to the Hebrews*, Edinburgh, 1913.
——, *The Faith of the New Testament*, London, 1920.
Nauck, *Die Tradition*: W. Nauck, *Die Tradition und der Charakter des ersten Johannesbriefes*, Tübingen, 1957.
Neil, *Thessalonians*: W. Neil, *Commentary on I and II Thessalonians*, London, 1950.
Neuenschwander, U. *Protestantische Dogmatik der Gegenwart und das Problem der biblischen Mythologie*, Bern, 1949.
Neufeld, J. J. *Wenn der Herr Kommt*, Wuppertal, 1956 (4th ed.).
Newbigin, L. and others, 'The Nature of Christian Hope', in *Ecumenical Review*, III, 1952, pp. 282ff.
Nicoll, W. Robertson, ed. *The Expositor's Greek Testament* (5 vols.), London, 1905f.
Nicklin, *Gleanings*: T. Nicklin, *Gospel Gleanings: Critical and Historical Notes on the Gospels*, London, 1950.
Niebuhr, H. Richard, *Christ and Culture*, London, 1952.
Niebuhr, Reinhold, 'The Christian Faith and the Economic Life of Liberal Society', in *Goals of Economic Life*, ed. A. Dudley Ward.
Nineham, D. E. ed. *Studies in the Gospels: Essays in Memory of R. H. Lightfoot*, Oxford, 1955.
——, 'The Case against Pauline Authorship', in *Studies in Ephesians*, ed. F. L. Cross, pp. 21ff.
Niven, W. D. 'After 50 Years: 6. Eschatology and the Primitive Church', in *E.T.* L, 1938, pp. 325ff.
Nock, *Paul*: A. D. Nock, *St. Paul*, London, 1938.
North, C. R. *The Suffering Servant in Deutero-Isaiah: an historical and critical study*, Oxford, 1948.
——, *Interpretation*: *The O.T. Interpretation of History*, London, 1946.

Noth, M. 'History and the Word of God in the O.T.', in *B.J.R.L.* XXXII, 1949, pp. 194ff.

Nygren, *Romans*: A. Nygren, *Commentary on Romans*, London, 1952.

Oepke, *Thessalonicher*: A. Oepke, *Die Briefe an die Thessalonicher*, Göttingen, 1959 (8th ed.).
——, 'Der Herrenspruch über die Kirche: Mtt. 16, 17-19, in der neuesten Forschung', in *S.T.* II, 1948, pp. 110ff.

Oesterley, *Apocrypha*: W. O. E. Oesterley, *The Books of the Apocrypha: their Origin, Teaching and Contents*, London, 1914.
——, *Parables*: *The Gospel Parables in the light of their Jewish Background*, London, 1936.
——, *Introduction*: *An Introduction to the Books of the Apocrypha*, London, 1935.
——, *The Jews and Judaism during the Greek Period*, London, 1941.
——, *Judaism and Christianity* (3 vols.), London, 1937-8.

O'Neill, *Theology of Acts*: J. C. O'Neill, *The Theology of Acts*, London, 1961.
——, 'The Use of Kyrios in the Book of Acts', in *S.J.T.* VIII, 1955, pp. 155ff.
Orr, J. art. 'The Kingdom of God', in *H.D.B.* II, pp. 844ff.
Otto, *Kingdom of God*: R. Otto, *The Kingdom of God and the Son of Man*, London, 1938.
Owen, H. P. 'The Parousia in the Synoptic Gospels', in *S.J.T.* XII, 1959, pp. 171ff.
Pallis, *Romans*: A. Pallis, *To the Romans, A Commentary*, Liverpool, 1920.
——, *Notes on St. Mark and St. Matthew*, London, 1932.
Parker, T. H. L. ed. *Essays in Christology for Karl Barth*, London, 1956.
Parry, *Pastoral Epistles*: R. St. J. Parry, *The Pastoral Epistles*, Cambridge, 1920.
Peake, A. S. *The Problem of Suffering in the O.T.*, London, 1904.
——, ed. *A Commentary on the Bible*, London, 1925.
Pedersen, *Israel*: J. P. E. Pederson, *Israel, its life and culture* (2 vols) London, 1947.
Percy, *Botschaft*: E. Percy, *Die Botschaft Jesu*, Lund, 1953.
Pfeiffer, *Introduction*: R. H. Pfeiffer, *Introduction to the O.T.* London, undated.
——, *Apocrypha*: *History of N.T. times with an introduction to the Apocrypha*, London, undated.
Plummer, *Luke*: A. Plummer, *The Gospel according to St. Luke*, Edinburgh, 1896.
Powell, W. 'Spatial imagery in the N.T. teaching about the Kingdom of God' in *E.T.* LX, 1948, p. 194.
Preiss, T. *Life in Christ*, London, 1954.
Prestige, *Fathers*; G. L. Prestige, *Fathers and Heretics*, London, 1940.
——, *God in Patristic Thought*, London, 1936.
Prideaux S. P. T. 'The Second Coming of Christ', in *E.T.* LXI, 1949, pp. 240ff.
Quin, E. 'The Kingdom of God and the Church in the Synoptic Gospels', in *Scripture*, IV, 1949, pp. 237ff.
Quispel, E. in *The Jung Codex*, ed. F. L. Cross.
Quistorp, H. *Calvin's Doctrine of the Last Things*, London, 1955.
Rackham, *Acts*: R. E. Rackham, *The Acts of the Apostles*, London, 1901.
Ramsey, *Glory*: A. M. Ramsey, *The Glory of God and the Transfiguration of Christ*, London, 1949.
——, *From Gore to Temple*, London, 1960.
Rankin, *Wisdom*: O. S. Rankin, *Israel's Wisdom Literature*, Edinburgh, 1936.
Ratschow, C. H. 'Anmerkungen zur theologischen Auffassung des Zeit-problems', in *Z.T.K.* LI, 1954, pp. 360ff.
Rawlinson, *Mark*: A. E. J. Rawlinson, *St. Mark*, London, 1925.
——, *Essays*: *Essays on the Trinity and the Incarnation*, London, 1928.
Redlich, *Mark*: E. B. Redlich, *St. Mark's Gospel*, London, 1948.
——, *Form Criticism*: *its value and limitation*, London, 1939.
Reicke, B. *Diakonie, Festfreude und Zelos*, Uppsala, 1951.
——, 'A Synopsis of early Christian Preaching', in *Root of the Vine*, ed. A. J. Fridrichson, pp. 128ff.
Reitzenstein, R. *Die hellenistische Mysterienreligionen nach ihren Grundge-danken und Wirkungen*, Leipzig, 1927 (3rd ed.).
Rengstorf, *Lukas*: K. H. Rengstorf, *Das Evengelium nach Lukas*, Göttingen, 1949 (5th ed.).

Rich, *Die Bedeutung*: A. Rich, *Die Bedeutung der Eschatologie für den christlichen Glauben*, Zürich, 1954.

Richardson, *T.W.B.* A. Richardson, ed. *A Theological Word Book of the Bible*, London, 1950.

——, *Introduction*: *An Introduction to the Theology of the N.T.* London, 1958.

——, and W. Schweitzer, *Biblical Authority for To-day*, London, 1951.

——, *Miracles*: *The Miracle Stories of the Gospel*, London, 1941.

Ridderbos, *De Komst*: H. N. Ridderbos, *De Komst van het Koninkrijk*, Kampen, 1950.

Riesenfeld, *Gospel Tradition*: H. Riesenfeld, *The Gospel Tradition and its Beginnings; a study in the limits of Formgeschichte*, London, 1957.

Rigaux, *Thessaloniciens*: B. Rigaux, *Saint Paul. Les Épitres aux Thessaloniciens*, Paris, 1956.

——, 'Révélation de Mystères et Perfection à Qûmran et dans le nouveau Testament', in *N.T.S.* IV, 1958, pp. 237ff.

Ringgren, H. *The Messiah in the Old Testament*, London, 1956.

——, 'König und Messias', in *Z.A.W.* LXIV, 1952, pp. 120ff.

Rissi, M. *Zeit und Geschichte in der Offenbarung des Johannes*, Zürich, 1952.

Roberts, *Kingdom of God*: H. Roberts, *Jesus and the Kingdom of God*, London, 1955.

Roberts, C. H. 'The Kingdom of Heaven, Lk. 17, 21', in *H.T.R.* XLI, 1948, pp. 1ff.

Robertson-Plummer, *I Corinthians*: A. Robertson and A. Plummer, *The First Epistle of Paul to the Corinthians*, Edinburgh, 1911.

Robinson, *Religious Ideas*: H. Wheeler Robinson, *The Religious Ideas of the Old Testament*, London, 1913.

——, *Inspiration and Revelation in the Old Testament*, Oxford, 1946.

Robinson, *Coming*: J. A. T. Robinson, *Jesus and His Coming*, London, 1957.

——, *Body*: *The Body*: *a study in Pauline Theology*, London, 1952.

——, *In the End, God* . . . . London, 1950.

——, *Twelve New Testament Studies*, London, 1962.

——, 'The Parable of the Sheep and the Goats', in *J.T.S.* II, 1955, pp. 225ff.

——, 'The Most Primitive Gospel of All?' in *J.T.S.* VII, 1956, pp. 177ff.

——, 'The Parable of Jn. 10, 1-5', in *Z.N.W.* XLVI, 1955, pp. 233ff.

Robinson, *Ephesians*: J. A. Robinson, *St. Paul's Epistle to the Ephesians*, London, 1941 (2nd ed.).

Robinson, *Problem*: J. M. Robinson, *The Problem of History in Mark*, London, 1957.

——, *New Quest*: *A New Quest for the Historical Jesus*, London, 1959.

Robinson, *Matthew*: T. H. Robinson, *The Gospel of Matthew*, London, 1928.

——, *Prophecy and the Prophets in Ancient Israel*, London, 1923.

——, 'The Old Testament and the Modern World', in *The Old Testament and Moden Study*, ed. H. H. Rowley, pp. 346ff.

Ropes, *James*: J. H. Ropes, *The Epistle of St. James*, Edinburgh, 1916.

Rops, D. *Israel and the Ancient World*, London, 1949.

Roux, H. *L'Évangile du Royaume*: *Commentaire sure l'Évangile de Matthieu*, Paris, 1942.

Rowley, *Relevance*: H. H. Rowley, *The Relevance of Apocalyptic*, London, 1947 (2nd ed.).

——, *Missionary Message*: *The Missionary Message of the Old Testament*, London, undated.

——, *Faith*: *The Faith of Israel*, London, 1956.

——, *Israel's Mission to the World*, London, 1939.

Rowley, *The Zadokite Fragments and the Dead Sea Scrolls*, Oxford, 1952.
——, ed. *The Old Testament and Modern Study*, Oxford, 1951.
——, ed. *Studies in O.T. Prophecy, presented to T. H. Robinson*, Edinburgh.
Rupp, G. 'Doctrine of Man: the Christian and Secular Eschatologies', in *E.T.* LXI, 1950, pp. 100ff.
Russell, J. S. *The Parousia: a critical enquiry into the N.T. doctrine of our Lord's Second Coming*, London, 1878.
Rust, E. C. 'Time and Eternity in Biblical Thought', in *T.T.* X, 1953, pp. 327ff.
Sanday, *Life of Christ*: W. Sanday, *The Life of Christ in Recent Research*, Oxford, 1907.
——, ed. *Studies in the Synoptic Problem*, Oxford, 1911.
Sanday and Headlam, *Romans*: W. Sanday and A. C. Headlam, *The Epistle to the Romans*, Edinburgh, 1902 (5th ed.).
Sanders, J. N. 'The Case for Pauline Authorship', in *Studies in Ephesians*, ed. F. L. Cross, pp. 9ff.
Sanders, J. O. and Wright, J. S. *Some Modern Religions*, London, 1956.
Savage, H. E. *The Gospel of the Kingdom*, London, 1910.
Schattenham, J. 'The Little Apocalypse of the Synoptics and the 1st Epistle of Peter', in *T.T.* XI, 1954, pp. 193ff.
Schlatter, *Matthäus*: A. Schlatter, *Das Evangelium nach Matthäus*, Stuttgart, 1935.
——, *Lukas: Das Evangelium des Lukas*, Stuttgart, 1931.
——, *Markus: Markus der Evangelist für die Griechen*, Stuttgart, 1935.
Schmauch, W. ed. *In Memoriam E. Lohmeyer* Stuttgart, 1951.
Schmaus, M. *Dogmatik* (III, pt. 2) München, 1941.
Schmid, *Markus*: J. Schmid, *Das Evangelium nach Markus*, Regensburg, 1950.
——, 'Der Antichrist und die hemmende Macht (II Thess. 2, 1-12)', in *T.Q.* CXXIV, 1949, pp. 323ff.
Schmidt, *Johannesapokalypse*: K. L. Schmidt, *Aus der Johannesapokalypse*, Basel, 1946.
——, 'Die Kirche des Urchristentums', in *Festgabe für A. Deissmann*, pp. 258ff.
Schmiedel, P. W. 'The Gospels', in *Encyclopaedia Biblica* II, London, 1901 col. 1857.
Schniewind, *Markus*: J. Schniewind, *Das Evangelium nach Markus*, Göttingen, 1947 (4th ed.).
——, *Matthäus: Das Evangelium nach Matthäus*, Göttingen, 1950 (5th ed.).
——, *Nachgelassene Reden und Aufsätze*, Berlin, 1952.
Schoeps, *Paul*: H. J. Schoeps, *Paul: The Theology of the Apostle in the light of Jewish religious history*, London, 1961.
Schofield, J. N. *The Historical Background of the Bible*, London, 1938.
Schuster, H. 'Die konsequente Eschatologie in der Interpretation des N.T. kritisch betrachtet', in *Z.N.W.* XLVII, 1956, pp. 1ff.
Schweitzer, *Mystery*: A. Schweitzer, *The Mystery of the Kingdom of God*, London, 1925.
——, *Quest: The Quest of the Historical Jesus*, London, 1910.
——, *Mysticism: The Mysticism of Paul the Apostle*, London, 1931.
——, *My Life and Thought*, London, 1933.
——, *Paul and His Interpreters*, London, 1912.
——, 'Die Idee des Reiches Gottes im Vorlaufe der Umbildung des eschatologischen Glauben in den uneschatologischen', in *S.t.U.* 1953, pp. 7ff.

Schweitzer, W. *Eschatology and Ethics*, Ecumenical Studies 51E/132, Geneva, 1951.

Schweizer, E. *Spirit of God*, London, 1960.

——, 'Der Menschensohn', in *Z.N.W.* LIX, 1959, pp. 185ff.

Scott, *Tributaries*: E. F. Scott, *The Gospel and its Tributaries*, Edinburgh, 1928.

——, *Colossians*: The *Epistles of Paul to the Colossians, to Philemon and to the Ephesians*, London, 1930.

——, *Pastoral Epistles*: The *Pastoral Epistles*, London, 1936.

——, 'Gnosticism', in *E.R.E.* VI, pp. 233ff.

Scott, R, B. Y. 'Behold he cometh with the clouds', in *N.T.S.* V, 1958, pp. 127ff.

Seaver, *Schweitzer*: G. Seaver, *Albert Schweitzer, the Man and his Mind*, London, 1947.

Selbie, J. A. 'Cananean', in *H.D.B.* I, pp. 348ff.

Selby, D. J. 'Changing Ideas in N.T. eschatology', in *H.T.R.* L, 1957, pp. 21ff.

Selwyn, *I Peter*; E. G. Selwyn, *The First Epistle of St. Peter*, London, 1946.

Sevenster, J. N. 'Some Remarks on the Γυμνος in II Cor. 5,3', in *Studia Paulina*, pp. 202ff.

Sharman, *Son of Man*: H. B. Sharman, *Son of Man and Kingdom of God*, London, 1943.

Simpson, *Patoral Epistles*; E. K. Simpson, *The Pastoral Epistles*, London, 1954.

Simpson, M. A. 'The Kingdom of God has come', in *E.T.* LXIV, 1952, p. 188.

Sjöberg, *Menschensohn*: E. Sjöberg, *Der Menschensohn im Äthiopischen Henochbuch*, Lund, 1946.

——, *Verborgene Menschensohn*: *Der verborgene Menschensohn in den Evangelien*, Lund, 1955.

Sledd, A. 'The Interpretation of Lk. 17, 21', in *E.T.* L, 1938, pp. 235ff.

Smith, *Parables*: B. T. D. Smith, *The Parables of the Synoptic Gospels*, Cambridge, 1937.

Smith, *Isaiah*: G. A. Smith, *The Book of Isaiah*, (3 vols.) London, 1927.

——, *The Book of the Twelve Prophets* (2 vols.), London, 1928.

Snaith, *Distinctive Ideas*: N. H. Snaith, *The Distinctive Ideas of the O.T.*, London, 1944.

——, *Cyrus to Herod*: *The Jews from Cyrus to Herod*, Wallington, 1949.

——, *Studies in the Psalter*, London, 1934.

——, 'The Servant of the Lord in Deutero-Isaiah', in *Studies in O.T. Prophecy*, ed. H. H. Rowley, pp. 189ff.

Sparks, *Formation*: H. F. D. Sparks, *The Formation of the N.T.*, London, 1952.

Spencer, F. A. M. 'The Advent Hope', in *E.T.* XLIV, 1937, pp. 106ff.

Spicq, *Hébreux*: C. Spicq, *L'Épitre aux Hébreux*, Paris, 1952 (3rd ed.) (2 vols).

——, *Pastorales*: *Saint. Paul*: *Les Épitres Pastorales*, Paris, 1947.

Stählin, G. 'Die Endschau Jesu und die Mission', in *E.M.* 1950, pp. 97ff., 134ff.

——, 'Zum Problem der johanneischen Eschatologie', in *Z.N.W.* XXXIII, 1934, pp. 225ff.

Stauffer, *Theology*: E. Stauffer, *New Testament Theology*, London, 1955.

——, *Jesus*: *Jesus and His Story*, London, 1960.

——, *Christ and the Caesars*, London, 1955.

——, 'Das theologische Weltbild der Apokalyptik', in *Z.s.T.* VIII, 1931, pp. 201ff.

Stebbing, S. *A Modern Introduction to Logic*, London, 1930.
Steere, D. V. 'The Hope of Glory and this present life', in *T.T.* X, 1953, pp. 367ff.
Stewart, J. *A Man in Christ*, London, 1935.
Stibbs, *I Peter*: A. M. Stibbs, *The First Epistle General of Peter*, London, 1959.
Stonehouse, *Matthew and Mark*: N. B. Stonehouse, *The Witness of Matthew and Mark to Christ*, Philadelphia, 1944.
Strachan, *Fourth Gospel*: R. H. Strachan, *The Fourth Gospel: its Significance and Environment*, London, 1943.
Stratton, C. 'Pressure for the Kingdom', in *Interpretation*, VIII, 1954, pp. 414ff.
Strack, H. L. and Billerbeck, P. *Kommentar zum Neuen Testament aus Talmud und Midrash* (4 vols.), München, 1922-28.
Strawson, W. *Jesus and the Future Life*, London, 1959.
Streeter, *Four Gospels*: B. H. Streeter, *The Four Gospels: A Study of Origins*, London, 1930 (revised ed.).
——, 'On the Trial of our Lord before Herod', in *Studies in the Synoptic Problem*, ed. W. Sanday, pp. 229ff.
——, 'Synoptic criticism and the eschatological problem', in *Studies in the Synoptic Problem*, ed. W. Sanday, Appendix, pp. 425ff.
Strobel, *Untersuchungen*: A. Strobel, *Untersuchungen zum eschatologischen Verzögerungsproblem*, Leiden, 1961.
——, 'Zum Verständnis vom Rom. 13', in *Z.N.W.* XLVII, 1956, pp. 67ff.
Studia Paulina in honorem J. de Zwaan, Haarlem, 1953.
Sundwall, J. *Die Zusammensetzung des Markusevangeliums*, Åbo, 1934.
Swete, *Mark*: H. B. Swete, *The Gospel according to St. Mark*, London, 1898.
Synoptischen Studien: *Alfred Wikenhauser zum 70. Geburtstag am 22. Februar, 1953 dargebracht von Freunden, Kollegen und Schülern*, München, 1953.
Tasker, *John*: R. V. G. Tasker, *The Gospel according to St. John*, London, 1960.
——, *II Corinthians*: *The Second Epistle of Paul to the Corinthians*, London, 1958.
——, *James*: *The General Epistle of James*, London, 1956.
——, *Matthew*: *The Gospel according to St. Matthew*, London, 1961.
Taylor, *Names*: V. Taylor, *The Names of Jesus*, London, 1953.
——, *Mark*: *The Gospel according to St. Mark*, London, 1952.
——, *Life and Ministry*: *The Life and Ministry of Jesus*, London, 1954.
——, 'The Apocalyptic Discourse of Mk. 13', in *E.T.* LX, 1948, pp. 94ff.
——, 'The Origin of the Markan Passion Sayings', in *J.T.S.* I, 1954, pp. 159ff.
Temple, *Readings*: W. Temple, *Readings in St. John's Gospel*, 1st and 2nd series, London, 1947.

Thurneysen, *Philipper*: E. Thurneysen, *Der Brief an die Philipper*, Basel, 1958.
——, *Jakobus*: *Der Brief des Jakobus*, Basel, 1942 (3rd ed.).
——, 'Christus und seine Zukunft', in *Zwischen den Zeiten*, IX, 1931, pp. 187ff.
——, 'The End of all Things', in *Interpretation*, XII, 1958, pp. 407ff.

Titius, *Jesu Lehre*: A. Titius, *Jesu Lehre vom Reich Gottes*, Leipzig, 1895.

Tödt, *Menschensohn*: H. E. Tödt, *Der Menschensohn in der synoptischen Überlieferung*, Gütersloh, 1959.

Torrance, *When Christ comes*: T. F. Torrance, *When Christ comes and comes again*, London, 1957.

Torrance, *Kingdom and Church*: a *Study in the Theology of the Reformation*, Edinburgh, 1956.
——, 'A Study in N.T. Communication', in *S.J.T.* III, 1950, pp. 298ff.
——, 'The Place of Christology in Biblical and Dogmatic Theology', in *Essays in Christology*, ed. T. H. L. Parker, pp. 11ff.
Turner, *Mark*: C. H. Turner, 'The Gospel according to St. Mark', in *A New Commentary on Holy Scripture*, ed. C. Gore, H. L. Goudge, A. Guillaume.
Turner, *Pattern*: H. E. W. Turner, *The Pattern of Christian Truth*, London, 1954.
——, *Jesus, Master and Lord*, London, 1953.
Vaux R. de. 'Fouille au Khirbet Qûmran', in *R.B.* 1953, pp. 88ff.
Vidler, A. R. *Essays in Liberality*, London, 1957.
Vielhauer, P. 'Zur Paulinismus der Apostelgeschichte', in *Ev.T.* X, 1950, pp. 1ff.
Vincent, *Philippians*: M. R. Vincent, *The Epistles to the Philippians and to Philemon*, Edinburgh, 1897.
Volz, *Jüdische Eschatologie*: P. Volz, *Jüdische Eschatologie von Daniel bis Akiba*, Tübingen and Leipzig, 1903.
Vriezen, *Theology*; T. C. Vriezen, *An Outline of O. T. Theology*, Oxford, 1958.
Wade, J. H. *New Testament History*, London, 1922.
Walker, *Hebrew Religion*: T. Walker, *Hebrew Religion between the Testaments*, London, undated.
Wallace, R. S. 'The Parable and the Preacher', in *S.J.T.* II, 1949, pp. 13ff.
Walter, E. *Das Kommen des Herrn*, Freiburg, 1941.
Wand, *General Epistles*; J. W. C. Wand, *The General Epistles of St. Peter and St. Jude*, London, 1934.
Ward, A. Dudley, ed. *Goals of Economic Life*, London, 1953.
Warfield, B. B. *The Inspiration and Authority of the Bible*, London, 1959 (18th ed. edited by S. G. Craig).
Warren, M. *The Triumph of God*, London, 1948.
Weber, *Eschatologie und Mystik*: H. E. Weber, *Eschatologie und Mystik im N.T. Ein Versuch zum Verständnis des Glaubens*, Gütersloh, 1931.
Weiss, *Predigt*: J. Weiss, *Die Predigt Jesu vom Reiche Gottes*, Göttingen, 1906 (2nd ed.).
——, *Das Urchristentum*, Göttingen, 1917.
——, *Die Schriften des Neuen Testaments*, Göttingen, 1906 (2nd ed.).
Welch, *Visions*: A. C. Welch, *Visions of the End, a Study in Daniel and Revelation*, London, 1958.
Wendland, *Eschatologie*: H.-D. Wendland, *Die Eschatologie des Reiche Gottes bei Jesus*, Gütersloh, 1931.
Wendt, H. H. *Die Lehre Jesu*, Göttingen, 1886.
Werner, *Formation*: M. Werner, *The Formation of Christian Dogma*, London, 1957.
——, *Der protestantische Weg des Glaubens*, I, Bern and Tübingen, 1955.
——, 'Die Hoffnung der Kirche auf die Wiederkunft Christi, in *V.s.P.* 1942, pp. 25ff.
——, 'Ein neuer vaticanischer Entscheid über die Lehre von der Wiederkunft Christi', in *S.t.U.* 1944, pp. 117ff.
Westcott, *John*: B. F. Westcott, *The Gospel according to St. John*, London, 1902.
——, *Johannine Epistles*: *The Epistles of St. John*, London, 1886 (2nd ed.).
——, *Ephesians*: *St. Paul's Epistle to the Ephesians*, London, 1906.

Westcott, *Hebrews*: *The Epistle to the Hebrews*, London, 1889.

Whitehouse, W. A. 'Christ and Creation', in *Essays in Christology*, ed. T.H.L. Parker, pp. 113ff.

——, 'The Modern Discussion of Eschatology', in *Eschatology*, W. Manson and others, pp. 63ff.

Whitley, C. F. *The Exilic Age*, London, 1957.

Wickham, *Hebrews*; E. C. Wickham, *The Epistle to the Hebrews*, London, 1910.

Wilder, *Eschatology and Ethics*: A. N. Wilder, *Eschatology and Ethics in the Teaching of Jesus*, New York, 1950 (revised ed.).

——, 'Mythology and the N.T.' in *J.B.L.* LXIX, 1950, pp. 113ff.

——, 'Eschatological imagery and earthly circumstance', in *N.T.S.* V, 1958, pp. 229ff.

Wiles, M. F. 'Early Exegesis of the Parables', in *S.J.T.* XI, 1958, pp. 287ff.

Williams, *Acts*: C. S. C. Williams, *A Commentary on the Acts of the Apostles*, London, 1957.

Williams, N. P. 'A Recent theory of the origin of St. Mark's Gospel', in *Studies in the Synoptic Problem*, ed. W. Sanday, pp. 389ff.

Windisch, *Bergpredigt*: H. Windisch, *Der Sinn der Bergpredigt*, Leipzig, 1929.

——, *Der Hebräerbrief*, Tübingen, 1931 (2nd ed.).

——, *Die katholischen Briefe*, Tübingen, 1930 (2nd ed.).

Winter, P. *On the Trial of Jesus*, Berlin, 1961.

Woods, G. F. *Theological Explanation*, Welwyn, 1958.

Wood, *Jesus*: H. G. Wood, *Jesus in the 20th Century*, London, 1960.

——, *Christianity and the Nature of History*, Cambridge, 1934.

Wrede, D. W. *Das Messiasgeheimnis in den Evangelium*, Göttingen, 1901.

Wright, C. J. 'The Fourth Gospel', in *The Message and Mission of Jesus*, ed. H. D. A. Major, T. W. Manson and C. J. Wright.

Zahn, *Lukas*: T. Zahn, *Das Evangelium des Lukas*, Leipzig, 1913.

SELECT INDEX OF N.T. REFERENCES